The Quality of

The Quality of the Urban Environment

Essays on "New Resources" in an Urban Age

EDITED BY HARVEY S. PERLOFF

Published by Resources for the Future, Inc.

Distributed by The Johns Hopkins Press, Baltimore and London

RESOURCES FOR THE FUTURE, INC.

1755 Massachusetts Avenue, N.W., Washington, D.C. 20036

Resources for the Future is a nonprofit corporation for research and education in
the development, conservation, and use of natural resources and the improvement
of the quality of the environment. It was established in 1952 with the cooperation
of the Ford Foundation. Part of the work of Resources for the Future is carried
out by its resident staff; part is supported by grants to universities and other
nonprofit organizations. Unless otherwise stated, interpretations and conclusions
in RFF publications are those of the authors; the organization takes responsibility
for the selection of significant subjects for study, the competence of the
researchers, and their freedom of inquiry.

This book is based on papers prepared for presentation at a conference
sponsored by Resources for the Future, Inc., Washington, D.C., November 1967.
At the time of the conference, Harvey S. Perloff was director of RFF's
regional and urban studies.
Charts were drawn by Clare and Frank Ford.

RFF editors: Henry Jarrett, Vera W. Dodds, Nora E. Roots, Tadd Fisher.

ISBN 0-8018-1028-0

Originally published, 1969
Second printing, 1970
Third printing, 1971

Preface

The quality of the environment in which people live, work, and play influences to no small degree the quality of life itself. The environment can be satisfying and attractive and provide scope for individual development or it can be poisonous, irritating, and stunting.

The papers in this volume are concerned with the urban environment — in which the majority of Americans live — or, more accurately, with the environment of urbanites, for the concern extends to outlying areas where urban dwellers visit and play.

The papers were initially prepared for a conference on the urban environment sponsored by Resources for the Future, Inc. The conference was organized to evaluate the current "state of the art" and to stimulate research in the field. Its main objective was to review (1) both the established concepts and those now evolving or needed to advance work in the field; (2) the existing sources of information and the new kinds of information which are required, particularly in measuring improvement or degradation of the environment; and (3) public policy issues related to environmental improvement.

No attempt was made to provide a comprehensive overview of thinking and research in the field (much significant work in progress is not reported). Rather, the choice of subjects and authors was highly selective: essentially a *sampling* — with a strong economic-cum-planning focus — was made of some of the more interesting current work dealing with issues and methods directly relevant to public policy-making. The main purpose was to expose conceptual probings that would be of particular interest both to scholars concerned with environmental research and to policy makers concerned with narrowing the gap between intellectual speculation and practical application.

It should be stressed that the papers report on research that has been, and still is, under way. They have all the weaknesses — and excitement — of progress reports. Some ideas are well developed, others represent early speculation. Some of the research is theoretical or conceptual, some is largely empirical, while some is essentially "observational" in approach (if this is a legitimate way of describing Wilfred Owen's comparisons of U.S. and European styles of developing transportation environments and the Atkisson-Robinson provocative aesthetic evaluations).

No attempt has been made to bring the papers into a uniform pattern, since this would have been impossible or, if it had been possible, it would have been certain to take the edge off the special thrust and originality of each paper. They should be taken for what they are: individual probings into different corners of a vast and largely undefined field.

There were, however, three themes that emerged early in this joint effort that had at least *some* unifying impact. In inviting the authors to the conference, I had suggested the value of looking at the quality-of-the-environment questions on the urban scene as largely concerned with a set of "new resources in an urban age." The urban environment, it was suggested, as is true of the rural environment, involves an important group of natural resources; that is, features of the natural environment which, by definition, are in relatively scarce supply. Examples of these are: relatively "pure" air and water; urban space, including overground and underground space; the radio spectrum; amenity resources; and the like. Here, however, as compared to the rural environment, the natural resources are much more intimately tied in with the man-made features of the urban community, a difference of degree that begins to amount to a difference in kind.

Because several of the authors found the "new resources" theme fitted well into their own conceptual frameworks and research, the convergence effect can be noted in some of the essays.

Further, it was suggested earlier that there is conceptual value in seeing some of the man-made features as providing an important kind of environment, a "microenvironment," and that for many purposes and for many situations microenvironments serve as actual or potential substitutes for the "macroenvironment." The most familiar example is the airconditioning of homes, places of work, and automobiles; while the Houston Astrodome points to significant possibilities for the future in creating highly controlled "mini" environments. The question of tradeoffs between micro- and macroenvironments thus becomes a critical one in the urban setting. The discussion at the conference stimulated Richard Frankel to work out (with the help of his wife, who was called on to provide a "housewife's view" of environment) a set of macro-micro environmental categories, and several of the authors, particularly Irving Hoch, elaborated several facets of this important theme.

A third theme provides the largest part of whatever unity there is to be found in these individual essays. Most of the authors took up the challenge posed by the first paper — highlighted by the current effort within the federal government to develop social indicators that would provide a base for presidential reporting on the environment as well as on other "social" areas — to suggest measures of environmental condition and change. Thus, to the extent that there is any unifying element in this volume, it is the search for better informational and measurement tools which would ultimately be useful for decision making.

The most characteristic feature of the essays in this volume is the effort to conceptualize the subject matter at hand. The first paper attempts to set up a decision-making framework for studying, reporting on, and making policy about the urban environment. The Ayres-Kneese paper on pollution involves a conceptual tour de force demonstrating how the "production" of waste is an integral feature of our urban activities and how all forms of waste must be treated as part of a highly inter-related system, choosing those control and disposal methods that offer the greatest overall net benefits. Implementation of the proposed model, which is feasible even if demanding, would provide a significant part of the information called for by the policy framework proposed in Chapter 1. It thus effectively demonstrates the kind of systems approach and information inputs that would be needed to cope with the problems and potentialities of the urban environment.

Five of the nine papers in the volume are concerned with urban space, the most characteristic of the "new resources" and the most valuable of all our natural resources, viewed from the standpoint of national wealth accounting. (Anyone who doubts this would do well to examine the figures on the subject presented in the Hoch paper.) The ways in which urban space is used two-dimensionally and three-dimensionally, the extent to which and the manner in which it is covered or uncovered, how we move about in it and tie activities together, its value in various uses and locations, and its amenity features are examined in these papers with care and, in most cases, with conceptual freshness. These are large subjects. Even in the case of the longer papers, there is no attempt to be exhaustive. Rather, an effort is made to highlight the features that are particularly pertinent to the subject at hand.

Two of the papers suggest broad settings within which the problems of the urban environment might be fruitfully viewed. The Berry-Neils paper points out that the urban environment is to a large extent the embodiment of national developments — in technology, industrial expansion, changes in modes of life — and that these must be understood and traced through in order to grasp what is behind environmental conditions and environmental change. The Chapin-Logan paper suggests that the way people use their environment is directly related to the character and rhythm of their activities. An understanding of time use is therefore essential to appreciate what is important for people in the environment and provides some of the knowledge needed to deal with questions of tradeoffs between micro- and macroenvironments. For example, the large amount of time spent in home activities and the very much shorter time periods spent outside are clearly suggestive of at least one important reason why it seems hard to get most people really excited about the "external" environment, and again highlight the significance of the micro-macro tradeoff theme.

In general, while the papers help provide a better understanding of the natural resources elements in the urban environment, and while they do treat some of the issues touching on the interrelationship of the natural and man-made features, a full-bodied discussion of the latter remains for the future. There are many interesting questions to be asked about the "utilities environment," the "community-or-neighborhood environment," and the various microenvironments (using the categories of the first paper), to fill out the broad environmental picture.

HARVEY S. PERLOFF

Contents

Preface   v
Harvey S. Perloff

1 **A framework for dealing with the urban environment: introductory statement** . .   3
Harvey S. Perloff
    Extending the concept of resources *4*
    The urban environment as a subsystem *10*
    Elements within the environmental system *13*
    The urban environment and the environment of urbanites *15*
    Policy measures and a decision framework *16*
    Elements to be covered *18*
        The natural environment 18,   *The spatial environment* 18,   *The*
        transportation-utilities environment 18,   *The community-or-*
        neighborhood environment 19,   *The microenvironments* 19
    Indicators, accounts, and policy measures *20*
    Final note *25*

    Appendix: Microenvironmental responses to changes in the urban
    environment   26
    Richard J. and Beverly F. Frankel

2 **Pollution and environmental quality**   35
Robert U. Ayres and Allen V. Kneese
    A materials balance approach *35*
    Residuals associated with energy conversion *40*
        Thermal power 41,   *Transportation* 42,   *Industry and households* 45
    Residuals from materials processing and industrial production *46*
        Potential improvement through process change 52
    Residuals associated with final consumption: households *55*
        The whole sector—interdependencies 62
    Planning and policy *64*
        General considerations 64,   *Controls and environmental*
        management 65,   *Management planning* 68
    Needed data and research *69*

3 The three-dimensional city: contained urban space 75
Irving Hoch
    Some simple models *75*
    Real-world confirmations and complications *81*
        The macro level: the overall spatial pattern 81, *The micro level: individual firm behavior—model elements* 84, *Land viewed as space* 89, *A revised statement of firm decision making* 89, *Externalities and zoning* 91, *Other regulations and restrictions* 93
    Externalities *95*
        General issues 95, *Specific cases* 97
    Urban space indicators *105*
    Recent developments in three-dimensional space use *118*
        High-rise developments 119, *Underground developments* 121, *Elevated structures and the use of air rights* 124
    Long-term forecasts and visions *129*
        Increased dispersal 129, *Dispersal reversal* 130, *Dispersal and concentration* 132, *Conclusion* 133
    Appendix *133*

4 Open (uncovered) space as a new urban resource 139
Marion Clawson
    Functions and forms of open space *140*
    Need and demand for open space *143*
    Crowding and space *152*
    Efficiency in use of open space *156*
    Landforms best suited for open space *160*
    Open space as part of grand urban design *161*
    Parks, playgrounds, and similar areas *161*
    Man-made water bodies as open space *164*
    Urban open space as an externality situation *168*
    Open space on the city margin *168*
    Public control over urban open space *171*
    Appendix: References to the literature *173*

5 Amenity resources for urban living 179
Arthur A. Atkisson and Ira M. Robinson
    The objects of amenities planning and management *179*
        Amenity response system 182, *Amenity responses and respondents* 185, *Economic and political responses to amenities* 186, *Amenities, disamenities, and their precipitants* 189
    Demand for amenities *190*

The amenity decision system *193*
   The physical context of amenity decisions 194,   *A management
   system for urban natural amenities* 195,   *Inventory of natural
   amenity precipitants* 195,   *Amenity demand curves* 196,   *Research
   into decision-making criteria* 199*

6 **Transport: key to the future of cities** 205
  Wilfred Owen
    Underlying causes of congestion *206*
    Urban development and transport technology *209*
    The implications of economic growth *210*
    National policy and urban planning *213*
    Traffic patterns and their meaning *215*
    Horizontal, vertical, and time separation *217*
    Non-transport functions of transport facilities *219*
    Transport solutions through urban design *221*
    Needed institutional changes *223*
    A program of research *225*
    In conclusion *227*

7 **The value of urban land** 231
  Edwin S. Mills
    Classical and neoclassical land rent doctrine *231*
    Land rents in recent models of the urban economy *234*
    Empirical studies of urban land values *237*
    A model of urban land values *241*
    Empirical estimates and tests *245*
    Concluding comments *251*
      Data availability 253

8 **Location, size, and shape of cities as influenced by environmental factors:
  the urban environment writ large** 257
  Brian J. L. Berry and Elaine Neils
    Evolution of the American urban system *258*
     Mercantile beginnings 258,   *Industrial transformation* 262,
     Cumulative heartland-hinterland relationships 262,   *Amenity
     resources and the service sector* 265
    Patterns of urbanization and urban influence in 1960 *270*
    The system of cities and the characteristics of different categories *284*
     Typology of cities, 1960 288
    System generating and maintaining mechanisms *291*
    City and environment under post-industrial conditions *301*

9 Patterns of time and space use 305
       F. Stuart Chapin, Jr., and Thomas H. Logan
          Household activity patterns as a behavioral system *306*
             The conceptual framework at the micro level 308,   *A macro*
             adaptation of the schema 310
          A snapshot view of household activity patterns in the United States *313*
             The analysis 314,   *Findings—an overview* 316,   *Findings—clues*
             to differential activity choices 318,   *General measures* 318,
             Measures of specific activity categories 320,   *Interpretative*
             observations 324
          Implications of activity patterns for policy *327*
             A note on spatial patterns of activity 327,   *Activity systems and*
             environmental resources policy 330

The Quality of the Urban Environment

1

**A framework for dealing with the urban environment:
introductory statement**

Harvey S. Perloff

Dean, School of Architecture and Urban Planning
University of California, Los Angeles,
and Associate, Resources for the Future

A framework for dealing with the urban environment: introductory statement

Harvey S. Perloff

The current interest in the quality of the urban environment is in large part a convergence of two other evolving public concerns. One is a concern with the quality of the natural environment — the quality of air, water, land, wilderness areas, and other resources. The other is a concern with the development of our urban communities — with all the matters coming under the rubric of more traditional city planning, but recently refocused to a special concern for the human beings in the city. The quality of life of all the people who are clustering into urban communities is clearly influenced by what happens to both the natural and the man-made environments in direct interrelationship with each other.

Our capacity to deal effectively with the enormously complex problems of the urban environment — problems that become more complex with each passing year — will certainly be much increased if we can sharpen our concepts, clarify the nature of the problems, improve our measurement tools (including the measurement of alternative proposed solutions), and be inventive about new institutional arrangements to cope with new situations. The present paper merely points, in an introductory vein, to some conceptual and measurement issues that deserve attention within such a policy-oriented probing of the subject.

We know from experience that it is difficult to make much progress in the realm of public policy and co-ordinated public-private action unless there is fairly substantial common ground of understanding and agreement as to just what the public interest is and why group action is called for. This is true whether we are talking about cleaning up the rivers, improving mass transportation, or eliminating slums (or, for that matter, providing financial aid overseas). The importance of such common ground is particularly great where most proposed solutions involve governmental restraints on the use of private property and the making of profits, or the imposition of extra costs on private groups, or the expenditure of large sums of public money. In spite of the fact that some people see the United States as increasingly subject to creeping or galloping socialism, it takes quite a bit of doing to get the necessary public backing to enable a governmental agency to impose limitations on private activities.[1]

This paper owes a great deal to the valuable comments made by Irving Hoch on earlier drafts. I am also indebted to Stuart Chapin, Mancur Olson, and Benjamin H. Stevens for their suggestions. — AUTHOR'S NOTE

[1] A good example is the difficulty that state agencies have experienced in carrying out existing water pollution control legislation. The private interests in such a situation — the polluting industries — are specific and known (restrictions by a state pollution control agency can be very costly indeed for a specific firm), while the public interest is much more diffuse and vague. Not surprisingly, the energy that the state agency will normally exert will be more or less in direct proportion to the interest that the public, or representatives of the public, take in the matter. Matthew Holden, Jr., suggests,

The rationale on which public action is based — and the breadth and depth of its acceptance — thus has a great deal to do with the ability of governments to carry out a coherent set of policies over a substantial period of time. This normally calls for rather broad social concepts which in their very essence point to the objectives involved, the nature of the problems or difficulties, and the kinds of solutions which would seem to follow logically. Concepts of this type are sometimes rather vague and at times might even have contradictory elements within them. They can also linger long after the situation has changed. But whatever the difficulties and dangers, such broad social concepts tend to play an important role in providing a foundation for public policy and action in given matters.[2]

In dealing with problems that are as numerous, diverse, and complex as those involved in the quality of the urban environment, there is a clear gain if we can have concepts that serve simultaneously a simplifying and unifying role, since they contribute to the development of a common ground of understanding.

I would like to suggest two concepts that can play such a simplifying and unifying role with regard to the quality of the urban environment. One is an extension of the meaning and scope of natural resources, to encompass what I have called "new resources in an urban age." The other is a view of the urban environment as a contained (but not closed), highly interrelated system (or subsystem) of natural and man-made elements in various mixes.

Extending the Concept of Resources

For a very long time — in fact, for many centuries — natural resources have been thought of essentially as the elements of the natural environment needed for the production of certain basic commodities (farm, forestry, fishing, water, and mineral *products*) and, to a much lesser extent, of certain services (especially recreation and water transportation). My colleagues and I have described elsewhere[3] the slowly changing meaning of natural resources ("the resources that matter") as the nation's economy has evolved from an agricultural to an industrial base and, more recently, as tertiary activities have grown in importance. The ever greater capacity for substi-

---

in an interesting monograph, that the whole matter of degree of application of state pollution legislation is the subject of *negotiation* between the agencies and the polluting industries. *Pollution Control as a Bargaining Process: An Essay on Regulatory Decision-Making* (Cornell University Water Resources Center Publication No. 9, October 1966).

[2] In an earlier period, for example, one thinks of the role of the concept centering on "the settlement of the West" encompassing notions of national stature, new opportunity, and the individual farmer as the backbone of democracy — all of which provided a base for governmental action "in the general interest" over a substantial period of time. In a more recent period, we have observed the role that the concept of full employment has played as a basis for public action in coping with problems of the business cycle and economic growth.

[3] Harvey S. Perloff and Lowdon Wingo, Jr., in Joseph J. Spengler (ed.), "Natural Resource Endowment and Regional Economic Growth," *Natural Resources and Economic Growth* (Resources for the Future, 1961), pp. 191–212; and Harvey S. Perloff, Edgar S. Dunn, Jr., Eric E. Lampard, and Richard F. Muth, *Regions, Resources, and Economic Growth* (The Johns Hopkins Press, 1960).

tution among natural resource commodities (through developments in science and technology), the increasing elaboration of commodities so that the economic value of the "first stage" is a small part of the total value added, and the fabulous growth in the demand for services have all joined to reduce the relative importance of natural resources commodities. The extent of this reduction is suggested by the fact that contribution of the so-called natural resources industries to GNP has declined from a third of the total in 1870 to some 11 per cent roughly a hundred years later.[4]

In the process, the concept of natural resources has been broadened somewhat. Thus, in recent decades, the notion of "amenity resources"— particularly as it reflects a special juxtaposition of climate, topography, coast and seashore, etc., especially attractive for the location of economic activities and family living — has been incorporated into the resources concept. Similarly, there have been increasing references to "open space resources," i.e., open areas, particularly on the outskirts of cities, that offer breathing space and recreation possibilities for city residents.

The time has arrived, however, to rethink the basic concept of natural resources in a more general way so that it has the greatest possible relevance to our own day and to the foreseeable future.

At the core, the more traditional commodity resources *and* the newer environmental resources ultimately yield services to consumers; to use the jargon of economics, they enter the individual's utility function. However, the newer environmental resources are much more subject to externalities than are the commodity resources: the activities of all kinds of production and consumption units — whether family, business firm, or governmental — may generate either direct or indirect external effects on other units. This is the case when a firm emits wastes into the air or into streams, when one building cuts out the sunlight from other buildings, when planes roar over a residential section of the city, when a car adds to the congestion on a highway, or when a great new subdivision uses up a beautiful open area on the edge of town. In each case, costs or "illfare" are imposed on others. Analysis of the newer resources thus forces us to face up to a basic defect in classical economics: the assumption that the utility functions of individual human beings are independent of one another. Actually, resource economics has been concerned with this issue for some time, but now the questions of externalities and of collective goods must be brought front and center.

It has long been accepted that, in a socioeconomic sense, natural resources are those elements of the natural environment that have a use to man, and are therefore in demand, but whose supply falls short of the demand. Thus, as developments occur in science and technology, new resources (uranium, for instance) come continually into being; or existing resources greatly increase in value (for instance, with advances in construction, vertical transportation, and communication technology, airspace becomes more valuable), while others pass out of use. Where an element of the natural

---

[4] Neal Potter and Francis T. Christy, Jr., *Trends in Natural Resource Commodities: Statistics of Prices, Output, Consumption, Foreign Trade, and Employment in the United States, 1870–1957* (The Johns Hopkins Press for Resources for the Future, 1962), as revised by Potter.

environment is in demand but supply is either plentiful for all or cannot readily be packaged for individual ownership and exchange, we have the case of a "free good" which is not considered a natural resource in the socioeconomic meaning of the term.[5] In almost all earlier economic texts, the classic case of a free good was fresh air. While in technical economic terms fresh air remains a free good, in a social accounting sense this is no longer the case in cities, where it entails large personal and group expenditures. If the meaning of natural resources is to be tied to the basic concept of features of the natural environment that are in relatively scarce supply, then it becomes necessary to invent a new category for those elements that, although they are in relatively scarce supply, still are not subject to individual ownership and exchange. This category would usefully serve to distinguish fresh air from, say, sunlight. The concept of free goods will clearly require rethinking.

Because natural resources have been associated with basic commodities important in national production for so long, there has been a lag in general appreciation of the extent to which the scarce elements of the natural environment today are of a non-commodity character. It takes quite a wrench in thinking to get away from the commodity view of natural resources and to be able to include in the resources category such elements as relatively pure air and water, three-dimensional space (including airway space, radio-spectrum space, city land, and underground space) and valued amenity features of the natural environment. Yet, in our crowded urban age, these are resources that count.

In trying to absorb the new resources elements into our conceptual scheme of things, and yet retain the major features of the more traditional interpretation of natural resources, there has been a tendency to associate these new elements almost exclusively with qualitative aspects of the environment and interpret this as essentially important for consumption rather than production. While the qualitative and consumption considerations certainly must loom large in any view of the newer resource elements, the quantitative and production aspects must also be seen as significant. A more complete view of the newer resource elements is provided most readily when we see them in terms of an extension of the basic natural resources concept — that is, when we accept an uninhibited interpretation of "needed elements of the natural environment that are in relatively short supply." This becomes particularly salient when we begin to grasp how different the whole production process is in the United States today compared to the past. Thus, less than 30 per cent of the labor force is engaged in commodity production and the proportion continues to decline.[6] The

---

[5] A feature of free goods has been that they do not become property. Insofar as they have value, they are expected to be capitalized as a component of land value. "Land" is thus viewed as a *collection* of fixed-to-a-place natural environmental features, including not only the geographic territory and soil, but also the associated water, climate, sunlight, air quality, and other amenity features.

[6] Even this figure is too high in a realistic sense. A substantial part of what the census puts in the commodity (or product) category actually involves service activities, ranging from R&D activities to paper work and promotional activities.

service industries loom increasingly large. The recreation and education industries, for example, will soon pass farming in importance in both labor force and GNP terms. Project these trends another generation and the picture of the economy has very little resemblance to the one that was pertinent when the early conservation movement in the United States first gathered momentum.

All this is familiar and yet we have a hard time getting away from the more traditional picture of the "productive plant" or the "economic base" as represented largely by the farms, the mines, and the factories. These are certainly still very important, but the productive plant must now be seen increasingly as a series of *interrelated networks* of training, research, communication (which is at the heart of an automated plant), transportation, water and air use, and many other processes, together with their capital embodiments, established mainly in an urban setting. Productivity changes are increasingly influenced by the efficiency of the urban "plant" or urban environment.

In the past, when agriculture was at the center of the economic stage, both the quantity and quality of the land and water resources in an intimate interrelationship (as well as the know-how and vigor applied in the production processes) were important to the results obtained. Similarly, when industrialization took hold, the quantity and quality of mineral as well as forest and farm resources were of central importance. Today, even if in a different setting, quantitative as well as qualitative factors are significant (always in an inextricable mix): e.g., the volume of water available for drinking, cooling, and waste disposal; the volume of air for waste disposal; the space available for the movement of planes or trucks; the land available for the construction of efficient industrial plants and for parking; the space available for radio-spectrum communications; and many other similar elements are a critical part of the production picture.

It is no trivial matter to establish the fact that the newer resource elements involve not only highly significant consumption and quality-of-living aspects but also equally significant production considerations. For example, if public annoyance with air and water pollution and traffic congestion should result in severe restrictions on industrial location, extremely heavy costs in industrial waste disposal, or severe limitation on the use of trucks, we may indeed pay a high price in rising costs of production. This is not to suggest, of course, that restrictions may not be appropriate under certain conditions; what is important is that the policy decisions should be made with a full appreciation of the production as well as the consumption factors. For in dealing with matters of the city, we are dealing with the very foundations of the nation's productive plant.

Once we begin to view features of urban land, air, and water, and space and amenity as significant natural resources, certain well-established principles, long associated with natural resources, come readily into play. These associations are not only significant intellectually (to the extent that meaningful classification is always important in the study of a subject), but also have important policy overtones. In the United States, the concept of natural resources carries certain strong connotations that influence the way in which we tend to approach an item that comes under the resources rubric. These connotations stem both from the impact made by the conservation movement, especially in the first third of this century, and from our experience with the use of our material (commodity) resources. They center on the well-established trinity of "conservation, development, and use of natural resources" and on at least some appreciation of the requirements and limitations posed by ecological considerations. Thus, in the United States, the term natural resources sets up an image encompassing several principles:

1. Resources are part of the national heritage; they should not be used unthinkingly and selfishly by any one group at the expense of others or by any one generation at the expense of future generations.

2. The value that the nation can receive from its resources depends on its willingness to *invest* in the *development* of such resources, whether it is a matter of enriching the soil, harnessing river basins or harnessing the atom, or experimenting with the best means for desalinization of water.

3. To get the most value out of the nation's resources, development wherever possible and appropriate should seek to achieve *multiple uses*. The multiple-purpose development of river basins comes most readily to mind, but the same principle applies to the use of farm land at the outskirts of cities for open space and recreation as well as for agricultural output.

4. While man has demonstrated a remarkable capacity for manipulation of nature for his own ends, there are basic ecological principles he must understand and respect if he is to achieve his objectives over an extended period of time and without extremely high costs in real terms. Optimum returns can be obtained only through a knowledgeable and thoughtful mix of natural and man-made elements.

These principles can be described in other ways, but the core elements would be similar. The main point to be made here is that such principles have direct and important relevance to the "newer" non-commodity elements of the natural environment discussed here. Thus, by encompassing these "newer" elements into the natural resources rubric we achieve a unifying and simplifying end which, as suggested earlier, is extremely important in laying a foundation for coherent and consistent public policy and administration.

Thus, for example, under the first principle, the question can legitimately be raised as to whether certain resources — urban land, air, water, etc. — should be considered to be in the public domain[7] (or at least whether private holding and use should be extensively controlled) in order to protect the more general interest. Reference to established legal and traditional principles with regard to the "older" resources, while by no means binding, is instructive and helps to firm up the basis for public policy. Experience with law and policy touching on the more traditional resources, for example, can have important implications as we begin to make extensive

[7] As Mason Gaffney has suggested for air.

use of air rights and underground or tunnel rights. Some legal scholars are beginning to make just this kind of extension; for example, with regard to air rights.[8]

In a similar light, the well-established principle of the desirability of *development* of natural resources to maximize social returns over time comes readily into play in thinking about the newer resources. Thus, for example, even in the face of a severe congestion problem in airways over and near cities, the existing approach is largely limited to the *regulation* of private commercial airlines, with limited investment in safety features and runways at the major airports. When airspace is viewed as a critically important natural resource, the desirability of addressing the problem through a developmental approach is immediately visible. The form and character of future city building should be examined in terms of achieving objectives with regard to the airways, as well as other objectives. For example, some airspace might well be set aside for the use of small airplanes only, to create what might be called air-commuting zones; this would clearly call for the development of a full ground-and-air approach to city building, in sharp contrast to the present two-dimensional approach.

The principle of multipurpose use of resources, which has evolved from, and has played such an important role in, river basin development, has great relevance for the urban-oriented resources. In fact, if sensibly applied, it is likely to achieve greater importance here than with regard to the more traditional resources. Communication and frequent interchanges are critical for most functions carried out in the city. The friction of space (transportation cost) not only produces the clustering of people and activities — that is, relatively high density — but in fact suggests that multiple-purpose use of space is at its essence a cost-saving device. Seen in this light, city building today tends to be highly inefficient. The present basically two-dimensional rather than three-dimensional city planning simultaneously promotes an outmoded single-purpose view of urban space (regulated by a simple set of zoning principles) and permits a wild jumble of incompatible uses, particularly on city streets.[9] Efficient and compatible multiple uses in a city require expert multiple-dimension planning. This is clearly a highly important area for additional thought and research. We urgently need principles that might guide decisions on when and how much multiple use is appropriate.

Finally, the importance of careful attention to ecological considerations in "conserving, developing, and using" urban-oriented resources should hardly need any special stress. It is evident that water and air can handle different amounts of pollution in different mixes under varying natural conditions; the capacity to make multiple use of these critically important resources is dependent in no small part on our knowledge of these natural conditions and the extent to which they can be modi-

[8] Michael M. Bernard, *Airspace in Urban Development, Emergent Concepts*, Technical Bulletin 46 (Urban Land Institute, July 1963).

[9] As Lawrence Halprin has put it: "It is too much to ask of a street that it serve, at the same time, for pedestrians and traffic and parking and shopping and children's play, and also provide amenity and quiet to the inhabitants along its way." *Cities* (Reinhold, 1963), p. 11.

fied. Builders who have constructed artificial lakes as space- and vista-providers often learn some quite interesting lessons about the ecology of still waters as algae emerge in abundance. The same is true of those who use or provide other amenity resources. A nice item along this line comes from Honolulu. It seems that Waikiki Beach may someday soon be scratched off the tourist's guide list because it is losing its sand. New shore-front hotels have been built where there are no beaches, so the hotel owners have created their own. These synthetic beaches have upset the normal action of the ocean tides and currents off Waikiki's shoreline so much that the ocean is reclaiming the sand. Beaches far from these hotels are also being denuded. (Incidently, sand costs about $6 a cubic yard in the islands.)

City people may find it a little harder than their country cousins to grasp the importance of ecological principles, but it will be a little easier to get the lessons across if they can first grasp the notion that natural resources are a significant part of their environment, not things way out there in the countryside. And once these lessons are learned, it might even be easier to talk publicly about externalities, and about costs imposed on others, and why new rules of the game may be needed if we are to achieve desirable urban environments.

The Urban Environment as a Subsystem

At an earlier point, I suggested that two concepts could play a useful simplifying and unifying role in creating a foundation for coherent and effective public policy with regard to the urban environment: in addition to the extension of the "natural resources" concept, there is need to see the urban environment as a contained highly interrelated system or subsystem. (Damage one part of it and other parts are immediately or soon affected; improve one part and other parts may be improved as a result.) In one sense, the "system" concept is an extension of the ecological considerations discussed above, but because of the importance of man-made features in the urban environment, the man-made as well as the natural elements must be seen as part of the relational system. Good and bad results are normally obtained as a result of the special *mix* of the two and therefore the two must be seen in all of their complex interrelationships.[10]

All urban units, whether city, metropolis, or megalopolis, are an integral and intimate part of the national scheme of things. None of them functions in isolated glory. It is not surprising, therefore, that all urban features, including the urban environment, comprise *open* systems. Roads, trains, and planes tie one city to others; messages go out and come in from everywhere; polluted water is carried from cities upstream to those downstream; polluted air is transported to distant areas; the size of the downtown of a given city will depend in no small part on how much of the nation's business is carried on there (thus, there is only one New York); urbanites vacation all over the country and the world; and so it goes. But the important consideration here is that the urban environment does comprise a meaningful and impor-

---

[10] This is true, of course, of the rural environment as well, but the sheer volume of man-made items in the urban setting is so great that the question of mix has a special relevance.

tant system, signifying that, as with all systems, the internal elements — in this case, the main features that characterize the urban environment — have greater and more intimate relations among themselves than they do with units or features outside the identified system. Geographers, economists, human ecologists, and other students of the city generally define the urban unit itself in terms of its nodal characteristics; that is, in terms of the quantity and intensity of the interactions. For example, they may define it in terms of the movement of persons and goods (while there is a great deal of movement *between* urban units, it does not compare to the daily movement back and forth *within* such units), in terms of the volume and frequency of messages sent, in terms of the extent of the local labor market, and the like. The physical areas covered by such intensity-of-flow items do not coincide exactly, but while the edges may be fuzzy, the urban community emerges as an identifiable nodal-type unit.

The nodal characteristics, while physically presenting a seemingly chaotic picture in our metropolitan and megalopolitan regions, have a clear and understandable logic. This has been an important part of the field of study of urban economics. The importance of centrality of location of economic activities stems from a number of factors, key among which is the significant — and generally increasing — specialization of function in manufacturing and service industries. Such specialization calls for the shipping of goods to and from a large number of producers, each adding value through specialized activity and sending them on. Thus, clustering is an important cost-saving device. Most of the production activities, in turn, call for the assistance of many specialized services, including professional services. The services themselves are linked not only with manufacturing activities but among themselves, with forward and backward and lateral linkages of every imaginable type. Those who ship goods need ports, railheads, highways, and airports that are linked with other major centers, and these facilities are, of course, necessarily localized to achieve the economies of scale to which they are subject.

The highly sophisticated manufacturing and service industries that are characteristic of our day require a wide and varied set of worker skills, and call for large labor pools. These are to be found only in population centers. Members of the skilled work force — including the managers — who are in demand choose to work in areas that they find pleasant for family living, and industry adjusts to this preference. Since many such persons prefer to live in communities which provide a large number of services, facilities, and amenities, cities draw activities for this reason as well. Here, centrality is a factor, since the costlier services and facilities (for instance, a symphony hall) must draw on a large population, but with urban growth many of the services and facilities can be provided in subcenters. This, however, only means that although centrality is somewhat more complex than in an earlier day, the economies-of-scale factor still comes strongly into play.

Taken together, all this adds up to the creation and maintenance of an elaborate *system* of people, capital, and movement with an inherent logic.

Nodality is a physical as well as economic phenomenon. This is true of the key elements in the *urban environment*. Thus, we can usefully speak of an airshed and a watershed encompassing an urban community, each with a focal zone; we can demarcate the open spaces and amenity areas reachable within, say, a Sunday's drive (an open-space-recreation zone if you wish) on the basis of a "gravity model"; we can separate the city into characteristic areas such as the central business district (CBD), inner city residential areas, suburbs (including high-income enclaves), and exurbia; we can demarcate the major transportation movements in nodal terms; and we can characterize work environments — downtown, in industrial estates, and scattered.

Systemic elements of the urban environment are generated not only by interrelations of natural and man-made features, but by *trade-offs* between these features (as well as within them). For example, more airconditioning of homes and workplaces can serve as a substitute for more air pollution control (that is, controlling the micro- rather than the macroenvironment). Polluting plants can be moved to the edge of or beyond the local air- or watershed instead of providing waste removal features within these plants. More open space might be provided in town, or people may be encouraged (by good roads, etc.) to drive out to the natural open spaces at the edge of town.[11]

Urbanites are not accustomed to thinking of their environment as a contained, highly interrelated system. Thus, they will complain loudly about air pollution conditions and yet vote for a mayor who promises to bring new manufacturing plants into town and to build superhighways right into the heart of the city. They will complain about the rapid loss of open space and yet vote for severe restrictions on the height of apartment and office buildings, for large-lot zoning, and for building highways through parks in order to reduce their cost. They will decry the loss of amenity resources nearby and yet permit private building right up to the beach edge and the pollution of nearby lakes. Of course, all this is not simply a matter of overlooking an important concept or a lack of understanding of systems analysis. Diverse interests are involved (different people are affected differently by these seemingly contradictory policies) and there are profits to be made, costs to be avoided, and elections to be won. But the point still needs to be made that the creation of a common ground of

[11] The trade-off notion is not always readily accepted. Thus, for example, a *Washington Evening Star* editorial (16 September, 1967) concerned with airplane noise, states: "The Los Angeles Department of Airports has come up with an unusual solution to the problem of noise from jet aircraft. . . . Officials are planning to award contracts soon for soundproofing a dozen homes around International Airport and measuring the before-and-after level of decibels. The project, which will cost some $200,000, seems designed to prepare the way for soundproofing of many dwellings with the help of local government subsidy. . . . But one can't help wondering if this isn't exactly the kind of solution that the airlines would like best, since it involves no effort on their part. By the same reasoning, why not put a filter on every homeowner's faucets to cope with water pollution, or install universal air-conditioning to 'solve' the question of polluted atmosphere?"

Why not indeed? The editorial writer has overlooked the fact that most homes in the United States are individually heated while group heating is practiced in Sweden and elsewhere and that many other services have gone one way or the other over the years (including movie watching). The Los Angeles Department of Airports is indeed to be congratulated for carrying out a sensible experiment. I would hope that they are simultaneously looking into another alternative — that of location and relocation policy to cope with the noise problem — as well as into the question of the relative cost of building quieter planes.

understanding of what is involved in working towards a desirable urban environment is essential for the building of a foundation for sensible, coherent public policy concerned more with a broad range of interests than with powerful but limited special interests.

Elements within the Environmental System

If we are to develop an understanding of the urban-environment system, it will be necessary as a starting point to identify the key elements involved; that is, those elements whose relationships and interactions define and give special character to the system. This is a complex matter and can probably be done at various levels and in various frameworks. As a starting point and at a very general level, it is helpful, in order to sharpen the contrast between open and closed systems, to think of the key environmental elements involved in collective-living, high-density situations of an essentially *closed* character so as to identify similarities and differences with a more open situation of the type we are discussing.

At a very simple level, one thinks of the cavedweller situation (which evidently comprised the human environment for a certain group of early man over a very long period of time, possibly a million years). Key elements in such cave environments evidently were the maintenance of relatively pure air (smoke pollution must have been a serious problem); acquiring and storing drinkable water; provisions for warmth and general bodily comfort; and division of space between family living quarters, work activities, recreation, and other clan activities. (Development of different types of enclosures for various groups and activities was related to technology; for example, the use of animal skins as cave dividers.) Environmental aesthetics were evidently not neglected, as suggested by the numerous cave paintings which have been found.

Essentially the same elements are identifiable when we think of other relatively closed environmental systems, such as that of the present day submarine, bathysphere, and space capsule.[12] At the other extreme of complexity from the old cave environment, diving into the wild blue yonder, are the environmental elements involved in a space satellite of the far distant future. In *Beyond Tomorrow*,[13] D. M. Cole (a senior space scientist at General Electric's Space Technology Center) gives some attention to the environmental factors. His vision of "a new home among the stars" accommodates between 10,000 to one million people in a hollow asteroid, possibly 20 miles long, 10 miles in diameter. Such colonies, Cole suggests, could cruise space in their self-powered, closed cycle worlds by using new forms of macro-ecological relations and by developing flexible and extremely attractive interior environmental conditions. Here, too, air, water, weather conditioning, sunlight, space, and amenity features are pictured as key elements of the environment.

[12] A lively and informative treatment of the problems and possibilities in the realm of closed ecological systems is provided in "2000+," the February 1967 issue of *Architectural Design*, John MacHale, Guest Editor.

[13] D. M. Cole, *Beyond Tomorrow* (Amherst Press, 1965).

The closed-system view not only helps to highlight the basic elements that are essential for man's survival and comfort, but also suggests the many varieties of collective-living, high-density environments that are conceivable at different levels of technological development and different kinds of socioeconomic patterning. There is a strong tendency in our cities today to accept existing forms and relationships as given, merely because they are familiar. We simply do not think about these matters unless some problem emerges which makes us uncomfortable, such as excessive air pollution or noise. Actually, with vast opportunities for achieving varied and attractive urban environments, the key elements of the environment and the ways in which they are interrelated, or can be made to interrelate, should be subjects of continuing study and private as well as public concern. The existing uses made of urban and nearby land; of three-dimensional space; of air and water; of structures for living, working, and collective activities; of climatic elements; and of amenity features of the environment must be recorded in meaningful ways, so that the interrelationships and interactions can be highlighted as a base for decisions that will influence the environment in desired directions.

While discussing elements of the environment, it is well to note also that for the greatest part such elements do not interact only at the scale of the urban unit as a whole — say, the metropolis — but are found in different intensities and in special mixes at smaller scales. Thus, air and water quality (or degrees of pollution) are different in different parts of the metropolis (air pollution, for example, will be more intense at congested transportation points or in parts of the metropolis dominated by manufacturing industry). Similarly, availability (nearness) of open space is different for every section of the urban unit; the condition of structures and their spacing will be different in each neighborhood; and the condition of the water, sewerage, and waste disposal facilities will differ from section to section. A careful recording of these differences and of the total impact of the special mixes to be found in each identifiable section of the urban unit is critical for sound policy making. The issue is generally not how some hypothetical average individual is faring, but the quality of the environment within which different real groups are living, working, and moving about. Information on distribution of qualitative levels should not be overlooked. This can be summed up by saying that the reality of the slum, as well as of the magnificent high-income enclaves, must be recognized in any meaningful approach to the problems of the urban environment.

Differentiation must not only be provided in geographic terms, but also in terms of the various groups making up the urban society. Different groups react differently to various aspects of the environment and also make different contributions to the environment or detract from it. This is seen most readily when the question of crowding in the urban environment is considered. Edward T. Hall, a student of the subject, has pointed out:

The degree to which peoples are sensorially involved with each other, and how they use time, determines not only at what point they are crowded but the methods for relieving crowding as well. Puerto Ricans and Negroes have a much higher involvement ratio than New Englanders and Americans of German or Scandinavian stock. Highly involved people apparently require higher densities than less involved people, and they may also require more protection or screening from outsiders. It is absolutely essential that we learn more about how to compute the maximum, minimum, and optimum density of the different cultural enclaves that make up our cities.[14]

Hall suggests that the various ways in which different groups handle time is reflected in their need for space. "Monochronic" and "polychronic" styles of time-use are characteristic of what he calls low-involvement and high-involvement groups and this in turn influences their relative degree of need to separate activities in space.

Beyond group characteristics, there are important individual differences that must also be taken into account.

The Urban Environment and the Environment of Urbanites

It has been noted that the urban environmental system is an open one. It is open in various ways. Thus, instead of ending discernibly at one line, the built-up relatively dense sector of a city or metropolitan region fades gradually out into the countryside. City and countryside intermingle in a rather wide belt. Villages, towns, and farms provide a somewhat different setting for living and working than does the more built-up portion: open space is hardly in scarce supply, travel distances tend to be longer, water and sewerage facilities are often not tied in to the core systems. Yet the people living in such zones are largely urbanites (or farmers much concerned with the question of the appropriate time to sell their land) and these zones are mainly areas for future building. Roads and utility lines built here, open space set aside, and other activities (or lack of them) will influence the future urban environment in important ways.

The system is also open, as suggested earlier, in its direct transportation and communication linkages with other urban centers. This deserves particular attention because of the tendency for "string" construction along highways in many parts of the country to provide a very special — and in many cases aesthetically horrendous — urban environment. Often such string developments are found in the outer zone mentioned above and are thus an integral part of the general exurban picture.

Finally, the system is open in the sense that urbanites living within the built-up, high-density areas — that is, within the core urban environment — spend greater or lesser periods of time away from that environment, largely for recreation purposes, and particularly for vacations. Some have vacation homes in recreation environments. In this regard, amenity resources achieve particular significance. The quality of these resources and their closeness to urban centers (which has a great deal to do with frequency of visits) thus is part of the "environment of urbanites" if not part of the urban environment itself. These resources, of course, also comprise part of the

[14] Edward T. Hall, *The Hidden Dimension* (Doubleday and Company, Inc., 1966).

environment of rural populations, but for present purposes we are limiting attention to the urban population. The problems are clearly different for the rural population.

The value of recognizing these factors in any full-bodied treatment of environmental issues suggests that we have to be concerned not only with spatial elements — that is, the extent of the urban environment that is being described, analyzed, or controlled by public policy and action — but also with function, time, and intensity dimensions. We want to know how much time during the week, month, or year various groups in the population are "exposed" to the different kinds of environments and, if possible, the intensity of the exposure. These matters will be touched upon at a later point.

Policy Measures and a Decision Framework

It seems evident that the quality of the urban environment — as well as the environment for urbanites — will increasingly be a matter for public concern. The caliber of governmental policy and action with regard to environmental issues can be expected to be improved as our knowledge of the environment increases and as we develop better tools for decision making. It therefore seems appropriate to devote major attention to the question of reporting on the environment and on means for evaluating public action with regard to the environment.

Reporting on and evaluating the urban environment presents different problems from those presented by the more traditional commodity natural resources. While in the latter case there are usually some externalities to be considered and complex systemic interrelational elements to be dealt with, these features are so much greater in the case of the urban environment that it is a matter of kind more than of degree. The interrelationships among the elements of the environmental system and the externalities are so central in the scheme of things that we must come to grips with the question of how these can be highlighted meaningfully. This underlines the importance of a useful reporting and analytical framework. The problem of creating such a framework is hardly new. City planners have been struggling with the issue for over half a century. However, city planning has emphasized — almost to the exclusion of other considerations — past, present, and future *land uses.* Other urban natural resources (air and water, for example) have rarely received major attention; this is true also for systemic elements within the urban environment, such as the multiple relationships between land use and man-made structures.

We can probably go a substantial distance toward providing a useful reporting-and-evaluation framework through the use of what have come to be known as social indicators and social accounts. I have found particularly stimulating the proposal for an annual Social Report of the President, parallel to the Economic Report, but concerned with a different set of issues, including the quality-of-the-environment question. A system of reporting which would fulfill the requirements of such an annual report would have to characterize changes in environmental quality through the use of a few particularly pertinent measures, and to evaluate the results obtained through various public and private efforts to improve the environment. A national reporting scheme would necessarily have to be quite broad — and essentially limited — in scope. It should, logically, be supplemented by reporting on a local basis, that is, by state-of-the-region reports, which can provide a useful foundation for policy making and governmental action at the local and metropolitan scale. The problem of reporting at the national level would be much eased if the appropriate information was available for all the urban units within the nation.

What might such a system of reporting appropriately contain?[15]

First, it is necessary to decide just how much is to be included under the environmental rubric. It is evident, at one extreme, that it cannot be limited merely to physical (including natural) factors if the information is to provide a useful foundation for decision making. At the other extreme, it cannot usefully cover all matters that at one time or another are referred to as "environmental." The latter would bring in just about everything. The term environment is often used not only to cover the natural and man-made surroundings but also much of the social-political-economic ambience — i.e., frequent references are made to "a democratic environment," "a competitive environment," etc. These types of issues can be covered more appropriately under other headings in either a Social Report of the President or a state-of-the-region report at the local level, say, with regard to a discussion of "equality of opportunity" or under "political participation."

Any delimiting of a field, even for reporting purposes, involves all sorts of cultural (including language) and political considerations, particularly the explicit and implicit public objectives or goals that are currently dominant. For present purposes — mainly to introduce some ideas for discussion in a preliminary way — it may be appropriate to start with an attempt to look at the more important elements that directly influence *conditions of living and working of the urban population* and particularly where they influence *the health, comfort, safety, and aesthetic satisfaction of individuals.* This would suggest limiting coverage to those aspects that are necessary to *differentiate localized situations* of some importance to the lives of the people; for example, those aspects that are essential to describe either slum conditions in our cities or the relative purity of the air within given metropolitan regions, but not those features that are common for people everywhere, the host of essentially *national* economic, social, cultural, and political factors in the quality of American life.

The differentiation of localized situations would have to proceed at various levels to distinguish between significantly different *settings.* Thus, as already suggested, it would be necessary to distinguish between metropolitan and non-metro-

[15] The materials presented here are based on a "Preliminary Report on Environment" which I prepared for the Panel on Social Indicators of the U.S. Department of Health, Education, and Welfare (May 1967) with the help of Joseph L. Fisher and Robert Gold. I want to acknowledge the many useful suggestions I have received on the earlier report from my colleagues, Irving Hoch, Lowdon Wingo, and Blair Bower, which I have incorporated in the present statement, as well as from Fisher and Gold.

politan (basically, small town) settings; between built-up and low-density zones, residential and nonresidential areas; and among the various characteristic types of communities, such as slum areas, middle-class areas, and the like.

Elements to Be Covered

It is proposed that the following items be included under the environmental rubric for metropolitan areas:[16]

THE NATURAL ENVIRONMENT

1. The airshed (to describe relative purity of air and air pollution);
2. The watershed (to cover water supply and water pollution);
3. The open space-recreation "shed" (to cover conditions within an area that can be reached on a one-day recreation trip);
4. Quiet-and-noise zones (to describe relative degree and time-span of noise exposure);
5. Olfactory zones (to describe relative degree and time-span of exposure to unpleasant smells);
6. "Micro-climate" zones (including uncomfortable heat, wind blockage, etc.)[17]
7. Sunlight exposure (relative condition of buildings with regard to good, bad, or indifferent sunlight exposure).

THE SPATIAL ENVIRONMENT

While basically part of the natural environment, it differs enough from the items under "The Natural Environment" to deserve special treatment. This category would attempt to characterize the use of underground space,[18] land, and overground space in terms of standards of efficient use (e.g., relative congestion and duration of what might be called low-quality conditions), changes in values of space, and degree of allocation of space in terms of relative values (thus, amount of subsidy would be highlighted).[19]

THE TRANSPORTATION-UTILITIES ENVIRONMENT

These have the characteristic of tying the metropolitan area into an integrated unit through a series of superimposed networks (or what might be called the skeletal features of the region). They tie directly into the natural environment through those

---

[16] The metropolitan region is highlighted here because it calls for the most extensive coverage.

[17] Because of traditional usage, "micro" is used here, although on a different scale from that employed in the case of home and work environments, where the term is also employed.

[18] It is reported that in about a hundred cities in the U.S.S.R., 35 per cent or more of the investment in structures is in the portion that lies underground. American Public Works Association Research Foundation, *Better Utilization of Urban Space* (Chicago, June 1967), p. 7.

[19] Urban ground and near-ground spaces cover a remarkable (and fascinating) variety, including: streets of various kinds; alleys; freeways; minor and major plazas; gardens; playgrounds; neighborhood, central, and regional parks; waterfronts; rooftops; open parking lots; etc., etc.

utilities that provide water supply and provide for sewerage and solid waste disposal; also as they use underground, land, and overground resources. The latter is additionally significant in the case of electric and gas utilities, as well as telephone utilities. Aesthetic considerations with regard to such facilities have come increasingly to the fore.

The transportation network is particularly important for the urban environment. Accessibility, including relative accessibility to amenity resources, is a basic consideration in many aspects of the environment. The reporting should cover such items as availability of mass transit and other forms of transportation and the conditions surrounding movement in general, including considerations of trip-time, congestion, safety, and stress.

THE COMMUNITY-OR-NEIGHBORHOOD ENVIRONMENT

This item would cover the main environmental elements within markedly differentiated communities or neighborhoods — for example, slum areas, other central city areas, and suburban and exurban areas. The term community or neighborhood here is intended simply to imply the existence of distinguishable common characteristics of physical elements, together with important interactions between people and physical environment within a contiguous geographic area by the fact of juxtaposition and "mix." At the same time, in order to provide adequate coverage of public service and facility conditions, it would be desirable not to restrict the areas too narrowly in geographic terms. The services environment is necessarily variable (since different services extend over different zones) so that in defining areas some fuzziness at the edges might well be appropriate.

THE MICROENVIRONMENTS

The family or household shelter and the workplace are the settings for the individual's most intimate social relations as well as for his most direct and frequent contacts with the man-made physical environment.

The framework that is thus provided can be described as one of several environmental "envelopes" (although the term should not be taken too literally) through which the quality of the urban environment can be characterized: the large natural resources and space-use envelope, the community-neighborhood envelope, and the home and work microenvelope, all tied together in various ways and literally tied together through the transportation-utilities set of networks. Each of these is characterized by different underlying conditions, the first through the special role of urban-oriented natural resources, the second by the interrelations of group behavior patterns and these with the man-made physical environment, and the third — the microenvironment — by the primacy and intimacy of social relationships as well as by the special needs and characteristics of a limited group (the household in one case, and employees of specific workplaces in the other). The importance of the microenvironment is attested to by the fact that some 68 per cent of the total time of urban adults, on the average, is spent at home. The figure is 76 per cent for the total urban population.[20] Of the remaining time, almost two-thirds is spent at work.

Indicators, Accounts, and Policy Measures

A broad framework for what I would call a system of "policy measures for the environment" is suggested here (see Table 1). First, let me make some comments about the terms used. "Indicator" is normally used to describe the condition of a single element, factor, or the like, which is part of a complex interrelated system (employment, cost of living, production, etc., in the case of economic indicators). It is evident that in the case of the urban environment equally revealing indicators can be provided to describe existing conditions — say, with regard to air pollution, quality of housing, amount of open space available, etc.

"Accounts," on the other hand, refer to comprehensive systems of data characterized by a balance between inputs and outputs or inflows and outflows (such as national income accounts, input-output accounts, or flow-of-funds accounts) or providing the value of the total stock of various items in a total system, as in the case of wealth accounts. We have a long way to go before we are able to work out comprehensive social accounts for the environment. However, as noted at a number of points, it is important to provide a broad picture of the urban environment because it is essential to be able to highlight interrelationships and externalities. What seems possible at the present time is the provision of rather comprehensive "policy measures" or "decision measures" that, while not fully comprehensive or characterized by balanced two-way flows, could nevertheless serve a unifying purpose in reporting on the environment specifically as an aid to governmental policy decisions. These must include both stock and flow items and, because of the focus on public policy, emphasize outlays and investment and the returns on these.

Table 1 on pages 22–23 outlines the main elements of the data framework proposed.

The first task involved would be to work out meaningful "indicators of present condition" (column 1) for each of the items listed. These would reflect present goals and standards (both legislative and informal) with the data attempting to indicate where we stand with regard to these goals and standards. The establishment of standards is no mean task. It would require a good bit of research as well as a sensitive reading of the standards that have the broadest and most strongly-held acceptance. This clearly is an evolving task. In the first instance, the best standards at hand would be employed. At the same time, it would be useful to highlight the weaknesses of existing standards, particularly where too narrow an interpretation of objectives to be achieved could be misleading, and to explore the special characteristic of measures within the different categories.

As Joseph Fisher has pointed out (in his chapter in the "Preliminary Report on

---

[20] Taken from a time budget study of forty-four U.S. cities. See Alexander Szalai, "Multinational Comparative Social Research," *American Behavioral Scientist*, Vol. 10, No. 4 (December 1966).

Environment" for the Panel on Social Indicators of the U.S. Department of Health, Education, and Welfare), the quality characteristics of the environment tend, to a considerable extent, to be subjective, with considerable variation in the views of different individuals. Further, air pollution and recreation opportunities, for example, affect different individuals quite differently, both physiologically and psychologically.

Another point deserves attention: The various aspects of the natural environment are interrelated in numerous and sometimes confusing ways. One way of abating industrial air pollution is by filtering and washing smoke to prevent contaminants from going into the atmosphere, and instead sluicing them out into the water courses, thereby adding to water pollution. The interrelations extend beyond the realm of natural resources. For example, one way of reducing pollution from automobiles would be to discourage or prohibit certain uses, but this would greatly affect transportation and might also drastically alter the microenvironment in which people live and work. Just as the various kinds of environmental pollution tend to be interconnected, so also the measures for abating and controlling them tend to be interconnected. And one should be cautious about interpreting a favorable movement over time in an indicator of air pollution lest it is accompanied by an equal or greater movement in the opposite direction in an indicator of water pollution.

Concern for arriving at some overall indicator of environmental quality in which the various interrelations and trade-offs can be included leads one toward the concept of net social benefit — that is, total (or incremental) social benefit less social cost. This concept of net social benefit can be applied to a particular kind of environmental disturbance or it can be thought of in connection with a large range of environmental effects.

The social indicators alone can provide only a limited part of the story. If we are looking ultimately to policy, it would be essential to get a picture also of the costs of our shortfalls, as well as the costs and anticipated benefits of actually fulfilling existing goals and standards, or higher-level goals and standards. But this calls for more than indicators; here we would have to put policy measures to work. The key categories that might be employed are suggested in Table 1.

Thus, the reporting system proposed would set out, as a second item, "costs of environmental maintenance at present levels" (column 2), broken down by private and public costs wherever possible. In almost every instance, substantial sums are already being spent in order to maintain existing environmental conditions — no matter how unsatisfactory. This is true of the present expenditures involved in keeping down air and water pollution; it is also true of the costs involved in trying to create a relatively safe street environment and transportation environment. The setting down of current cost figures would provide a rough measure of the relative amount of effort directed at any one of the items of interest in the environment. It would raise issues about the priorities attached to the various subjects and it would also raise questions such as whether we are getting our money's worth. There is a tendency in most discussions of the environment to think only in terms of the additional expenditures necessary to achieve somewhat higher levels. This can be misleading, certainly as regards

Table 1. *Framework for Evaluating Policy Measures for the Environment*

Elements in the environment	Indicators of present condition	Costs of environmental maintenance at present levels		Costs (or other adverse consequences) of environmental abuses and shortfalls		Costs of achieving standards at various levels		Benefits of achieving standards at various levels	
		Private	Public	Private	Public	Private	Public	Private	Public
	(1)	(2)		(3)		(4)		(5)	

A. *The natural environment*
   1. The airshed
   2. The watershed
   3. The open space–recreation "shed"
   4. Quiet-and-noise zones
   5. Olfactory zones
   6. Micro-climate zones
   7. Sunlight exposure

B. *The spatial environment*
   1. Underground space
   2. Uncovered land
   3. Covered land
   4. Radiospectrum space
   5. Airways space

C. *Transportation–utilities environment*
   1. Transportation:
      a) commuting time; b) alternative modes, including mass transit;
      c) congestion; d) safety; e) stress;
      f) aesthetics (e.g., billboards, landscaping)
   2. Water supply facilities
   3. Sewerage facilities
   4. Solid waste disposal

5. Electricity facilities
6. Gas facilities
7. Telephone facilities
8. Other communication facilities

D. *Community–neighborhood environment*
 1. Community characteristics:
  a) mix (e.g., degree of segregation);
  b) types and condition of structures and land uses;
  c) community stresses; d) design environment (densities, street lighting, billboards, interest points, landscaping, zoning, etc.)
 2. Services environment (measures of quality and nearness):
  a) educational–cultural environment; b) personal safety and protection; c) health facilities and services; d) commercial facilities and services; e) recreation facilities and services; f) "caretaker" functions

E. *Household shelter*
 1. Housing condition
 2. Crowding
 3. Rats, roaches, and other pests
 4. Plumbing
 5. Household equipment

F. *Workplaces*
 1. Safety
 2. Amenities (e.g., eating facilities, sanitation)
 3. Work challenge indicators (assembly line, freedom of movement, etc.)

the relative emphasis to be given to different activities. As in the other major items to be covered, breakdowns in terms of the various sections of a metropolitan region (slums, suburbs, etc.), would provide a useful picture of the relative attention being given to the various parts of the region.

Column 3 in the proposed reporting system calls for estimates of the costs — or other adverse consequences — of environmental abuses and shortfalls. In this, an attempt would be made, not only to obtain rough estimates of such items as the costs resulting from air pollution, but also of inadequate public services. Such costs would be recorded in dollar terms wherever possible, even if some heroic assumptions have to be made. In cases where dollar costs are simply not to be had, sharply focused descriptions or indicators of a non-cost nature would be useful.[21]

Here, again, the specification of the standards to be achieved would be essential, particularly in measuring shortfalls. It is necessary to establish a wide variety of fairly narrow and specific standards — e.g., for housing quality — as well as broader, more aggregative goals, such as a satisfactory home and community environment. Not only must standards be quite specific in the case of the environment, but they are also inevitably rather variable, that is, they often have to cover a wide range. Thus, it is possible to set up standards for various degrees of "purity" in the case of air and water and to measure the cost of achieving such standards as well as the cost of falling short of their achievement. The same is true in the case of housing standards, standards of congestion, and many other features that might be included under the environmental rubric. To round out the picture, then, it would be necessary to provide estimates of costs of achieving standards at various levels (column 4).

Thus, the whole system is built on a recognition of the fact that the quality of the environment is judged by the values of the society, that different levels of achievement are possible, that each of these has cost features attached — both in achieving the given levels and in falling short of achieving them — and that benefits are also to be derived from improvements in the environment. Unfortunately, these benefits are very much harder to define. In some cases they can be fairly firm, particularly when the benefit amounts to an avoidance of the cost of abuse or shortfall. But in other cases they are much more general. Over time, however, it might be increasingly possible to provide benefit estimates. Even short of such figures, it would be possible to describe in general terms the benefits of achieving specified standards and, thereby, to provide a better basis for public judgment.

At a later stage it might be possible to introduce additional types of indicators or other measures to round out the picture and provide a better basis for evaluating the present and alternative futures. One of these would be a "time budget" or measure of time expenditures, which would provide a picture of the time spent in major activities by various categories of individuals, and thus, in a general way, suggest the

[21] A sense of how much information can be conveyed by focused description is provided by the statements in the Supreme Court 1954 school decision on the losses attendant on a "separate-but-equal" education system.

relative importance of different kinds of environments and the uses made of them.[22] Such a measure, together with direct measures of intensity of use of services and facilities as well as of homes, workplaces, and transportation, would provide the basis for measurement of relative "exposure" and the development of risk ratios. This, for example, would tend to show the tremendous importance of the street in poor neighborhoods, the extent to which some public facilities are overutilized and others underutilized, and the relative exposure of people to various areas of the city (thus emphasizing, for example, the relatively great importance of small intown open spaces — such as squares and school playgrounds — as compared to vast open spaces far beyond the reach of most people). An intensity index could be a very powerful tool for decision making in some of the environmental items.

Differentiation in the "policy measures" not only needs to be made with regard to various classes of communities within a metropolis but also with regard to various age groups, income groups, and racial and ethnic groups. Wherever pertinent, the indices or measures should be in terms of age, income, and race and ethnic categories as in the educational-cultural environment, in health, and in recreation.

The indicators of present conditions should, wherever possible, provide information on three kinds of items: (1) the *average* situation in the various communities for the key items, as well as group distribution around the average; (2) improvement or deterioration over time, and (3) extreme situations that deserve special attention. In general, treatment of extreme situations is necessary so that significant *special* problems are not overlooked: without such items any reporting scheme would tend to be much too bland. If the scheme is to serve policy and action purposes realistically, a description of community stresses when the situation is explosive or of pollution conditions when health is directly threatened should not be lost in a mere deluge of data on averages.

Final Note

The information framework proposed here is essentially a decision-making "model," highlighting the present state of affairs, what is deemed good and bad about it, the costs we suffer as a result of the shortcomings, and what is needed to bring the situation up to higher standards. The implementation of such a model would clearly require substantial effort but, when operational, it would provide an extremely valuable decision-making tool. It has the clear advantage of being close to policy and operations both in terms of its inputs and outputs; that is, on the one side, administrative or operating data could be used as the main sources of information while, on the other, it would provide a basis for policy decisions in a direct and meaningful framework. It is taken as an article of faith that governmental policy and action will be improved as knowledge about the urban environment increases and alternative possibilities can be reviewed in a broad and meaningful decision framework.

---

[22] See the Chapin-Logan paper on pp. 303–32.

Appendix: Microenvironmental responses to changes in the urban environment

Richard J. and Beverly F. Frankel

Harvey Perloff, in his paper, defines the possible arrays of environmental elements and their trade-offs, both natural and man-made, which give special character to the urban-environment system. He suggests that a study of the trade-offs surrounding these basic elements would not only quantify the multiple levels of high-density living, but could conceivably define levels of technological development and socioeconomic patterning formed in urban environments. In an effort to record the interactions of urban living that influence policy making, Perloff presents a comprehensive framework of several environmental "envelopes."

Without taking into account the ethnic and socioeconomic differences found among urbanites, the writers have attempted to qualify Perloff's environmental envelopes by listing and defining in some detail several of the environmental characteristics of concern in urban environments. What is deemed important is the individual or private microenvironmental response as opposed to the public or governmental-control approach to a change in the quality of the macroenvironment. Our thesis is that the individual tends to replenish in his microenvironment what the macroenvironment lacks or makes scarce. The individual responses to changes in the macroenvironment fall into four distinct and rather independent groups: individual responses to himself (mental attitudes and dress); home environment (indoors); surroundings of the home environment (outdoors); and translocation of or moving from the macroenvironment. Table A–1 suggests some of the "individualized," microenvironmental responses to macroenvironmental conditions.

At the time the paper was written, Richard J. Frankel was a visiting scholar at Resources for the Future.

Table A–1. Policy Measures for the Environment: Responses to Macroenvironmental Conditions

Elements in the environment	Attribute of macroenvironment	Societal–governmental approach	Private or individual microenvironmental approach	
			Family	Workplace (firm)
	(1)	(2)	(3)	
A. THE NATURAL ENVIRONMENT				
1. The airshed	Air quality (smoke, soot, smog, gaseous waste); smells or odors	a) Emission or ambient air standards; b) Fuel or combustion equipment standards; c) Taxation on emissions.	(*Self*) Shift from outdoor to indoor physical activities. (*Household*) a) Ventilation control (air filters, air conditioning in car and house); b) Greater frequency of cleaning (clothes, household items, and car) and earlier replacement of goods due to more rapid deterioration; c) Increase in outdoor maintenance (repairs, repainting, and vegetation replacement); d) Relocation to another neighborhood or city. (*Transport*) More frequent trips (from polluted areas).	a) Process change or product substitution to reduce waste; b) Waste treatment to reduce pollution; c) Air conditioning of entire plant (closed windows); d) Relocation of factory.
2. The watershed	Water quality (pH, hardness, turbidity, dissolved solids, BOD, organisms, etc.)	a) Water quality standards; b) Municipal water and waste treatment plants; c) Effluent charges or user fees; d) Regional transfers of water.	(*Self*) Bottled water or preferences for other drinks. (*Household*) a) Individual wells; b) Home water softeners; c) Greater consumption of soaps; more rapid deterioration of clothes; d) Outdoor vegetation affected (change in types of shrubbery). (*Transport*) Change in type and location of water sports.	a) Change in water source (new wells or water intake points); b) Industrial water and waste treatment plants; c) Change in water consumption per unit of output, recirculation, and reuse; d) Relocation of industry.

Table A-1. (Continued)

Elements in the environment	Attribute of macroenvironment	Societal–governmental approach	Private or individual microenvironmental approach	
			Family	Workplace (firm)
	(1)	(2)		(3)
3. Open-space–recreation "shed"	Lack of vegetation, scrubby open areas (due to asphalting, density, and buildings).	a) Urban redevelopment programs (tree-lined avenues, parkways, playgrounds, shopping malls, etc.); b) Change in transport system (subways, commuter trains, buses, off-street parking, underground highways, center-strip plantings).	(*Household*) a) Plants in lobby, entrance ways, and around house; b) More flowers, flower pots, flowery wallpaper. (*Transport*) a) Frequent trips to gardened parks; b) Relocation to suburbia.	
4. Quiet–and–noise zones	Noise	a) Zoning regulations (quiet around hospital areas); b) Muffler standards (car inspections, construction equipment, planes, diesel trucks); c) Flight patterns or routes around cities; d) Laws of nuisance pertaining to noise	(*Self*) Ear plugs. (*Household*) a) Air conditioning of home and car; b) Thicker wall construction, more insulation, closed windows; c) Competitive background noise from radio, TV. (*Transport*) a) Premiums on certain locations of private homes or high apartment units away from street level; b) Relocation of home (or construction of units at far end of lots, away from street).	a) Insulation or heavier construction; b) "Musak" or other background music programs; c) Complete air conditioning (closed windows).
5. Olfactory zones (see airshed)				

6. Micro-climate zones	Weather variations (differences in climate between areas and seasons as distinguished from small changes due to air pollution or heat sinks in urban areas)	a) Building codes or standards for construction materials; b) School sessions varied to suit weather; c) Snow removal operations; d) Geodesic domes.	(Self) a) Individual dress—light reflective color in heat; dark, heavy material in cold; b) Reapportionment of leisure time between inside and outside activities; c) Sports change between indoor and outdoor. (Household) a) House design includes basement for recreational areas when weather does not permit outdoor playground; b) Stress on indoor activities for family (TV, reading, games, exercise groups).	a) Cropping patterns or plants grown varied depending on climate; b) Enclosure of facilities (construction) varied; c) Number of working days or school days per year varied.
7. Sunlight exposure	Amount of sunshine	Building codes (requiring space between buildings, maximum height).	(Household) a) Larger window areas; b) Lighter colors in decorating.	a) More glass construction, increased artificial light; b) Lighter and brighter colors in decorating.

B. THE SPATIAL ENVIRONMENT (partially covered under "D")

C. TRANSPORTATION–UTILITIES ENVIRONMENT

1. Transportation	Traffic congestion	a) Change in transport form (rapid transit, commuter trains, subways, shuttle planes); b) Easing of traffic situation (traffic reports, roadnet regulations, changing of one-way direction during rush hours, off-street parking, highway program).	(Self) Individual preference for car, public transport, or walking. (Transport) a) Compensation by living downtown or further out; b) More mobile public demands increase in recreational area accessibility.	a) Shopping centers located in suburbia to cut travel time; b) More on-site parking important factor in accessibility; c) Staggered work hours and shifts to accommodate off-peak traffic.
2. Sewerage facilities (example of one of multiple utility types)	Sewage	a) Sewerage system for collection; b) Municipal sewage treatment plant;	(Household) Outhouse or septic tank.	a) Tie-in with municipal facilities; b) Wastewater treatment plant; c) Disposal system.

Table A-1. (Continued)

Elements in the environment	Attribute of macroenvironment	Societal–governmental approach	Private or individual microenvironmental approach	
			Family	Workplace (firm)
(1)		(2)		(3)
		c) Reclamation plant for water reuse; d) Conveyance system for disposal; e) Waste treatment plant performance criteria.		
3. Law enforcement	Crime	a) Law enforcement agencies (police, FBI); b) Civil codes of justice; c) Institutions for confinement and correction;	(Self) a) Stay in at night; b) Carry firearms for protection; c) Deposit valuables in bank or home safe. (Household) a) Insurance; b) House safe, locks. (Transport) a) Travel in pairs or groups; b) Avoidance of dangerous or undesirable neighborhoods; c) Relocation of home.	a) Burglary and protection systems installed (including safes, locks, etc.) b) Relocation of business.
	Civil riots	d) Military interventions; e) Curfews; f) Licensing of protests (marches or sit-ins).		
D. COMMUNITY–NEIGHBORHOOD ENVIRONMENT				
1. Community characteristics	Space	a) Building codes (height of buildings, distance between structures, vision regulations); b) Zoning of low and high density areas and uses.	(Household) a) Idea of living space altered (living-sleeping quarters combined, efficiencies, roll-out beds, one-half kitchens); b) Physical reshaping of space (dividers for visual spacing, more windows, porches, or sundecks to extend space, light colored walls). (Transport) a) Join clubs which offer space facilities (tennis, swimming, gym, etc.); b) Rent space for parties, recreational activities.	

Population density	a) Rezoning of low and high density dwellings; b) Birth control programs; c) Greater emphasis on educational and recreational facilities (impact on services environment).	(Self) a) Seek privacy by renting single apartments; b) Off-hour working schedules; c) Recreational interests indoors (development of the arts—painting, music). (Household) a) Limit number of children; b) Social activities within home (bridge groups, etc.) (Transport) a) Frequent walks or trips away; b) Greater use of individualistic transportation modes; c) Travel at off-peak hours.	
2. Services environment / Education	a) Federal and state assistance programs (loans, scholarships, research and development funds, construction grants); b) Federal and state standards (compulsory education, hiring policies); c) Job training; d) Social work agencies; e) Pay differential in educational systems for advanced degrees.	(Self) Education time lengthened (time horizon requiring supplementary income expanded). (Household) a) Pressure on children to excel (rebellion, competitiveness of school children); b) Exposure to media (TV, newspapers); c) Private tutors; d) Reclassification of job status by education level.	a) Job training, school-work programs, apprenticeships; b) Competitiveness for job positions based on education level; c) Higher salaries for higher education levels.
Health (physical and mental)	a) Medicare programs; b) Physical fitness (other preventive medicine) programs; c) health-education programs; d) Social work agencies; e) Hospitals, clinics, medical centers; f) Pest control and eradication programs.	(Self) Personal physical fitness (yearly checkup, vitamins, weight consciousness); (Household) a) Medical insurance; b) Accident prevention by safeguards (netting, screens, sprays, protective clothing).	Safety programs, medical insurance, independent medical staff.

2

Pollution and environmental quality

Robert U. Ayres and Allen V. Kneese

At the time the paper was written, Robert U. Ayres was
a visiting scholar at Resources for the Future.
Allen V. Kneese is Director of the Quality of the Environment Program,
Resources for the Future.

Pollution and environmental quality

Robert U. Ayres and Allen V. Kneese

Environmental pollution has usually been observed and studied in rather rigidly defined separate classes based on the environmental medium into which waste residuals are discharged. This tendency has also been evident with respect to governmental institutions devised to control these problems. Thus we have at the federal, state, and often at the municipal level, independent units of government to deal with waterborne wastes, wastes discharged to the atmosphere, and solid wastes. Such a division of responsibilities can, perhaps, be justified on the basis that specialized skills are needed to deal with different problems and the differing areal extent of the geographical "problems sheds" involved. In large part, however, this segmentation results from a failure to recognize the strong interdependencies which exist between the various waste streams and the control measures appropriate thereto.[1]

In this chapter the subject of environmental pollution is not considered in terms of the usual air-water-solids categorization. Rather, the discussion is organized in terms of the main sectors of the economy which present the nation, and particularly its urban areas, with a waste disposal problem and an attempt is made to look at that problem in its entirety. The approach suggested is designed to help in dealing with policy issues touching on the quality of the urban environment and the interest of society in its critical resources of air, water, and land in an urban setting.

A Materials Balance Approach

Environmental pollution and its control can usefully be viewed initially as a materials balance problem for the entire economy.[2] A highly simplified schematic of how the goods and residuals production process works is indicated in Figure 1.

We are indebted to many persons for help in the preparation of this paper. Among them, our associates at Resources for the Future, Blair T. Bower and Richard J. Frankel, merit special mention. We are also indebted to George O. G. Löf, Richard McKenna, and Erna Belton for research assistance.—AUTHORS' NOTE

[1] In the last few years there have been several studies which took a more comprehensive view of the waste residuals problem. Among them are *Waste Management and Control* (National Academy of Sciences–National Research Council, 1966); *Restoring the Quality of Our Environment*, Report of the Pollution Panel of the President's Science Advisory Committee (1965); and *Environmental Pollution: A Challenge to Science and Technology*, Report of the Subcommittee on Science and Astronautics, House of Representatives, 89 Cong., 2 sess. (1966). An additional study incorporating more empirical information and with a regional focus (New York metropolitan region) is Walter M. Phillips, Blair T. Bower, Gordon P. Larson, and Abraham Michaels, *Wastes Management: Generation and Disposal of Solid, Liquid, and Gaseous Wastes in the New York Region* (Regional Plan Association, September 1967).

[2] As far as we know, the idea of applying materials balance concepts to waste disposal problems was first expressed by Frank Smith in *The Economic Theory of Industrial Waste Production and Disposal* (draft of a doctoral dissertation, Department of Economics, Northwestern University). We

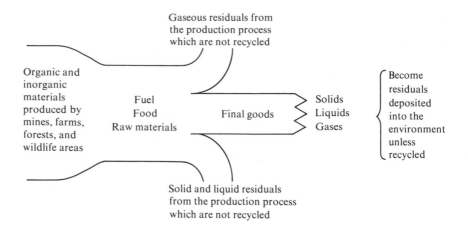

Figure 1. Schematic of the goods-residuals production process.

Final goods in the schematic can be either consumer goods, like food and automobiles, or intermediates in the productive process. The inputs to the system are fuels, foods, and raw materials: these are partly converted into final goods and partly become waste residuals. Except for increases in inventory and recycling, final goods also ultimately enter the waste stream. For the sake of simplicity, and also because it isolates the problems of greatest significance for urban areas, we will ordinarily begin our consideration of the materials flow after the basic fuel, food, and raw materials have been produced by mines, farms, forests, and wildlife areas, but before they enter into processing. It must be noted, however, that this does neglect some significant discharges of wastes into the environment — for example, mine tailings, acid mine drainage, and salt water pumped up with crude oil. However, the streams included are the most relevant for urban environments.

In an economy which is closed (no imports or exports) and where there is no net accumulation of stocks (plant, equipment, inventories, consumer durables, or residential buildings), the amount of residuals which is inserted into the natural environment must be approximately equal to the weight of basic fuels, food, and raw materials entering the processing and production system, plus oxygen taken from the atmosphere.[3] This result, while obvious upon reflection, leads to the rather striking corollary that residuals disposal — in terms of sheer tonnage — is an even larger operation than basic materials production.

---

also benefited from an unpublished paper by Charles Headley in which a pollution "matrix" is suggested. One of the authors of this chapter has previously used a similar approach in ecological studies of nutrient interchange among plants and animals: see Robert U. Ayres, "Stability of Biosystems in Sea Water," Technical Report No. 142 (Hudson Laboratories, Columbia University, August 1967).

[3] To simplify our language, we will not repeat this essential qualification at each opportunity, but assume it applies throughout the following discussion. In addition, we must include residuals such as oxides of nitrogen (NO_x) arising from reactions between components of the air itself, but occurring as combustion by-products.

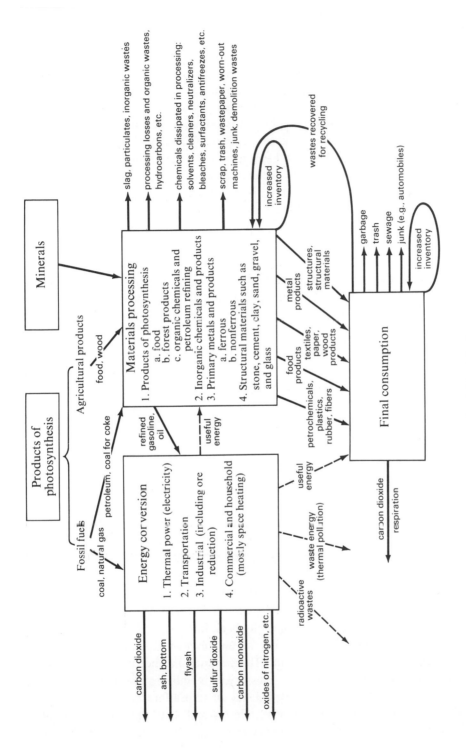

Figure 2. Materials flow.

Figure 2 shows a materials flow of the type we have in mind in greater detail and relates it to the various sectors of the economy. In an open economy (such as any city, state, or nation engaged in trade across its boundaries) it would be necessary to add flows representing imports and exports. Similarly, in any economy undergoing stock or capital accumulation, the production of residuals in any given year would be less by that amount than the basic inputs. In the United States, accumulation would account for about 10 to 15 per cent of basic annual inputs, and there is some net importation of raw and partially processed materials — amounting to 4 or 5 per cent of domestic production. Table 1 shows the weight of raw material produced in the United States in several recent years, plus net imports of raw and partially processed materials.

Of the "active" inputs,[4] perhaps three-quarters of the overall weight is eventually discharged to the atmosphere as carbon [combined with atmospheric oxygen in the form of carbon monoxide (CO) or carbon dioxide (CO_2)] and hydrogen [combined with atmospheric oxygen as water (H_2O)] under current conditions. This results from combustion of fossil fuels, and from animal respiration. Discharge of CO_2 can be considered harmless in the short run. There are large "sinks" (in the form of vegetation and large water bodies, mainly the oceans) which reabsorb this gas, although there is some evidence of net accumulation of CO_2 in the atmosphere. Some experts believe that the latter is likely to increase greatly (as much as 50 per cent) by the end of the century, possibly giving rise to significant — and probably, on balance, adverse — weather changes.

The remaining residuals are either gases [like CO, nitrogen dioxide (NO_2), and sulfur dioxide (SO_2) — all potentially harmful even in the short run]; dry solids like rubbish and scrap; or wet solids like garbage, sewage, and industrial wastes suspended or dissolved in water. In a sense, the solids are the irreducible limiting form of waste. By the application of appropriate equipment and energy, all undesirable substances can be removed from water and air streams[5] — but what is left must obviously be solid. From this viewpoint, a primary interdependence between the various waste streams is clearly revealed.

But solid residuals, or for that matter those that remain in a liquid or gaseous state, do not necessarily have to be discharged to the environment. In many instances, it is possible to recycle them economically back into the productive system. We shall note some outstanding examples later in the discussion, along with a number of unexercised opportunities of this kind. The materials balance view underlines the fact that the total materials throughput necessary to maintain a given level of production and consumption decreases as the efficiency of utilization (i.e., recycling) increases. Similarly, the useful lifetime of goods is closely related to the net throughput of the system. The longer cars, buildings, machinery, and other durables last, the fewer new

[4] Excluding stone, sand, gravel, and other minerals used for structural purposes, ballast, fillers, insulation, etc. We also disregard gangue and mine tailings in this tally.

[5] Except CO_2, which, as noted above, may be harmful in the long run.

Table 1. *Weight of Basic Materials Production in the United States*
plus Net Imports, 1963

(million tons)[a]

Basic materials	1963	1964	1965
Agricultural (including fishery, wildlife, and forest products)			
Food { Crops (excluding livestock feed)	125	128	130
Food { Livestock	100	103	102
Other products	5	6	6
Fishery	3	3	3
Forestry products (85% dry weight basis)			
Saw logs	53	55	56
Pulpwood	107	116	120
Other	41	41	42
Total	434	452	459
Minerals, other than mineral fuels			
Iron and ferroalloys	204	237	245
Other metals	161	171	191
Construction materials	1,579	1,668	1,763
Other nonmetals	125	133	149
Total	2,069	2,209	2,348
Mineral fuels	1,337	1,339	1,448
Grand total	3,840	4,060	4,255
Total "active" materials[b]	2,261	2,392	2,492

[a] Throughout this paper, the measurement "ton" indicates "short ton" unless otherwise designated.
[b] Excluding minerals used for structural purposes, ballasts, fillers, etc.

Source: Compiled and inferred from official statistics.

materials are required to compensate for depreciation or to sustain a given rate of capital accumulation.

Finally, the more efficient fuel combustion processes can be made (in the strict energy conversion sense), the fewer waste products there will be for the environment to receive, for a given total energy production. Perfect utilization of carbonaceous fossil fuels would leave only water and carbon dioxide as residuals, while nuclear energy conversion need leave no chemical residuals at all (although thermal pollution and radiation hazards cannot be dismissed).

One might reasonably protest that this is a very mechanistic and simplistic view of the problem: after all, improving combustion is not costless, and increasing the durability of goods requires more expensive inputs. It may be cheaper to buy new raw materials than to recycle used ones, and it may cost less to buy additional gasoline than to achieve further increase in the efficiency of combustion. All this is of course true. It would also be to the point if the functioning of the economy gave rise to incentives (like prices) which fully reflected the cost of disposing of residuals, including

Table 2. *Fuel Consumed in Energy Production[a]*

Fuel source	Contribution to total primary energy	1965 consumption as fuel
	(Per cent)	*(Million tons)*
Coal	23	465
Petroleum and natural gas liquids	43	503
Natural gas, dry[b]	30	337

[a] Figures from W. A. Vogely and W. E. Morrison, "Pattern of Energy Consumption in the United States, 1947–65 and 1980 Projected," *Transactions* of the 15th Sectional Meeting of the World Power Conference, October, 1966 (Tokyo, Japan: Japanese National Committee of the World Power Conference, 1966).

[b] Assuming an average molecular weight of 16 (methane, CH_4), whence 16 grams (1 mole) occupies 22.4 liters; thus 337 million tons of natural gas is equivalent to 15.2 trillion cubic feet.

any costs to the overall society associated with their discharge into the environment. But it is clear that, whatever other normative properties the functioning of a market economy may have, *it does not reflect these costs adequately.* Market economies are effective instruments for organizing production and allocating resources, insofar as the utility functions associated with two-party transactions affect only the parties. But, in connection with waste disposal, the automatic market exchange process fails because the utility-functions involve third parties.[6] Before elaborating on this point and suggesting some directions for public policy, we turn to some empirical estimates of the actual discharges of residuals to the environment and a discussion of some technologies for their modification.

Residuals Associated with Energy Conversion

In the United States in 1965, the energy conversion sector, as a whole, obtained 4 per cent of its output from hydroelectric generators and 0.1 per cent from nuclear fuel (although the latter contribution is increasing rapidly). The remainder was derived from fossil fuels, as shown in Table 2.

In 1965, electric utilities consumed 20 per cent of all primary energy, 24 per cent went to transportation (mainly as gasoline), 32 per cent was used in industry, and 21 per cent in households and commercial establishments. At present, coal dominates the electric power generating field and plays an important role in industry, especially in the smelting of ferrous metals; petroleum even more heavily dominates the transportation area. These two fuels also cause the most serious residuals problems, as will be seen later.

[6] There have been many explorations of how externalities give rise to market failure. For one pointed directly at the matter of environmental pollution, see Allen V. Kneese and Blair T. Bower, *Managing Water Quality: Economics, Technology, Institutions* (The Johns Hopkins Press, for Resources for the Future, Inc., 1968), Chapter 4.

Table 3.   Thermal Power Combustion Residuals, 1965

Residuals	Million tons
Carbon dioxide (CO_2)	807.0
Water (H_2O)	231.0
Sulfur dioxide (SO_2)[a]	13.6
Ash (total)	25.0
Flyash not collected[b]	2.4
Oxides of nitrogen (NO_X)[c]	3.7

[a] The Public Health Service estimates that 12 million tons of SO_2 were emitted into the atmosphere by electric utilities, which might suggest that 1.7 million tons are being removed from stack gases at present; however, it appears that SO_2 removal at present is actually much less than this.

[b] Data from Richard J. Frankel. Based on an industry-wide collection efficiency of 86.5 per cent for flyash in the stack, and allowing about 20 per cent for bottom ash.

[c] Assuming 28.4 lb NO_X produced per ton of oil burned (Los Angeles). If carbon is the controlling factor (as seems to be the case), then we would expect 33.3 lb NO_X per ton of contained carbon, or 3.7 million tons NO_X on a nationwide basis.

THERMAL POWER[7]

As noted above, over half the utility electric power produced in 1965 used coal as the primary energy source: about 251 million tons out of a total U.S. domestic supply of 465 million tons were used for this purpose.[8] Most of the remaining electric energy was produced in the West and Southwest with hydropower and natural gas. Combustion of natural gas produces comparatively small amounts of potentially harmful residuals.

Some 16.5 million tons of (high sulfur) residual oil were also burned by electric power plants, mostly on the East Coast. A variety of residuals which can result in external costs are associated with the use of coal. Among them are acid and turbid waste waters from coal cleaning at the mine, losses as soot or dust during transport, flyash (fine inorganic particulates in flue gases), gaseous stack emissions [primarily CO_2, sulfur oxides (SO_X), and NO_X] and, if flue gases are scrubbed, liquid and solid residuals result from this process. Indeed, coal and residual oil burning thermal plants contribute major fractions of the total amounts of SO_2 ($\sim$50 per cent), NO_X ($\sim$53 per cent), and particulates ($\sim$25 per cent) emitted to the atmosphere in the United States. In the case of particulates this remains true despite the major control efforts that have already been introduced. These controls include limitations in the allowable sulfur content of utility coal or residual oil, plus increased use of precipitators and other devices for removing sulfur and flyash from stacks. A summary of the (non-nuclear) residuals from thermal power production in 1965 is shown in Table 3.

An obvious substitute for emissions control for "dirty" fuels is to use an inherently "clean" fuel like natural gas or to convert to atomic energy. A growing trend toward the use of atomic energy is now clearly evident. The amount of residuals produced by nuclear fuels is quantitatively very small compared to that produced by

[7] Much of the information for this section was obtained from an unpublished research report by Richard J. Frankel.

[8] About 100 million tons each were used by the steel industry and other industries.

fossil fuels, since energy released per unit of material throughput is vastly larger. There are no significant discharges of residuals to the atmosphere from nuclear plants[9] but some of the small amounts of liquid residuals are so radioactive that they must be put in permanent storage. All the ramifications of this apparently have not been fully explored.

Despite the rapid growth of the use of atomic energy, the use of fossil fuels for power generation will continue to increase until at least 1975 or 1980. During this period the use of natural gas is also likely to increase.

TRANSPORTATION

In 1965, the transportation sector accounted for 24 per cent of all primary energy produced in the United States, and all but an insignificant percentage was accounted for by petroleum products: the sector consumed 308 million tons as fuel, plus substantial quantities of additives, notably 2 million tons of lead.[10]

In the United States, transportation is overwhelmingly automotive. In 1965, 82 per cent of all workers used private automobiles en route to work and a majority of the rest traveled on buses. Intercity travel is even more heavily dominated by motor vehicles: in 1965, 89.4 per cent of intercity passenger miles were accounted for by private cars, and a further 2.5 per cent by motor coaches. The movement of freight is still largely by railroads, but in 1965 trucks were the second most important mode, with 24.4 per cent of all freight ton-miles, and a virtual monopoly of local distribution of goods. Domestic airlines accounted for just under 6 per cent of passenger miles and 0.1 per cent of freight ton-miles.[11]

More than 300 million tons of petroleum fuels and lubricants were consumed for transportation purposes in 1966. About 224 million tons, of which 200 million tons were gasoline, were used by automobiles, trucks, buses, and off-highway equipment. Aviation—a rapidly increasing sector[12]—used 39 million tons; marine and railroad uses accounted for 28 million tons. The remainder is unaccounted for in the statistics. Most fuel used in aviation, primarily by jets, is consumed above 3,500 feet in altitude; most fuel used by ships is consumed away from harbors. Apart from marine and aviation uses, fuels other than gasoline—mainly diesel oil—amounted to about 13 per cent of the total petroleum fuels used. The use of these diesel fuels can be assumed to result in comparatively small emissions. Hence, it seems reasonable to focus on the emissions picture for internal combustion engine vehicles.[13]

[9] Although the long-lived isotope krypton 85, which may be released in nuclear fuel processing plants, could pose a serious problem if not controlled.

[10] Vogely and Morrison, "Patterns of Energy Consumption . . . ."

[11] From "Automobile Facts and Figures" (Automobile Manufacturers Association, 1966).

[12] In 1955, airlines accounted for 3.42 per cent of domestic intercity passenger miles. By 1965 this had risen to 5.96 per cent.

[13] For a more detailed discussion of the data and sources, see Robert U. Ayres and Allen V. Kneese, "Environmental Pollution," in *Federal Programs for the Development of Human Resources*, A Compendium of Papers submitted to the Subcommittee on Economic Progress of the Joint Economic Committee, 90 Cong. 2 sess. (1968), Vol. 2, pp. 626–84.

Table 4. Major Emissions Per Pound of Fuel Consumed (1965)

(pounds)

Emission	CO	HC	NO_X	Particulates	SO_2 H_2S
Spark Ignition ICE[a] (Otto cycle)					
Los Angeles data	0.500	0.093	0.024	0.00022	0.00014
New York data	0.472	0.104	0.018	0.00018	0.00014
Morse Panel estimate	0.560	~0.100	0.031	—	—
	(35,000 = 3.5%)	(900)	(1,500)		
Diesel engine					
Los Angeles data	0.0045	0.018	0.018	0.0045	0.0045
New York data	0.0067	0.020	0.025	0.0125	0.0045
Gas turbine[b] (Rover 2S–140)	~0.02	(neg.)	~0.0003	(neg.)	0.002
	(340)		(5.5)		(60)
External[c] combustion					
Steam (Williams)	~0.0075	~0.0016	~0.001	(neg.)	0.0045
	(500)	(20)	(70)		
Steam (Thermo-Electron)	≲0.0002	(neg.)	≲0.003	(neg.)	0.00042
Stirling (Philips)	~0.0015	(neg.)	~0.002	(neg.)	0.0045
	(100)	(1.5)	(150)		

[a] Calculated by assuming volumetric emissions shown in parenthesis (in ppm), 15 lb of air/lb of fuel and molecular weights as follows: CO = 28 (= air); HC = 86 ($\cong$ 3 × air); NO_X = 36 (= 1.3 × air).

[b] Calculated by assuming 63 lb of air/lb of fuel, volumetric emissions in ppm as shown in parentheses and molecular weights as above, plus SO_X = 64 (= 2 × air).

[c] Calculated by assuming volumetric emissions shown in parentheses (in ppm) 15 lb of air/lb of fuel and molecular weights as above. Sulfur emissions assumed to be the same as diesel, with similar fuel. If external combustion engines use more than 15 lb air/lb of fuel, coefficients should be increased by the corresponding ratio. Coefficients for Thermo-Electron steam engine supplied by letter from Robert J. Harvey, Manager, Advanced Programs and Planning, Thermo-Electron Engineering Corporation.

Source: Automobile Steam Engine and Other External Combustion Engines, Joint Hearings before the Committee on Commerce and the Subcommittee on Air and Water Pollution of the Committee on Public Works, 90 Cong. 2 sess. (1968), p. 7.

Using the calculated coefficients in Table 4 and the total gasoline consumption in the transportation sector (disregarding diesel and aircraft uses) we obtain the results shown in Table 5.

It will be noted that our estimates of CO production and HC are greater than the official Public Health Service estimates. The discrepancy seems to be due to the use of different bases for the derivation in the two cases.

Potential control techniques have been discussed at great length in recent years. The major possibilities consist of:

1. Recycling the "blow-by" gases which formerly escaped from the cylinders past the rings and were released from a vent under the engine (this change has been made since 1963 on all U.S. cars; it eliminates about 20 per cent of the unburned hydrocarbons and carbon monoxide).

2. Improving the efficiency of the combustion process by improved carburetion (or fuel injection). This is a matter of matching the fuel and air intake more accurately

Table 5.   Estimates of Residuals from Automotive Transportation (1965)

(million tons)

Residual	Present authors[a]	U.S. Public Health Service
Carbon monoxide (CO)	100	66
Unburned hydrocarbons (HC)	20	12
Oxides of nitrogen (NO_X)	5.7	6
Lead compounds	0.2	0.2
Oxides of sulfur (SO_X)	0.4	1
Total	126	85

[a] Robert U. Ayres and Allen V. Kneese, "Environmental Pollution," in *Federal Programs for the Development of Human Resources*, A Compendium of Papers Submitted to the Subcommittee on Economic Progress of the Joint Economic Committee, 90 Cong. 2 sess. (1968), Vol. 2, pp. 626–84. (Revised.)

to the instantaneous demands of the engine, and particularly preventing excessively rich mixtures. Evaporation losses from the carburetor can also be considerably reduced by simple redesign.

3.   Unburned components in exhaust gases can be more completely consumed, either in the manifold or the tailpipe, by some type of "afterburner." The simplest method may be to introduce excess air into the hot manifold, where unburned gases will have an additional opportunity to burn completely. Catalytic mufflers or "reactors" can also reduce exhaust emissions, although catalysts tend to be "poisoned" by the lead in the combustion products. Hence the latter approach is not much in favor at present.

4.   Evaporation losses from the gas tank can presumably be reduced by various means, such as an absorbent charcoal buffer.

It seems likely that, by a combination of these means, about 90 per cent of the emissions from a typical gasoline internal combustion engine may ultimately be eliminated at an acceptable cost (less than $100). Engines may even achieve somewhat better results than this while they are comparatively new; the level of control tends to be degraded with age and wear. The problem of keeping emissions low throughout the life of the car, under conditions of little or poor maintenance, remains a very difficult one. Meanwhile, if emissions control is effective primarily during the first half of a vehicle's life, the net gain would ultimately be something like 50 per cent. However, an expected rapid increase in the number of cars on the roads would nullify most of this gain. Indeed, present approaches are unlikely to achieve much, if any, reduction in present air pollution levels. More radical approaches would seem to be required, such as greater emphasis on mass transportation and rail — rather than highway — transportation of goods.

As an example of what can be achieved by switching automotive traffic to rails, each 100 million passenger miles on electrified mass-transit would result in saving

16,000 tons of gasoline, a net decrease of 8,000 tons of CO; 1,600 tons of vaporized HC; and 320 tons of NO_X. Assuming the power is produced in thermal plants, there would be a compensating increase of 350 to 500 tons in oxides of sulfur (assuming fuel with a 2.5 per cent sulfur content). This shift might be accomplished in part by public subsidy of conventional or unconventional mass transit systems, tax or other disincentives to drive or park private cars in areas where alternatives exist, and construction of convenient (possibly automated) parking facilities near transit termini. Automated comprehensive underground goods distribution systems utilizing electric minirails, pneumatic tubes, and/or moving belts may find a place in densely populated areas.

Another possible solution would involve a (partial?) switch to alternative power sources for vehicles, including gas turbines or turbo-electric hybrids for large buses and articulated trucks, and external combustion (e.g., steam) engines or battery-fuel cell electric propulsion for automobiles and taxis. Remote (i.e., wired or radiated) external power sources in a dual mode (e.g., road-rail) configuration are also conceivable possibilities for private vehicles in the longer time frame.[14]

In general these latter technological alternatives can render transportation services with less throughput of materials and fuel than conventional motor vehicles and/or involve combustion of fuels in central power plants where it is more efficient and residuals can be more efficiently treated and disposed of. They can be encouraged by public sponsorship of research, public investment, tax incentives such as faster writeoffs, effluent taxes on pollutants, enforcement of air quality standards, and by directed purchase of appropriate vehicles for the use of government agencies. Thus the Post Office alone would provide a sizable market for an electric truck, and city, state, and federal agencies could provide an initial market for a steam engine or battery-fuel cell (electric) vehicle. Once the economies offered by such vehicles are proven, fleet owners such as rent-a-car concerns, taxi companies, and finally private individuals might be induced to switch.

INDUSTRY AND HOUSEHOLDS

Coal is an important source of energy in industry, particularly in the metallurgical field and in the manufacture of lime and portland cement. Thus in 1965 the industrial sector consumed 188 million tons of coal, of which 96 million tons were first carbonized to yield 77 million tons of coke plus coal gas. The best quality low-sulfur (~ 1 per cent) bituminous coals normally are used for coking.[15] Thus the average sulfur content of all industrial coal (2 per cent) is less than the average for utility coal (2.5 per cent). This implies a total SO_2 emission from coal burned in industry

---

[14] Robert U. Ayres, "Technology and Urban Transportation: Environmental Quality Considerations" (Hudson Institute, H1–949/1, 2–KK, January 1968). See also U.S. Department of Commerce, *The Automobile and Air Pollution: A Program for Progress*, a compilation of Sub-panel reports to the Advisory Panel on Electrically Powered Vehicles (December 1967), Vols. I and II.

[15] These low-sulfur coals, mainly from western Pennsylvania and West Virginia, sell for much higher prices than utility coal, and supplies are largely pre-empted by long-term contracts.

of 7.4 million tons in 1965.[16] Total particulates (flyash) produced by industrial and coking coal is estimated at 14 million tons, based on the average 7.5 per cent ash content. Assuming an average collection efficiency of 62 per cent implies residual particulate emissions of the order of 5.3 million tons.[17] The U.S. Public Health Service estimates a total of 6 million tons of particulate matter from all industrial operations.[18] Although we have no quantitative basis of verification, the same source also estimates that 2 million tons of NO_X and 2 million tons of CO are produced annually by industry in the United States.

Space heating in industry and households creates the other major demand for energy. The fuels used in this application are mainly distillate oils ($\sim$177 million tons) and natural gas (286 million tons), both of which are comparatively clean. About 26 million tons of coal are still used in the household sector, although this amount is decreasing rapidly. The latter contributes on the order of 1 million tons of SO_2 and — because of the virtually complete lack of flyash collection in small heating plants — probably 1.7 million tons of particulates. The ash content (0.5 per cent) of fuel oil probably contributes a further 1 million tons. Fuel oil burned in industry and for space heating also contains a small amount of sulfur — perhaps 0.25 per cent — which would result in about 1 million tons of SO_2. (This may be somewhat underestimated.)

A figure on NO_X can be extrapolated from a coefficient of 33.3 lb per ton of contained carbon, or 1.33 per cent by weight. The industry and household category altogether consumed about 522 million tons of contained carbon in fuel in 1965, which would imply a production of 7 million tons of NO_X. Information on CO and HC during combustion is hard to find, but one may probably assume coefficients for distillate oil in the industry-household sector similar to that for external combustion engines (see Table 4); viz., 0.75 per cent for CO and 0.006 per cent for HC, by weight.

By applying these coefficients indiscriminately to the total quantities of fuel burned for which no other data are available, we obtain the quantities shown in Table 6. This is too mechanical an extrapolation; in particular, it may be too high for CO and too low for HC, at least where natural gas is the fuel. It is, however, suggestive of general orders of magnitude.

Residuals from Materials Processing and Industrial Production

It is particularly difficult to describe materials flow and residuals production in manufacturing industries for several reasons. First, there is a notable lack of direct information which is both comprehensive and dependable about quantities and

---

[16] The Public Health Service estimated 9 million tons of SO_2, which presumably includes SO_2 from other sources, such as sulfide ore treatment.

[17] Richard J. Frankel, unpublished research report.

[18] This is certainly too low if additional contributions from mineral ore beneficiation (particularly copper) and phosphatic fertilizer plants are considered.

Table 6. Summary of Residuals from Energy Conversion, 1965

(million tons)

Energy conversion	Carbon Monoxide (CO)	Hydro- carbons (HC)	Sulfur Dioxide (SO₂)	Oxides of Nitrogen (NOₓ)	Particu- lates
Utility power	1	neg.	13.6	3.7	2.4
Industry and households	5	neg.	8.4	7.0	7.0
Transportation	100	20	0.4	4.8–8.4	0.2
Total	106	20	22.4	15.5–19.1	9.6

Source: W. A. Vogely and W. E. Morrison, "Patterns of Energy Consumption in the United States." Based on calculations in Robert U. Ayres and Allen V. Kneese, "Environmental Pollution." These figures are somewhat larger than figures given by the Public Health Service, due to differences in estimates of the contribution from motor vehicles.

qualities of industrial inputs, processes, and waste residuals.[19] Second, industry generates an immense variety of residual products including most of those ultimately discarded by households, plus numerous others. Finally, while household, thermal power, and transportation activities are reasonably comparable across the country, the industrial mix of metropolitan areas varies drastically from place to place. For these reasons it is difficult to generalize meaningfully about industrial residuals (although some broadly applicable statements are possible). Thus, at this point in time, the following discussion is necessarily more illustrative than definitive. In many ways, materials balance concepts are more clearly applicable to industrial processes than to those in other economic sectors. But their comprehensive application on a meaningful (i.e., regional) basis must, like much other relevant analysis, await greatly improved data. At the end of this section we show, as an illustration, a detailed computed materials balance for one type of industrial plant under various conditions. This analysis yields some rather interesting conclusions.

The materials balance approach can be applied with particular effectiveness in the analysis of organic wastes from the processing of food and forest products. A simplified "flow chart" for these activities is shown as Figure 3. From the detailed statistics compiled by the U.S. Department of Agriculture, it can be determined that the total fresh weight of crops harvested for human consumption in the United States (excluding exports and industrial uses) is roughly 125 million tons. This corresponds to about 59 million tons of dry organic matter (O.M.). An additional 210 million tons of vegetable matter (dry weight) is harvested by and for livestock. Wood and forest products harvested for consumption in the United States account for a further 207 million tons (dry O.M.).

[19] For instance, only now is the first inventory of the content of industrial waste water discharges being assembled on a national basis (by the Federal Water Pollution Control Administration). Existing estimates are both old and somewhat ambiguous as to meaning. See, for example, William Rudolfs (ed.), Industrial Wastes — Their Disposal and Treatment (L.E.C. Publishers, Inc., 1953).

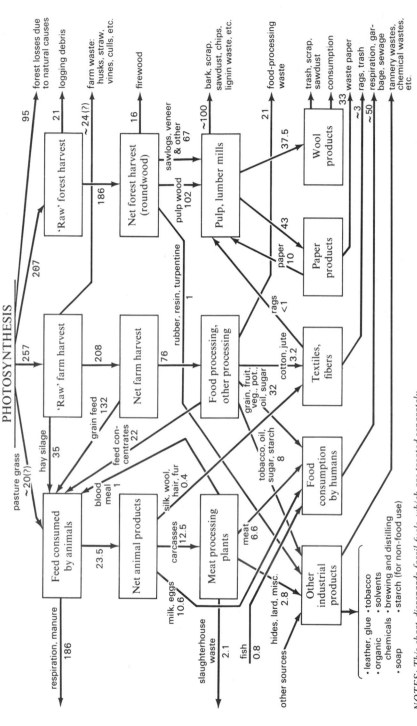

Figure 3. *Production and disposal of products of photosynthesis.*

NOTES: *This chart disregards fossil fuels, which are treated separately. All figures refer to millions of tons of dry organic matter.*

Prior to the concentration of animal feeding activities in commercial feedlots and poultry farms near major cities, *animal wastes* (*manure*) were automatically recycled, thereby satisfying a major part of the nitrogen and phosphorus requirements of agriculture. Today, however, large quantities of manure are produced and accumulated where there is no natural market for the material, and as a consequence disposal has become an increasingly serious problem.

Apart from the major (tonnage) residuals arising essentially from inefficiencies in the conversion of plant to animal calories, there are substantial residuals at the *slaughtering* stage. Although large meat packers have stated that they utilize every part of the animal "but the squeal of the pig," this is an exaggeration. The edible portion of the animal is about 63 per cent for hogs, 59 per cent for beef cattle, and 48 per cent for sheep, or about 60 per cent overall. An additional 15 per cent consists of other useful or utilizable products such as hides, tallow, glue, bloodmeal, etc. The remainder, about 25 per cent of the total, is essentially waste. Major meat packers have achieved higher rates of economic recovery by incorporating some or most of this material in animal feeds and fertilizers; smaller local slaughterhouses cannot attain this degree of efficiency. Statistics in this area are difficult to find, but on a national basis probably at least 10 per cent of the live weight is not recovered and is discharged to the environment — usually in urban areas.

The utilization of hides to manufacture leather products is also a major source of unrecycled residuals. *Tannery wastes* can be particularly obnoxious sources of water pollution. The technology exists to reduce tannery wastes now discharged to watercourses by using organic solvents and enzymes to remove unwanted material such as hair and fat from the hides, thus producing a much more compact residue than is now the case. This is not done in general because the high capital investment required does not seem justified in a static or declining industry. Moreover, to some extent this would mean trading a water pollution problem for an air pollution problem.

The *processing of food* from plant origins for direct human consumption involves a smaller absolute quantity of organic waste. Table 7 shows the figures for harvested crops, excluding fibers, tobacco, crops destined for animals, and exports; it also shows the quantities of processed food available "for consumption" (prior to home preparation and cooking). The differences represent statistical inaccuracies, plus various processing losses including spoilage due to vermin. In some cases, such as sugar beets, most of the weight of residuals is recovered (for cattle feed, for instance) but the residuals discharged to the environment, especially near centers of population, may be capable of exerting a highly degrading effect. Wastes from the processing of food products, for instance, tend to be high in organics which reduce dissolved oxygen and cause unpleasant odors in rivers.

In the *processing of forest products*, there are also substantial wastages. In paper making, for example, which absorbed 102 million tons of pulpwood in 1965 (dry O.M.), about 32 per cent of the input organic material is utilized as pulp; the remainder is lost—much of it in ways which have never been accurately catalogued. In a large modern integrated pulp and paper mill, some of this loss can be recovered and used

Table 7. Materials Balance for Processing Foods of Vegetable Origin[a]

(million tons)

	Inputs		Outputs			
	Net crops harvested for human consumption (in United States)		Food available for consumption		Processing losses[b] and waste	
Origin of food	Fresh weight	Dry weight	Fresh weight	Dry weight	Fresh weight	Dry weight
Grain	21.4	18.9	13.4	11.8	8.0	7.1
Potatoes and root crops	12.1	2.6	10.4	2.5	1.7	0.1
Beans and peanuts	2.2	2.0	1.6	1.4	0.6	0.6
Green vegetables	21.0	2.9	19.2	1.5	1.8	1.4
Fruits and nuts	16.7	2.4	14.1	1.8	2.6	0.6
Sugar (cane and beet)	49.3	27.7	10.2	10.2	39.1	17.5
Oil[c]	2.8	2.8	2.8	2.8	—	—
Total	125.5	59.3	71.7	32.0	53.8	27.3

[a] *Agricultural Statistics*, 1966.

[b] A major part of these are recovered as by-products.

[c] Vegetable oil is derived mainly from soybeans, cottonseed, and flaxseed; the pulp and meal are used as animal feed concentrates.

as a raw material for organic chemicals — notably surfactants (detergents) — or as a growth medium for yeasts or bacteria which can, in turn, be used for animal feed. However, this degree of recovery is still relatively rare in the industry, and only about 15 per cent of the lignin waste liquors, for instance, are recovered.[20] Accompanying the 1965 production of 33.3 million tons of paper pulp (dry weight) was a residual bark, cellulose, and lignin liquor waste of 69 million tons (dry O.M.), plus a large number of other chemicals used in the processing. This clearly puts a heavy demand on the assimilative capacity of the rivers and streams which are the major means of disposal at present.

Sawmills, plywood, and veneering plants do not contribute large amounts of processing wastes but there are substantial residuals in the form of bark, sawdust, chips, and scrap. In areas of low population density the disposal of these poses no particular problem. However, in dense conurbations the disposal of bulky demolition wastes especially (a major constituent of the "trash" category of refuse) can be quite awkward.

The *chemical industry* — both inorganic and organic — subsumes a large number of products which are used, or used up, in the preparation of other goods. A rather useful distinction can be found here between chemicals whose actual substance will ultimately become part of a final product, in some form, and chemicals serving other intermediate functions which do not appear physically in the final product.

The public is now well enough aware of the fact that agricultural chemicals such as pesticides, fungicides, and herbicides only serve their purpose (as presently used)

[20] See C. F. Gurnham, *Industrial Waste Water Control* (Academic Press, 1965).

when they are degraded and/or dispersed. Surface active agents used in detergents (1 million tons/yr) have also attracted a good deal of attention. It should be obvious, although it seldom seems to be pointed out, that the same is true of some dyes and pigments, virtually all industrial solvents[21] and "carriers" ($\sim$10 million tons), softeners (1 million tons), fluxes ($\sim$3 million tons), flotation agents, neutralizers, antichlors, bleaches, pickling agents ($\sim$1.3 million tons), antifreezes (0.5 million tons), lubricants, abrasives, fillers, explosives, and so forth.

Apart from the existence of important dissipative uses in the chemical sector, there are also inevitable losses in production and refining. This also applies, of course, to food processing and metallic ore reduction. However, as regards chemicals, it is noteworthy that there are often a number of intermediate stages *at each one of which there may be significant losses.*

A large number of important chemical products are derived via multistage processes, including synthetic fibers, synthetic elastomers (rubber), polyethylene, polypropylene, polyesters, PVC, polyurethane, insecticides, surfactants, etc. Needless to say, if 1 per cent of the material processed is lost at each stage, the total wastage in producing a complex product may be 5 per cent or so of the final weight. Of course the loss-rate varies, depending on a number of factors, notably the mode of handling and the volatility of the material. Thus, light petroleum and natural gas fractions are particularly subject to evaporative losses during refining and processing. If the overall loss rate to the atmosphere is only 1 per cent in each case (this may be a low estimate), the total quantities of hydrocarbons dissipated would be of the order of 8 million tons, although it is hard to see how this figure could be very closely checked.

Unlike the products of the chemical industries, the output of the *mineral and metallurgical industries* is almost entirely non-dissipative. Residuals consist of bulky solids (e.g., slag), gaseous emissions associated with the energy conversion aspect of ore reduction — plus substantial quantities of particulates — and liquid wastes resulting from cleaning ("pickling") the metal during various phases of fabrication or treatment from ingot to final product, usually to remove oxide scales which form when the hot metal comes in contact with air. Sulfuric acid is the major pickling agent for steel, but hydrochloric, nitric, and hydrofluoric acid are also used.

Slag, which once created a serious disposal problem for steel mills, has become a valued by-product. It consists of a mixture of impurities from the ore plus fluxing agents such as limestone (used mainly for smelting iron), cryolite, or fluorspar and is used mainly for road ballast and as aggregate for concrete products.

Substantial quantities of particulates are produced by foundries, both as "flue dust"— which, because of its high metal content, is largely recovered by Cottrell precipitators and wet scrubbers — and as soot from coal burning.[22] The latter is a major cause of SO_2 and particulate emissions. The U.S. Public Health Service estimates

[21] Dry cleaning and paint plants, for instance, constitute a major source of vaporized HC in the atmosphere. Most of these activities are in urban areas.

[22] Blast furnaces usually use coke, but other metallurgical operations such as reheating furnaces and rolling mills normally use coal.

that 2 million tons of CO, 9 million tons of SO_2, 2 million tons of NO_X, and 6 million tons of particulates are produced by industry as a whole. Presumably the majority of these pollutants come from the energy consuming ore-reduction, refining, and other operations in the primary metals sector.

Water-borne residuals from the metallurgical industry are extremely difficult to recycle, because of the large bulk involved and the low price of the constituents. The spent pickle-liquor from steel mills consists primarily of ferrous sulfate ($FeSO_4$) plus some excess sulfuric acid (H_2SO_4). The latter can be neutralized with lime, but further treatments such as ponding or evaporation have not proved economically feasible to date. The quantity of such residuals can be deduced roughly from the amount of acid used for pickling. About 0.75 million tons of H_2SO_4 were used in the iron and steel industry in 1963: this would correspond to roughly 1.1 million tons of $FeSO_4$, and a loss of about 0.35 million tons of metallic iron. Similar processes are used in other metallurgical operations, particularly copper and brass mills. Other metallic sulfates discharged annually probably add an additional 0.75 million tons, although the economics of recovery might be better in some cases. Apart from sulfate wastes, there are smaller but locally important quantities of other salts (chlorides, nitrates, and fluorides) and oily wastes from rolling operations.

Among the nonferrous metals (copper, lead, zinc), ore beneficiation causes additional problems: roasting of sulfide ores creates very concentrated SO_2 fumes which are lethal to vegetation and have literally created sizable deserts around copper smelters in Tennessee and Montana. However, it has recently become economically feasible to recover most of this sulfur in the form of dilute sulfuric acid, for which there is a market, and many of these blights have already been substantially reduced (although their ecological consequences have by no means disappeared as yet).

POTENTIAL IMPROVEMENT THROUGH PROCESS CHANGE

It should be emphasized that technological changes affecting residuals have not been, and are not now, usually instituted in order to avoid water pollution or other environment problems. In fact, almost all changes in production technology have been stimulated by factors unrelated to environmental quality, and have been developed without consideration for their external costs. On the other hand, in the few instances where they have been used, various stimuli to management — such as effluent charges — have resulted in process modification greatly reducing waste loads.[23] As more systematic means are developed to bring to bear on industry the external costs associated with the discharge of waste materials into the environment, waste residuals generation and control factors including recycling of recovered materials and production of usable by-products will receive more prominent consideration in process design. Studies of several industries have made clear that process design changes leading to residuals recovery or their conversion to usable by-products can, in some instances, profoundly affect wastes generation.

[23] For a detailed treatment of this experience, see Kneese and Bower, *Managing Water Quality* . . . .

Table 8.   Selected Figures from Materials Balance for Two Beet Sugar Processes
[All quantities in lb per (long) ton of beets processed]

Inputs and outputs	High residual	Low residual
Inputs		
Beets	2,200	2,200
Limestone	60	60
Coal	260	350
Sulfur	0.28	0.28
Products outputs		
Sugar	285	285
Pulp	100 (Dry weight of wet pulp)	100 (Dry)
Concentrated Steffens filtrate (used for stock feed to recover monosodium glutamate and potassium sulfate)	—	100
Waste residuals		
Sulfur dioxide (SO_2)	10	14
Calcium carbonate ($CaCO_3$)	120	120
Coal ashes	29	39
Organics	122	25
Soil	200	200

Source: Personal communication from George O. G. Löf, August 18, 1967.

In the following discussion we lean heavily upon the beet sugar industry as an illustration. This is not because this industry has the most important waste problem [although in 1950 it was estimated to discharge about 15 per cent of the organic wastes, measured in terms of "biological oxygen demand" (BOD) coming from all industries] but because its processes are comparatively simple, it has recently been intensively studied,[24] and we have been able to estimate a complete materials balance for representative plants using different processes.

The water-borne waste load generated in pounds of BOD per ton of beets processed has been reduced greatly in the beet sugar industry as a whole in the last two decades by comparatively simple and economical alterations in processes. The main changes are (1) the substitution of drying beet pulp for storage, instead of storing wet beet pulp in silos and (2) the use of Steffens process waste for the production of by-products. These changes reduce BOD generation by about 60 per cent. The other process change is related to recirculation of water. This further reduces the BOD generated by about 10 per cent.

Figure 4 indicates the main process and waste water residuals streams in representative beet sugar plants.

Table 8 summarizes the materials balance picture for two processes, a "high residual" process involving little or no recycling and a more efficient "low residual" process involving a more or less closed cycle.

[24] See George O. G. Löf and Allen V. Kneese, *The Economics of Water Utilization in the Beet Sugar Industry* (Resources for the Future, Inc., 1968). The materials balance described in later pages was calculated by George Löf.

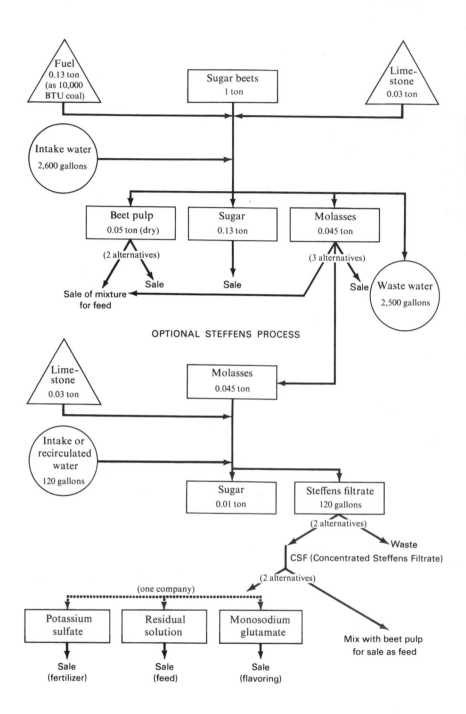

Figure 4. Main processes in a beet sugar plant.

Source: George O. G. Löf and Allen V. Kneese, *The Economics of Water Utilization in the Beet Sugar Industry* (Resources for the Future, Inc., 1968).

It should be noted that the "closed" plant requires treatment (in the form of clarification) for its recirculating water stream, despite the fact that materials recovery and by-product production have greatly reduced water-borne residuals. Even where there are favorable opportunities to utilize process changes and increase recovery, some waste residual usually remains. The stream containing this residual may be treated, thus producing a solid or gaseous residual or changing the chemical composition of the water-borne residual.

It can be seen from Table 8 that, from the point of view of waste residuals, a large reduction in organic residuals was purchased at the expense of a comparatively small increase in potentially harmful gas and inert solids. Again the interdependency between the residual waste streams is revealed. Considering the environment in which most beet sugar factories operate — away from large cities but near small streams with very limited capacity to assimilate organic wastes — the trade-off shown is probably favorable.[25] If air, water, or solids problems were studied individually, such tradeoffs would never be revealed or examined from the point of view of the full range of industrial costs — internal and external.

Residuals Associated with Final Consumption: Households

Most final (consumer) goods are utilized in the household, and thus give rise to the residuals found at the end of the materials flow through the economy. We have already considered one important class of household activities which results in large amounts of residuals — the transportation of its members. We included this discussion in the section on energy conversion because the interdependencies between the various types of residuals and possible methods for control can better be analyzed in the context of overall urban transportation systems.

The other major residuals from household activities are the gases which result from space heating and home incineration or other combustion; sewage (solids in water suspension but also containing dissolved solids like chlorides and nitrates); and solid wastes, including garbage and refuse as well as junk automobiles and the like.

Generally speaking, the space heating and incineration[26] activities of households do not appear to contribute a major portion of the gaseous residuals found in the atmosphere of cities — with the exception of flyash or soot — nor are gases generally a very significant portion of the weight of residual materials stemming directly from households. However, there is considerable variation among cities in this regard. The dominant position of automobiles in regard to gaseous emissions is clearly evident in Table 9, which shows atmospheric emissions in Sacramento County, reflecting conditions perhaps characteristic of areas that have little heavy industry and use relatively clean fuels, and where decentralized incineration is relatively uncommon.

---

[25] Combustion of coal in beet sugar plants is conducted on too small a scale to make recovery of sulfur practical. (See pp. 41–42). However, fuel substitution might be feasible in certain instances.

[26] We do not include here the residuals from incinerators *after collection* of solid wastes. These are discussed below.

Table 9. *Atmospheric Emissions in Sacramento County, California, 1964*

(tons/day)

Source	Contaminant			
	Carbon monoxide (CO)	Hydrocarbons (HC)	Sulfur dioxide (SO₂)	Oxides of nitrogen (NOₓ)
Stationary sources				
Downtown business	2	18	1	4
Railroad and airport	1	3	1	3
Travis Air Force Base	7	5	<0.5	1
Wood burning	3	<0.5	<0.5	<0.5
Asphalt plants	2	4	1	4
Aerojet-General Corporation	2	1	<0.5	1
Residential and incinerators	2	3	0.3	2
Municipal refuse	1	1	<0.5	<0.5
Motor vehicles	760	140	2	45
Approximate total	780	175	6	60

Source: Aerojet-General Corporation, *California Waste Management Study,* A Report to the State of California, Department of Public Health, Report No. 3056 (Final), Azusa, California, August 1965.

However, the type of fuel used in homes is very significant in regard to atmospheric emissions. Natural gas (used in Sacramento) is a relatively "clean" fuel in the sense that combustion is almost complete. For example, the relative quantities of particulates emitted to the atmosphere per Btu of fuel are 1 for coal, 0.6 for oil, and 0.15 for natural gas. In addition, natural gas is relatively free of sulfur compounds while, as we have already seen, certain coals and residual fuel oils contain up to 3 per cent or 4 per cent of sulfur. Consequently, in cities where space heating with lower quality fuels is dominant, the contribution of households to overall emissions may be considerably greater. Table 10 shows, for example, estimates of emissions from various sources in New York City, where natural gas is scarce and residual oil is the major fuel. In general it is difficult and expensive to control harmful emissions from households by treatment at the source. Fuel substitution or centralized provision of heating services — via central steam plants or electricity — would usually be more practical.

Another point illustrated by Table 10 is the importance of decentralized refuse incineration as a source of emissions — especially of particulates and hydrocarbons. Some of these emissions come from central incinerators but in New York (and other large cities) apartment house incinerators also contribute significantly. Combustion processes in these incinerators are usually inefficient and particulates are poorly controlled, if at all.

In the control of gases from household activities, there are important tradeoffs with other residual discharges, both as to type and spatial distribution. We will return to this point later.

Table 10. Atmospheric Emissions in New York City, 1964

(tons/day)

Source	Contaminant				
	Carbon monoxide (CO)	Hydrocarbons (HC)	Sulfur dioxide (SO$_2$)	Oxides of nitrogen (NO$_X$)	Particulates
Stationary sources					
Electric power	1	4	754	254	35
Industrial	2	2	140	54	26
Commercial, institutions,					
and large apartments	76	21	678	212	37
Small residential	4	4	67	78	24
Refuse combustion	291	120	6	7	75
Miscellaneous[a]	750	31	—	705	7
Motor vehicles	3,784	695	14	162	22
Total	4,908	877	1,659	1,472	226

[a]Mainly gasoline marketing, commercial dry-cleaning, etc.

Source: Electric Power and Fuel Consumption, 1965–1985 (Tri-State Transportation Commission, New York, July 1967; mimeo.).

One of the major components of household residuals is sewage. Most of the dry weight of sewage from households not using garbage grinders (about 0.55 lb per person per day) is composed of human excrement. In addition there are various organic and inorganic substances which result from cooking and washing operations. From households using garbage grinders, the total dry weight of sewage is about doubled. Actually the materials balance implies that the total dry weight of all organic wastes (sewage plus garbage) must be equal to the dry weight of food products entering the household, less the carbon content of CO$_2$ produced by respiration and minor corrections for annual accumulation (increase in population) and deaths.

Of most direct concern in connection with household wastes are the degradable organic materials which impose a demand on the dissolved oxygen of waters to which they are discharged. This is usually measured in terms of the five-day biochemical oxygen demand or BOD$_5$. It is convenient to think of BOD$_5$ as a substance in the water — a measure of the degree of waste residual which can be added or removed. Of increasing significance too are the plant nutrients which are the final stage of the breakdown of degradable waste (in addition to the nitrogen- and phosphate-rich contributions from human excrement there are the phosphate builders used in commercial detergents).

In addition to gaseous residuals and sewage, households produce wastes which are in solid form, including garbage, rubbish, and ashes:

1. Garbage wastes from preparation, cooking, and serving of food.

2. Rubbish: (combustible) paper, plastics, cartons, boxes, barrels, wood, excelsior, tree branches, yard trimmings, wood furniture, bedding, dunnage, etc.; (noncombustible) aluminum foil, tin cans, metal furniture, dirt, glass, crockery, etc.

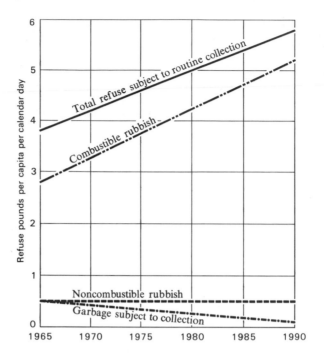

Figure 5. Projection of refuse production trends.

Source: Aerojet-General Corporation, *California Waste Management Study*, A Report to the State of California, Department of Public Health, Report No. 3056 (Final), (Azusa, California, August 1965).

3. Ashes: incombustible residue from fires used for heating and on-site incineration.

Altogether the average member of a household will throw away somewhere between 3.5 and 4.5 lb of solid wastes per day (see Figure 5).

These wastes are disposed of in a variety of ways in our urban areas. Backyard burning and burial has greatly diminished and the pattern has shifted historically to neighborhood dumps, and then to central incinerators and countryside landfills. But the present practices still give rise to major external costs — indiscriminate dump sites still litter the countryside; odor, smoke, insects, and rodents accompany open dumps (which are often burning to reduce volume and help control insects and rodents); contributions to air pollution arise from improper incineration and uncontrolled burning; and water quality degradation results from drainage through dumps and direct disposal of solid wastes into waterways.

As part of a very good study of the solid waste problem by the Maryland Department of Health, a survey was made in July 1966 of solid waste disposal practice in all twenty-three Maryland counties and the City of Baltimore.[27] Practices in the state could perhaps be considered typical of those in the megalopolitan East. At least 40 per cent of the 155 disposal sites were producing significant external costs.

As presently practiced, solid wastes collection and disposal costs are high. It is estimated that annual local government costs for collection and disposal are $1.5 billion. This is exceeded in local government budgets only by expenditures for schools and roads. In addition, it has been estimated that the annual expenditures of the private sanitation industry are nearly as high.[28] Of the total cost of disposal, about 80 per cent is for collection. Collection is labor-intensive and technologically primitive. One of the several significant external costs associated with disposal of solid wastes is the high rate of injuries among sanitation workers: for example, in New York, the injury frequency rate is reported at seventy injuries per million man-hours worked, as contrasted with twelve injuries per million man-hours in manufacturing as a whole.[29]

Collection costs are also highly sensitive to certain variables. A cross-section statistical analysis of St. Louis found that an increase from two to three weekly pickups increased collection costs by nearly one-third, while moving pickup location from the curb to rear of the house almost doubled the cost.[30]

Because collection is such an expensive and cumbersome process, it is attractive to think in terms of different and less labor-intensive collection systems. One proposal that recurs frequently in the literature is that solid wastes should be ground and delivered to the sewers. Since over 99 per cent of sanitary sewerage is now composed of water, the existing sewers could accommodate a considerable increase in solids without an expansion in capacity. Additional grinding could be done in the home or at grinding stations located relatively close to the points of pickup. In the latter cases, various organic substances in addition to garbage could be ground up. This would reduce (but certainly not eliminate) collection costs, and what was collected would require additional sorting.

This procedure would, of course, increase the waterborne wastes and put an additional loading on the sewage treatment plants and/or the stream. (The inter-dependency of various waste streams and means of control is again evident.) On the other hand, it would reduce the load on the transportation system by reducing the number of collection trucks and thus increasing the overall speed of surface traffic.[31]

[27] See *Collection and Disposal of Solid Wastes — A Maryland Program* (Maryland State Department of Health, August 1, 1966).

[28] Wesley E. Gilbertson and Ralph Black, *Solid Wastes* (National Commission on Community Health Services, 1964).

[29] *Ibid.*

[30] Werner Z. Hirsch, "Cost Functions of an Urban Government Service: Refuse Collection," *The Review of Economics and Statistics* (February 1965).

[31] Experiments at the University of Pennsylvania indicate that ground-up solid residuals (including metal and glass) can be successfully pumped as a liquid slurry through surprisingly small diameter pipes. A 2-inch pipe would suffice for a city with a population of 10,000 or 15,000. This might provide an alternative to conventional collection and transportation but would present a problem of liquid disposal.

Savings realized at the collection end might possibly compensate for increased treatment costs.

As far as disposal is concerned, combustion looks promising because, as shown in Figure 5, a large portion (80 per cent) of the total rubbish and garbage is combustible. Incineration reduces the total volume of the solid wastes to about one-fifth of that before combustion.[32] Consequently, from a narrow cost minimization point of view, it would be desirable to conduct the incineration very close to the source (e.g., in apartment house incinerators and back yards). This, however, results in converting the major part of the residuals to gases and airborne particulates which, in highly developed areas, are likely to give rise to large external costs. If efficient techniques for controlling emissions from small incinerators could be worked out, burning close to the source would have much to commend it.

In recent years, solid waste residuals from households have been substantially increased by a heavy trend toward nonreturnable containers of all types. For example, the use of one-way bottles almost doubled between 1965 and 1966.[33] In many instances, also, nonreturnable containers are being made of less degradable materials than previously — primarily plastic and aluminum. Overall, 48 billion cans, 26 billion bottles and jars, and 26 billion metal and plastic caps are produced each year, and virtually all of these are eventually discarded. Rates of reclamation and reuse are rather low. About 10 per cent of the plastic produced is recovered and about 15 per cent of the rubber products (mostly automobile and truck tires).[34] Of the 43 million tons of paper products produced each year, about one-third is reclaimed.

Worn out and discarded automobiles are a major source of solid wastes and pose quite special problems. At the present time there are about 90 million automobiles and trucks operating in the United States, with an annual production of about 9 million vehicles; 6 million to 6.5 million vehicles are scrapped each year; and about 2.7 million vehicles are added to inventory.[35]

The recycle picture is mixed. About 6.8 million tons of steel was recovered in 1965 from scrap auto, bus, and truck bodies.[36] It is difficult to say exactly what hap-

[32] At several locations in Europe, incineration is carried out in thermal electric plants. At Munich's Nord power station, for example, refuse is burned along with powdered coal. Electrostatic precipitators are used to control particulate emissions in the stack gases. The electric power system charges the refuse collection agency $1.50 per ton to burn the refuse delivered to the plant.

[33] *Chemical Week*, Vol. 99, No. 19 (1966), p. 44.

[34] *Environmental Pollution, a Challenge to Science and Technology*, Report of the Subcommittee on Science Research and Development of the Committee on Science and Astronautics. 89 Cong., 2 sess. (1966), p. 44.

[35] Based on the anticipated growth in total vehicle population from 1960 to 1970. Estimates published by the Federal Power Commission, February 1967, based on various projections by the Bureau of Public Roads, the Bureau of the Census, Resources for the Future, and the American Automobile Association.

[36] Testimony by Wesley E. Gilbertson, Public Health Service, in *Air Pollution — 1966*, Hearings before a Subcommittee on Air and Water Pollution of the Senate Committee on Public Works, 89 Cong., 2 sess. (1966), pp. 344–50. Mr. Gilbertson estimated that this accounted for

pened to the remainder. Presumably some was lost during manufacturing processes and probably most of this was returned to production as "new" scrap of unidentifiable origin. Essentially all of the lead in storage batteries is ultimately recovered, and the majority of tires are apparently re-capped at least once. About 0.3 million tons, or 15 per cent of all rubber, is recycled (mostly old tires); however, a substantial tonnage of rubber — possibly half a million tons a year — is powdered. Some enters the air as organic dust, which may be a health hazard, and is ultimately mostly washed into rivers and streams. The remainder is probably burned or added to the growing inventory of old tires which are accumulating haphazardly in garages, on vacant lots, etc.

At present prices, not all discarded automobile bodies can be utilized as open hearth or oxygen-process scrap, because of the presence of awkward contaminants, such as copper ($\sim$30 lb per automobile), lead (30–40 lb), aluminum (30–90 lb), zinc (30–45 lb), nickel, and chromium as well as nonmetallic impurities. Iron and steel constitute only about 79 per cent of the curb weight of an average automobile, and, even with tires, fluids, and batteries removed, about 15 per cent of the residual weight consists of materials which the potential scrap user does not want.[37] Thus, the annual supply of discarded motor vehicles (close to 6.5 million per year) is increasing faster than demand for this resource. The surplus piles up in automobile "graveyards" or as abandoned hulks scattered over the countryside, or, when the concentration of eyesores reaches the threshold of toleration, the junk cars are sometimes incinerated and/or compressed and used in landfill operations. However, a major outlet in recent years has been to increase the inventory of junk cars in automobile graveyards.

Where a potential demand for scrap exists locally and the supply is large enough — as in a large metropolitan area — new technology makes it possible to improve the quality of the scrap metal at an economic cost. The method utilizes giant shredders which automatically fragmentize the automobile bodies (minus engines, radiators, and gas tanks) and magnetically sort the ferrous from the nonferrous materials. Combustible material is burned off, and the ferrous residue is heated and rolled to increase its density. The resultant product is equivalent in quality to desirable No. 1 heavy melting scrap (e.g., steel rails) in quality and degree of contamination. About 2.5 million tons were processed in this way in 1965; unfortunately the capital investment required for such equipment is such that it can only be justified in densely populated areas.

The processing required to return the solid wastes (junk automobiles) to the production cycle results in a discharge of residuals to the air, as contrasted with com-

---

94 per cent of the vehicles scrapped in that year, but this assumed an average weight of steel per vehicle (2.131 lb) based on automobiles alone. In actual fact, the average weight per vehicle must be somewhat higher since about 12 per cent of the vehicles scrapped were trucks or buses, some of which were equivalent to several automobiles in weight. Hence, it might be fairer to assume that 90 per cent of the vehicles were accounted for.

[37] This suggests the possible designability of a disposal tax graduated to take account of the ease with which the materials contained in the automobile lend themselves to recycling.

pression and sanitary landfill *without* incineration, or dumping in shallow coastal waters where the hulks can become convenient breeding grounds for marine fauna. At the present annual rate of motor vehicle discard, about 2.5 million tons of non-metallic materials must be disposed of.

THE WHOLE SECTOR — INTERDEPENDENCIES

Figure 6 shows a schematic residual materials flow for the household sector, excluding automobiles. From it one can obtain a conception of the interdependencies of the various waste streams. For instance, if waste waters are given high-level treatment and if all sewage sludges and the maximum amount of garbage and refuse are incinerated, the majority of the final residual waste load from households, which must be disposed of into the environment, is gaseous. On the other hand, if no incineration is conducted at all and sewage treatment is pressed to the point where all solids are removed from the waste water stream, all but a small percentage (gases from space heating) of the weight of residuals flowing from households become a solid or semi-solid waste. Finally, should garbage and refuse grinding and discharge to the sanitary sewers be practiced on a large scale and no waste water treatment to remove solids be conducted, very little gaseous waste would flow from households and perhaps half the weight of residuals would be deposited into the aquatic environment. The remainder would be solids.

A general alternative to trying to "throw away" these residuals is to reincorporate them into the productive process, thus reducing the overall throughput of the production-consumption system. At some cost, virtually all the household residuals could be recaptured for useful purposes. Thus sewage solids and wet garbage could be composted and recovered for fertilizer. Metals and some other durable materials (including glass) can be, and sometimes are, recovered for reuse. Plastics pose perhaps the most difficult recycling problem. Still, application of known recovery technologies could reduce the net outflow of residuals from the household sector to a very low level.

We are *not* proposing that this is necessarily the appropriate solution. The cost of recovering the material may be, and often is, considerably higher than the cost of obtaining new materials from nature, even when external costs associated with disposing of residuals into the environment are taken into account. But there are reasons to think that the present system for organizing production (the market combined with rather ad hoc controls) does not produce the optimum degree of reuse possible with today's technology, nor does it stimulate an appropriate rate of improvement in that technology. Under current conditions, few, if any, individuals and private or public agencies systematically bear the external costs of disposing of waste residuals into the environment. Water and air pollution control are in separate agencies and solid waste disposal in still another. Restrictions relating to water pollution usually say nothing about air pollution or disposal of solids. Often the water pollution authority is pushed to protect watercourses by producing gases or solids which it "throws away" into the environment. We will not here pursue the matter of how the matrix of controls and regulations might be altered to improve the situation but we

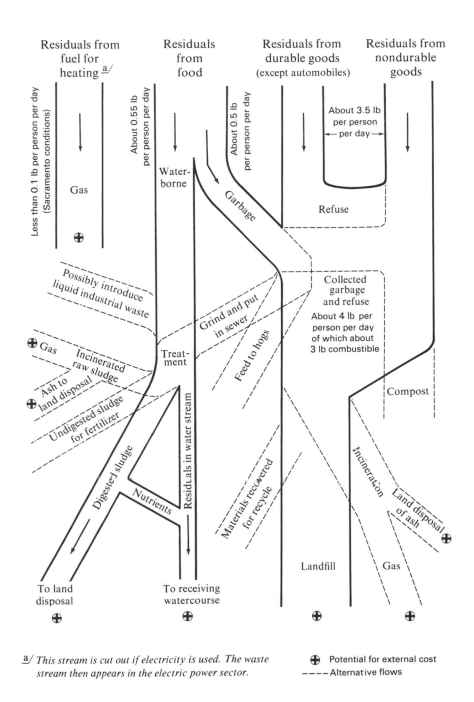

Figure 6.   Household residual materials flow (per capita).

do want to emphasize that arrangements which fully reflected all external costs would tend to lead to higher rates of reuse, less net throughput, and a more rapid rate of technological improvement in recovery systems.

Planning and Policy

GENERAL CONSIDERATIONS

In a necessarily partial and illustrative way we have applied an approach to the problem of calculating and forecasting residuals which does not use as central categories the conventional division between liquid, gaseous, and solid residuals. Rather it attempts to account for the residual materials, regardless of form, which result from the various materials- and fuel-using economic processes and functions in national and regional economies.

As explained in the introductory section, this approach provides certain general insights concerning the quantity of residuals generated, the factors bearing on this quantity, and about the failure of the market mechanism to deal appropriately with the entire resources allocation problem. The interdependencies between residuals streams, which become so clear in this approach, also suggest that the conventional organization of governmental media to which residuals are discharged — air, water, and the solid earth — needs re-examination.

To recapitulate, given the population, industrial production, and transport services in a region, it is possible to visualize combinations of social policy which could lead to quite different relative burdens being placed on the various residuals-receiving environmental media; or, given the possibilities for recycle and less residual-generating production processes, the overall burden to be placed upon the environment as a whole. To take one extreme, a region which went in heavily for electric space heating and wet scrubbing of stack gases (from steam plants and industries), which ground up its garbage and delivered it to the sewers and then discharged the raw sewage to watercourses, would protect its air resources to an unusual extent, but only at the sacrifice of placing a heavy residuals load upon water resources. On the other hand, a region which treated municipal and industrial waste water streams to a high level but relied heavily on the incineration of sludges and solid wastes would protect its water and land resources, but at the expense of discharging waste residuals predominantly to the air. Finally, a region which practiced high-level recovery and re-cycle of waste materials and fostered low residual production processes to a far-reaching extent in each of the economic sectors might, as we have seen, discharge very little residual waste to any of the environmental media.

In the transportation sector — which is the greatest single source of gaseous residuals and also a very significant source of solid wastes — a variety of waste and cost tradeoffs is also possible. For example, powering automobiles electrically and supplying power from conventional steam plants would tend greatly to reduce emissions of carbon monoxide and hydrocarbons to the atmosphere, but at the same time would increase sulfur dioxide emissions unless the waste gases from the power plant were treated. If treatment took the form of wet scrubbing, discharges to the water environment would be increased. If dry sulfur recovery processes were used, overall discharges to the environment would be lessened, but NO_x emissions would be reduced less than the others. If nuclear power were used, residuals discharges would be practically eliminated, but the small quantities of radioactive solid waste would require special and expensive disposal methods. If mass transit were substituted for individual cars, emissions would be greatly reduced, as would also be the case if steam (external combustion) engines were substituted for conventional internal combustion engines. If electric vehicles, as has been suggested, had longer lives than conventional automobiles, another major residuals problem would be significantly reduced in intensity.[38]

The approach sketched out in this paper is clearly experimental at this point. But we feel it could be developed and refined into a much more powerful technological-economic tool than has previously been available for projecting and analyzing environmental quality problems of type A. 1 and A. 2 in the classification presented in p. 22 of Perloff's introductory essay to this volume.[39] A regional or metropolitan area focus is appropriate for this effort, since it is at this level that the analysis of residuals flows can be brought into a meaningful relationship with the geographical, meteorological, and hydrological systems into which the waste residuals flow. An understanding of this relationship and operational mathematical modeling of these natural systems permits the analysis of concentrations, durations, and probabilities.[40] The latter must be obtained as a basis for gauging external costs and devising appropriate mechanisms and levels of control. Damages, or external costs, must also be evaluated on a regional basis. Mere calculations of residuals on a national level tell us little of specific value in devising efficient management schemes.

CONTROLS AND ENVIRONMENTAL MANAGEMENT

If we wish to realize the very great advantages of the decentralized decision-making mechanism — in other words, the market — we must find appropriate ways to control the external environmental effects associated with residuals discharge. This means that in some fashion the external costs imposed by residuals discharged to the environment (be they liquids, solids, or gases) must be weighed against, and balanced with, the costs of controlling the amount of these residuals, including any external

[38] Ayres, "Technology and Urban Transportation . . . ."

[39] A significant first step toward the type of approach we have in mind is found in Phillips *et al.*, *Wastes Management*. For a more formal mathematical development of the ideas in this paper, see Robert U. Ayres and Allen V. Kneese, "Production, Consumption, and Externalities," *American Economic Review* (forthcoming).

[40] There has been much progress in providing useful models of these natural systems. For applications, see Robert K. Davis, *The Range of Choice in Water Management* (The Johns Hopkins Press, for Resources for the Future, Inc., 1968), and an unpublished dissertation by Azriel Teller, "Air Pollution Abatement: An Economic Study into the Cost of Control" (The Johns Hopkins University, 1967).

costs which may result from increased levels of residuals in one environmental medium as a result of control exercised in another.

There are two potentially workable ways whereby decisions on how much to produce and how to produce it (and, similarly, decisions on consumption) can take better account of all the costs and benefits (private and external or social) flowing from the economic activity in question.

The first is to internalize the problem so that a single economic unit will take account of all of the costs and benefits associated with the external effects. One way to do this is to enlarge the size of the economic unit. Where external effects are limited in scope, there tends to be some incentive for merger,[41] because — as we implied earlier — overall costs are properly taken into account. For example, combining a rolling mill with a blast furnace in an integrated plant facilitates the recycling of "home" scrap and saves on fuel and combustion residuals. But waste products are often so widely dispersed in nature and affect so many diverse interests that the merger route is not feasible. Also the decisions of individuals and households bear upon the extent to which external costs occur and these decision units are not subject to merger in the usual economic sense.

The second approach is closely related to the first but involves the formation of a co-operative agency or governmental authority to induce (or require) systematic "internal" consideration of all costs and benefits by changing the framework within which the individual or firm would otherwise be operating. This is sometimes achieved by mutually negotiated restraints, but more frequently by external regulations enforceable at law. For example, certain emission standards may be required for automobile exhausts. There are numerous examples of public agencies placing regulations on economic activities such as production, purchase, and sale of property or goods to limit the external effects involved. Another means which is usually preferred by economists, but little used in practice, is to put an actual price (or tax) on the externality-causing activity. Examples of this approach are a tax on sewage effluents which is related to the quality and quantity of the discharge, or a surcharge on the price of fuels with high sulfur content which is meant to take account of the broader costs to society external to the fuel-using enterprise. These procedures use economic incentives to allocate the resource (the waste assimilative capacity of the environment) similar to those generated where market mechanisms can balance costs and returns. But whichever route is adopted, the interdependency between various waste residual streams must be recognized. A tax or other restraint on one in isolation does not necessarily optimally control external costs or even necessarily reduce them when all waste streams are considered simultaneously.

Internalization of external costs by one means or another presents complex problems, but even the best techniques for doing this cannot guarantee that environmental quality will be managed in the most economical way; i.e., in such a fashion that the combined cost of controlling or alleviating the ill effects of residuals, plus the

---

[41] An extreme form of this approach would be nationalization of all economic activity.

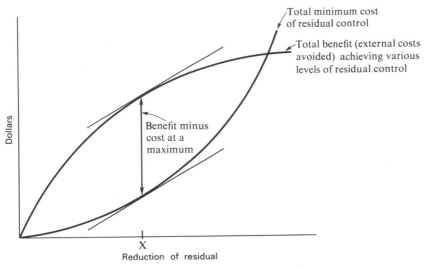

Figure 7.

external damages imposed by uncontrolled final discharges, is minimized. In Figure 7, this optimum level is shown at point X, which is defined mathematically as the point at which the slopes (the derivatives) of the cost and benefit functions are equal. But for this to be the true economic optimum, the costs must be the lowest possible for a given level of residual control. In this connection, it is important to recognize that in most, if not all, fields of environmental quality management there are potentially effective and efficient measures which cannot be achieved either by setting standards or by imposing taxes upon the activities of individual decision makers that cause externalities (discharge residuals). In other words, there are potentially efficient environmental quality control measures unavailable to the individual firm, or even the individual municipality, not to mention the individual person.[42]

Examples of such measures are reservoir regulation of the low flow of rivers to improve their residuals assimilation capacity, land-use restrictions to achieve a similar objective as regards the atmosphere (or airshed) over an area, or co-ordinated solid waste disposal for a megalopolitan region as a whole. Economic efficiency requires that such measures be executed on a geographic scale which would normally encompass a number of political subdivisions, and our society is institutionally ill-equipped to accomplish this. Moreover, existing institutions for environmental management have no machinery or authority to allocate the external cost associated with residuals (or other external effects) to the originating activities or, indeed, even to identify them unambiguously. This is true even when air, water, and solid wastes control are each considered in isolated categories and very much more so when the integral interdependencies between them are recognized.

[42] For a rigorous theoretical treatment of the relationships between external costs of waste discharge and economically optimal collective investment, see Hayden Boyd, "Collective Facilities in Water Quality Management," in Kneese and Bower, *Managing Water Quality*.

MANAGEMENT PLANNING

The kind of approach to planning for regional environmental management we have in mind is the following: As a first step, a more or less refined materials balance would be estimated for the area. This would involve some major complications since regional economies are very "open." In other words, all material imports and exports (including goods at various stages through the manufacturing process) would have to be accounted for. Getting this information as well as that needed to estimate materials balances for various industries would involve considerable primary data collection. But, once completed, the materials balance would provide a picture of the residuals flows in the area. Economic base input-output models[43] could then be used to project levels of activity and industry mixes into the future — as well as transportation requirements, population, and other parameters of interest in constructing a new materials balance. In the first instance, present technology and low levels of materials recycle and by-product recovery could be assumed. This procedure would differ from conventional approaches in that it would relate levels of residuals generation logically to the industrial and population base and account for all residuals in an internally consistent model. Conventionally, levels of emissions to the air, liquid-borne residuals, and solid wastes are extrapolated separately.

As a further step, the procedure would permit analysis of the overall impact on all residuals of control measures instituted for one or more of them. As we have seen, for a given level of economic activity, a given efficiency of energy conversion, and a given degree of recycle and by-product recovery, reduction of one type of residual must come at the expense of creating another. Moreover, as a basis for economic analysis of this alternative, residuals should be classified and quantified in terms of their potential recoverability,[44] and the overall residuals implications of projected changes in waste treatment and recovery technologies could be tested.

Another major effort would have to go into mathematically simulating the natural system, especially the meteorological and hydrological systems, in such a way that concentrations and their probability and duration could be estimated, as well as secondary effects of residuals discharges. The latter might include photochemical reactions in the atmosphere and the reduction of dissolved oxygen in water courses resulting from the discharge of organic wastes to them. Where possible, concentrations of residuals and their secondary effects should be related to quantitative monetary measures of damage. Where this is not possible, they may be compared with conventional standards of environmental quality. But such standards should be subjected to cost sensitivity analysis before a final working standard is adopted. These activities would cover the range of operations shown in Table 1 of Perloff's introductory essay.

[43] See John R. Meyer, "Regional Economics: A Survey," *The American Economic Review* (March 1963). See also Ayres and Kneese, "Production, Consumption, and Externalities."

[44] A distinction should be drawn between recycle and by-product recovery processes which market conditions will make internally profitable to the firm and those which might be stimulated by public policy — residuals taxes, for example.

A further step in the planning process would be to examine the potential of larger-scale control systems in the region. Research on water quality management has shown clearly that such measures as reservoir regulation of river flows, mechanical aeration of residuals-receiving watercourses, and treatment of municipal and industrial wastes together in collective regional treatment plants can enter efficiently into regional water quality management systems.[45] Changes in regional transport systems and altered design and operation of electric power systems might also enter efficiently into regional environmental quality management systems.

The final result of such a planning activity would be a coherent set of projections of residuals, estimates of optimal emissions control equipment and procedures (including recycle and by-product recovery and treatment to change the form of wastes where appropriate to maximize net benefits or achieve standards), and large-scale measures which would fit integrally and efficiently into a regional management system.

Finally, it might be necessary to design an institution or institutions to perform management functions and to supply it with appropriate policy instruments.[46] The latter would include authority to regulate emissions, levy charges or taxes on them, and implement (or encourage the other agencies to implement) large-scale regional measures. Management would also include continuing operating, co-ordinating, and planning responsibilities.

Needed Data and Research

The implementation of the kind of planning study sketched above would be hindered by many problems of insufficient or inaccurate data and less than fully satisfactory operational mathematical models. For example, models of the pertinent atmospheric and hydrological systems could stand much improvement. We will not attempt to provide a comprehensive list of needed data and research but will discuss briefly three areas on which we feel information is most deficient and is likely to be hardest to improve.

1. The first is the area of residuals from industrial operations. Very little organized information on this matter is available and the few studies which have provided pertinent information of a reasonably dependable type have been difficult and costly. Simple coefficients of residuals per unit of output will not suffice. Depending on production processes and by-product recovery, the waste residuals of particular types from different plants in the same industry can differ by orders of magnitude. One must be able to forecast how particular residuals are influenced by such factors as raw materials prices and effluent controls and how overall manufacturing costs vary with changes in these factors. Further studies along the general lines of the beet sugar study described on pp. 53–55 are badly needed and some of these are under way. It is also possible that some of the needed information could be obtained

[45] For an example, see Robert K. Davis, *The Range of Choice in Water Management.*

[46] There is already clear evidence that rethinking of the traditional government approach to these problems is going on. A case in point is the new Environmental Protection Administration of New York City. A somewhat similar arrangement has been recommended for Washington, D.C.

from data collected by the Bureau of the Census but not published in the *Census of Manufacturers*. This possibility is also being investigated. The objective of the needed industry studies would be to provide information on the economic tradeoffs (from the industry point of view) between discharges to the various environmental media on the one hand, and materials recovery on the other.

2. The second and even more difficult area of information deficiency relates to the provision of estimates of the benefits (external costs avoided) to be achieved by reducing discharges to the various environmental media. Although this matter has received a considerable amount of attention,[47] we are far from being able to make all the desired estimates of benefits on a routine basis for the type of study outlined in the previous paragraph. Acceleration of work on this matter by economists and social psychologists is urgently needed. In the meantime it will be necessary to use optimization models which accept whatever information on benefits can be made available and also additional constraints representing alternative environmental standards.

3. The third bundle of problems relates to the selection of an appropriate region for planning and management and involves many difficulties which cannot be pursued in any depth here. In general it will be necessary to conceive of at least two regional areas of interest. One may be termed the "source and control area" and the other, the "impact" area. The source and control area will include the region where residuals emissions are concentrated and affect a natural environmental system or systems in a substantial way (usually a metropolitan area or groups of areas). If it is possible to affect environmental quality by controlling the natural system (e.g., release from storage reservoirs to improve the assimilative capacity of streams), the point at which control can be exercised should also be included. This is why it is appropriate, for instance, to encompass portions of a watershed which may not be affected adversely by residuals discharges but where reservoir sites exist that could be used to store water to augment low flows. The impact area is the region over which external costs occur as a result of emission in the source and control area. Clearly the two may not correspond. For example, air pollution may (and does) damage crops outside a source metropolitan area and even outside the airshed in which the source area is located. Such damages should be identified and evaluated wherever they occur and weighed against control cost in the source and control area. From the technical economic point of view of achieving optimum level and techniques of environmental control, it is only necessary that the source and control area be under some kind of unified management. But, as the political scientists remind us, it may not suffice to obtain a "constituency" for control. Effective and efficient environmental management requires "institutional design" and our ability to do this is very primitive. The design of an institution which would manage efficiently and equitably and would be politically viable is perhaps the most difficult and important problem in the environmental

---

[47] For a review of the current situations, see Allen V. Kneese, "Economics and the Quality of the Environment — Some Empirical Experiences," in M. E. Garnsey and J. N. Hibbs (eds.), *Social Sciences and the Environment* (University of Colorado Press, 1967), pp. 165–293.

management field. But problems of this type are now being explicitly addressed by several planning studies in the United States and accelerating research in the "new" political economy and in political sociology should yield useful results over the next few years.

Even though the approach we have outlined has many deficiencies in data and technique, we do not feel it would be unrealistic to implement it experimentally in some suitable region over the next few years. Such a study could yield useful results in its own right and provide excellent guidance to future environmental quality research by revealing both gaps and opportunities.

3

The three-dimensional city: contained urban space

Irving Hoch

Research Associate, Resources for the Future

The three-dimensional city: contained urban space

Irving Hoch

This chapter is concerned with the use of enclosed space in the urban environment and with the basic alternatives of growing up versus growing out. Obviously, a full treatment of the subject would be a rather monumental undertaking. An attempt is made here to provide an introductory and preliminary overview and to bring into focus some specific topics of interest.

Enclosed urban space is contained within structures. The major kind of structure, in terms of value and use, is the building. However, enclosed space is a general enough category to justify giving some attention to non-building items, such as tunnels, elevated highways, sewers and conduits, shopping malls, domed stadiums, etc.

This chapter is divided into six parts. The first develops some simple allocation models, applying theory of the firm to land and building mix on both the micro and macro levels. (It can be skimmed by the non-technical reader.) The second part confronts theory with the real world and particularly stresses the concept of land as three-dimensional space. One of the real-world complications noted is the matter of externalities, and these are discussed in the third part. Next, some measures of urban space are presented; these constitute a first approximation to a set of indicators of the spatial environment. In the fifth part, recent developments in three-dimensional space use are discussed — specifically, high-rise developments, underground development, and elevated structures and the utilization of air rights. Finally, some long-term forecasts are noted, and some visions of the three-dimensional city are contemplated.

Some Simple Models

We can obtain insight into why, where, and how structures occur by means of a highly simplified economic model. The model hinges on factor substitution; with good reason, Mills sees factor substitution as the most dramatic characteristic of the urban scene.[1]

Let us begin with a Cobb-Douglas production function, and examine life on the micro level. We will then move from the individual firm to the market, within the general context of this model. That discussion then leads into some general remarks on the spatial organization of the urban economy.

I am indebted to my colleagues at Resources for the Future for encouragement and helpful reviews during the writing of this paper. In addition, Mason Gaffney and William Pendleton developed a number of useful comments and references in discussions of a previous draft of the paper.— AUTHOR'S NOTE

[1] Edwin S. Mills, "An Aggregative Model of Resource Allocation in a Metropolitan Area," *American Economic Review* (May 1967), p. 197.

At the micro level, let output be enclosed rentable space and inputs be land and building input,[2] denoted as follows: land = a; building input = b; rentable space = x. Corresponding prices are P_a, P_b, and P_x, assumed constant at the firm level. For simplicity, we peg the discussion in terms of building space, but the argument will be applicable to structures in general. (It might be noted that at the present level of abstraction, the individual firm corresponds to the individual building. More involved model building would distinguish between these entities.)

Write $x = Ka^\alpha b^\beta$; and assume $\alpha + \beta < 1$. An elasticity sum below one is a necessary condition for profit maximization, by way of the second order condition of the calculus. This can be interpreted as reflecting a factor fixed to the firm, often labeled "management" or "entrepreneurial capacity" for convenience.

Profit maximization leads to the usual value-of-marginal-product equals price of input statements for a and b; in this context, the explicit equations may be written for each factor as a function of the other:

$$a = \left(\frac{P_x}{P_a}\alpha K\right)^{\frac{1}{1-\alpha}} b^{\frac{\beta}{1-\alpha}}$$

$$\text{and}\quad b = \left(\frac{P_x}{P_b}\beta K\right)^{\frac{1}{1-\beta}} a^{\frac{\alpha}{1-\beta}}$$

Since $\alpha + \beta < 1$, it follows that the exponent $\beta/(1-\alpha)$ is less than one, as is $\alpha/(1-\beta)$.[3]

Geometrically, these equations plot as shown, with equilibrium values a_1 and b_1 for a given set of prices.[4]

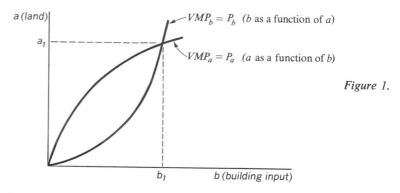

Figure 1.

---

[2] Building input is the aggregate of building materials, labor, and maintenance. Of course, this sort of simplification is ultimately defensible only if the components of the aggregate are used in fixed proportions.

[3] Thus, $\alpha + \beta < 1$, hence: $\beta < 1 - \alpha$ and $\dfrac{\beta}{1-\alpha} < 1$.

[4] Algebraically, let x_1 be the equilibrium value of x; then:

$$x_1 = [K\alpha^\alpha\beta^\beta P_x^{\alpha+\beta}P_a^{-\alpha}P_b^{-\beta}]^{\frac{1}{1-\alpha-\beta}}$$

and

$$a_1 = \alpha x_1 P_x P_a^{-1}, \quad b_1 = \beta x_1 P_x P_b^{-1}$$

As we move toward a center of economic activity, the firm will be faced with higher levels of P_a and P_x, and our equilibrium shifts to (a_2, b_2) involving increased building per unit of land. Note that P_b here is assumed unchanged but the b relation shifts because of the change in P_x; the a relation shift reflects both P_x and P_a changes.

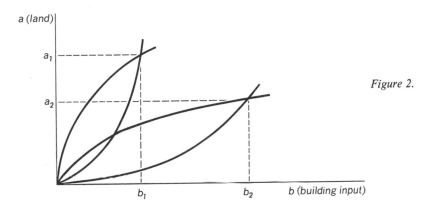

Figure 2.

If there is a technological advance in construction that can be represented as a decrease in P_b, the model indicates this will increase both land and building input, though the relative increase will be greater in building input. This is shown in Figure 3 below.

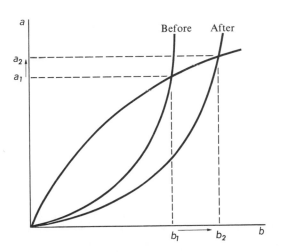

Figure 3.

There is empirical evidence that the size of new office buildings has been increasing over time, and that site increases, as well as greater height and changed design, are involved.[5] This can be viewed as consistent with the diagram above.

[5] Robert Moore Fisher, *The Boom in Office Buildings*, Technical Bulletin 58 (Urban Land Institute, 1967), pp. 21, 22. "With larger sites, greater height or changed design — or a combination

Maximization is carried out subject to institutional constraints, however, so that the equilibrium point may not be attainable. Some forms of zoning fit in this category. Thus, zoning sometimes involves a specific height limitation (for example, the maximum permissible building height in Washington, D.C., is 130 feet[6]). If this is viewed as equivalent to an upper bound on building inputs, $b \leq b_0$, we obtain a restricted equilibrium (a_0, b_0) as shown in Figure 4.

More often, zoning takes the form of a restriction on floor space relative to site area — e.g., a ratio of 15:1[7] — which implies a prohibited set of input combinations, as shown by the shaded area in Figure 5. (The shape of the curve dividing the a, b plane follows from the assumption of decreasing returns to scale.) The restriction is often referred to as the FAR — an abbreviation for Floor Area Ratio, that is, ratio of floor space to site area.

If the FAR restriction is effective, the firm will operate with less than optimal levels of building relative to land, since the Cobb-Douglas expansion path is a straight line through the origin and (a_1, b_1), the unrestricted equilibrium. Given land level a_1, building input will be b_0. It is not obvious from the diagram where the restricted equilibrium will be. However, this can be determined by means of algebraic manipulation.

Using the Lagrangian multiplier, with side condition $x/a = C$, to represent the restriction $x/a \leq C$, the following solution for output and inputs is obtained in terms of parameters:

$$x = \left[\frac{K}{C^\alpha} \frac{\beta^\beta}{P_b^\beta} \ (P_x - D)^\beta \right]^{\frac{1}{1-\alpha-\beta}}; \quad D = \frac{P_a - \alpha C P_x}{C(1-\alpha)}$$

$$b = \left[\frac{\beta(P_x - D)}{P_b} \right] x$$

and, of course, $a = x/C$

Although zoning can imply lack of optimality for the individual firm, a rationale for its use is that it accounts for externalities not handled otherwise, and an increase

---

of these elements — typical office buildings completed in the postwar years have contained more floor space than those built in previous booms." In Chicago, "the average size of new office buildings has increased during nearly every decade since the 1870's. Buildings completed since 1960 have averaged 7¾ times the size of buildings erected nine decades earlier."

[6] Cf. Harold M. Lewis, *A New Zoning Plan for the District of Columbia* [prepared for the Commissioners of the District of Columbia] (New York: Harold M. Lewis, 1956), p. 54. The 130-foot limit applies to commercial buildings. Residential buildings have a 90-foot limit.

[7] Cf. Fisher, *The Boom in Office Building*, p. 21: "The advantages of making the most of a particular site by building offices in the sky have been offset in part by zoning ordinances. Many codes restrict the intensity of development by setting a maximum permitted ratio of gross floor area to total site area."

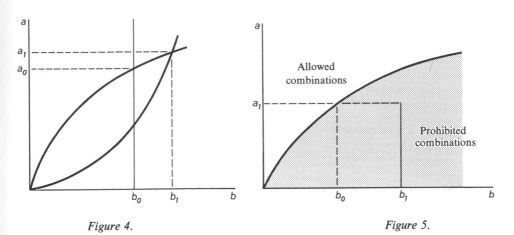

Figure 4.   *Figure 5.*

in community welfare is thereby generated.[8] In addition, some elements of protection-
ism and the consumption of merit goods[9] seem to be involved.

Let us now attempt to move from firm to market. (This is not an easy move
operationally, given conventional theory.) This will be essayed as follows. Assume
(1) the profit maximizing conditions hold at the firm level; (2) there is a fixed
amount, A, of urban land available in a particular area of interest; (3) there are N
firms; (4) P_b is fixed to this market, that is, the supply of b is perfectly elastic (in
contrast to a, which is perfectly inelastic); and (5) all firms have the same production
function. By assuming (5), it follows that at equilibrium all firms will have the same
amount of a. If one firm has less than the average amount, its value of marginal
product (VMP) will exceed P_a and it will bid a away from other firms. Hence, we can
state $A/N - a_0$ is a fixed level of land per firm. We can then proceed to determine b
and P_a in terms of individual firm equations. Algebraically, we have specified a, P_b,
and P_x and can solve for the remaining three variables x, P_a, and b from our three
equations (production function and profit maximizing relations). In effect, we find
that P_a which is consistent with profit maximization.[10] Algebraic manipulation yields

$$b = [P_x K \beta a_0^\alpha P_b^{-1}]^{\frac{1}{1-\beta}}$$

$$P_a = [P_x P_b^{-\beta} a_0^{\alpha+\beta-1} K\alpha^{1-\beta} \beta^\beta]^{\frac{1}{1-\beta}}$$

---

[8] In the case of the land-building mix, an analogous lack of optimality occurred in western
U.S. agriculture by virtue of the 160-acre limitation on the individual farm firm. Cf. Murray Benedict,
Farm Policies of the United States, 1790–1950 (Twentieth Century Fund, 1953), Chap. I, pp. 21–22
in particular.

[9] For a recent discussion of merit goods, see Julius Margolis, "The Demand for Urban Public
Services," in Harvey S. Perloff and Lowdon Wingo, Jr. (eds.), *Issues in Urban Economics* (The Johns
Hopkins Press for Resources for the Future, 1968) pp. 541 ff.

[10] The theorizing here might be extended by arguing that equilibrium occurs only if profit
obtained is equal to the entrepreneur's opportunity cost. Put another way, N can be viewed as variable
in the longest run.

The P_a equation yields some interesting implications: (1) The elasticity of land price with respect to output price, P_x, is $1/(1 - \beta)$. Empirical evidence[11] leads to a crude estimate of β as around 2/3; this means that land prices vary roughly as the cube of output price; thus, a doubling of floor space price generates an eightfold increase in land price. Hence, a range of product prices will correspond to a much wider range of land prices.[12] (2) If quantity of land, A, is increased exogenously, there is a not surprising drop in P_a; the elasticity is $(\alpha + \beta - 1)/(1 - \beta)$. As an empirical example, we might consider landfill occurring on a body of water fronting on the central business district (CBD). (3) The elasticity of b with respect to P_x is exactly the same as that of P_a; in this model, then, the equilibrium level of building quantity and land price are perfectly correlated.

To this point, we have taken P_x as given. Certainly, the value of P_x will have a vital bearing on land utilization. It was argued earlier that P_x will increase with movement toward a center of economic activity. One can get good first approximations to real-world urban structure by assuming that there is one city center and that access to the center is valuable; for example, transportation costs decline as one locates closer to the center. Thus, x viewed as building floor space is used in producing other things whose value is a function of access to the center. Again, x is used in conjunction with other inputs, and the costs of assembling these inputs in one place increases with distance from the center. Hence, it becomes reasonable to write $P_x = P_c - T$, where P_c is price at the center and T reflects transportation and assembly costs which increase with distance from the center.[13]

By specifying the existence of different products or activities yielding different P_c and T values, we can obtain a von Thünen type of model with concentric circles of land use around the city center. A given concentric ring is devoted to the specific activity that can pay the most for land in the area.[14]

[11] Based on Table 1, p. 85, and an assumption that $\alpha + \beta$ equals approximately .9.

[12] If we are concerned with rental value of floor space, then maintenance charges ought to be included; in this formulation, the elasticity of land price with respect to output price may be 5 or 6, rather than 3.

[13] The insertion of $P_x = P_c - T$ into the P_a equation above yields a result quite similar to Mills' equation (8). (See p. 243 in this volume.) Thus, $1/(1 - \beta)$ corresponds to his $1/\alpha_1 = 1/(1 - \beta_1 - \gamma_1)$. Mills' model is more complex, in that a transportation production function is introduced explicitly. This is commendable in that there is simultaneous concern with land use and transportation facilities. It is common to treat one as given exogenously to the other. That may sometimes be necessary, given real-world complexity, but it can lead to unfortunate policy results. For example, Edgar M. Hoover notes, "The danger in models based simply on existing origin-destination patterns . . . is that they tend to make the status quo into the ideal. This is objectionable if we believe that the 'status is nothing to quo about'." From "The Evolving Form and Structure of the Metropolis," in Perloff and Wingo (eds.), *Issues in Urban Economics*, p. 260.

[14] For a detailed statement of theory, see Edgar S. Dunn, Jr., *The Location of Agricultural Production* (University of Florida Press, 1954). Some examples of urban application include: W. Alonso, "A Theory of the Urban Land Market," in Regional Science Association, *Papers and Proceedings* (1960), Vol. 6, pp. 149–57; L. S. Burns and F. G. Mittelbach, "Location — Fourth Determinant of Residential Value," *The Appraisal Journal* (April 1964), p. 238 in particular; and

Brigham and Tiebout, among others, argue that this pattern needs modification because access is better near transportation networks, with consequent local peaking of values and floor space near those networks; this will be particularly pronounced at the intersection of major arterials.[15] Other writers focus on multiple centers;[16] some are concerned with the attraction of different kinds of centers (employment, recreation, etc.) or of the mutual attraction of all points in urban space, eventuating in the construction of gravity and potential models.[17]

Nevertheless, there is general agreement that distance from the center yields good first approximations to empirical reality. From the center outward, then, we get a "density gradient where density is a negative function of radial distance."[18] Along a radial, then, many variables of interest fall off from a peak in a monotonic, negative exponential fashion. This description of behavior is seen as applicable to land value, floor space, employment, and population density, and to associated variables such as trips generated and traffic congestion. Here, then, is the three-dimensional city from the macroscopic point of view.

Real-World Confirmations and Complications

In this section an attempt is made to compare real-world phenomena to aspects of the model presented above. Empirical confirmations will be noted, as will absences of agreement, indicating the need for qualification, extension, or further explanation.

THE MACRO LEVEL: THE OVERALL SPATIAL PATTERN

In the discussion that follows, consideration of the overall spatial pattern will touch on centralizing and decentralizing forces, the center, density gradients, and concentric rings. Centralizing forces may be cataloged under such headings as: need for

---

Edward L. Ullman, "The Nature of Cities Reconsidered," in H. W. Eldredge (ed.), *Taming Megalopolis* (Anchor Books, Doubleday, 1967), Vol. 1, p. 84. See also Norbert J. Stefaniak, "A Refinement of Haig's Theory," *Land Economics* (November 1963), pp. 429–33, for some suggestive remarks on industry locations given the distribution of site rentals.

[15] Brigham treats this as a relatively minor qualification; Tiebout sees it, in conjunction with externalities, as a major caveat. Eugene F. Brigham, "The Determinants of Residential Land Values," *Land Economics* (November 1965), p. 327; and Charles M. Tiebout, "Intra-Urban Location Problems: An Evaluation," *American Economic Review* (May 1961), p. 274.

[16] Cf. Ullman, "The Nature of Cities . . . ," and Hoover, "The Evolving Form . . . of the Metropolis," p. 262.

[17] In "Information for Land-Use Models," Highway Research Board, *Highway Research Record 194* (Washington, 1967), p. 9, Robert E. Barraclough writes: "Distance from the region's main center is the simplest measure [of accessibility]. Other measures have been used or suggested, such as the sum of distances from several centers weighted according to size of center; the sum of airline distances from each small area to all other small areas; gravity-type measures . . . . Recently, there have been expressions of doubt as to the efficacy of these measures." For a discussion of gravity and potential models, see Walter Isard, *Methods of Regional Analysis* (M.I.T. Press, 1960), Chapter 11.

[18] Hoover, "The Evolving Form . . . of the Metropolis," p. 248; see pp. 248–53 for a detailed discussion of the literature on density gradients.

face-to-face contact, specialization, and external (or agglomeration) economies. (These might be viewed as exogenous sources of demand for output produced near the center.)

Hoover sees the underlying rationale of the city as that of providing and facilitating close, easy, and multifarious contact, so that decision units may interact in fruitful and efficient ways.[19] Clearly, the importance of such interaction will differ for different activities, industries, groups, and individuals. Where the communication of information through face-to-face contact is an important component of an activity, that activity will have an incentive for central location.

As cities grow, greater specialization becomes possible, since specialization depends on the size of the market.[20] Specialized activities serving the entire metropolitan region will also have an incentive for central location, thus minimizing their access costs.[21] Jean Gottmann notes the interdependence of "quaternary" activities, including administration, finance, research, advertising, and the mass media. Such activities fit under the headings of both face-to-face contact and specialized activities.[22]

Finally, there is often a clustering of firms in a given industry or of linked industries, reflecting external economies. The common advantage is "generally a pool of especially suitable labor, a variety of specialized business services, or the congregation of customers seeking to compare a variety of offerings."[23] All of these factors cause a concentration at the center and a decline in density with movement away from the center.

Some empirical evidence is available which confirms the existence of pronounced density gradients. Thus, examples of total floor space, total trip destinations, non-residential floor space, and land value data exhibit marked peaking in the CBD and essentially monotonic decline with movement out from the CBD.[24] (Some mappings appear almost spikelike in form.) Residential floor area is generally much flatter in its distribution, though net population density (population relative to residential land) shows a more pronounced pattern.[25]

[19] *Ibid.*, pp. 237, 241, 246, 277.

[20] Dennis Cox, in his unpublished Ph.D. thesis draft, "Two Essays in the Distribution of Population," Stanford University, lists a number of specific examples to be found in the literature. They include medical specialties, the theater, libraries, fur repair shops, and diaper services.

[21] An interesting discussion of both face-to-face contact and specialized functions appears in Environmental Goals Committee, *Environmental Goals for the Los Angeles Region* (Los Angeles, 1967), pp. 57–62.

[22] Jean Gottmann, "Rising Demand for Urban Amenities," *Planning for a Nation of Cities* (M.I.T. Press, 1966).

[23] Hoover, "The Evolving Form . . . of the Metropolis," p. 245.

[24] Some examples may be noted. Transportation studies have developed a good deal of information. Thus, for the New York region, see Barraclough, "Information for Land-Use Models," figs. 1 through 5; for the Chicago region, see Chicago Area Transportation Study, *Final Report*, Vol. I, *Survey Findings* (Chicago, 1959), figs. 5 through 9; for the Pittsburgh region, see Pittsburgh Area Transportation Study, *Final Report*, Vol. I, *Study Findings* (1961), figs. 36, 41, 50, and 53. For a mapping of assessed property values, see Duane S. Knos, *Distribution of Land Values in Topeka, Kansas* (Center for Research in Business, University of Kansas, 1962), p. 6. See also Chapter 6 in this volume.

[25] Chicago Area Transportation Study, *Final Report*, Vol. I, p. 22.

Net population density gradients in a number of cities have been estimated by Colin Clark and by Richard F. Muth.[26]

A mapping of Chicago industrial floor area relative to industrial land by quarter square miles has been published, and it shows good agreement with expectations. The highest ratio class (above 2.5) occurs in the CBD and environs; the ratio generally declines with distance from the CBD, though some secondary cases of high ratios appear near rail and water facilities.[27]

There is some evidence of concentric rings of activity, although patterns are affected by accessibility factors other than distance, by zoning, and by the somewhat gross classification of land use usually employed. Thus, in Chicago, the Chicago Area Transportation Study shows that commercial land is concentrated in the CBD, with scattered nodes reflecting shopping centers; that as distance from the CBD increases, the percentage of all land in residential use also increases; and that major concentrations of industrial land occur outside the CBD in clusters, generally in close relation to rail and water facilities. Industrial zoning clearly limits the location of industry to areas near such facilities.

Improvements in transportation and communication can have a decentralizing effect. Thus, the general movement of industrial plants from central city to suburb probably reflects the growth of interstate highways and of trucking. Often, most of a factory's sales will be outside the local market, so that shipping goods from the central railroad depot, say, would be much more expensive than shipping from a truck yard outside the city. Again, Webber argues, "The patterns in Washington, Detroit and Los Angeles clearly suggest that the walking-precinct type of CBD, with its restricted radius...is not the only effective spatial pattern for face-to-face communication.... In Los Angeles...few linked establishments are within walking distances of each other, and an auto trip is thus an adjunct to a face-to-face meeting."[28]

With respect to the center, it should be noted that there may be different centers for different activities, and that a given center is not necessarily fixed through time. "The concept of a single most central focal point in an urban area is...significant and useful..., [but] there is in principle a variety of distinguishable central points of this sort, depending on what kinds of people or things are...assembled with a minimum of total expense or effort."[29]

Schultz and Simmons note that Chicago's CBD covers three-eighths of a square mile, and is enclosed by a river, a lake, and rail yards; hence, "The CBD wasn't likely to wander off, as similar districts elsewhere had, to the annoyance and embarrassment

[26] Colin Clark, "Urban Population Densities," *Journal of the Royal Statistical Society*, Series A, CXIV, Part IV (1951), pp. 490–96. Richard F. Muth, "The Spatial Structure of the Housing Market," in Regional Science Association, *Papers and Proceedings* (1961), Vol. 7, pp. 207–20.

[27] Mayor's Committee for Economic and Cultural Development, *Mid-Chicago Economic Development Study* (Chicago, 1966), Vol. I, plate 22.

[28] Melvin M. Webber, "Order in Diversity: Community Without Propinquity," in Lowdon Wingo, Jr. (ed.), *Cities and Space* (The Johns Hopkins Press for Resources for the Future, 1963), p. 43.

[29] Hoover, "The Evolving Form...of the Metropolis," p. 240.

of investors. . . . Because of its small, limited area its growth was inevitably vertical."[30] They feel that most CBD's have separate shopping and office centers, reflecting the two major functions of the CBD.[31]

Homer Hoyt holds that the main office center of most cities is moving in the direction of high-income residential areas.[32] In Washington, D.C., there has been a steady movement of office development westward; 67 per cent of land zoned for offices is contained in the older downtown area, but only 20 per cent of new space was constructed there during the period 1960–67.[33]

Increased accessibility brought about by the development of urban radial and belt expressways is a factor in the movement of industry to the outer portion of the metropolitan area, as well as in the growth of suburban shopping centers.[34] It also seems to be an important factor in the growth of apartments in the suburbs.[35]

The situation appears similar to that in the location hypothesis formulated by T. W. Schultz for agricultural areas.[36] Some points more distant in miles from the central market are nevertheless more accessible. Access to markets rather than distance from them is the primary determinant of income differences. The lagging areas cut off from the center in the Schultz formulation seem to correspond to the "gray blighted" areas discerned in the cityscape by a number of writers.

THE MICRO LEVEL: INDIVIDUAL FIRM BEHAVIOR — MODEL ELEMENTS

With regard to the form of the production function, data presented by Goldsmith show marked differences in the mix of land and building values for broad property categories. These are summarized in Table 1.

Assuming the Cobb-Douglas function, these data indicate marked differences in production functions between classes of property. For a given Cobb-Douglas function, at equilibrium, $aP_a/bP_a = \alpha/\beta$. Hence, variations in aP_a/bP_b indicate variations in α and β.[37]

A similar argument leads to the conclusion that the movement of industry from central city to suburb may involve a change in production function as well as factor substitution. Thus, on the suburban fringe, land was substituted for labor and capital; the sprawling one-story plant, using less labor, was substituted for the multi-story

---

[30] Earle Schultz and Walter Simmons, *Offices in the Sky* (Bobbs-Merrill, 1959), p. 22.

[31] *Ibid.*, p. 209.

[32] Homer Hoyt, "Recent Distortions of the Classical Models of Urban Structure," *Land Economics* (May 1964), p. 204.

[33] District of Columbia Redevelopment Land Agency, *Office Building Construction in Washington, D.C., 1960–67* (Washington, 1967), pp. 5 and 10.

[34] Cf. Ullman, *The Nature of Cities Reconsidered*, for some detailed data.

[35] Cf. Max Neutze, *The Suburban Apartment Boom: Case Study of a Land Use Problem* (Resources for the Future, Inc., 1968); and Hoyt, "Recent Distortions . . .," p. 208.

[36] T. W. Schultz, *The Economic Organization of Agriculture* (McGraw-Hill, 1953), Chaps. IX and X.

[37] Alternatively, of course, we can worry about (1) the applicability of Cobb-Douglas here, and (2) the accuracy of Goldsmith's data.

Table 1.   Value of Land Relative to Value of Structures, United States, 1958, by Type of Property

Type of property	Land value/structure value (aP_a/bP_b)
Single-family homes	.200
All non-farm residential	.155
Industrial	.176
Commercial	.667
Miscellaneous non-residential	.667
Public utility	.111
Social-recreational	.667

Source: Raymond W. Goldsmith, *The National Wealth of the United States in the Postwar Period* (Princeton University Press, 1962), Tables A–35, A–40, B–11, B–123, B–124, B–125.

plant. "In the end, although land was considerably cheaper on the fringe, the total dollars spent on land (or the annual rent) was *higher* than previously.... At the same time, the proportion of dollars spent on capital and labor was lower than previously."[38] Some observers focus on the technical changes. Thus, Hoover notes that new technologies in materials handling and distribution radically changed plant layout.[39] Again, "industry looks at any building taller than one story as internally inefficient. Every added story is said to increase truck stopping time and labor costs, and promote inefficient scheduling and handling."[40]

But the technical change noted may be effect rather than cause. In practice, it may be difficult to distinguish between production function change and factor substitution.

The entrepreneurial factor has been treated as fixed to the firm, but a good share of total costs might be subsumed under this heading. Thus, "in 1954, one large builder estimated that 40 per cent of his costs were attributable to planning, finding and assembling land and dealing with local controls."[41] Again, Neutze notes: "The operations of local government are...sufficiently complex that only someone who has invested a good deal of time can evaluate the possibility of getting a plot of land rezoned and serviced by sewers, roads, and other public facilities, and can know whom to contact to get these things done."[42]

Risk is a particularly important element in real estate. For example: "Papa Mizner...made one major miscalculation. He believed that the coming great city of the Pacific Coast was Benicia, not San Francisco. He acquired enormous real-estate

[38] Mayor's Committee, *Mid-Chicago Economic Development Study*, Vol. I, p. 8.

[39] Hoover, "The Evolving Form . . . of the Metropolis," p. 272.

[40] *Christian Science Monitor*, October 15, 1965, p. 59. See also Real Estate Research Corporation, *Analysis of Development Potential in the Chicago Central Area* (November 1966), pp. 17–19.

[41] Martin Meyerson, Barbara Terrett, and William L. C. Wheaton, *Housing, People and Cities* (McGraw-Hill, 1962), p. 117.

[42] Neutze, *The Suburban Apartment Boom*, p. 122.

holdings there and waited in vain for Benicia to become the California metropolis and make him the John Jacob Astor of the West."[43]

Risk can be used to explain such phenomena as adjacent buildings of different height. Thus, in Pittsburgh, "The Golden Triangle contains most of the highrise office buildings in the region. . . . But while it has many skyscrapers, it also has numerous structures of only one, two or three stories."[44] Neutze addresses the general problem and decides that ". . . there is a good deal of *ex ante* uncertainty. . . [so that] the optimal height can vary over wide ranges, depending on the developer's estimates of the values of the key parameters."[45]

Additional factors involved probably include lack of instantaneous adjustment in the real world, the impact of the business cycle, and differences in accessibility on the micro level. Thus, Winnick notes, "Even in the. . . venerable European weekly market, differential land values arise. . . . Favored sites may be on the shadier side of the square or closer to the mainstream of consumer traffic."[46]

It is sometimes argued that tall buildings "cause" high land values. This is probably a crude version of the case developed above in which both tall buildings and high land values are "caused" by a relatively high price for floor space. Further refinement of this case can be based on the role of real-world imperfect information and risk. If an entrepreneur decides that the market now calls for a taller building than existed previously on a site, takes a chance, and is in fact successful, he will obtain profits reflecting his sagacity or luck. These profits will be capitalized into land values, but the entrepreneur does have title to the land. Hence, risk effects can be viewed as a component of the entrepreneurial factor, at least in an *ex ante* sense. They will be part of the land price, *ex post*.

An alternative set of assumptions leads to an argument that tall buildings "cause" low (or lower) land values. Thus, Winnick quotes Alfred Marshall as arguing that aggregate land values will be reduced "as building technology permits higher structures with lower land coverage."[47] The argument appears to hinge on the characteristics of the demand for output (floor space). In the model variants treated in

---

[43] Alva Johnston, *The Legendary Mizners* (Farrar, Straus, and Young, 1953), p. 5. Rather extensive documentation of similar examples can be had; a few more are worth noting. Thus, "Henry Cobb, associate of I. M. Pei, found that in most admirable private developments, the individual investor had gone broke." Joseph R. Passonneau, "A Planning Inventory for the Metropolis," in Sam Bass Warner, Jr. (ed.), *Planning for a Nation of Cities* (M.I.T. Press, 1966), p. 182. And, "When his own land gamble failed, Charles Dickens . . . got some satisfaction — and perhaps some of his losses back — by writing the novel *Martin Chuzzlewit* in which Cairo [Illinois] is thinly disguised as Eden, and the land jobbers not disguised at all. It is not likely that the butts read the book; they were too busy drawing maps of new cities." Eugene Rachlis and John E. Marqusee, *The Land Lords* (Random House, 1963), pp. 38–39.

[44] Pittsburgh Area Transportation Study, *Final Report*, p. 43.

[45] Neutze, *The Suburban Apartment Boom*, p. 84.

[46] Louis Winnick, "Development Values and Controls," in Derek Senior (ed.), *The Regional City* (Aldine, 1966), p. 126.

[47] *Ibid.*, p. 129.

the previous section, P_x was fixed; demand was perfectly elastic. But a general advance in building technology should have national impact. In this case, a sloping demand curve seems appropriate. Hence, the results in Figure 3 can be viewed as a limiting case; a perfectly inelastic demand is the other extreme. If land is assumed to be fixed to the market, the ultimate equilibrium price of land may be higher or lower than its initial price, depending on elasticity of demand for output. A relatively inelastic demand for output seems an essential element of the argument that increasing building size will cause land values to decline. And this, of course, is an empirical question.

The decision to build tall buildings may involve consumption — in terms of expressing rivalry and presumably enhancing prestige — as well as profit maximization. However, as Jay Starrett Berger notes, "many or all of the so-called monuments have been designed to contribute value through advertising,"[48] so that monument building may pay off in pecuniary as well as in nonpecuniary returns.

Even within specific categories of construction (residential, office, etc.), land, building inputs, and output are anything but homogeneous. There is heterogeneity in land input because of physical characteristics (slope, bearing properties, drainage, etc.). Land heterogeneity also stems from differences in infrastructure. Roads and utility lines can be viewed as capital components of land. The value of access to them is capitalized into land values. Thus, a Philadelphia study indicates that obtaining access to sewers doubles the value of land.[49]

At the firm level, land prices were treated as constant to competitive firms. But, because site assembly involves the consolidation of contiguous parcels, the last parcels obtained are often more expensive per unit than the first, as the owners hold out for higher prices. Davis and Whinston emphasize this in developing an argument for urban renewal.[50] This could be criticized, perhaps, as the discovery of differences in risk preference among small-parcel holders. The holdouts are willing to gamble that they will receive a higher price against the possibility that the assembler may give up and cancel the project.[51] The problem might be viewed as reflecting real-world time lags or capital rationing. Because instantaneous adjustment does not occur, some small-parcel owners become aware of the assembly operation and begin to raise their prices. If the assembler had the resources to carry out all his negotiations at the same

[48] Jay Starrett Berger, *Determination of the Economic Height of High Rise Buildings* (Ph.D. thesis, University of California, Los Angeles, 1967), p. 81. See pp. 78 through 86 for a detailed discussion of advertising and "noneconomic" motives in high-rise construction.

[49] Grace Milgram, "Transactions, Prices and Development of Land in an Urbanizing Area of Philadelphia" (University of Pennsylvania, Institute for Environmental Studies, August 1966). Quoted by Neutze, *The Suburban Apartment Boom*, p. 55.

[50] Otto A. Davis and Andrew B. Whinston, "The Economics of Urban Renewal," a reprint of a 1961 article appearing in James Q. Wilson (ed.), *Urban Renewal: The Record and the Controversy* (M.I.T. Press, 1966), pp. 58–59.

[51] On occasion, the assembler may build around a holdout. Thus, "sometimes no offer is high enough — in the early nineteen-thirties the RCA Building in Rockefeller Center was erected around Hurley Brothers and Daley's bar and grill, which is still on 49th Street and the Avenue of the Americas." Sidney E. Zion, *New York Times*, January 20, 1968.

time, the problem might not arise. This situation can be approximated by restricting the availability of information. Thus Victor Gruen, in discussing a large Rochester redevelopment project, notes that if the private developers had approached the city officially, "news of the plan would necessarily leak out, and in that event it would become extremely difficult to acquire the land for the project area."[52]

Building input includes construction inputs and operating and maintenance inputs after the building has been constructed. Hundreds of inputs are involved in the construction and operation of office buildings.[53] As many as sixty building trades are involved in high-rise office building construction. The scheduling of access to the hoists lifting materials is an intricate — and emotion-charged — decision process. If a contractor misses his scheduled hoist time, it may be several days before he can be rescheduled. In general, then, a good deal of optimization at various levels is involved in choice of designs, materials, processes, and labor.

Output also involves a number of dimensions; it consists of floor space plus a variety of "quality" characteristics.

For a given land area, output equivalent to one floor area can be obtained by completely filling the site with one story, or by building two stories on half the site, or three stories on one-third of the site, etc. At first blush, this increase in stories seems uneconomic, because some land is unutilized, and because, in fighting gravity, more building inputs are required to obtain the same amount of floor space as building height increases. This involves both increased costs in the construction process and space loss per floor because elevators are installed beyond a certain height. Hence, "it is cheapest to build any given floor area in the fewest possible floors,"[54] taking as given the quality of the output in terms of materials used, decorative finishes, reputation of architect, etc. But raising the issue of quality of output leads to quality considerations involving height and space use. Thus, access to light, air, and unobstructed view may be valued by the space consumer. Some consumers are willing to pay a height premium which may reflect less noise and dust, less air pollution, a better view, or the increased prestige presumed to be associated with increased height.[55] (Of course, such considerations are relevant in office and residential building, but probably have little relevance in industrial building.)

Hence, if the seller of space is concerned with maximizing profits, rather than minimizing costs, it may pay him, even in the absence of building and zoning restric-

[52] Victor Gruen, *The Heart of Our Cities* (Simon and Schuster, 1964), p. 308.

[53] Schultz and Simmons, *Offices in the Sky*, p. 218.

[54] Daniel Seligman, "The Future of the Office Building Boom," *Fortune* (March 1963), p. 87. Berger, *Determination of the Economic Height . . .* , p. 188, notes: "The square foot cost of construction increases with building height."

[55] Some examples: Century City, a high-rise residential development in Los Angeles, charges an increment in rent of five dollars per floor per month; high-rise apartments in Washington, D.C., suburbs have a similar increment of five dollars every two floors; rentals in new San Francisco office buildings range from 53 cents per square foot for lower floor space to 85 cents per square foot for upper floor space. *Sources:* Personal interview and Brian W. H. Taylor, *San Francisco Examiner*, September 15, 1966.

tions, to throw away (in effect) some of his land, either by the use of setbacks or by leaving part of his site in open space.

These comments open some major lines of inquiry, including (1) land viewed more generally as space, (2) a revised statement of firm decision making, and (3) externalties and zoning.

LAND VIEWED AS SPACE

Perhaps, as a residual of agricultural applications, there is a tendency to think of land in terms of two dimensions — as the surface of the earth. But land in urban uses is a three-dimensional resource, in practice as well as principle. A given site can be thought of as divisible vertically into space "slabs" of a given thickness — say one story thick in both an upward and a downward direction. The value of a given slab can be viewed as the residual of income produced within it minus the costs of all other inputs involved (the building inputs). Hence, as the slabs move upward in space their value will eventually decrease, reflecting a narrowing of the gap between the increments of revenue and cost. Net space income at the peak of the New York World Trade Center (at 1,350 feet) no doubt is low, and probably becomes negative at greater heights. Frank Lloyd Wright's mile-high building must be uneconomic at present.[56]

The multiple use of urban "land," the lease or sale of air rights, and the purchase of apartments in condominiums can then be viewed as particular topics under the general heading of land seen in the broad as space.[57]

A REVISED STATEMENT OF FIRM DECISION MAKING

The process of high-rise decision making may now be viewed in more detail. In general, for a given site area and a given quality or level of building inputs per floor, we would expect costs to increase with building height as an expression of the usual "law of variable proportions."[58]

A good deal of empirical verification of this expectation is given both by Berger

---

[56] *Architectural Record* (July 1966), p. 229, notes that the mechanical system needed to enable such a building to function does not yet exist. And see Schultz and Simmons, *Offices in the Sky*, pp. 254–55, on the elevator problems of a mile-high building.

[57] Bernard develops a similar view: "It would seem upon reflection, that more than anything, it is the *space* itself that contains the essence of real property." Michael M. Bernard, *Airspace in Urban Development, Emergent Concepts*, Technical Bulletin 46 (Urban Land Institute, July 1963), p. 13.

[58] This is implicit in the Cobb-Douglas production function with individual elasticities below one. The sum of elasticities below one, as employed here, corresponds to the real-world observation that both land and building inputs cannot be increased indefinitely without an eventual relative falling off in output increase. There are not many Pentagon buildings. (The Pentagon impresses Ada Louise Huxtable as "a thriving, functional success in 1968" though originally labeled "Somervell's folly." *New York Times*, January 16, 1968, p. 41. But it has relatively high operating costs, according to Schultz and Simmons, *Offices in the Sky*, pp. 300–301.)

and by Stone.[59] Some cost specifics may be noted. As a building increases in height, foundation costs and window-wall costs do not increase proportionately; however, mechanical costs, elevator costs, specialized equipment, and scheduling costs increase at a greater than proportionate rate.[60]

Kingston and Clark present data showing that elevators consume 2 per cent of gross floor area at eight stories, 5 per cent at thirty stories, and 10 per cent at seventy-five stories.[61]

On the revenue side, a 1933 analysis (the Sheridan-Krakow formula) attempted to relate square foot rental value of office space to exposure to sunlight, height, width of office, depth of office, and corner influences. "For instance, one per cent was added for each story above the eighth floor, and one per cent deducted for each floor below. Two per cent was deducted for each foot over a depth of 25 feet, and one per cent added for each foot under 25 feet down to 15 feet."[62]

Berger notes that, despite advances in artificial illumination and ventilation, rents today remain correlated with exterior access.[63]

Hence, a profit equation for high-rise buildings might be written:

$$\pi = R(x, H, h, D, d, E, M) - aP_a - C(b_1, \ldots, b_N, P_{b_1}, \ldots, P_{b_N}, H, h, D, d, E, M)$$

where π is profit, R is revenue, C is building cost, and land value is aP_a. Revenue is written as a function of floor space (x), building height (H), room height (h), room depth (D), decor (d), elevator quality in terms of average elevator trip time, involving number and speed of elevators (E), and maintenance level (M). Building costs are written as a function of N building inputs and their respective prices; some of the input quantities and prices will depend on the quality variables, H, d, etc. There will be corresponding extensions and complications for production and decision equations in a revised model.

This formulation brings into focus a number of points at which trade-offs may occur. Thus, it can imply some smoothing out of the profit relation even though there are cost discontinuities "because of the indivisibility...of elevators, air conditioning systems, and heating plants which must be added or converted to more costly types when building height reaches certain points."[64] However, at the cost discontinuity

[59] Berger presents information on both high-rise office and residential construction, *Determination of the Economic Height . . .* , pp. 177–209. P. A. Stone presents similar evidence on residential construction in "The Economics of Housing and Urban Development," *Journal of the Royal Statistical Society*, Series A, Part IV (1959), pp. 417–83; and in his *Housing, Town Development, Land and Costs* (London: Estates Gazette Limited, 1963). Some key tables from Berger and Stone are presented later in the text.

[60] Charles Thomsen, "How High to Rise," *The Appraisal Journal* (October 1966), p. 588.

[61] J. L. Kingston and W. C. Clark, *The Skyscraper* (American Institute of Steel Construction, 1930), p. 66. Quoted by Berger, *Determination of the Economic Height...*, p. 181. And see Schultz and Simmons, *Offices in the Sky*, p. 47.

[62] Schultz and Simmons, *Offices in the Sky*, p. 207.

[63] Berger, *Determination of the Economic Height...*, p. 89.

[64] Berger, discussion of "breaking-points," *ibid.*, pp. 159–60, 196.

point, there is probably some compensating jump in revenue, reflecting the higher quality of service.

EXTERNALITIES AND ZONING

The matter of access to light, air, and vista can be viewed as involving externalities that the builder can internalize to some extent by setbacks. This sometimes occurs beyond the confines of the immediate site. Thus, Meyerson notes,

From within, Manhattan House offers fine views of the city; from surrounding areas it constitutes such a view. If, however, other buildings of the same mass and size were to rise near it, its elegance would be dissipated. By setting the upper floor wings back from the street and controlling development in the immediate vicinity the developer has ensured that some of the view, both from and of the building, will be preserved.[65]

This was done by acquiring enough surrounding property to limit development on all sides of the building.

In general, external economies and diseconomies are a pervasive and important feature of the urban scene. Some benefits or costs flowing from a particular action are borne by an economic decision unit independent of the unit pursuing the course of action.[66] As noted earlier, the existence of externalities is a major rationale for zoning.[67]

Zoning regulations can be classified under two main headings: land use regulation and building bulk regulation.[68] Land use regulation involves the definition of districts or zones on a map; a hierarchy of use is specified and "lower order" land uses are prohibited from locating in higher order zones. Generally the zoning order, from highest to lowest, runs: single-family residential, multiple-family residential (apartments), commercial, and industrial. Minimum lot size regulations often apply within a given zone.

Building bulk regulations include building height limitations, the percentage of a lot the structure may cover, setbacks, and side space regulation and are based on the assumption that the builder will not or cannot account for access to light, air, and vista on his own volition.

Over time, there appears to have been an evolving interaction between bulk

---

[65] Martin Meyerson, *Face of the Metropolis* (Random House, 1963), pp. 109–10. Other examples of this process are noted by Schultz and Simmons, *Offices in the Sky*, pp. 63, 176, 253.

[66] Allen V. Kneese, *The Economics of Regional Water Quality Management* (The Johns Hopkins Press for Resources for the Future, 1964), p. 41. In his introductory paper to the present volume, Perloff sees externalities and interrelationships as much greater in the urban environment than in the rural environment; this is so pronounced that it amounts to a difference in kind.

[67] Cf. Tiebout, "Intra-Urban Location Problems...," pp. 275–76.

[68] Cf. John C. Bollens and Henry J. Schmandt, *The Metropolis* (Harper & Row, 1965), pp. 282–84; James Marston Fitch, *American Building 1: The Historical Forces that Shaped It* (2nd ed.: Houghton Mifflin Co., 1966), pp. 242–43; and Stephen Sussna, "Bulk Control and Zoning: New York City Experience," *Land Economics* (May 1967), p. 161.

regulation and urban building. Thus, prescribed and voluntary setbacks yielded the wedding cake architecture of Manhattan. It appears that much of this was involuntary.[69]

Given space restrictions, there will be economic incentive to develop more floor area within the space available. This has led to a number of building design and technical innovations; for example, the elimination of space between the ceiling of one story and the floor of the next.[70] Again, Fisher notes that postwar Manhattan office buildings "have provided an average of three-fifths more rentable floor space than buildings erected between 1925 and 1933. These postwar buildings have contained more floor space even though they are squatty with setbacks and have fewer stories than the tall tower-type buildings of the twenties."[71]

These developments might have furnished a motive for the change to the floor area ratio (FAR) mode of zoning regulation, which New York City instituted in 1962. Other technological changes have reduced the economic rationality of setbacks, and the new zoning regulations appear to reflect the new state of affairs. Air conditioning and improved artificial lighting implied fuller utilization of potential building space. "The result was the modern slab building with uniform size floors top to bottom which provided larger rentable floor areas on the desirable upper floor."[72] In brief, the modern slab building is now economic.

The New York Port Authority's World Trade Center exhibits the influence of the new regulations. The twin towers, which will be the world's tallest buildings, are square shafts. The Trade Center meets the FAR requirements by a large open plaza. The *New York Times* architecture critic foresees the plaza as being "vast, desolate, dull, windswept and empty most of the time."[73] James Marston Fitch argues, "The current tendency to place the high-rise office building in a plaza of its own is commendable, so far as it goes. But it has not gone nearly far enough.... What is called for is a new kind of urban space, neither fully open like a street nor fully enclosed like a building." This urban space would contain retail services and provide a place for relaxation, sun and air, and light recreation.[74]

---

[69] Fitch, *American Building I*, p. 242, writes: "Zoning was directly responsible for the spectacular setback design of modern skyscrapers." And see "Zoning: New York Tries Again," in *Architectural Forum* (April 1959), p. 123: "The cake-mold which has been the city's maximum zoning envelope since 1916 has forced any builder who wanted a full return on his investment to put up a contorted ziggurat whose shape was determined not by structural or aesthetic considerations but solely by a complicated and arbitrary law of setbacks." (A ziggurat is a staged tower in which each story is smaller than that below it.)

[70] Cf. *Architectural Forum* (June 1964), p. 6, advertisement for an air electric floor system to eliminate bulky ductwork and achieve a maximum number of stories for a given building height.

[71] Fisher, *The Boom in Office Buildings*, p. 21.

[72] Lyndon H. Lesh, "Office Building Development," *Journal of Property Management* (May–June 1965), p. 131, quoted by Fisher, *ibid.* And see George Becker, "The Valuation of Office Buildings," *The Appraisal Journal* (October 1967), p. 497.

[73] Ada Louise Huxtable, *New York Times*, April 16, 1967, Section D, p. 30.

[74] Fitch, *American Building I*, pp. 295–96.

OTHER REGULATIONS AND RESTRICTIONS

A wide variety of government regulations other than zoning, if effective in practice, impose constraints on allocation in construction. These include subdivision regulation, housing codes, and building codes. Further, most observers discern monopoly elements on the supply side in construction. This constraint implies the need for further extension of the models developed above, which assumed competitive markets.

The regulation of construction by building codes is often viewed as a major source of inefficiency, though there is marked absence of consensus (perhaps typical for such issues).[75] Milton Friedman sees building codes as a form of local political support which serves "craft unions as a means of preventing non-union workers from engaging in their fields through substitution or elimination of materials or techniques."[76]

Galbraith saw construction as a special case contrary to his general notion of countervailing power.[77] Monopolies on the supply side (unions and suppliers of building materials) had not generated countervailing monopoly on the producer side. But this monopoly power may now be generating both countervailing power and competition by other industries.

Thus, a trend toward the growth of large corporations in construction seems to be emerging. The editors of *House and Home* see these patterns:[78]

1. building markets entered by giant corporations with interests outside housing; e.g., Alcoa, Reynolds, Humble Oil;[79]
2. a growth in equity financing;
3. horizontal and vertical integration.

[75] The editors of *House and Home* see "the chaotic plethora of local building codes as the biggest roadblock" in construction—William L. C. Wheaton, Grace Milgram, and Martin Meyerson (eds.), *Urban Housing* (Free Press, 1966). J. A. Reidelbach of the Home Builders Association agrees: he argues that the consumer ought to be protected against fire and unsafe structures, but that varied building codes stifle technical advance — *Oakland Tribune*, September 28, 1966. However, Douglas E. Parsons, former chief of the Building Research Division, National Bureau of Standards, argues that the present system is functioning well. He does agree that codes specifying materials and processes should be replaced by "performance type" codes — *Los Angeles Times*, January 1, 1967. A proposed revised building code for New York City was the product of a six-year joint effort by the Polytechnic Institute of Brooklyn and city and building industry representatives, at a cost of roughly a million dollars. (This code, in its entirety, consisted of 1,700 pages weighing 15 pounds.) Frederick Frost estimates that the adoption of this code would reduce construction costs by 3 to 5 per cent — *Building Research Journal* (January–February, 1967). But William Tabler, head of the New York chapter of the American Institute of Architects, argues that the new code is more restrictive than the old and will lead to "utter chaos" — *New York Times*, October 12, 1967.

[76] Milton Friedman, *Price Theory* (Aldine, 1962), p. 161.

[77] John Kenneth Galbraith, *American Capitalism* (Houghton Mifflin, 1952).

[78] "New Direction for the Housing Industry," in Wheaton, Milgram, and Meyerson (eds.), *Urban Housing*, pp. 325–26.

[79] In "Lure of the Land," *Time* (February 5, 1965) lists some large firms moving into real

Peterson has developed some detailed information on the trend, particularly on planned community development by large corporations.[80] (By way of qualification, it must be noted that there seems to be a high degree of risk in these corporate activities.)[81]

Some critics see small scale as a cause of inefficiency. The construction industry in its "small-scale, localized, inefficient profusion" is seen by Andrews as incapable of standardization or mass production.[82] Hence, a trend toward large-scale operation would be welcomed by such critics as a move toward greater efficiency and "rationalization." But countervailing monopoly (or oligopoly) is not necessarily an unmixed blessing. Countervailing monopolists may decide to combine forces, with the consumer countervailed upon.

Prefabrication can be viewed as competition from an outside source in response to monopoly. This takes several forms. First, "A conspicuous trend is the relative de-emphasis of onsite craft activities in favor of offsite fabrication in industrial plants. Many new factory based power tools now produce prefabricated building products which formerly were made and installed at the site with hand tools. Prefinishing has increased markedly, in the case of aluminum alone, tripling in 1957–61."[83]

A second form of outside competition (and prefabrication) can be seen in the development of the mobile home industry. According to available sources, sales of mobile homes increased from 118,000 units in 1962 to 216,000 units in 1965; the dollar value of these sales moved from $660 million in 1962 to $1.2 billion in 1965.

---

estate: Weyerhaeuser (summer homes, recreation, ski resorts); Goodyear (the new town of Litchfield Park); Great Lakes Carbon; Castle & Cooke; Alcoa ($41 million invested in ten projects in six cities); Kaiser Industries; Reynolds Metals; General Electric; Humble Oil; Gulf Oil; Union Oil; Sunset Petroleum (with 73 per cent of its 1964 income from real estate); Puget Sound Power & Light Co. The connection may sometimes prove embarrassing. For instance, tenants protesting rent increases hung aluminum foil from Alcoa's Lincoln Towers development in Manhattan; *New York Times*, July 8, 1967.

[80] David Lee Peterson, *The Planned Community and the New Investors: Economic and Political Factors in Corporate Real Estate Development* (Center for Real Estate and Urban Economics, University of California, Berkeley, 1967).

[81] Thus, Donald A. Schon notes that large corporations now in the "city business" have not yet achieved major success, and that in the late 1950's Monsanto, Union Carbide, Koppers, and Johns-Manville lost a good deal of money upon attempting to enter the building system field; address by Schon at the Building Research Institute Spring Conferences, Washington, D.C., April 1968. Again, "Sunset International Petroleum is selling its way out of housing for good reason: Its new-town program was one of home building's all time misadventures"; *House and Home* (February 1968), p. 10.

[82] Richard B. Andrews, *Urban Growth and Development* (Simmons-Boardman Publishing Company, 1962), pp. 205, 207–10. See also Meyerson, Terrett, and Wheaton, *Housing, People and Cities*, pp. 116–17.

[83] U.S. Department of Commerce, Business and Defense Services Administration, *Construction Review* (March 1967), p. 9.

This contrasts with total housing starts of 1,469,000 in 1962 and 1,520,000 in 1965, with a sales value of $18.6 billion in 1962 and $20.4 billion in 1965.[84]

So far, the discussion has focused on enclosed space within buildings. However, the occurrence of other forms of enclosed space can be correlated with the occurrence of building space. This can either be viewed as an aspect of the general substitution of capital for land, given an increase in the price of land relative to capital, or as a consequence of increased demand for infrastructure, viewing demand for utility and transportation networks as derived from demand for building space. In any event, these enclosed space forms (subway tunnels, sewer pipes, utility cables, etc.) will increase with movement toward the urban center.[85]

Generally, then, the study of these other space forms should be amenable to the same sort of economic analysis that is applied in the case of building space.

Externalities

As externalities are pervasive and important in the urban environment, it seems advisable to devote a section to discussing them.

GENERAL ISSUES

It may be that concern with externalities goes too far. Bowman argues this point: "There is a widely held notion that every market result is suspect because of the inevitable benefit or harm it might cause to others.... But all actions have side effects." But it is more likely, as Coase contends, that concern with externalities may miss some salient points.[86] His argument may be summarized as follows:

1. Externalities are reciprocal. Smoke producers impose a burden on white-shirt wearers. But charging for this imposes a burden on smoke producers.

2. It is necessary to weigh the harm against the good that will result, in both directions. "Nothing could be more 'antisocial' than to oppose any action which causes any harm to anyone.... In devising and choosing between social arrangements, we should compare the total product yielded by the alternative arrangements."

3. The resolution of externalities by private negotiation has much to recommend it over public coercion, because it leads to "right" amounts of output. This works

[84] Sources include U.S. Department of Commerce, *Construction Review* (March 1967), p. 25, and (August 1967), p. 11; and State of Minnesota, Highway Interim Commission, *Mobile Homes and the Mobile Home Industry* (St. Paul, 1967), p. 45.

[85] Thus, under Market and Powell streets in downtown San Francisco, there are eleven utility systems: electric, gas, steam, municipal railway power, street light power, water, high pressure water (for major fires), sewer, traffic signal power, telephone and telegraph lines, and blockhouses. In New York City, the utility network is so dense "at Wall and Broad Street, that there isn't room to bury a pencil. Excavation is impossible, and the dirt has to be spooned out." See *San Francisco Chronicle*, "The Steel Jungle Under Market Street," January 3, 1967, p. 6, and Fred J. Cook, "Dig They Must — Find They What?" *New York Times Magazine*, May 19, 1963, p. 69.

[86] Ward Bowman, "The New Haven, A Passenger Railroad for Nonriders," *Journal of Law and Economics* (October 1966), pp. 49, 50. R. H. Coase, "The Problem of Social Cost," *Journal of Law and Economics* (October 1960), pp. 1–44; in particular, pp. 26–28, 35, 40, 42–44.

best when a few, easily identified, parties are involved and where the cost of negotiation is relatively low.

4. The laws on nuisance cover many externalities. "The courts, in cases relating to nuisance, are...making a decision on the economic problem and determining how resources are to be employed. While statutory enactments add to the list of nuisances, action is also taken to legalize what would otherwise be nuisances under common law." In particular, negative externalities are often caused by public enterprise or government action.

The core of the Coase argument can be presented by a simplified version of one of his illustrative cases. Assume that a factory moves into a district previously free from smoke and causes $100 worth of annual damage to wearers of white shirts. Further, location of the factory at this site is worth at least $100 annually to the factory owner, for we assume he is willing to pay a tax equal to the damage he causes. Assume that locating here relative to the next best location is worth $110 to him. Then $110 minus $100 leaves a net increment of $10. The matter of who bears the damage is irrelevant; $100 of damage occurs and is borne by the factory owner if a tax is imposed or by white-shirt wearers if a tax is not imposed. Now, assume that white-shirt wearers can move to a new smoke-free neighborhood at an annual cost of $40. In this event, the increment becomes $110 minus $40, or $70; hence, *this* is the proper solution. If the white-shirt wearers move out, total product is maximized, and this is therefore the optimum solution. "The belief that it is desirable that the business which causes harmful effects should be forced to compensate those who suffer damage is undoubtedly the result of not comparing the total product obtainable with alternative social arrangements." There is a "similar error in the suggestion that smoke-producing factories should, by means of zoning regulations, be removed from the districts in which the smoke causes harmful effects.... The aim of such regulation should not be to eliminate smoke pollution but rather to secure the optimum amount of smoke pollution, this being the amount which will maximize the value of production."

Coase brings to the discussion of externalities an awareness of the mobility of resources, of the possibility of substitution, and of the central importance of opportunity costs. But some issues need probing.

Coase sets as his central (and perhaps his only) value, the maximization of society's total output. But this seems to disregard an element of distributive justice. It would appear that many, perhaps most, people feel that "who got there first" should bear on what happens next. Thus, when a person buys property in a smoke-free neighborhood, it can be presumed that he feels this condition is a component of his property and a source of some of its value. It may be objected that the right to retain things as they are can generate vested interests in Veblen's sense: The legitimate right to something for nothing. Barriers to change *can* be barriers to progress. Nevertheless, a good case (in terms of generally held values) can be made for compensation of white-shirt wearers for costs of moving. More generally, a case can usually be made for compensation of an initial group harmed by the action of a group appearing later on the scene, with the compensation equal to the adjustment costs involved. It may be that this is implicit in the laws of nuisance and in the call for negotiation. It might be made more explicit. Thus, some people may not want to negotiate, either because it is not in their interest to negotiate, or because rational action is not part of their behavior pattern. Institutional arrangements and constraints would be needed if the initial group did not have clear title to the property rights involved. The elucidation of just what the property rights are is probably the nub of the problem. Negotiation becomes more and more difficult as parties to external effects become more widespread and as the effects become more diffuse.

Finally, maximization of output may not be a universal value, even among policy makers; this may be so even if we define output broadly to include such things as utility derived from sentimental attachment to their old neighborhood by white-shirt wearers.

Some of these issues lie behind Neutze's advocacy of bargaining through a local government body, so that a formal organization is responsible for representing the total interests of the group. "The role of law is to specify the initial position from which bargaining starts; i.e., the rights of each partner."[87]

Coase believes that economists, and policy makers generally, have overestimated the advantages of government regulation in handling externalities. "But this belief does not do more than suggest that regulation should be curtailed. It does not tell us where the boundary line should be drawn." Satisfactory views on policy can come only from a patient study of individual cases; e.g., the operation of zoning in practice.[88]

The remainder of this section essays a preliminary, partial, and probably impatient approximation to this patient study in the context of the three-dimensional city.

SPECIFIC CASES

The following cases will be discussed here: Structures and air flight; tall buildings and radio-television transmission; aesthetic and historic values; tall buildings and zoned height limits; and density and land use zoning.

Structures and Air Flight. Michael Bernard notes:

The traditional concept of property ownership was that one owned a piece of land down to the center of earth and up to the heavens ... [with] the owner's parcel a sort of inverted pyramid projecting out from the center of the earth, embracing the land surface and the heavens above it.[89]

This "unlimited" property ownership was restricted by air travel. The Supreme Court decided: "Airspace is a public highway. Yet the landowner owns at least as much of the space above ground as he can occupy or use in connection with the land."[90]

---

[87] Neutze, *The Suburban Apartment Boom*, p. 134.
[88] Coase, "The Problem of Social Cost," pp. 18, 19.
[89] Bernard, *Airspace in Urban Development...*, p. 7.
[90] *United States v. Causby*, 328 U.S. 256 (1945) quoted in Bernard, *ibid.*, p. 11.

About half the states have enacted legislation which vests ownership of the space above the surface in the owners of the surface beneath; aircraft flight over the land is lawful unless at such a low altitude as to interfere with land or space use.

In an attempt to reconcile these uses, government agencies have been given the power to limit height and location of surface developments in the vicinity of airports. Airport commissions have extensive authority and thus can zone in their own benefit. The Federal Aviation Agency (FAA) fixes standards for determining obstructions to air navigation. In federally aided airports, FAA obstruction standards are mandatory. "Landowners, on the other hand, have been permitted to recover damages for property 'taken,' as if in eminent domain for [air] highway purposes."[91]

As noted in the general discussion, the core of the problem lies in defining respective property rights when conflict occurs. Although, as air travel increases and as tall buildings grow taller, such conflict will probably also increase, it seems likely to be relatively minor for the present and near future. But the problem of noise, in general, and sonic boom, in particular, could become major.[92] And technical advances (in helicopters and planes that take off and land vertically, for example) could create the need for a good deal of planning and organization.[93]

Tall Buildings and Radio-Television Transmission. Tall buildings interfere with radio and television reception. This is particularly pronounced in Manhattan. In response, a firm franchised by the city of New York is developing a system of underground cable television transmission. It plans to install 50 miles of cable under Manhattan streets at a cost of ten million dollars (or $200,000 per mile). Coverage would extend from 86th Street South on the east of Central Park, and from 79th Street South on the west. Subscribers to the system would pay an installation cost of $20 and a monthly charge of $5 and would receive every channel broadcasting in New York plus three extra channels featuring local news and weather.[94]

There was concern that the World Trade Center would interfere with TV transmission from the top of the Empire State Building.[95] The television broadcasting companies handled this problem by deciding to move to the Trade Center. Would compensation for external effects make sense here? Perhaps loss in quality of television

---

[91] *Ibid.*, pp. 16–17.

[92] There have, of course, been cases of airplanes hitting urban structures, with subsequent loss of life. On rare occasions skyscrapers have been involved: in 1945, a B-25 bomber crashed into the Empire State Building, killing fourteen persons. The heliport on top of the Pan Am Building in New York City has been opposed as hazardous and noisy, but its license was renewed in December 1967. An official noted that noise had been reduced through new routes and operating practices. *New York Times*, May 6, 1966; October 21, 1966; and December 1, 1966.

[93] Note Perloff's discussion of air-commuting zones in Chap. 1 of this volume.

[94] Wired television for all cities has been advocated by Barnett and Greenberg as a means of improving diversity and quantity of television programming. Many more channels are possible. H. J. Barnett and E. Greenberg, "On the Economics of Wired City Television," *American Economic Review* (June 1968), pp. 503–8.

[95] For example, see *New York Times* editorial, "Ghost Hunting," August 18, 1966.

reception is too minor or too diffuse, or the legal issues too complex, to entertain the suggestion that television set owners be compensated by those constructing tall buildings after the introduction of television. And perhaps the Empire State Building's loss of television revenue can be viewed as a normal risk of business enterprise.[96] In considering policy, we might ponder the distinctions between this kind of case and others where regulation or compensation is advocated.

Aesthetic and Historic Values. Individual buildings, collections of buildings viewed as an organized design, and the cityscape as a whole can be sources of pleasure or displeasure as art forms. Historical landmarks can be viewed in a similar fashion.

It is likely that most people are only mildly concerned about such matters, though an articulate minority is deeply concerned. Beauty is a matter of taste, and the discussion could be closed by arguing that there is no accounting for taste. But even within this relativistic frame, it can be argued that there is value in giving expression to all tastes. Of course, there are externalities; your taste may make me wince, and mine may make you furious. It is not obvious that anything can or should be done about such externalities.

However, there may be certain aesthetic considerations common to humanity as a species; for instance, our pleasure in trees may reflect our evolutionary past. (Man's eye is most sensitive to the yellow-green part of the spectrum.) Many people are willing to pay for a view of trees or greenery. But perhaps there is market failure here — perhaps trees are a collective good and more trees than we now possess would make everyone better off.

Again, there may be certain aesthetic considerations and values common to members of a particular culture, so that there is some basis for at least a limited consensus.

Meyerson does not define beauty or good design explicitly, but presents a series of examples he sees as falling in the category, and adds a highly perceptive commentary.[97] Thus, some element of externality and collective good is intrinsic in the urban scene: "Urban design, architecture and landscape are...the only arts that cannot be avoided. People cannot avoid exposure to the design of buildings and open spaces or to...urban design: the design of combinations of buildings and space."[98]

Architectural excellence can be viewed as one of a competing number of goods, and hence subject to economizing. Thus, "there is a point at which the practical purpose

[96] The Empire State Building will probably lose some tourist revenue as well. There were attempts to influence public opinion against the Trade Center by "The Committee for a Reasonable World Trade Center" headed by Lawrence A. Wien, also head of a group owning the Empire State Building; *New York Times*, February 16, 1967 advertisement, p. 27; and May 2, 1966.

[97] Meyerson, *Face of the Metropolis.*

[98] *Ibid.*, p. 7. Peter Blake, in *God's Own Junkyard* (Holt, Rinehart, and Winston, 1964), p. 141, makes the same point with more feeling in this quote of Vincent Scully: "The buildings along our streets belong to and affect all the people who use those streets." (Presumably this is not meant too literally.) Blake adds: "The trouble with most of the eyesores created in America is that they are impossible to ignore."

for which a structure is being built is in conflict with aesthetics.... In order to build a more beautiful building, the developer would have to sacrifice some measure of his practical purpose such as profit."[99]

But because of the collective nature of architectural beauty, private returns for such sacrifices are generally not forthcoming: "If we expect a firm to spend more than it normally would for good design, we are...asking it to give the public (or that part ...which enjoys urban design) something for nothing. Unless firms can be reimbursed for the expense of providing the public with beauty, they will not have the financial incentive to provide it."[100]

Meyerson feels that government can play a role in improving the quality of design, but notes that government bodies will have difficulty in defining good design and that "few city dwellers are likely to be ready to tax themselves to make cities more beautiful."[101] Nevertheless, he advocates that government agencies be patrons of the great architects, that government spend lavishly for good design, and that local ordinances (zoning, etc.) be used to promote aesthetic goals. But it is worth emphasizing that even these relatively modest policy proposals must involve economizing and trade-offs in practice, and some efforts at identifying the benefits and costs, and the beneficiaries and cost-bearers, might well be attempted.

Tall Buildings and Zoned Height Limits. Earlier, we examined height limits and building bulk regulation in terms of access to light, air, and vista. There seems to be fairly general agreement that such access externalities are accounted for by setback provisions. For instance, Schultz and Simmons, writing as representatives of the National Association of Building Owners and Managers, note that there is something to be said for the argument.[102]

But little in the way of negotiation and compensatory payments for the reduction of access has occurred, of course. This may reflect a value position that private ownership or control of certain natural resources is immoral: light and air are seen as free goods that should not be subject to private expropriation.[103] However, regulation of high-rise buildings seems to have gone well beyond accounting for such access externalities, in terms of restrictions imposed. Thus, Schultz and Simmons suggest that New York City's height restrictions were fairly flexible, relative to Chicago's, and that

[99] Meyerson, *Face of the Metropolis*, p. 233.

[100] *Ibid.*, p. 236.

[101] *Ibid.*, p. 237.

[102] Schultz and Simmons, *Offices in the Sky*, pp. 277–78.

[103] For a similar interpretation, see Berger, *Determination of the Economic Height...*, p. 90. This kind of argument has been applied to the protection of "scenic resources" against high-rise construction. Thus, "the people of Hawaii are waging a bitter battle against a millionaire land developer who wants to build a high rise complex on Diamond Head's seaward slope." *Newsweek*, January 22, 1968, p. 29. "Conservationists, planners, and others fear the proposed buildings would mar the view of Diamond Head from the sea. A spokesman for one development group has denied the scenery would be harmed." *Washington Post*, February 13, 1968, p. A2.

Chicago's growth (in both skyscrapers and economic activity) was inhibited thereby.[104] In a broader comparison, Berger notes that fifty cities had building height restrictions by 1917, but that, unlike other cities, New York had no absolute height limitation. Towers of unlimited height were authorized, provided they did not cover more than 25 per cent of the lot.[105]

It was suggested earlier that height involves prestige. This can be viewed as an example of the lack of independence of consumer utility functions — something more common in real life, perhaps, than in economic thought. Up and down, top and bottom seem rather profound symbols in Western — perhaps human — consciousness, involving notions of subordination-superiority, and of achievement. "To be at the top," "to look up to," "to look down upon (in scorn)," "the ladder of success," are some phrases that fit the hypothesis. It is not surprising, then, that executive suites are generally penthouse offices. The pervasive attitudes involved can be presumed to establish height as a status symbol, and height premiums must reflect this to some extent.

An attempt to ration prestige may be part of an anti-height syndrome. This seems the case in the District of Columbia. Harold M. Lewis notes that the provisions of an act of 1910 establish District height controls at 130 feet in business districts and at 90 feet in residential districts "in order to assure the continued dominance of the Capitol and the Washington Monument. . . , the major public symbols of the national government."[106]

Again, Percy Johnson-Marshall is unhappy with "degeneration. . .in the centres . . .of large cities." One form of degeneration is "the overthrow of the older building hierarchy. Churches and other public buildings which formerly had stood over surrounding buildings *of lesser importance*, were now submerged, usually by commercial over-building." [Italics added.][107] Perhaps this involves concern with a symbolic "defiance" of temporal and spiritual authority.

A motive for constructing tall buildings is often alleged to be a striving for prestige at the expense of rivals.[108] Perhaps some see this as "wasteful."

In the early days of skyscrapers, it was argued that they were fire hazards and that germs would proliferate and diseases flourish in their shadow. These alleged exter-

---

[104] Schultz and Simmons, *Offices in the Sky*, pp. 281–87.

[105] Berger, *Determination of the Economic Height. . .*, p. 97.

[106] Lewis, "A New Zoning Plan for D.C.," pp. 5 and 54. Residential districts are located in the hills in the outlying city areas, "and thus start from an altitude of as much as 200 feet above the base of the Capitol," which is 305 feet at its peak.

[107] Percy Johnson-Marshall, *Rebuilding Cities* (Aldine, 1966), p. 11. A tower of Babel argument may be implicit in this.

[108] See Meyerson, *Face of the Metropolis*, p. 73, on the Prudential Building in Boston versus the John Hancock Building; Seligman, "The Future of the Office Building Boom," p. 87, on the Chase Manhattan Bank Building in downtown Manhattan versus the First National City Bank Building; and statement attributed to Cass Gilbert, architect for the Woolworth Building, *Chicago Tribune*, May 3, 1967, on the Woolworth Building versus the Metropolitan Tower. The Metropolitan Tower was the world's tallest at 700 feet, and Woolworth allegedly outbuilt it because the Metropolitan Insurance Company had refused him a loan.

nalities turned out to be nonexistent. It is also often argued that skyscrapers cause congestion, and that negative externalities are involved. This is probably true, though there are some who doubt it.[109] But the argument tends to miss the Coasian point that the increment of benefits from another high-rise downtown may well exceed the increment of costs, including these external diseconomies; similarly, prohibiting the high-rise on these grounds may well reduce total product.

Further, increased density may well make new transportation facilities economic.[110] (It *is* somewhat perplexing that planners tend to favor low density development *and* mass transit.)

Sentiment against high-rise buildings has a public housing variant. For instance, in 1966, New York City decided that it would no longer build high-rise public housing projects because these were seen by some poor people as "symbols of second-class citizenship." Its new emphasis was to be on structures of six to eight stories (approximately half the height of older projects) and on the rehabilitation of old buildings. In testimony before the Tydings Committee, Dorn McGrath, an official of the U.S. Department of Housing and Urban Development (HUD), said that HUD questions concentrating low-income families in large air-rights housing projects and prefers to scatter such families in smaller subsidized housing units throughout the city.[111] Daniel Van Sweat, Atlanta model cities administrator, is quoted as stating, "We don't want to swap a vertical ghetto for the one we have now, with elevator crime and all that."[112] And Martin Luther King reached an agreement with the city of Chicago that future public housing would be limited to eight stories in height.[113]

Policy here may be based on a belief that high density leads to antisocial behavior. But Christopher Alexander argues: "It is true that there is often a positive correlation between high population density and various indices of social disorder, like crime, delinquency, ill health, and insanity. But there are places — Boston's North End and Hong Kong, for instance — which have exceptionally high densities and exceptionally low indices of social disorder.... Those social disorders apparently caused by density

---

[109] Berger, *Determination of the Economic Height...*, p. 91, "the degree to which building height contributes to traffic congestion...is largely unknown." Schultz and Simmons, *Offices in the Sky*, pp. 274–75, point out that skyscraper elevators are "an indispensable part of municipal transportation" and that eliminating them would generate more traffic. Mason Gaffney, in reviewing this chapter, developed a similar argument. In a marginal sense, however, an increment of space at the urban center, with street use at "capacity" is likely to add more in travel congestion costs than an increment at the outskirts of town, where street use is below "capacity."

[110] Vincent Ponte notes recent Montreal developments: "The sudden mushrooming of downtown Montreal produced an urgent transportation problem. Fortunately, the new millions in tax revenue generated by the new buildings supplied an important part of the means to borrow funds for a subway." Ponte, "Man and His Buildings," in National Association of Building Owners and Managers, *Montreal Convention Papers* (Chicago, 1967), p. 110.

[111] *Use of Air Space in the District of Columbia*, Hearings before the Subcommittee on Business and Commerce of the Committee on the District of Columbia, 90 Cong. 1 sess. (1967), p. 148.

[112] Quoted in Priscilla Dunhill, "Model Cities," *Architectural Forum* (December 1967), p. 36.

[113] Bertrand Goldberg, "The Architect's Reaction to Federal and Local Influences on Multifamily Housing" (Address, 1967 Fall Conferences, Building Research Institute, November 14, 1967).

are in fact caused by low income, poor education, and social isolation."[114] It may be that high density intensifies the effects of the causes Alexander specifies, yet he argues, "I predict the partial correlation between density and social disorder, when controlled for income-education and for social isolation, will disappear altogether."

Density and Land Use Zoning. The focus of the argument has shifted from height to density. As indicated above, there tends to be animus against both height and high density among planners. In the case of high-density residential uses, both external diseconomies and merit goods are cited as reasons for preventive zoning:

- Congestion reduces the level of public services: e.g., schools, playgrounds, traffic, parking, and sewers.
- Congestion harms individual consumers by reducing quiet, privacy, amenity, recreation, and the "pleasant residential character" of a community.[115]

The latter argument involves external diseconomies that are imposed on people who particularly prefer privacy, quiet, and so on; it also involves an element of "merit-goodism" for consumers who may wish to consume less of these goods than they "ought." Zoning forces them to do "better." There is a belief that consumers may be "exploited" if left to their own devices. Thus, Sussna notes that antipathy toward tenements has been cited as one of the sources of the first zoning ordinance.[116]

Counterarguments might touch on the possibility of economies of scale for some public services, and of proper assessment of costs on those who cause congestion. Merit goods can be countered by an appeal to consumer sovereignty: there may be doubt as to the merit of these goods for *all* consumers. People who prefer "closeness" or "togetherness" ought to be allowed these goods so long as they do not reduce neighbors' privacy and quiet thereby. This then evolves into an argument for the existence of neighborhoods of varying density, and the toleration of some neighborhoods of very high density. This, in turn, raises the interesting question of how far externalities, or neighborhood effects, extend — in terms of over-the-road distance.

In practice, it seems quite likely that land use zoning imposes some important externalities by limiting high densities, segregating land uses, and imposing minimum lot sizes in single-family residence zones. This generalization, of course, has many exceptions, including both legal evasion of the rules by variances and rezoning, and illegal evasion, which leads to occasional zoning scandals. But such exceptions, and the scandal attached, indicate that effective restrictions hold more generally, so there is scope for black markets or "gray" markets (more or less legal evasion). Some of Neutze's evidence fits this interpretation. He concludes that "the zoning decision determines both density and land values to a very large degree." Thus, "allowable density appears to control... [land] price.... Both government assessors and lenders

---

[114] Christopher Alexander, "The City as a Mechanism for Sustaining Human Contact," in William R. Ewald, Jr. (ed.), *Environment for Man* (Indiana University Press, 1967), pp. 98–99. Also see the Hall quotation on density and culture on pp. 14–15 of this volume.

[115] Cf. Lewis, "A New Zoning Plan...," pp. 22, 29–30.

[116] Sussna, *Bulk Control and Zoning...*, p. 161.

value apartment-zoned land at so much per unit permitted, adjusted for the location of the site."[117] He discusses the case of "apartment hotels," which involved developers who took advantage of a loophole in the Montgomery County, Maryland, zoning ordinance to construct apartments at a density well above the apartment maximum (120 versus 43 units per acre). Under the zoning ordinance, as long as 10 per cent of the units were available to transient tenants, apartments could be built without the "normal controls over density, height, setback and site coverage.... For the first time apartments could be built in the county at densities which permitted builders to bid for the high-cost sites in or near important suburban centers.... Some of the highest land prices recorded in the county ($10–$20 per square foot) have been paid by these developers."[118] (The ordinance was later amended.)

Seligman cites a study on the Philadelphia area which "suggests an average market value in the Cheltenham suburb of around $20,000 an acre for property developed into single-family houses, versus about $120,000 an acre for garden apartments, and well over $200,000 for high-rise apartments."[119]

This suggests that there is an effective artificial constraint on the supply of apartment housing; gains from this restricted supply are capitalized into land values. This argument views the land value increment as analogous to that occurring for tobacco acreage allotments, or for taxicabs in New York City, or for liquor licenses in California. In all such cases, supply is restricted, and benefits are capitalized into the right to engage in the activity. It seems reasonable to conclude that zoning restricts the supply of multiple-dwelling units both in location and in quantity.

Further, areas zoned for single-family residences generally have minimum lot size restrictions. This is often viewed as a segregation device, in terms of both income and race.[120]

In sum, at least some of Coase's skepticism on the universal efficacy of regulation seems warranted. Given a majority view that the goals of zoning are a good thing, future regulation might nevertheless attempt to account for these artificially induced externalities with an approach permitting a wider spectrum of choice in living pattern. One element of revised policy might consist of Marion Clawson's suggestion that, in some cases, governments ought to sell zoning and rezoning through open, competitive bidding.[121] (Such a market would reduce windfall gains as well as improve allocation.)

[117] Neutze, *The Suburban Apartment Boom*, p. 55.

[118] *Ibid.*, Chap. 1, Chap 4.

[119] Daniel Seligman, "The Move to Apartments," *Fortune* (April 1963), p. 101.

[120] See C. W. Griffin, Jr., book reviews, "The State of the Cities," *The Reporter* (December 16, 1965), p. 53; Leon N. Weiner, *The American City* (August 1967), p. 16; Harvey S. Perloff, "Modernizing Urban Development," *Daedalus* (Summer 1967), p. 789; Bernard J. Frieden, "Housing and National Urban Goals," in James Q. Wilson (ed.), *The Metropolitan Enigma* (U.S. Chamber of Commerce, 1967), p. 179; and Mason Gaffney, "Containment Policies for Urban Sprawl," in Richard L. Stauber (ed.), *Approaches to the Study of Urbanization*, Governmental Research Series, No. 27 (University of Kansas, 1964). A similar point is made in all these references.

[121] Marion Clawson, "Why Not Sell Zoning and Rezoning? (legally, that is)," *Cry California* (Winter 1966–67), pp. 9, 39.

Urban Space Indicators

A major concern of this volume is the question of reporting on the quality of the urban environment. In the concluding section of Chapter 1, Perloff emphasizes the importance of providing a broad picture of the urban environment in terms of social indicators and social accounts. Within that general orientation, this section attempts to develop some preliminary measures that will be useful as indicators of contained urban space.[122] The emphasis here is on indicators of present conditions in quantitative terms, viewing these as essential to the development of indicators of the quality of the urban environment. (The latter would also involve specification of value weights, policy standards, definition of optimal conditions, and attempts to measure deviations therefrom.)

Considering the interest inherent in the subject, reliable data on urban land and building prices and quantities in the United States are relatively sparse. Perhaps the economist tends to be the reverse of Oscar Wilde's cynic: he knows the value of everything and the price of nothing. With the disclaimer, then, that there will be many gaps, let us view the following available measures: (1) property value (land and structures) in asset terms; (2) land prices and building prices; (3) some building quantity data; (4) some infrastructure items.

Property values are presented for the United States as a whole; for urban and nonurban areas; and for individual cities (interurban results). Then some intracity items are presented. The relation of height to building price and quantity is investigated in passing.

Goldsmith has developed a number of series estimating components of national wealth over time. For 1958, the last year for which data are available, he estimates that land and structures comprise roughly 70 per cent of all tangible assets and 50 per cent of all equities (assets minus liabilities).[123]

Table 2 gives a detailed breakdown of the Goldsmith data for land and structures, classified by function. Broad categories appear in the upper part of the table and a finer breakdown for some of the categories is given in the lower part. Non-farm residential property accounts for roughly 40 per cent of total value, government and business equal about 20 per cent each, and agriculture and "all other" account for about 10 per cent each.

---

[122] Items developed here will generally fall under Perloff's "Spatial environment" classification, though some fall under the "Transportation-utilities" heading. Additional measures are provided in the other chapters in this volume. See Chapters 6 and 7, in particular, for material related to the measures presented here.

[123] Tangible assets include machinery, equipment, and inventories. Structures include buildings *and* roads, underground mining structures, etc., but the non-building items are relatively minor in terms of total value. Values, in billions of dollars, are $1,145 for land and structures, $1,653 for tangible assets, and $2,247 for total equities. See Raymond W. Goldsmith, Robert E. Lipsey, and Morris Mendelson, *Studies in the National Balance Sheet of the United States; II, Basic Data on Balance Sheets and Fund Flows* (Princeton University Press for National Bureau of Economic Research, 1963), pp. 68–69.

Table 2. *Distribution of Property Values by Function, United States, 1958*

Categories	Structures	Land	Land plus structures	Fraction of total	Goldsmith table (source)
	($----$ *Billions of dollars* $----$)				
Non-farm residential	392.0	60.7	452.7	.389	A–35, A–40
Agriculture	36.0[a]	87.6	123.6	.106	B–91
Business	175.1	45.0	220.1	.189	B–123, B–124
Institutional and social–recreation	30.4	10.2	40.6	.035	B–41, B–125
Civilian government nonresidential	168.2	39.2	207.4	.178	B–150, B–151
Federal government–military	20.7	1.6	22.3	.019	B–175
All other	31.8	66.4	98.2	.084	(See below)
Total	854.2[b]	310.7	1,164.9	1.000	
Additional detail					
Business					
Industrial	37.5	6.6	44.1	.038	B–123, B–124
Commercial	38.0	25.4	63.4	.054	" "
Miscellaneous	3.6	2.4	6.0	.005	" "
Public utility	96.0	10.6	106.6	.092	" "
Social–recreational	6.3	4.2	10.5	.009	B–125
Non-profit institutions	24.1	6.0	30.1	.026	B–41
All other					
Vacant lots	—	32.8	32.8	.028	B–17
Underground mining structures	31.8	—	31.8	.027	B–126
Subsoil assets (minerals)	—	19.9	19.9	.017	A–43
Private forests	—	13.7	13.7	.012	A–42
Civilian government					
Federal forests	—	7.4	7.4	.006	B–150, B–151
Other federal	35.0	3.8	38.8	.033	" "
State and local government	133.2	28.0	161.2	.139	" "

[a] Includes 19.3 residential and 16.7 nonresidential.
[b] "Total structures" here includes federal government-military structures. In some of Goldsmith's summary tables, this item is omitted.

Sources: Indicated tables in Appendixes A and B, Raymond W. Goldsmith, *The National Wealth of the United States in the Postwar Period* (Princeton University Press for the National Bureau of Economic Research, 1962).

For land alone, agriculture accounts for roughly 30 per cent, non-farm residential for about 20 per cent, business for 15 per cent, vacant lots and government for about 10 per cent each, and all other categories make up about 15 per cent.

Property value figures for urban versus non-urban areas, and for individual cities, were developed from data appearing in the *Census of Governments* and in Netzer's *The Economics of the Property Tax.*[124] The basic data pose a number of prob-

[124] Data on assessed values appear in the U.S. Bureau of the Census, *Census of Governments: 1962* (Washington, 1963). For the United States as a whole and for Standard Metropolitan Statistical Areas (SMSA's), this source gives enough information on assessment ratios (the ratio of assessed

Table 3.   Real Estate Values for United States, All SMSA's, and Nineteen Large Cities, 1961

	Resi-dential	Industrial-commer-cial	Acreage and farms, vacant, other	Total real estate value	Popula-tion (1960)	Real estate value	
						Per capita	Per capita relative to U.S. level
	(------- billion dollars -------)				(*millions*)		
United States	510.2	230.0	223.4	963.6	179.3	$5,374	1.000
All SMSA's	391.7	180.9	65.9	638.5	112.3	$5,686	1.060
Non-SMSA	118.5	49.1	157.5	325.1	67.0	$4,852	0.903
19 large cities	91.4	54.5	6.9	152.8	28.0	$5,457	1.020

Primary Sources: Data in U.S. Bureau of the Census, *Census of Governments: 1962*, Vol. II, *Taxable Property Values* (Washington, D.C., 1963); and Dick Netzer, *Economics of the Property Tax* (The Brookings Institution, 1966). See text for procedures.

lems in terms of sampling variability, possible bias, and differences in definition among units. The results, consequently, are not "good," but are probably the best available. A summary of estimating procedures appears as an appendix (pp. 133–35).

City results obtained are aggregated and compared to United States, SMSA, and non-SMSA results in Table 3. Aggregated values appear for nineteen of the twenty-one largest U.S. cities. New Orleans and San Antonio were excluded because data on them were not available.

Table 3 results indicate a fair correspondence between population and value of real estate. Thus, SMSA population was .626 of U.S. population (in 1960); the value of real estate in SMSA's was .663 of the U.S. total (in 1961). Put another way, per capita real estate value for SMSA's was 1.06 of the U.S. per capita figure. Relative to non-SMSA per capita real estate, the ratio was 1.17, so a fairly substantial difference existed. For the nineteen large cities, real estate value per capita was slightly above the U.S. figure and slightly below the SMSA figure. In ratio terms, the per capita levels were 1.02 the U.S. level and .96 the SMSA level.

This is in line with evidence Netzer presents, indicating a general tendency for

---

value to market value) to permit estimation of market values for the broad classes of property: (1) residential; (2) industrial-commercial; and (3) acreage and farms, vacant land, and all other. Assessment ratios are based on sample information developed by the *Census of Governments*.

For individual cities, some data are available, but generally estimation will be unsatisfactory because assessment ratios usually vary between classes of property, and information on individual cities is generally lacking. However, Dick Netzer had some special census tabulations run for a set of cities and results are presented in his *The Economics of the Property Tax* (The Brookings Institution, 1966), Table 4–1 and Table 7–3. These were employed as a major source of information, and, in conjunction with a set of mildly heroic assumptions, allowed estimation of property values for each city.

Table 4. *Estimated Property Values by Class of Property for Nineteen Large Cities, 1961*

(millions of dollars)

City	Single-family houses (*Given*)	Other residential (*Estimate*)	Commercial–industrial (*Estimate*)	All other (primarily vacant land) (*Estimate*)	Total
New York	5,870	17,428	13,741	1,593	38,632
Chicago	4,930	5,860	5,350	839	16,979
Los Angeles	10,368	4,059	7,225	1,043	22,695
Philadelphia	3,582	658	2,576	158	6,973
Detroit	3,427	1,049	3,209	100	7,785
Baltimore	1,979	118	851	15	2,962
Houston[a]	3,471	57	2,667	1,070	7,266
Cleveland	2,045	64[b]	1,892	107	4,108
Washington, D.C.	1,888	1,043	1,485	610	5,026
St. Louis	1,492	409	2,641	128	4,669
Milwaukee	1,900	208	1,278	43	3,429
San Francisco	2,973	1,134	1,488	190	5,785
Boston	417	1,192	2,111	137	3,857
Dallas[a]	3,131	279	2,249	181	5,839
Pittsburgh	1,504	168	829	125	2,625
San Diego[c]	2,124	543	1,076	238	3,981
Seattle	2,052	347	1,134	205	3,738
Buffalo[c]	817	1,189	1,870	50	3,926
Cincinnati	1,367	225	817	82	2,491
Total	55,335	36,030	54,488	6,913	152,766

[a] County figures; i.e., county in which central city is located.

[b] Available evidence suggests that much "other residential" was included in other categories — most probably in single-family residential.

[c] City figures, although county assessment ratios were employed.

per capita taxable values to be higher in the outlying portion of the SMSA than in the central city.[125]

Table 4 presents estimates of property value by class of property for each city in the group of nineteen large cities. Aggregate property values were divided by 1960 populations to obtain property value per capita. Results appear in Table 5. Niedercorn and Hearle have developed estimates of land use acreages by city,[126] and by dividing their data into the corresponding property value totals, property value per acre could be estimated. These results also appear in Table 5.

Property values per capita will reflect value per acre, the distribution of housing between single-family and multiple-family units, and the size of the city (in particular, the amount of vacant land within city boundaries). In Table 5, it can be seen

[125] Netzer, *The Economics of the Property Tax*, Table 5–7. Historically, on a per capita basis, higher suburban residential property values were somewhat offset by nonresidential values, but by 1960 both categories were higher for the suburbs; *ibid.*, pp. 119–20.

[126] John H. Niedercorn and Edward F. R. Hearle, *Recent Land-Use Trends in Forty-eight Large American Cities*, Memorandum RM–3664–FF (The RAND Corporation, 1963).

Table 5.   *Estimated Property Value Per Capita and Per Acre Property Value by Class of Property, Nineteen Large Cities, 1961*

City	Property value per capita	Per acre values			Date of land use survey
		All residential	Industrial–commercial	Vacant	
		(– – – – – *thousand dollars* – – – – –)			
New York	$4,964	490.2	633.2	61.2	1959
Chicago	4,782	238.8	186.6	68.3	1961
Los Angeles	9,155	135.5	226.9	11.5	1960
Philadelphia	3,482	110.1	135.2	11.7	1960
Detroit	4,661	126.0	339.6	13.5	1954
Baltimore	3,155	89.5	93.1	1.7	1956
Houston[a]	5,844	—	—	—	—
Cleveland	4,689	114.0	186.6	16.6	1958
Washington, D.C.	6,578	260.0	634.0	350.2[b]	1955
St. Louis	6,226	148.2	375.5	28.4	1950
Milwaukee	4,626	87.3	173.9	4.8	1958
San Francisco	7,814	499.0	397.8	53.3	1948
Boston	5,533	166.3	463.2	78.9	1958
Dallas[a]	6,137	—	—	—	—
Pittsburgh	4,344	172.8	207.2	12.7	1959
San Diego	6,946	134.5	324.1	4.7	1958
Seattle	6,710	126.7	263.3	23.9	1953
Buffalo	7,369	242.1	303.9	28.0	1958
Cincinnati	4,956	101.8	143.4	6.5	1960
Weighted average, all cities	$5,457	201.4	277.7	21.1	—

[a] Per capita figures refer to county. City data not available.

[b] Anomalous result. Checking indicates large difference in census value figures and other sources. See Harold M. Lewis, *A New Zoning Plan for the District of Columbia* (New York: Harold M. Lewis, 1956), p. 81.

that most of the cities are fairly close to the average. But Los Angeles, with the highest per capita figure at around $9,000, and Baltimore with the lowest, at around $3,000, indicate that a substantial spread in average value exists.

Property values per acre seem fairly reasonable. Cities having high per acre values for both residential and commercial-industrial classes are New York, San Francisco, and Washington; this probably reflects both national importance and concentration.

A few items on intracity property value may be noted. The magnitude of CBD property values in Washington, D.C., is indicated by Lewis, who estimates that 19 per cent of the property tax was collected from the CBD in 1955.[127] Larry Smith developed a suggested pattern of intracity land values, presented here as Table 6.

[127] Lewis, *A New Zoning Plan...*, p. 79. The assessor defines the CBD as enclosed by 5th Street, N.W., Pennsylvania Avenue, N.W., 19th Street, N.W., and N Street, N.W. The Washington commercial assessment ratio is close enough to the residential ratio to make this a good estimate of relative property values.

Table 6.   Hierarchy of Land Uses and Land Values

Location	Land value supported (per sq. ft.)	Land uses	Comments
Core (office)	$50+ – $25	Prime multi-tenant office Prime single-occupancy office (prestige) Prestige retail Financial Other mixed uses (not freestanding) Service Food (eating and drinking)	High density primary core space use; prestige a highly important factor—convenience and central location controlling factors
Core (retail)	$25 – $15	Large comparison retail (department stores)[a] Specialty and chain retail[a] Multi- and single-tenant office Hotel Entertainment Banks Service and support uses Luxury high-rise residential apartments	Somewhat lower density use
Fringe	$55 – $5	Secondary retail Other centrally oriented commercial Secondary office	Necessary CBD service uses form major portion of fringe
Fringe	$5 – $1	Wholesale Middle-income residential apartments Neighborhood—convenience retail Loft industrial	Marginal CBD uses
Non CBD or suburban	$1 – $0.10	Low-rise or single-family middle-income residential Low-income private and public housing Industry Warehousing Neighborhood—convenience retail Suburban retail (shopping center) Low-rise office—other commercial	Locate in CBD only as a result of utilization of obsolete space (warehousing industry low-income housing) or as a result of public policy offsetting space differential
—	—	Civic and institutional uses	Location and land price as a question of public policy—centrality guides many locational decisions

[a] The table must be taken as an illustration of the relationship which frequently exists rather than an absolute statement of values, or ranking order of land values. In practically all cities, certain types of retail will be found on limited areas of land of greatest value. The size of the city under consideration will influence the absolute values.

Source: Larry Smith, "Space for the CBD's Functions," reprinted by permission of the *Journal of the American Institute of Planners* (February 1, 1961), Table 4, p. 38. There are 43,560 square feet per acre.

This table demonstrates the broad range of urban land value — land value at the center is worth 500 or more times that at the fringe.

In a national context, the square of that figure (250,000) is the ratio of peak CBD value in New York City to the average value of U.S. farmland. This is based

Table 7. *A Collection of Estimated Land Values Indicative of the Range in Value for the United States*

Kind of land, place, and date	Price per acre
All U.S. farmland, 1959 (excluding buildings)[a]	$ 85
All California farmland, 1959 (excluding buildings)[a]	300
California citrus land, 1965[b]	6,500
Suburban raw land, Fort Worth, Texas, 1964[c]	2,550
Suburban developed land, Fort Worth, Texas, 1965[d]	9,580
Suburban raw land, Los Angeles, 1964[c]	17,200
Suburban developed land, Los Angeles, 1965[d]	35,700
CBD, peak value, Los Angeles, 1961[e]	3,000,000
CBD, peak value, New York, 1961[e]	9,000,000
CBD, peak value, New York, 1965[f]	22,000,000

[a] Irving Hoch, *Estimates of Value of Agricultural Land by State*, Information Series in Agricultural Economics, No. 66–5 (University of California, December 1966), p. 15.

[b] United States Department of Agriculture, *Farm Real Estate Market Developments*, CD–68 (July 1966), Table 9, p. 20.

[c] A. Allan Schmid, *Converting Land from Rural to Urban Uses* (Resources for the Future, Inc., 1968), Appendix Table A–8.

[d] Based on data developed by Max Neutze from *FHA Homes* and a special tabulation supplied to Neutze by the FIIA Statistical Section. See Neutze, *The Suburban Apartment Boom*, pp. 86–90, for details on the series involved.

[e] Frank G. Mittelbach and Phoebe Cottingham, "Some Elements in Interregional Difference in Urban Land Values," *Regional Science Association, Western Section, Second Annual Meeting, Papers* (University of Oregon, 1963), p. 17.

[f] Robert Moore Fisher, *The Boom in Office Buildings*, Technical Bulletin 58 (Urban Land Institute, 1967), p. 20.

on data in Table 7, which presents a collection of national land prices. Estimated prices are given for farmland, suburban raw land, suburban developed land, and peak-value CBD land. Figures for Fort Worth and Los Angeles are listed because they had the low and high values, respectively, in a set of forty-one SMSA's examined by Neutze.

Some notion of average levels of building costs per square foot, by building type, is given in Table 8. Broad categories of buildings have quite comparable costs per square foot, though commercial building does exceed industrial, which in turn exceeds residential. The spread is only about one dollar. In New York, estimated costs per square foot for office buildings are generally well above those for commercial structures. It may be inferred that a good deal of the difference reflects the cost increment involved in building high-rise structures.[128] The Seagram Building costs reflect the "high quality" inputs used in its construction; presumably, the difference between $45 and $30 may be interpreted either as advertising expense, or as consumption, conspicuous or otherwise.

Some additional information bearing on cost and height is available for industrial, residential, and office buildings. Alschuler and Footlik estimate that, for industrial buildings, "the structural costs of multi-story buildings will exceed single-

[128] Estimates for high-rise buildings, nationwide, are usually around this level, running from $20 to $30 per square foot.

Table 8.   *Estimated U.S. Building Costs per Square Foot*

Building type	Estimated cost per square foot
All residential, 1963[a]	$11.70
Industrial, 1963[a]	12.20
Commercial, 1963[a]	12.80
High-rise office buildings (New York), 1964[b]	30.00
Seagram building (New York), 1958[c]	45.00

[a] Robert E. Lipsey and Doris Preston, *Source Book of Statistics Relating to Construction* (Columbia University Press, for the National Bureau of Economic Research, 1966), p. 20. Based on Dodge Series Data.
[b] Real Estate Board of New York, Press Release No. 2809, June 22, 1964, p. 2.
[c] Martin Meyerson, *Face of the Metropolis* (Random House, 1963), p. 51.

story costs by $1.00 to $3.00 per square foot."[129] They present estimates of costs per square foot of net floor area (usable space) for a single-story industrial building located in the suburbs, and for a ten-story industrial building located in an urban center. Land costs per square foot of land are set at $0.70 and $1.25, respectively, for these locations. Figures developed appear in Table 9. The high-rise building costs about 20 per cent more per square foot in the comparison.

Some of Stone's estimates of residential construction costs are noted explicitly in Table 10. Costs refer to a three-bedroom dwelling unit, and rise with height from two to twelve stories. (Costs for a single-family house are somewhat higher than those for a two-story apartment building, but almost all of the difference appears to reflect differences in quality which Stone introduced, apparently for the sake of realism.)[130]

Berger presents some regression results on high-rise office construction costs and efficiency with height as one of the explanatory variables.[131] Efficiency is defined as net rentable area as a percentage of gross building area. The samples used are for Los Angeles County, 1964. The results are:

$$Y_1 = 17.38 + .142X_1 + .352X_2 - .037X_3; \quad R^2 = .33 \tag{1}$$

$$Y_2 = 80.99 - .469X_1 + .163X_2; \quad R^2 = .21 \tag{2}$$

where Y_1 is construction cost per square foot;
         Y_2 is building efficiency;
         X_1 is stories;
         X_2 is average floor area (horizontal dimension);
         X_3 is auxiliary building area (basements, attached parking structures, etc.).

[129] John Alschuler and Irving M. Footlik, "Industry Can Cut Costs with Multi-Story Buildings," *Mid-Chicago Economic Development Study*, Vol. I, p. 57. They argue that savings in land cost and in mechanical and electrical services will offset part of the differential.

[130] See P. A. Stone, *Housing, Town Development, Land and Costs* (London: Estates Gazette, Limited, ca. 1964), footnote to Table 19.

[131] Berger, *Determination of the Economic Height . . .*, pp. 184 and 198.

Table 9. A Comparison of Single-Story and High-Rise Industrial Building Costs, Chicago Area

	Costs per square foot	
Item	Single-story building in suburbs	10-story building in urban center
Architectural and structural	$3.50	$6.80
Mechanical and electrical	2.25	1.75
Landscaping and parking	0.70	1.10
Subtotal: building	6.45	9.65
Cost of land per square foot of building[a]	2.10	0.60
Total cost per square foot of building area	8.55	10.25

[a] Land cost per square foot of land is set at $0.70 in the suburbs and $1.25 in the urban center.

Source: John Alschuler and Irving M. Footlik, "Industry Can Cut Costs with Multi-Story Buildings," Mayor's Committee for Economic and Cultural Development, *Mid-Chicago Economic Development Study*, Vol. I, 1966, p. 70, Cases 1B and 3.

Table 10. Costs of Three-Bedroom Dwellings, England

(pounds sterling)

	Costs per dwelling		
Housing type and stories	Land, road, sewers, etc.	Construction costs	Total
Single-family house[a]	337	1,698	2,035
Apartment building			
2 stories	285	1,617	1,902
3 stories	250	1,940	2,190
4 stories	231	2,199	2,430
6 stories	212	2,539	2,751
9 stories	202	2,830	3,032
12 stories	199	2,992	3,191

[a] A footnote indicates the single-family house figure includes a 5 per cent allowance on the two-story price to allow "for the greater provision of fittings."

Source: P. A. Stone, *Housing, Town Development, Land and Costs* (London: Estates Gazette, Limited, ca. 1964), Table 19.

Statistically significant coefficients are obtained for X_2 and X_3 in equation (1) and for X_1 in equation (2). Signs of coefficients are generally consistent with expectations, though that of X_3 in (1) is not. In particular, costs increase and efficiency decreases with height.

Turning to building quantity data, Table 11 presents some information on non-residential and office floor space for central business districts. It is clear that New York City far overshadows other cities in terms of CBD floor space. In the eight square mile area of Manhattan below Central Park are the "headquarters for 109 of the

Table 11.   Some Information on Nonresidential and Office Floor Space for Central Business Districts

Locale	Floor space in thousand square feet, and date	
	Nonresidential	Office
New York	540,000 (1967)[a]	196,000 (1967)[b]
Chicago	85,432 (1956)[c]	41,000 (1965)[d]
Washington	75,000 (1967)[e]	20,500 (1964)[f]
Pittsburgh	32,000 (1960)[g]	Not available
Los Angeles	40,400 (1960)[h]	Not available

[a] Regional Plan Association, *The Region's Growth* (New York, May 1967), p. 40.

[b] Real Estate Board of New York, *Office Building Construction in Manhattan, 1947–67* (September 1, 1964), p. 4; and Press Release No. 2809, June 22, 1964, p. 2.

[c] J. Douglas Carroll, Jr., Roger L. Creighton, and John R. Hamburg, "Transportation Planning for Central Areas," *Journal of the American Institute of Planners* (February 1961), p. 29.

[d] Fisher, *Boom in Office Buildings*, pp. 14, 46. From records of Building Managers Association of Chicago.

[e] Regional Plan Association, *The Region's Growth*, p. 45.

[f] Washington Board of Realtors Research Department, *Office Building Construction 1965–1966* (Washington, D.C., 1967), p. 2.

[g] Pittsburgh Area Transportation Study, Vol. 1, p. 43. From Pittsburgh Regional Planning Association Golden Triangle Study, 1960.

[h] Los Angeles City Planning Department, *Centropolis: The Plan for Central City Los Angeles* (1961), p. 16.

nation's largest industrial firms, six of its ten largest banks, and nine of its 50 biggest insurance companies."[132]

Some idea of the distribution of building heights by cities can be gleaned from the following data. Table 12 presents the distribution of building heights of tall buildings for the United States. (Certainly most, and perhaps all, are office buildings.)

It is clear that New York and Chicago dominate the tall-building scene. For the next nineteen cities in population size, the number of buildings over 300 feet in size can be viewed as a high-rise index. For this measure the following values are obtained: San Francisco, 25; Philadelphia, 23; Dallas, 18; Detroit, 17; Houston, 17; Pittsburgh, 16; Los Angeles, 12; Boston, 9. The other cities in this group all had five or fewer buildings that were 300 feet or above.

Some information on residential units in high-rise buildings appears in the 1960 Census of Housing. Information is given on number of dwelling units located in (1) buildings with one to three floors versus (2) buildings having four floors or more. The latter group is broken down into buildings with elevators versus walk-up buildings. The information is summarized in Table 13.

Clearly, only a small fraction of total dwelling units are located in tall buildings and, of these, a very large proportion is located in New York City.

[132] Tristate Transportation Commission, *Regional Profile: Manhattan Business District Floor Space Trends* (New York, 1967), p. 1.

Table 12.   Distribution of Heights of Tall Buildings, United States, 1967

City or group of cities	Height				
	800 ft. and above	600 ft. to less than 800 ft.	500 ft. to less than 600 ft.	400 ft. to less than 500 ft.	Total 400 ft. and above
New York	7	19	36	40	102[a]
Chicago	2	4	10	17	33
Next nineteen in size[b]	0	5	14	35	54
Remainder of U.S.	0	0	4	22	26
Total U.S.	9	28	64	114	215

[a] Of the buildings, 101 were in Manhattan, one was in Brooklyn.

[b] In the next nineteen cities, Dallas had the largest total with eight, followed by Detroit with seven, Pittsburgh with six, and Philadelphia and Houston with five each. Washington, St. Louis, Milwaukee, San Diego, and Buffalo had no structures above 400 feet.

Source: The World Almanac and Book of Facts (Newspaper Enterprise Association, Inc., 1967), pp. 300–303.

Table 13.   Distribution of Dwelling Units by Height of Structure, United States, 1960

(thousands)

City or group of cities ranked by population	All units	Units in building of four floors or more	
		With elevators	Walk-up
New York	2,758.6	756.2	797.8
Next twenty cities	7,116.5	365.7	186.5
Next 238 cities	10,509.7	188.1	162.7
Remaining urban	20,379.1	100.0[a]	80.0[a]
Total urban	40,763.9	1,410.0	1,227.0
Categories as fraction of total, U.S.	1.000	.035	.030
New York value as fraction of total	.068	.536	.650

[a] Estimate based on rate of decline in previous cases.

Source: U.S. Bureau of the Census, *U.S. Census of Housing: 1960*, Vol. 1, *State and Small Areas, U.S. Summary Final Report*, HC (1)–1 (Washington, 1963), Table 21.

The underlying data for Table 13 were employed to calculate dwelling units in high-rise buildings as a fraction of total dwelling units for each of the nineteen large cities considered previously. Results appear in Table 14. In addition, the same sort of ratios are presented for some New York and Chicago suburbs.

There are some pronounced differences between cities. New York stands apart with 56 per cent of its dwelling units in tall buildings. Boston and Washington have somewhat over 20 per cent in this category; San Francisco has about 20 per cent; and Chicago has roughly 12 per cent. In Boston, a large proportion of the units are in walk-up buildings, as are about half of those in New York; the buildings involved must be four- to six-floor tenements. Dwelling units in high-rise buildings with elevators comprise 27 per cent of the total in New York, 18 per cent in Washington,

Table 14.   *Distribution of Dwelling Units by Height of Structure, by City, 1960*

City	Dwelling units in buildings with four floors or more as fraction of all dwelling units		
	With elevator	Walk-up	Total
New York	.274	.289	.563
Chicago	.077	.042	.119
Los Angeles	.044	.006	.050
Philadelphia	.038	.018	.056
Detroit	.047	.016	.063
Baltimore	.022	.016	.038
Houston	.004	.001	.005
Cleveland	.025	.032	.057
Washington, D.C.	.181	.044	.225
St. Louis	.039	.013	.052
Milwaukee	.025	.019	.044
San Francisco	.163	.033	.196
Boston	.073	.165	.238
Dallas	.006	.003	.009
Pittsburgh	.025	.014	.039
San Diego	.011	.005	.016
Seattle	.063	.021	.084
Buffalo	.030	.011	.041
Cincinnati	.017	.075	.092
Newark, N.J.	.100	.115	.215
East Orange, N.J.	.237	.095	.332
Yonkers, N.Y.	.187	.134	.321
Evanston, Ill.	.085	.007	.092
Gary, Ind.	.012	.013	.025
Oak Park, Ill.	.030	.004	.034

16 per cent in San Francisco, 8 per cent in Chicago, and 7 per cent in Boston. Other large cities have 6 per cent or less. The Washington case is interesting inasmuch as there is a fairly restrictive height limitation on residential building. This may have led to an increase in the number of individual buildings.

It is noteworthy that the values for the suburbs of New York and Chicago approach those of the central city, indicating that suburban land "nodes" with high land values are associated with high-rise buildings.

For individual large cities, if fraction of dwelling units in tall buildings (Table 14) is plotted against average residential property value (Table 5), a fairly linear scatter results. Least square regressions were run on the data as follows:

Let Y_1 = fraction in elevator buildings;
Y_2 = fraction in walk-up buildings;
X_1 = residential property value per acre (in million dollars);
X_2 = a dummy variable for area, with a value of 1 for Eastern cities, 0 for other cities.

Results obtained were:

$$Y_1 = -.0263 + .4933X_1; \quad t \text{ ratio} = 6.69$$
$$R^2 = .75 \ (X_2 \text{ not included}) \tag{1}$$

$$Y_2 = -.0182 + .2652X_1 + .0447X_2; \quad t \text{ ratio for } X_1 = 2.08;$$
$$\text{for } X_2 = 1.38; \quad R^2 = .62 \tag{2}$$

Some items on infrastructure conclude this inventory of indicators of present conditions.

Schmid has estimated average improvement costs in converting raw land to urban uses as $6,300 per acre. (This is a major component of an estimated $10,000 per acre sales price.) The per acre improvement costs can be broken down as follows: sanitary sewer, $1,000; water main, $700; storm sewer, $1,100; and concrete curb, sidewalk, and paving, $3,500.[133]

Cohn lists a Department of Commerce estimated capital value of public sewerage systems as $25.7 billion in 1955;[134] Clawson estimates urban acreage as 11 million acres;[135] these figures in conjunction yield a per acre value of sewerage as somewhat over $2,000, which squares well with the combined sanitary and storm sewer estimates listed above.

Turning to urban transportation systems, some data on transit developments, focusing on tubes and tunnels, appears in Table 15. Cost per mile is about $10 million for an elevated system, $15 million for subways, and around $50 million for underwater tunnels and tubes. Urban expressways range in cost from about $1 million to more than $100 million per mile.[136] Some equations have been fitted to expressway costs as a function of residential density. Construction costs, as well as right-of-way costs, increase with density, reflecting increased interchanges and overpasses. The equations are:

$$Y_1 = 1.233 + .1716X \text{ (Pittsburgh)}[137]$$
$$Y_2 = 0.999 + .0708X \text{ (Chicago)}[138]$$
$$Y_3 = -5.05 + 5.85 \log X \text{ (Chicago)}[139]$$

[133] A. Allan Schmid, *Converting Land...*, based on his Tables 5 and 13.

[134] Morris M. Cohn, *Sewers for Growing America* (Ambler, Pa.; Certain-teed Products, 1966), p. 12.

[135] This is land in urban use as opposed to a withdrawn acreage of 17 million acres. Marion Clawson, "Urban Land Use," in Elias, Gillies, and Riemer (eds.), *Metropolis: Values in Conflict* (Wadsworth, 1964), p. 144.

[136] The proposed 1.2-mile Lower Manhattan Expressway is estimated to cost $150 million or $125 million per mile. *New York Times*, March 8, 1968, p. 1.

[137] A. O. Lind, "Freeway Costs in the Pittsburgh Area," Pittsburgh Area Transportation Study, *Research Letter* (September–October, 1961), p. 17.

[138] George Haikalis and Hyman Joseph, "Economic Evaluation of Traffic Networks," in *Studies in Highway Engineering Economy*, Highway Research Board Bulletin No. 306 (Washington, 1961), pp. 39–63.

[139] Lind, "Freeway Costs...," p. 15; Chicago Area Transportation Study, p. 22.

Table 15.   *Some Cost Figures on Transit Developments Focusing on Tubes and Tunnels*

Transit development, 1966–67	Cost per mile
	(*million dollars*)
Subway tunnel under East River, New York City	70.0[a]
BART underwater tube, San Francisco Bay	45.0[b]
Philadelphia subway extension	13.1[c]
BART tunnel, East Bay Hills	10.0[d]
BART elevated, average, 71 miles	9.3[e]
Berkeley subway, total cost (estimate)	14.9[f]

[a] Based on data in *New York Times*, October 27, 1966.
[b] *San Francisco Examiner*, April 16, 1966.
[c] *Philadelphia Inquirer*, October 7, 1967.
[d] *San Francisco Chronicle*, March 7, 1966.
[e] *San Francisco Chronicle*, October 2, 1966. Total cost of BART system (initial estimate): $792 million for 75-mile network. Of this, 133 million was allocated to 4-mile underwater tube, in original estimate (*San Francisco Chronicle*, April 10, 1966). Hence, $792 - 133 = 659$; $659/71 = 9.3$.
[f] Based on subway costs listed in *San Francisco Chronicle*, October 2, 1966. A subway cost increment of 5.6 is added to the elevated cost of 9.3.

Y_1 is total cost (including right-of-way and construction cost) in millions of dollars; Y_2 is construction cost in millions of dollars; Y_3 is right-of-way cost in millions of dollars; and X is thousands of persons per square mile of residential land. The upper level of X is about 100 in the Pittsburgh study area, and 150 in the Chicago area.

Some idea of the total value of urban transportation infrastructure can be had by noting that the cumulative investment in New York Port Authority facilities totaled $1.5 billion at the end of 1966.[140]

These figures have been presented at this point primarily for descriptive purposes. Thus, they indicate some of the main magnitudes in urban space use, and serve as a first, very rough approximation to a meaningful set of indicators in Perloff's Table 1 in this volume.

In full development and application, such magnitudes can be of great use in assigning values to parameters in economic models, and hopefully, in deriving policy implications.

Recent Developments in Three-Dimensional Space Use

This section is concerned with recent developments in the use of three-dimensional urban space. Subsections are devoted to: high-rise developments, underground developments, and elevated structures and the use of air rights. Common themes throughout are multiple use (in its several senses) and the impact of technical advance.

[140] Port of New York Authority, *Annual Report* (1966), p. 50.

The discussion of recent developments is a catalog of what is new; but beyond that it indicates some of the experiments, innovations, and institutional devices that are shaping the future use of urban space.

HIGH-RISE DEVELOPMENTS

A good deal of high-rise construction has taken place in recent years. Building height records are being broken in most large cities and many massive development projects have been undertaken.[141]

There is a trend toward multiple use within one or a cluster of high-rise buildings. An example is the John Hancock Center tower building in Chicago which combines enough different functions to be a town in itself. There are 750 apartments on forty-nine floors, office space on thirty-four floors, and parking on seven floors. Thus, it will be possible to commute to work by elevator. Other examples include the Fox Plaza Building in San Francisco, combining a shopping center, fourteen stories of offices, and sixteen stories of apartments; Marina City in Chicago with a building complex containing 900 apartments, 900 parking spaces, shops, offices, a marina for 700 boats, a skating rink, and a swimming pool; and the Prudential Center in Boston, which includes offices, a 1,000-room hotel, 1,250 apartments, and parking for 5,000 cars.[142]

Factors behind these developments may include: an increase in the price of land relative to building inputs and technological innovations of advantage to high-rise construction.

With respect to land prices, marked increases have occurred in both central districts and suburbs. For the latter, Schmid presents unweighted average prices for raw suburban land in 1960 and 1964, using a sample of 259 cities.[143] The 1964 value is $3,030 versus the 1960 value of $1,995, involving a 52 per cent increase. When Schmid's data are restricted to the thirty-nine SMSA's appearing on Neutze's list of large SMSA's, the respective figures are $5,046 versus $3,181, a 59 per cent increase. Neutze's data on improved suburban land yields a 1965 simple average of $17,520 as compared to a 1960 average of $14,150, involving an increase of 24 per cent.[144] Hence, the difference between the Schmid and Neutze results indicates that the increase in value is concentrated in raw land as opposed to improvements transforming raw land to devel-

---

[141] Some examples: New York's World Trade Center will provide 10 million square feet of space at a cost of $575 million; Century City in Los Angeles is a planned $500 million development; San Francisco's Embarcadero Center and Golden Gateway development have an estimated cost of $125 million each; Philadelphia has a $500 million downtown renewal plan; Boston has its Prudential Center, a new government center, and a $400 million CBD program; Baltimore has its Charles Center development; and Chicago has Marina City, the John Hancock Center, and a new civic center.

[142] A number of other examples appear in *Business Week*, April 2, 1966, pp. 37–38, and in a *Christian Science Monitor* article, "New Patterns of Building Design," October 15, 1965, p. 9.

[143] Schmid, *Converting Land...*, Appendix Tables A–7 and A–8.

[144] Neutze, *The Suburban Apartment Boom*, data used in Chap. 5, based on *FHA Homes* data and unpublished information from the FHA Statistical Section.

oped sites. In contrast, a variety of construction cost indexes show an increase of from 7 to 10 per cent for the 1960–64 period.[145]

This change in relative prices may be a factor in the marked shift to multiple-family housing in recent years. Thus, during the 1940–49 and 1950–59 decades, an average of over 80 per cent of all housing starts were one-family starts; in 1959, the percentage started to drop, and from 1963 to 1965 it leveled off at around 60 per cent.[146]

With respect to technological advance, Neutze concludes that "the opinion of people close to the industry is that there has been much less than a revolution in techniques of building, even of high-rise apartments."[147]

Nevertheless, some innovations seem to have particular application to high-rise construction. (It might well be that, given these innovations, buildings rose higher, so that a cost index might show no decline in costs. Thus, the average cost of a building of a given number of stories might decrease, but if the average number of stories increased, the cost index would increase correspondingly.)

These innovations include prestressed concrete; other new materials (aluminum siding, gypsum board); the tower crane; standardization of dimensions of construction material (modular co-ordination); and prefabrication.[148] The introduction of prestressed concrete[149] into the United States appears to have been an important technological advance. This product was introduced in 1951, 5 U.S. plants were producing it in the early 1950's, and 200 plants were producing it in 1965. High strength, prestressed concrete has been an important factor in high-rise building since World War II.

The tower crane was introduced from Europe around 1959. There are now about 300 in use. They are especially useful in the construction of tall buildings; material is lifted from the ground and deposited anywhere on the construction floor.

[145] U.S. Bureau of the Census, *Statistical Abstract, 1965* (Washington, 1965), p. 745. Relevant indexes are U.S. Department of Commerce composite; American Appraisal Company; Associated General Contractors; E. H. Boeckh; Engineering News Record; and Turner Construction Co. If we subtract the Schmid figures from the corresponding Neutze figures, improvements net of raw land increase by 14 per cent for 1960–64.

[146] Neutze, *The Suburban Apartment Boom*, Table 1, p. 9.

[147] *Ibid.*, p. 29.

[148] The discussion draws on U.S. Bureau of Labor Statistics, *Technological Trends in Major American Industries*, Bulletin 1474 (Washington, February 1966), pp. 5, 32–37, 62, 66, 85; and U.S. Department of Commerce, Business and Defense Services Administration, "Innovations in Construction," *Construction Review* (November 1967), p. 8.

[149] "Nearly all concrete structures built today are strengthened with imbedded reinforcing rods. . . . Prestressed concrete is made by compressing concrete between pretensioned reinforcing rods so the concrete carries an initial compressive load." Paul Gugliotta, in R. Colborn (ed.), "Modern Concrete Design," *Modern Science and Technology* (D. Van Nostrand, 1965), p. 374. The steel is pretensioned by controlled stretching. The internal stresses produced counteract the stresses the structural member is expected to carry, permitting substantial reduction in the weight of the steel used. And structures using prestressed concrete can be erected faster than those using pour-in-place concrete. U.S. Department of Commerce, Business and Defense Services Administration, "Trends in Use of Prestressed Concrete," *Construction Review* (January 1965), p. 11.

As each floor is completed, the tower is jacked to the next level. On completion, the tower is disassembled and moved to another construction site.

There is an increasing use of prefabricated building components. The individual dwelling unit as a whole could eventually be prefabricated.

Thus, Moshe Safdie's Habitat 67 (at the Montreal Exposition) may be indicative of things to come. Safdie's units are concrete boxes which can be stacked on top of one another in almost any fashion desired. Up to five stacks are possible, and all apartments have outdoor living decks on the exposed parts of the roofs of lower boxes. However, the units cost about $100,000 per apartment (roughly five times the average) and it does not seem likely that this cost can be substantially reduced.[150]

But the editors of *Architectural Forum* see Safdie's concrete boxes as already somewhat obsolete. They weigh 27 pounds per cubic foot, while large containers of metal or of wood and metal weigh from 2 to 4 pounds per cubic foot. They suggest that, though the latter boxes could not be piled on top of one another, they "could be inserted in a simple structural cage" in a high-rise development. It is noted that there might be fireproofing problems with such boxes, but they are seen as inherently resistant to fire; hence, building codes might be revised.

The Iron and Steel Institute is carrying out research on the shipping of metal units one-story high which would furnish the floor deck for two floors, by virtue of a staggered honeycomb arrangement. There have even been musings about the stacking of mobile homes to form high-rise structures.

UNDERGROUND DEVELOPMENTS

Underground space is utilized primarily for utilities, sewers, and building foundations; transportation tunnels and subways, parking facilities, underground pedestrian malls, and floor space round out the uses. The underground development of floor space appears limited both by revenue and cost considerations. The revenue side involves the light and air amenities discussed above; the existence of "bargain basements" seems to correspond to a generally held notion of lower quality as one descends. On the cost side, Berger notes that the cost of subterranean parking increases in geometric progression when more than two levels are required.[151] Of course when site value is very high, some extension of a building in a downward direction may be feasible. Thus, the Chase Manhattan Bank has a six-level development below ground. The levels, in order downward, contain a cafeteria, bank facilities, building services, and vaults at rock level.[152]

Multiple use, an important aspect of underground space utilization, has two senses. The first involves the achievement of more than one purpose, so that joint production is involved; the second involves the separation and segregation of presumably

[150] *Architectural Forum*, "Habitat and After" (May 1967), p. 43, notes that much of the high cost is due to the fact the development is a prototype, but concludes, "mass production is not likely to reduce unit cost substantially."

[151] Berger, *Determination of the Economic Height...*, p. 147.

[152] Meyerson, *Face of the Metropolis*, pp. 53, 54.

conflicting activities, such as pedestrian and vehicle traffic, by means of devoting above-ground space to one activity and below-ground space to the other.

With respect to multipurpose uses of underground space, it has been suggested that such space could furnish fallout and nuclear attack shelters; manufacturing space free from vibration, temperature, and humidity fluctuations; the storage of surface water in floods; and the disposal of solid wastes (though contamination of underground water would be of concern).[153]

It is somewhat disquieting that in 100 Russian cities, 35 per cent or more of investment in structures is underground.[154] (Do they know something we do not?) Sweden has an extensive underground development program for civil defense purposes. About two billion dollars has been spent so far for underground installations, of which half are military, half civilian. Virtually all new buildings are constructed with underground shelters; present mass shelters are used for underground parking, convention rooms, and civic centers.[155] Sweden has one of Europe's great aircraft plants located 200 feet underground; a number of other manufacturing operations and sewage disposal plants are located underground, as is the bulk of the air force. A comparative study of an aboveground and an underground plant (with 500 workers each) revealed:

- absenteeism caused by illness was greater above ground; the accident rate was markedly lower below ground, but headaches and psychosomatic problems were greater below ground.
- the capital cost of putting a plant underground was 10 to 15 per cent greater than that of the conventional plant. However, operating and maintenance costs were so much lower that the underground plant was the better investment. (There were no exteriors to paint or repair and little heat was needed.)[156]

On a less dramatic level there are economies to be had by the co-ordination of utility installation; in particular, this involves installing all utilities in one trench or tunnel. Thus, in Oakland, California, the cost of putting electric services underground dropped from around $1,000 per lot to about $225 as a consequence of such co-ordination.[157]

Turning to the separation and segregation of conflicting activities, a number of developments may be noted. Several cities have built underground garages beneath a central-area park.[158] Rockefeller Center pioneered in the use of the first basement

[153] American Public Works Association Research Foundation, *Better Utilization of Urban Space, Summary of a Symposium on Research Needs* (Chicago, 1967), p. 7.

[154] *Ibid.*

[155] Oliver Clausen, "Sweden Goes Underground," *New York Times* (May 22, 1966), pp. 24, 111, 112.

[156] *Ibid.*

[157] Reported by James E. McCarty, Oakland City Engineer. A similar argument is made by Herbert I. Blinder, Director of Technical Services of the American Public Power Association in American Public Works Association, *Better Utilization of Urban Space*, p. 26.

[158] These include Pittsburgh, Los Angeles, San Francisco, and Chicago; Schultz and Simmons, *Offices in the Sky*, p. 181. See Meyerson, *Face of the Metropolis*, p. 96, for a detailed discussion of Mellon Square Park in Pittsburgh.

level of all its buildings as an underground pedestrian thoroughfare and shopping arcade. Escalators lead to the first floors of all buildings. This was seen as a means of reducing pedestrian traffic on the streets.[159]

The Rockefeller Center underground network links about 17 acres of buildings. A much larger area will be served by an underground system in Montreal, which now connects 50 acres of downtown structures and will eventually serve 100 acres.

Particular levels are devoted to subway transit, passenger trains, garages, pedestrian concourses and shopping, and to surface traffic. The first phase of the development is under the Place Ville-Marie; the shopping level here has fifty stores fronting on air-conditioned promenades through which an estimated 80,000 persons pass daily. Foot traffic at major intersections above ground has fallen by roughly 70 per cent. Office buildings tied into the underground network rented faster than those that were not. The total length of the pedestrian concourses is projected at 6 miles by 1977. The Eaton Center project in Montreal is a parallel development and a master plan for Philadelphia exhibits similar features, including a five-block underground shopping mall, a concourse connecting the mall and major department stores, and a transportation center connected by escalators to the mall, the streets, and new underground parking facilities.

Multiple use in the sense of separated uses can lead to conflict when the separation is incomplete. This is the case when maintenance and repairs of utility networks hinders street traffic, though utilities do attempt to co-ordinate their digging with the work of others, and try to schedule their work for hours of minimum traffic.[160]

A number of technical advances may bring about greater utilization of underground space. Thus, underground transmission systems are falling in cost relative to overhead lines and increased underground installation of utility lines can be expected.[161] Advances are occurring in tunneling and some important consequences are possible.

---

[159] Schultz and Simmons, *Offices in the Sky*, p. 177.

[160] Fred J. Cook, "Dig They Must...," p. 70. It has been noted, somewhat facetiously, that utilities in the United States (with greater vehicle traffic) open up the streets for repairs, while in Europe (with more pedestrians), sidewalks are liable to be torn up. American Public Works Association, *Better Utilization of Urban Space*, p. 42.

[161] This has been brought about in part by the use of aluminum in place of copper conductors. Estimates of the cost differential vary. DiMatteo and Stewart estimate that in 1955 the ratio of underground to overhead distribution cost was 10:1, but that this had dropped to 1.25:1 by 1967. But Consolidated Edison of New York estimates that for low-voltage distribution to consumers, it is two to five times more expensive to bury the lines than to build them overhead; and for high-voltage transmission, it is ten to fifteen times more expensive. More precisely, the ratio varies with population density. Thus, the Department of Interior estimates the high-voltage cost ratio as about 15:1 in rural areas, with equal cost in congested urban areas. "Undergrounding in highly congested areas is advantageous and is presently being done in metropolitan areas." See: U.S. Bureau of Labor Statistics, *Technological Trends...*, p. 233; L. P. DiMatteo and Mathew W. Stewart, "Prepare To Go 100 % Underground," *American City* (October 1967), p. 62; a report by Charles Luce, Chairman of Board, Consolidated Edison Co., advertisement, *New York Times*, October 3, 1967, p. 25, and U.S. Department of the Interior, *Report to the President, Program for Advancing Underground Electric Power Transmission Technology* (Washington, 1966), p. 13.

Thomas E. Howard[162] argues that surface excavation is the only acceptable option for building substructures and most highways. But for other cases, tunneling may become more economic. The bitter controversy surrounding urban expressway routing might vanish if there were a feasible subsurface alternative.[163] This alternative may appear in the form of the continuous tunnel borer, or mechanical mole, now under development, which involves the continuous penetration of a tunnel face with a single machine that simultaneously breaks away rock and scoops up fragments. If the hauling away of broken rock is added, the system becomes continuous. By 1964, the borer had been used successfully in some cases, but these were limited to tunneling through soft or medium rock. Though hard rock tunneling has not yet been achieved, Howard feels that the initial breakthrough to rapid excavation has now occurred.

Research is also being carried out on the use of laser beams in splitting rock; however, practical application appears to be twenty years away at the earliest.

Costs of urban expressways and underground automobile tunnels were compared over time by George A. Hoffman, who discerned a rise in the cost of the former and a fall in that of the latter.[164] He expected these cost trends to continue, with tunnel costs falling below expressway costs in the not too distant future. Hence, he suggested the possible construction of a vast subterranean transportation system, consisting of a large number of freeway tunnels and a very large number of underground parking spaces and/or a series of multistory parking garages.

The argument is open to some question because the data on expressways included a large number of New York City cases in the later years of the time series, while the data on tunnels included New York City cases in the early years. Because New York City values are probably above average in both applications, results may be biased. Yet the developments cited earlier support Hoffman's basic notions. Perhaps more serious is Webber's counter that "the problem of moving large numbers of cars into and out of garages during brief periods would call for so elaborate and costly a maze of access ramps as to discourage any serious effort to satisfy a parking demand of such magnitude."[165]

ELEVATED STRUCTURES AND THE USE OF AIR RIGHTS

Elevated structures are in bad repute. Although the cost per mile of subway transit is roughly 50 per cent higher than that of elevated transit,[166] there is a strong body of opinion that the higher costs should be borne. In Berkeley, California, 80 per cent

[162] Thomas E. Howard, "Rapid Excavation," *Scientific American* (November 1967), p. 74 ff.

[163] See B. Drummond Ayres, "White Roads Through Black Bedrooms," *New York Times*, December 31, 1967, p. E–7, for examples of such controversy.

[164] George A. Hoffman, *Urban Underground Highways and Parking Facilities*, Memorandum RM–3680–RC (RAND Corporation, 1963).

[165] Webber, "Order in Diversity...," p. 41.

[166] The Bay Area Rapid Transit District estimated the differential as roughly 100 per cent; the 50 per cent figure is based on an actual contract bid for a section of Berkeley subway. However, additional costs are entailed in the construction of subway stations. *San Francisco Chronicle*, October 2, 1966.

of the voters in a special election voted to bear the additional costs of subway construction. The following arguments were used to justify the subway:

- The elevated would divide the city along racial and income lines;
- It would tend to reduce access between sections of the city;
- It would cause noise and fumes not present with a subway;
- Elevated structures cause blight and a reduction in property values;[167]
- In contrast, a subway would generate an increase in property values. New structures will be built on some of the land above the subways, and the city of Berkeley has an option for air right construction above the subway stations.

The antipathy to elevated structures (anti-Chinese Wallism)[168] appears widespread. The *Chicago Tribune* wants the Loop elevated torn down;[169] Mayor Lindsay vetoed the elevated Lower Manhattan Expressway;[170] most New York elevated train structures have been torn down, their remnants and elevated highways are seen as having a negative influence;[171] the President of the American Institute of Architects argues that elevated expressways ruin real estate as well as architectural and visual values;[172] and Seattle businessmen now want the monorail torn down because it has depressed property values.[173] The antipathy seems well-founded: When such structures have been removed, an increase in land values and new construction has followed.[174] Clearly, the increase in light and air access, and reduction of noise and fumes have been valuable.

If "Chinese Walls" are out, air rights construction over transportation facilities is in. This kind of development has generated a good deal of interest and enthusiasm, probably reflecting the feeling that the problems posed by elevated transportation structures can be avoided, and that goodly amounts of income and taxes can be generated by air rights construction. Though there is some basis for this belief, it will probably prove to be somewhat optimistic. A brief survey of air rights development will be essayed here in support of this conclusion.[175]

[167] "This blighting...leads to increased cost for welfare, police, and equipment necessary to care for slum conditions and dwellers." ABC Campaign Committee, *Stop Elevated Tracks in Berkeley* (October 1966), p. 3.

[168] The original urban "Chinese Wall" apparently was a brick railroad structure in downtown Philadelphia, finally torn down after many years of promises to do so. Meyerson, *Face of the Metropolis*, p. 61.

[169] *Chicago Tribune*, May 7, 1967, editorial page.

[170] Present plans call for a combination of tunnel and open-cut surface road.

[171] W. Berger review, *Journal of the American Institute of Planners* (July 1967), p. 285.

[172] Morris Ketchum, Jr., quoted in *San Francisco Examiner*, July 4, 1966, p. 17.

[173] Berkeley Campus Committee on Border-to-Border Subway, Letter, September 1966.

[174] For example, "The tearing down of the Third Avenue El was followed by new high-rise buildings 'sprouting all over the place'." Fred J. Cook, "Dig They Must...," p. 69.

[175] References include: Bernard, *Air Space in Urban Development;* A. M. Hill, *Air Rights and Their Use in Los Angeles* (Los Angeles Bureau of Right of Way and Land, 1965); A. Hall, H. Harper, and R. Leyden, "Approaches to the Valuation of Air Rights," *Appraisal Journal* (July 1956), pp. 325–47; Walter R. Kuehnle *et al.*, *Case Studies in Air Rights and Subsurface Tunnel Road Easements*

Early air rights utilization involved air space over railroad yards and rights of way. The first major example was the New York development of the Park Avenue complex over an underground rail yard, beginning in 1903. Buildings involved included the Grand Central Station, the Waldorf-Astoria Hotel, the Biltmore Hotel, and a number of large apartment buildings recently replaced by office structures. Similar development over central city railroad yards later occurred in Chicago, with the construction of the Merchandise Mart (1929), the U.S. Post Office (1930's), the Prudential Building (1960), the Sun-Times Building, and the Marina City apartments (1960's). And the Montreal Place Ville-Marie development includes high-rise office buildings over rail yard and tracks.

Recent interest has focused on road transportation facilities. Thus, in Boston, the Prudential Tower, a hotel, auditorium, and six high-rise buildings are being built on air rights over a railroad yard and the Massachusetts Turnpike. A high-rise apartment development containing 960 units in four apartment buildings has been built over expressway approaches to the George Washington Bridge in New York City. The District of Columbia has proposed elevator apartments on a platform over the center leg of the Inner Loop Freeway. Philadelphia hopes to develop air rights construction over its crosstown expressway.[176] On a more modest scale, the San Francisco Housing Authority hopes to build public housing over neighborhood public parking lots.[177] On the national level, the Federal Highway Act of 1961 permitted the use of air space above interstate highways as well as below them, and the Bureau of Public Roads has acted to permit leasing of airspace over freeways constructed under a Federal Aid Program.[178]

Other policy instruments have been developed regarding the utilization of air rights. Thus, "The Housing Act of 1964 authorized federal grants-in-aid to urban renewal projects utilizing air space, if such projects eliminate a blighting influence and if they provide housing and related facilities for low- or moderate-income families. The 1966 Demonstration Cities Act extends this to include construction of foundations and platforms necessary for air rights sites for industrial development."[179]

The use of air rights can be labeled a multiple use of land — though this is a two-dimensional point of view. In a three-dimensional view, there may be tiers of use. Thus, the Pan Am Building is built on air rights over the Grand Central Building complex, in turn built on air rights over railroad facilities. The Pan Am Building has in turn allocated its air rights to a heliport on its roof.

(Chicago: American Institute of Real Estate Appraisers, 1965); Walter R. Kuehnle, "Air and Tunnel Rights, Yesterday and Tomorrow" (Speech given at American Institute of Real Estate Appraisers conference, Honolulu, 1967); District of Columbia Department of Highways and Traffic, *The Joint Development of Housing and Freeways* (1967); Alexandria, Virginia, Department of City Planning and Urban Renewal, *Air Rights*, Special Report No. 12 (1967).

[176] *Philadelphia Inquirer*, September 23, 1967, p. 19.

[177] Letter from San Francisco Housing Authority, August 31, 1967. The project has received tentative approval from the Housing Assistance Administration of HUD.

[178] Hill, *Air Rights and Their Use in Los Angeles*, pp. 1, 4.

[179] Alexandria, Virginia, Department of City Planning and Urban Renewal, *Air Rights*, p. 3.

Again, multiple benefits may be involved; for example, an apartment building, utilizing air rights, is scheduled to be built over a three-story school in the Bronx. Aside from the school and residential functions on the same site, presumably there is the benefit of increased safety for the schoolchildren because they will be able to go to school without crossing the street.

The value of air rights involves a number of factors. It will consist of the capitalized value of the use of the three-dimensional space involved (that is, the marginal product of the slabs of space discussed earlier) minus additional costs arising from that use. The additional costs will include: (1) costs of the structures needed to attain access to the space — platforms, stilts, piers, caissons, etc.; (2) additional costs imposed on the surface use of the space — thus, if airspace use involves setting an expressway in a tunnel, there will be additional costs of ventilating and lighting the tunnel; (3) externalities to both sets of uses. The externalities may involve both economies and diseconomies. Some will be internalized. Thus, apartments over an expressway will obviously have good access to the expressway, but may have access problems with respect to some other streets. Land development costs may be jointly shared. On the negative side, space users above an expressway will have pollution problems including noise, fumes, and carbon monoxide. The latter is disturbing since it will not be an obvious difficulty to those affected. Again, drivers are liable to be somewhat worse off in a tunnel than on an open stretch of road. (This involves ventilation, safety, and view.)

The George Washington Bridge apartment development is a case in point. John White developed an estimated value of air rights for this case, and his steps are presented in Table 16. He estimates air rights as $6.90 per square foot, which is .46 of his estimate of the full value of the land in question ($15.00 per square foot). The purchaser paid $8.15 a square foot; part of the discrepancy, however, can be explained by subsidies granted by the city and state. The city reduced the property tax by granting a 40 per cent tax abatement, and the state provided a 90 per cent loan on the total project cost at an interest rate of 5 per cent. (The investor, however, was limited to a 5 per cent return on his equity.) Further, some additional costs were borne in building the road so that air right construction was feasible. Finally, any additional costs imposed on drivers are neglected. Hence, in this example, the social value of the air rights are probably somewhat less than half the land value.

In addition, though the disutility of fumes and noise to apartment tenants was included as an offset item, it may have been underestimated. Some of the tenants have complained about the pollution problem, and a group calling itself "Citizens for Clean Air" is exploring ways of bridging the open spaces between buildings to cut down the noise and fumes.[180]

[180] *New York Times*, June 17, 1967. One tenant moved from the fourteenth to the twenty-eighth floor to get away from the fumes, but stated "we have to rent air conditioners from the management in order to keep the windows closed [to avoid fumes]." It was claimed that some tenants were moving with the expiration of their leases. The building manager acknowledged some tenant turnover, but would not give details.

Table 16. Air Right Value per Square Foot of Apartments Over George Washington Bridge on Approaches

Item	Value per square foot
Estimated land value (full value of ground and space)	$15.00
Concrete deck on reinforced columns	−11.50
Savings to air right buyer (excavation costs avoided, previous tenant relocation avoided)	+5.75
Estimated fume and noise effect: loss in utility to ultimate consumers and consequent loss in value to air rights builder	−1.00
Extra interest charges reflecting additional construction time involved	−1.35
Estimated value of air rights to purchaser	6.90
Actual value to purchaser; i.e., purchase price paid[a]	8.15
Additional costs borne by road builder, not included above	−1.50
Additional costs borne by drivers, not included above	?
Social value of air rights	$6.65−

[a] Discrepancy can be explained by city subsidy (reduced property tax) and state subsidy (low interest rate on large state mortgage).

Source: John R. White, "George Washington Bridge Approach," in Walter R. Kuehnle *et al., Case Studies in Air Rights and Subsurface Tunnel Road Easements* (Chicago: American Institute of Real Estate Appraisers, 1965), pp. 29–38.

Several generalizations emerge. First, the direct costs of utilizing air rights (platforms, stilts, etc.) can be quite high. This implies that for the present and for some time in the future, only central city locations are economically feasible for air rights construction. Thus, the George Washington Bridge case involved costs of around $8.50 per square foot. In Philadelphia, platform costs to cover three miles of the Crosstown Expressway are estimated at $12 to $15 per square foot.[181] The Philadelphia highway planners are now considering buildings on stilts. But this brings in the second generalization, which is that the costs of fumes and noise — either direct or indirect — can be quite high above expressways. Certainly, fumes and noise can be reduced, but the reduction involves a fair amount of cost — perhaps equal to the difference between the Philadelphia continuous platform costs and the George Washington Bridge costs, say around $5 per square foot.[182]

The development of air rights structures may be part of a discerned trend toward the integration of roads and buildings. Thus, Gutheim notes a number of cases moving

[181] *Philadelphia Inquirer*, August 23, 1967, p. 19. Bernard, *Air Space in Urban Development*, p. 13, quotes Nelson, *Appraisal Journal* (October 1955), to the effect that additional costs for air rights construction range from $4 to $20 per square foot in Chicago. Kuehnle, in his Honolulu speech, estimates central air rights value as 80 per cent of land values, indicating "costs" of $20 to $40 per square foot.

[182] Archibald Rogers of the American Institute of Architects argues that air pollution and noise problems can be solved by means of a platform consisting of a continuous slab, eliminating the open space between buildings. The *Washington Post*, July 26, 1967. He did not compare costs of alternatives, however.

toward this, including "an endless four-story building topped by a highway and related parking facilities [which] winds through the heart of Tokyo."[183]

A number of dome and mall developments can be fitted into this trend; there is an integration of "outside" and "inside" as well.

Thus, a number of cities plan to follow Houston's lead by constructing domed, air-conditioned, and heated sports stadiums.[184] And there are a number of examples of enclosed air-conditioned shopping malls, involving the glassing-in and air-conditioning of city streets.[185] Victor Gruen predicts that such developments will lead to the "rebirth of downtown core areas" in the United States.[186] Meyerson notes that conversion of streets to pedestrian malls is inexpensive, but that often the conversions are ineffective and short-lived.[187]

Long-Term Forecasts and Visions

Long-term forecasts about urban space can be grouped in terms of position taken on growing up versus growing out. There are those who foresee a continuing decline in centrality, at least in a relative sense, with much more spread over the urban plane. New town enthusiasts might be classified as a subgroup here. Others foresee a reversal of dispersion, greater concentration, and recentralization. And some take an in-between, perhaps best of both worlds, position. Let us consider some examples, both of forecasts of what is to come and visions of what ought to come.

INCREASED DISPERSAL

Around the turn of the century, Frank Lloyd Wright predicted that the future would involve a race between the elevator and the automobile, and the wise man would bet on the automobile.[188] This has been a fairly good bet for a number of years. The automobile, of course, has been a major source of urban dispersal. The dispersal predictors see the race becoming more one-sided, with reduced costs of communication, as well as transportation, involved. Melvin Webber takes this tack, albeit with some caution: "It is helpful to view the spatial city as a communication system. Space intervenes as friction, but transportation-communication changes are cost-reducing and space-expanding. The nodally concentric form could give way to nearly homogeneous dispersion. Recent and imminent developments are ambiguous, and a very hetero-

---

[183] Frederick Gutheim, "The Crunch of Concrete," *The Reporter* (September 28, 1961), p. 47. and cf. Hans Blumenfeld, "The Role of Design," *Journal of the American Institute of Planners* (September 1967), p. 308, on the assimilation of the skyscraper to the "extra human scale" of the expressway.

[184] The *Chicago Tribune* lists Atlanta, Pittsburgh, Philadelphia, New York, Boston, St. Louis, and Detroit in an editorial, "Will Chicago Be Left Behind?" July 15, 1967.

[185] Perhaps the most notable case is Rochester, New York. See Victor Gruen, *The Heart of Our Cities*, pp. 300–20; in particular, p. 312.

[186] Quoted in *Washington Star*, August 25, 1967.

[187] Meyerson, *Face of the Metropolis*, p. 190.

[188] Hugh Dalziel Duncan, "The Chicago School: Principles," in Arthur Siegel (ed.), *Chicago's Famous Buildings* (University of Chicago Press, 1965), p. 4.

geneous pattern is most likely. Yet the pressures for concentration and concentricity are ebbing, and the effects of counter processes will be increasingly manifest."[189]

Ullman takes a similar tack: "As Lovelace remarks, the underground system of sewers and water mains is about all that is holding the city together." He predicts that "the high grade activities characteristic of the top hierarchical position of the CBD will abandon it for centers better located to serve high income areas." The CBD will become one of many centers. Further, many activities apparently do not require the face-to-face contact that generates centrality. To the argument that sprawl is subsidized by government policy, he counters that (1) there are countervailing policies — e.g., urban renewal — and (2) this is the way things are, given the clash of interest groups.[190]

Paul Baran of The RAND Corporation forecasts that "buying-at-home-by-TV will be the last step away from the big city. Information consoles will be as commonplace as telephones. One or more wall panels in every kitchen will function as lighted blackboards to display information of the household's choosing. Cities will shrink to habitation maxima of 100,000 to 200,000."[191]

Put some of these innovations under a geodesic dome and you get Athelstan Spilhaus' Experimental City, an extreme variant of the new town. "Dispersal, not renewal, is the answer to the problems of the city." The old cities must go. "Without exception they are hopelessly bound by tradition and the abortions of their historical development." The Experimental City will have video phones; computers to unify shopping, charging, and banking; household computer terminals. Tunnels will serve autos and trucks entering from outside; all utilities will be routed through underground tunnels and ducts so that street excavations will be unnecessary. Travel within the city will be by some revolutionary form of public transport. There will be no need for zoning since factories will not be allowed to generate noise and pollution. Population will be limited to about 250,000, and each Experimental City will be separated from others by at least 100 miles of countryside.[192]

DISPERSAL REVERSAL

In response to the argument that advances in communication will greatly reduce differences in access, and hence lead to dispersion, Boris Pushkarev emphasizes face-to-face contact, and the centralizing impact of other innovations:

[189] Webber, "Order in Diversity...," pp. 42–46. The material quoted has been spliced together from a number of passages, with some incidental rearrangement.

[190] Ullman, *The Nature of Cities Reconsidered*, pp. 86–93. He refers to Eldridge Lovelace, "Urban Sprawl Need Not Be a Tragedy," *Landscape Architecture* (1961), pp. 230–31. For the opposite view on subsidies, see Gaffney, "Containment Policies for Urban Sprawl."

[191] Reported by John Lear, in "Science and the Peace Adventure," *Saturday Review* (September 23, 1967), pp. 64–65.

[192] This description is based on articles in *Newsweek* (January 8, 1968), pp. 44–45, Walter Sullivan, "A Smokeless, Noiseless, Trafficless City," *New York Times*, December 31, 1967, E. 7; and Athelstan Spilhaus, "The Experimental City," *Science* (February 16, 1968).

Group decisions and many life situations require a projection of personality, a commitment that calls for a face-to-face as well as voice-to-ear or eye-to-eye relationship. . . . [Again] increases in speed have required fewer, not more terminals due to scale economies. The automobile made a more even distribution of activities possible, but its short range confined its effects within metropolitan areas . . . . The possibility of a new decentralizing effect is raised by vertical take-off aircraft [but] . . . a much greater payoff can probably be expected from fixed path systems operating on the ground or under it. . . . The odds in the field of transportation technology seem to favor more clustering.[193]

In the race between the automobile and the elevator, the elevator is still in the running. Thus, a number of forecasters stress the megastructure. For example, Fitch argues:

The upper half of future skyscraper cities might well be residential, the middle zone institutional, the lower zone commercial and manufacturing. In such an urban structure, daily commutation would involve a vertical trip of thirty stories instead of a horizontal trip of many miles.

The skyscraper of the future should be served by aerial streets at every eight or ten stories. In office buildings, these aerial streets would offer the range of amenities and services required for a business district—restaurants, cafes, bars, specialty shops. . . . In residential skyscrapers, the flying streets would have the normal facilities of the neighborhood—shops . . . playgrounds . . . movies, churches, etc. Public and private transportation—wheeled traffic of all sorts— would be carried by special streets at some intermediate plane, e.g. at the thirtieth floor for a group of forty-five-story skyscrapers.[194]

Tyler and Asiala have applied systems engineering to the planning of the city of the future; in effect, they place megastructures in a circle and connect them with linear moving sidewalks and a circumferential transportation system. The circle would be a mile in diameter; the buildings would consist of 12 pairs of massive towers, about 100 stories high; population for this city would be 250,000; and "super modules of such clusters, say ten miles in diameter" would complete the circumferential metropolis. Automobiles would be banned from the center of the circle, which would be devoted to recreation. Building balconies would function as sidewalks.[195]

The megastructure can be viewed as the multipurpose building described above, grown bigger and better. Alternatively, air rights developments could evolve into "platform cities" as seen by Young:

The apparent "ground level" of whole towns—and in larger cities the central business districts, at very least—would be given over entirely to green landscapes and uncluttered side-

[193] Regional Plan Association, *The Region's Growth* (New York, 1967), pp. 18–19.

[194] Fitch, *American Building I*, pp. 296–98. And see the *Wall Street Journal*, "Shape of the Future," (January 30, 1967), pp. 1, 14: "Immense complexes may achieve heights of 200 or more stories, containing apartments for tens of thousands of families, along with offices, shops and recreational areas. In theory, residents would hardly ever have to step outside."

[195] Vernal M. Tyler and Carl F. Asiala, Jr., *The Aero Space Role in Planning Cities of the Future* (McDonnell Company, 1966).

walks. All or most buildings would be erected on stilts [and] automobiles could be shunted into underground parking areas, their drivers traveling by escalator onto the beautiful plateau [above].[196]

The underground developments in Montreal and Toronto appear to be in this line of development, save in a reverse direction: autos go above, and pedestrians below. Hoffman's massive tunneling projects might fit either variant.

In the megastructure vision, buildings take over some of the functions of the street and transportation system; in the multilevel vision, the street and transportation system is integrated into or becomes part of the buildings.

DISPERSAL AND CONCENTRATION

Some observers have it both ways, forecasting both greater dispersal (at the fringe) and greater concentration (at the center). Thus, for the city fifty years hence, Wheaton envisions "low density origin zones," "other activity zones," and "high-density zones."[197] The low-density zones will have low densities indeed, essentially involving sprawl as an accepted way of life. They will fill a large part of the space between the higher density zones. There will be detailed separation of land use at the street level, so that residential areas are unimpaired, but there will be a much higher mixture of land uses at the neighborhood level than has prevailed in the past. The "other activity zones" will contain mixed uses, but generally there will be focus on a specific function; e.g., education, health. The areas near airports will fit under this category; airports have a propensity to generate office and hotel building because of their convenience as regional meeting places. Finally, on the high-density zone, he writes,

It seems clear that in a city of 50 million there will be numerous high-density zones of a character quite different from the central business district as it is now known.

These high-density zones will probably ultimately consist of single or linked structures containing residential, office, and retail facilities for several hundred thousand people. . . .

In a four-block length of Sixth Avenue in New York City the equivalent of such a complex has been built within the last five years in the most primitive form imaginable. It consists of eight skyscraper office buildings and hotels. If that complex had been built on top of a ten-story parking lot with aerial ramps to the surrounding freeway system, mechanical walkways between buildings at the 20th- and 40th-story levels, and mechanical circulation from the underground subway serving it, we would today have the kind of high-density zone of which we will have many examples in the future.[198]

[196] Warren R. Young, "What's to Come," *Life* Magazine Special Issue: *The U.S. City* (December 24, 1965), p. 146.

[197] William Wheaton, "Form and Structure of the Metropolitan Area," in William R. Ewald, Jr. (ed.), *Environment for Man*, pp. 157–84.

[198] *Ibid.*, pp. 167–68. And see Hoover, "The Evolving Form. . .of the Metropolis," pp. 271–78, for a set of forecasts that fit into the intermediate category of both increased concentration and dispersion.

CONCLUSION

These prophecies and visions involve something more than social-science fiction. The line between what will be and what ought to be is generally a shifting thing, so that forecasts of fact often assimilate value elements and rather easily transmute into policy prescriptions. A few value positions, in response, seem germane. First, it seems worth the effort to make value positions explicit, that is, to note what values and whose values are involved in the vision of the good life in the future urban plane. As a variant, it is worth noting that different people have different life styles and personal visions of the good life, and planning and policy, ranging from mundane here-and-now matters to exciting prescriptions for Utopia, ought to take account of this. This sort of proposition tends to command universal assent, save in practice. Finally, economics as a discipline (and application thereof under the guise of benefit-cost analysis) has a great deal to contribute to the policy, planning, and prophecy process. In particular, it brings about a focus on such matters as substitution, mobility of resources, trade-offs, and a concern with foregone opportunities. For example, in the Spilhaus Experimental City, it seems likely that many of the infrastructure items postulated make economic sense only at the high density core of an urban complex. The complete suppression of pollution disregards the notion that some pollution is "optimal": suppression beyond that point generates more costs than benefits. Or another case in point: new zoning height regulations in many cities will generate high-rise buildings in large open plazas. Presumably, "amenity" is generated. Planners think so, anyway. But even if people, in general, enjoy and benefit from the large amount of open space (and that *is* open to question), there is a neglect of the cost side of the equation. Distance between buildings is increased to the pedestrian, and the construction of connecting passageways between buildings becomes more costly, perhaps impossible. Putting it generally, the full field of urban space planning and policy seems ripe for some tough-minded benefit-cost arithmetic.

Appendix

This appendix summarizes procedures used in developing estimates of property value for nineteen large cities. (These estimates appear in Table 5.)

Netzer presents information on single-family housing assessment ratios and on ratios for part of all other property.[199] This part refers to property with assessed values below a certain cutoff point (usually $300,000), and includes vacant land, multiple family housing, and commercial and industrial property. The assessment ratios for the cutoff group is divided by the single-family housing ratio and three classes are defined as follows: (1) cutoff/single-family above 1.05, (2) cutoff/single-family below .95, and (3) cutoff/single-family between .95 and 1.05.

The cities Netzer presents, by class, appear in Table A–1.

Cities with a population above 500,000 in 1960 were selected as a subgroup to be analyzed. Information was available for nineteen of the twenty-one cities in this group (only New Orleans and San Antonio were excluded).

[199] Dick Netzer, *The Economics of the Property Tax.*

Table A-1. *Classification of Cities by Relative Assessment Ratios*

Group	Assessment ratio of "other property" relative to assessment ratio of single-family housing	Cities
1	Above 1.05	New York, Chicago, Cleveland, San Francisco, Pittsburgh, Seattle
2	Below .95	Los Angeles, St. Louis, Dallas, San Diego (county), Atlanta (part), Kansas City
3	Between .95 and 1.05	Philadelphia, Detroit, Baltimore, Houston, Washington, Milwaukee, Boston, Buffalo (county), Cincinnati, Minneapolis, Newark

Source: Dick Netzer, *Economics of the Property Tax* (The Brookings Institution, 1966), Table 4–1 and Table 7–3.

The following procedures and assumptions were employed:

1. Data on Washington, D.C., were directly available in the U.S. Bureau of the Census, *Census of Government* statistics.

2. For the other cities, the assessment ratio for the cutoff group net of single-family homes was obtained on the basis of given information (*Census of Government* and Netzer).

3. State assessment ratios for vacant land generally were well below single-family housing ratios. The same situation prevailed for Washington, D.C.; on the basis of this evidence, it was assumed that the relative ratios for states applied to cities within those states. The assessment ratio for remaining classes of property was then obtained net of vacant land. Remaining classes of property included "other residential" (multiple-family housing), and commercial-industrial.

4. For cities with a cutoff ratio approximately equal to or below the single-family house ratio (cities in groups 2 and 3 in Table A–1), it was assumed that the "other residential" and the commercial-industrial assessment ratios were equal. For cities with cutoff ratio above the single-family house ratio (group 1 in Table 8), it was assumed that assessment ratios varied within the remaining classes of property. As a means of obtaining an initial approximation of these values, use was made of Netzer's conclusion[200] that, relative to single-family residential, the following assessment ratios held for multiple-family housing:

$$2\text{–}4 \text{ family ratio} = 1.0 \text{ single family ratio}$$
$$5\text{–}49 \quad\text{''}\qquad\text{''} = 1.25 \quad\text{''}\qquad\text{''}\qquad\text{''}$$
$$50+ \quad\text{''}\qquad\text{''} = 1.50 \quad\text{''}\qquad\text{''}\qquad\text{''}$$

In conjunction with *Census of Housing* data, and the assumption that the commercial-industrial assessment ratio equaled the 50+ family ratio, an iterative process moved

[200] *Ibid.*, p. 301.

Table A–2. Estimated Assessment Ratios by Class of Property for Nineteen Large Cities, 1961

City	Single-family homes	Other residential[a]	Commercial-industrial[a]	All other[a] (primarily vacant land)
New York	.476	.673	.800	.377
Chicago	.355	.493	.600	.269
Los Angeles	.202	.142	.142	.140
Philadelphia	.577	.588	.588	.357
Detroit	.429	.430	.430	.403
Baltimore	.667	.671	.671	.406
Houston[b]	.185	.211	.211	.118
Cleveland	.354	.386	.530	.216
Washington, D.C.	.472	.514	.538	.207
St. Louis	.356	.216	.216	.279
Milwaukee	.484	.487	.487	.388
San Francisco	.118	.188	.310	.082
Boston	.346	.351	.351	.234
Dallas[b]	.185	.130	.130	.118
Pittsburgh	.358	.493	.670	.221
San Diego[b]	.211	.140	.140	.146
Seattle	.139	.172	.200	.092
Buffalo[b]	.273	.274	.274	.216
Cincinnati	.433	.446	.446	.264

[a] Estimated.

[b] County assessment ratios employed. Assessment ratio information not available for central city.

from initial values to a final set of values, which checked with the net figures developed in step 3. Results appear in Table A–2.

Given assessment ratios, property values could be estimated directly by dividing property tax by assessment ratio. These results appear in Table 4 (page 108).

4

Open (uncovered) space as a new urban resource

Marion Clawson

Director of Land Use and Management Program,
Resources for the Future

Open (uncovered) space as a new urban resource

Marion Clawson

The rapid contemporary urbanization of the United States, and indeed of the whole world, has stimulated new and intense interest in "open space."[1] The term itself has several meanings, and under nearly any meaning there are various forms of open space. Later, we shall discuss various meanings and forms, but for the present we may consider open space as all geographical area (land or water), within or reasonably adjacent to a city or urban concentration, which is not covered by buildings or other permanent structures. From this very inclusive definition, we shall later exclude some kinds of uncovered space as not truly being "open."

The term "open space" is, in some respects, unfortunate; all too often its connotations have been negative — the absence of something, rather than the presence of a positive value. The positive features of open space might readily be emphasized more.[2] Open space is coming to be, in professional literature, a shorthand description of the many uses of land which require that there be no buildings upon the land; but, even within professional circles and still more within popular ones, it connotes lack of land use. This is one factor behind the frequent attempts to invade open areas with some type of nonconforming use. In spite of the limitations of the term, none seems to be better.

Space, to be meaningful at the level of personal experience, must be bounded, it must not stretch indefinitely. Interplanetary and interstellar space, it is true, does stretch indefinitely as far as human perception can determine, and that is one of the reasons that space programs are so difficult of true understanding. But space on the surface of the earth must have a boundary, an end, and the boundary may be established in any one of several ways. An open square within a city may be surrounded by high office or apartment buildings which effectively bound the space to the pedestrian; a suburban park may have only some unobtrusive trees or shrubs or even residences across the street as its boundary; and numerous intermediate degrees of bounding exist.

The interface between open and closed space may often be critical. The form and use of the outer edge of the closed space may greatly influence, if not determine, the use of the open space. It has often been remarked that the outside of a building belongs, in some sense, to the public, while the interior belongs to its occupants. Tall downtown buildings surely cast their shadow, figuratively as well as literally, over any open space that may lie between them. If one includes sidewalks and streets as open space, then advertising signs hung from buildings, as well as the actual store fronts, greatly influence the use of the open space — favorably as well as unfavorably. But,

---

[1] Bibliographic references are presented in the appendix to this chapter.

[2] Marion Clawson, "A Positive Approach to Open Space Preservation," *Journal of the American Institute of Planners*, Vol. XXVIII, No. 2 (May 1962).

aside from physical dominance, public or social control over private land use bordering open space surely provides some difficult problems of economics, administration, equity, and law. These problems, like all problems, would yield, at least in part, to determined and competent research.

The public always has major interest in open space within urban areas, even privately owned open space not available for entry by others than the owners. In this latter case, the perspectives of buildings and the vistas which the open space provides may be important. More commonly, at some time, some portion of the public uses the open space, in terms of occupancy and activity, even when legal title to the space is in other private hands. Some such privately owned open space has been made available for the use of other people voluntarily and upon decision by the owner; more commonly, however, it has been done to comply with some publicly determined rule, such as building setbacks from a street. Where legal title to the open space is in public hands, the public-private relationship shifts to the boundary of the open space. Under almost every imaginable circumstance of urban open space, there are unavoidable divergences of interest between some private property owners and some portion of the general public. The definition of the interests of each, reconciliation of differences, provision of the greatest total values achievable from the natural resources under the existing circumstances, and fair treatment of all interests provide many difficult problems which must be dealt with in some way.

Functions and Forms of Open Space

Open space within or adjacent to a city may perform one or more of the following functions:[3]

1. Provide light and air to buildings, especially to tall buildings in city centers;

2. Provide perspective and vistas of the urban scene, again especially in the more heavily built-up areas of a city.[4] This may alternatively be considered as a means of relief from the feeling of crowding, discussed below, or of the physical oppression which would result if all buildings were crowded to their physical limits;

3. Provide recreation in the broadest sense of that term, with a very wide range of specific activities;

4. Provide ecological protection of important values, such as recharge to groundwater, or prevention of flood damage in flood-prone areas, preservation of unique areas, and the like;

5. Serve as city-forming devices or influences, so that one part of a large metropolitan complex is distinguished from its neighbors, rather than merging completely with them; and

---

[3] Clawson, "A Positive Approach..."; see also Jeanne M. Davis, "Getting and Keeping Open Space," *A Place to Live: The Yearbook of Agriculture* (U.S. Department of Agriculture, 1963).

[4] Elizabeth Beazley, *Design and Detail of the Space Between Buildings* (London: Architectural Press, 1960); Kevin Lynch, *Site Planning* (M.I.T. Press, 1962).

6. Reserve presently vacant areas for one or more of these uses, or for more active public uses, such as schools, at some future date. In this case, the emphasis is not so much upon present use of the area as upon keeping it available for future use.

Transportation arteries — streets, highways, railroads, canals, airports, etc.— are open space in the sense that they are not covered by buildings. Even though their use for purposes other than transportation is limited, they do provide vistas of buildings and of other features of the landscape even in the most highly developed central business districts of our largest cities. Moreover, a great deal of recreation takes place on city streets, in the form of children playing, of children and adults visiting along the sidewalks, and in other ways. A considerable amount of business is often transacted upon the sidewalk, even in the United States where sidewalk merchants are controlled or prohibited. The importance of transportation arteries as open space lies in part in their extent: in most cities or urban groupings of population, transportation is the chief use of perhaps 30 per cent of the land.[5] In the United States, the various forms of transportation have almost never been planned, developed, and managed consciously as open space; the dominant consideration has always been the transportation function. Later, we shall suggest that streets could be designed to provide equally good transportation and also serve a valuable open space role in a much better way than most of them do today. The same viewpoint is expressed in different terms in the chapter of this book by Wilfred Owen.

Parks, parkways, open squares, and other publicly owned open space within or adjacent to cities often include areas of widely varying sizes, shapes, physical characteristics, and uses. Recreation, in the broadest sense, is a common chief purpose; but recreation in turn includes an extremely wide range of activities, from merely sitting down to enjoy a pleasant view to the most active kind of sports. The provision of a perspective or vista upon man-made improvements, or the sheer relief from sensations of crowding, may also be important values to such areas. Although at one time most park specialists felt that a park had to exceed some minimum extent if it were to be usable, in recent years we have seen that highly valuable parks could be created on very small tracks of land, particularly in the downtown parts of cities. Odd-shaped pieces of land, land too steep or too poorly drained for economical construction, land mined out for gravel or stone, and many other kinds of land situations lend themselves to open space uses.

Space around public buildings often has important open space values. Public buildings are usually built with a considerable amount of open land surrounding the actual structure — sometimes with quite extensive open grounds, landscaped in various degrees of excellence. Sometimes, indeed, such open space around public buildings constitutes parks or public use areas of the type described above; but, even where the grounds are not so extensive, they may still provide attractive views of surrounding buildings as well as of the space itself.

---

[5] Harland Bartholomew, *Land Uses in American Cities* (Harvard University Press, 1955). For an analysis of his data, see Marion Clawson, R. Burnell Held, and Charles H. Stoddard, *Land for the Future* (The Johns Hopkins Press for Resources for the Future, Inc., 1960).

In most cities, there is a substantial amount of open or unbuilt-upon space around private buildings. Setbacks from the sidewalk are required in American cities, both in business districts and in residential areas. Open backyards are very common in residential areas consisting of single-family dwellings, and apartment houses are often surrounded by some open land. A great deal of this privately owned open space is not available to any use by the public which involves the actual presence of the user upon the land. But sometimes it is open to some limited public use, such as walking; and even when it is closed to any occupancy, attractive and valuable vistas may be provided. The backyard of a single-family dwelling is usually open only to the owner and his guests; yet its trees may provide a pleasant general neighborhood environment and the absence of impervious covering may be important in watershed management for the whole community.

Open space on rivers, lakes, and other water bodies and along their shores often has special importance as an urban resource. Most of the larger older cities were built on navigable water. Today, although water navigation may be much less important to the cities than when they were built, the water body can still function as open space. Water as open space is so important that many artificial bodies of water have been created in recent years, specifically for an urban function. These will be considered in more detail later. Various kinds of direct use of water bodies may be possible — boating of many kinds, water sports, especially water skiing, fishing, hunting, and swimming. In addition to these activities on or in the water, many others are possible along the shore where relatively small strips of land may have high recreational value, in part because the water body contributes to the feeling of spaciousness. Sand beaches are especially prized when the water is fit for swimming, old piers and docks may be useful for sunbathing, and dikes or stream-side protection areas can often provide small parks or viewing areas of great attractiveness. Several cities, notably New York, have been rediscovering their waterfronts as positive open space assets. In any case, even if waterfront and water body alike have been neglected, the water body does provide vistas and perspective which may be lacking in other ways.

In each of the foregoing paragraphs, the recreational uses and vista-creating functions of open space have been stressed. In addition to these uses, open space may be used, consciously or without plan, to perform a city-forming function. In many an American city over the past century, the railroad tracks served to divide the city — "across the tracks" often being synonymous with lower class. Natural streams and lakes also perform this city-forming function; their location being more or less fixed, the city growth could be directed around them. The artificial bodies of water, referred to above, clearly have a city-forming aspect, whether by design or not. The most ambitious use of artificial water bodies to shape a city has apparently been made in Brasília; but Reston and other new American cities which have attracted attention have also used artificial water bodies as part of their planning mechanism.

The foregoing types of open space have been described as they can be seen from a pedestrian's eye-level. But we should not overlook the possibilities of open space at a higher elevation. If one views a city from an elevation of no more than 300 feet (for instance, from a low-flying helicopter or from a very tall building), the city is seen to have a great deal of open space — approximately as much as the site had before the city was built. A sea of rooftops may not be an exhilarating view, and ventilators, elevator housings, and other protuberances may interfere with many possible uses of such open space, although some uses, like sunbathing, do indeed take place. In looking to the more distant future, the urban rooftop may be the unexplored frontier: its use on a large scale, as open space, will present many problems, just as has the use of any frontier, but its areal extent and its location demand serious consideration.

In, and more particularly around, the modern American city there is comparatively a great deal of land not now covered with buildings, and thus open in this sense, yet not specifically reserved for future open space. Sprawl has characterized suburban growth in the United States, especially since World War II, and one major feature of sprawl has been that some lands have been developed while adjacent lands have not. We have estimated that as much land has been "withdrawn" but not used, as has been actually used for urban purposes.[6] These by-passed, leapfrogged, and vacant lands are found in tracts of widely varying size, shape, and physical character. Many of them would make excellent parks or other recreation areas; others would serve admirably as city-forming areas; others provide views and perspective for the developed city. But the fact that all are available for development of some kind makes their openness temporary or at least uncertain. We hesitate, therefore, to designate such lands as open space, although for the present they may serve this function very well.

Although the functions which open space within the urban framework is supposed to perform have been briefly described, it is clear that they have not been defined as precisely as could be wished, and certainly have not been measured in quantitative terms. We do not know what alternative arrangements might fulfill the same functions, possibly even more effectively. Above all, we do not know how much space is needed for any one of these functions. Standards have indeed been proposed, yet many planners and others have called for more objective and more defensible standards, or at least for a great degree of consensus among those who necessarily must use some kind of a standard in their planning work.[7]

Need and Demand for Open Space

An early question must be: Is there a clearly demonstrable and measurable need, or demand, for open space in any or all of its forms? Do the commonly asserted needs or demands merely reflect personal biases, without solid basis in fact — no more substantive than the idle talk of small boys discussing what they would do with a million dollars? While complex issues are involved, it is possible to give the concept of need and demand for open space both theoretical and analytical content.

[6] Clawson *et al.*, *Land for the Future.*
[7] A plea for consensus in open space standards is in Gerald F. Vaughn, "In Search of Standards for Preserving Open Space," *Public Administration Review*, Vol. XXIV, No. 4 (December 1964).

More analytical work has been done on the problems of open space for recreation than on those of open space for other uses; and recreation, imprecise though the term is, is a more clearly defined use of land and water than the other uses of open space that we have enumerated. The consideration of the need and demand for open space for recreation can therefore best precede the consideration of open space for other purposes.

The fact that man plays, as do many other animals, has been widely noted; it is asserted that play and relaxation are necessary for emotional and perhaps for physical and mental health. Recreation is supported by some as a necessary form of self-expression in a complex modern industrial age, when the individual is all too often submerged in an overwhelming and anonymous society. Recreation is also defended as a means of reducing juvenile delinquency and other socially deviant behavior. The frequency of assertion of these viewpoints, often by men of long and varied experience, and the obvious sincerity and conviction with which these views are held, should give even the most cynical critic pause.

There have indeed been many who doubted these claims for recreation in general and for use of outdoor natural resources for this purpose in particular. Whether or not the doubters have been as numerous as the advocates, one cannot say; they have been less vocal, at least in print. One can indeed safely say that the usual claims of human need for recreation rest on intuitive experience, not upon carefully devised and conducted experimentation; and quantification of such asserted need, which would be necessary if one were to judge the rationality of different amounts of expenditure for different kinds of recreation, has been totally lacking — if indeed not impossible.

There is another approach, however. Without either denying or affirming the asserted need, one can measure the demand for recreation — what people are willing to do, including what they are willing to give up, for it. Research in the past decade has shown clearly that it is possible to measure the demand for recreation of various kinds, and for the open space or other natural resources needed for it, as readily as it is possible to measure the demand for almost any other good or service; and, from such estimates of the demand curve, one can compare the value of resources or expenditures for alternative uses, of which recreation would be one.[8]

In order to measure the demand for recreation, it is necessary to start with the concept of the whole recreation experience.[9] This has five fairly identifiable phases:

[8] This is essentially the position which Jack L. Knetsch and I took in our book, *Economics of Outdoor Recreation* (The Johns Hopkins Press for Resources for the Future, Inc., 1966), see especially Chapter 3. See the footnote on page 51 which lists a number of studies published at the time this book was written. The article which preceded all these studies, and in some measure was the source of the methods used in all of them, was "Methods of Measuring the Demand for and Value of Outdoor Recreation," by Marion Clawson (RFF Reprint Number 10, 1959); for a fuller statement of the methodology, see Jack L. Knetsch, "Outdoor Recreation Demands and Benefits," *Land Economics* (November 1963).

[9] These ideas were first presented in published form, and are illustrated graphically, in Marion Clawson, *Land and Water for Recreation* (Rand McNally & Company, 1963); see especially Chapter 3.

(1) anticipation or planning, in which the person or group involved decides what it wants to do, where, when, and how much of its limited income or economic resources it wishes to commit to this activity (practically, this is the stage where most of the expenditures for outdoor recreation are made, before the recreationist ever leaves home); (2) travel from home to the site, however far and long that travel may be, and however much it may cost; (3) on-site experiences, which are often looked upon as if they were the whole of the recreation experience; (4) travel from the site home again, perhaps over the same route, perhaps over a different one, but in either case in a different psychological frame of mind and possibly in a different income situation; and (5) recollection, when the impressions of the earlier phases are relived, and often repeated verbally for others, and perhaps magnified or modified, yet from which perhaps more true satisfactions are received than from any other phase.

The whole recreation experience must be looked at as a "package deal," both on the income and on the cost sides. The costs may be one or more of several kinds: money, as for any other good or service purchased; time, which represents an expenditure or outlay against a fixed total supply available to the individual and is often far scarcer than money; travel, which might have a positive value but often has a negative one; effort, as when one walks to the recreation site; and possibly others. The satisfactions may also take various forms; and, since much recreation involves family or other groups, satisfactions may accrue to others as well as to the chief actor or evaluator. Poor food or a dirty rest room en route may, at least for some, detract from the inspiring view at the destination.

Demand for the whole recreation experience can be measured empirically in a given situation. Instead of the use of time-series data which is customary in most empirical studies of demand, the consumers (users) must be stratified geographically into groups whose costs of obtaining the recreation experience (or its price, to them) differ. (Theoretically, the time-series approach would be applicable to recreation demand analysis, although the problems of correcting for concurrent changes in income, leisure, personal tastes, etc. would be very great; practically, time-series cost data are unavailable and likely to remain so for the indefinite future.) Concentric zones, of equal distance or of equal time removed from the recreation site, can be established; and the numbers of visitors from each such zone determined for a specific period of time — annually, seasonally, or for sample days. Since the total population within each distance zone varies, numbers of visits must be reduced to a per-thousand-of-base-population basis, just as consumption of other goods is often placed on a per capita basis. The result is a schedule of volume (numbers of visits from each zone, in relation to total population residing there) and of prices (average cost per visit, for the whole experience) — these are the basic elements of a demand curve for any commodity or service.

This process and the relationships in one specific case are illustrated in Table 1. A substantial number of visitors to this area came from less than 50 miles away; since the total population in this zone was relatively small, visits per 1,000 base population were large, and costs per party visit were relatively low, measured either in dollars

Table 1.   *Visits to Lewis and Clark Lake in Relation to Total Population, and Expenditures per Visit (Party of Four), by Distance Zones, Summer 1959*

Distance zone[a]	Population 1950	Estimated visits June, July, August 1959	Visits per 1,000 base population	Average one-way distance	Estimated cost per visit (party of four)
	(thousands)	*(thousands)*		*(miles)*	
1. Less than 50 miles	88	333	3,784	18	$ 3.70
2. 50–100 miles	407	363	892	70	13.80
3. 100–150 miles	474	50	106	123	27.10
4. 150–200 miles	1,055	161	153	175	37.90
5. Over 200 miles, in survey area	5,558	20	4	228	41.25

[a] Determined from state highway maps; distance from county seat to power house at Gavins Point Dam.

Source: Adapted from Table 1 in "A Measurement of the Demand for Recreational Facilities at Lewis and Clark Lake," by John S. Evans and Carlton S. Van Doren, *Business Review Supplement* (Vermillion, S.D.: Business Research Bureau, School of Business, State University of South Dakota, February 1960).

or in miles travelled (and also in time, although this is not shown in the table). As one moves to more distant zones, the total number of visitors changes erratically, but visits per 1,000 base population change rather regularly and inversely to costs per visit. An irregularity between the third and fourth zones is indeed apparent; while complete data are lacking, this seems to be due to differences in the income levels of the population in these two zones.

This particular example is for outdoor recreation of a predominantly one-day outing type, these people must travel some distance, incur considerable costs in time, travel, and money; and get a bundle of satisfactions from the various phases of the whole experience. Few if any of them combine experience at this site with other experiences at other locations; in this respect, the one-day recreation experience is a cleaner and neater example than the typical vacation where friends are visited, sight-seeing is done in various places, and other recreational activities undertaken as part of a total package.

But this approach can be used for recreational activities within a city, which take but a few hours and involve no cash costs. In an as yet unpublished paper, Robin Mabey and Sylvia Law of the Greater London Council have shown that distances people are willing to walk to city parks is partly a function of the total number of people within the zone of origin. They have been able to establish volume (number of visitors in relation to number of residents within zone of origin) and price (distance walked) relationships for a considerable number of local parks in London.

When this approach to demand for outdoor recreation was first used, it was considered novel by some — and, indeed, may still be so considered by those who have not studied it carefully. The remarkable thing about this approach, however, is not its novelty but rather its close similarity to the empirical study of demand for any other service or commodity. A brief consideration of some of the factors involved in demand for any commodity or service will show how very similar is the demand for outdoor recreation to the demand for almost anything else:

1. Characteristics of the commodity or service are involved. One must define the commodity or service — Northern Hard Red Wheat, grade 2; or choice beefsteak; or the whole experience for outdoor recreation of the intermediate type.[10] There are problems of specifying units of volume — bushels, pounds, recreation days, etc. There are also matters of quality in the commodity or service; these obviously differ from one commodity or service to another.

2. Characteristics of the consumer are perhaps equally important. His income, his available leisure, his tastes (which often reflect his past experience), perhaps his age, education, occupation, or other socioeconomic characteristics, and other personal traits may or will affect his demand for the service or commodity under study. The characteristics which are important for outdoor recreation may or may not be important in the demand for bread, beefsteak, or automobiles; income is nearly always an important characteristic, others are more special to the particular commodity or service.

3. Alternative sources of supply of the same or closely similar commodity or service, or of other physically different commodities or services which may nevertheless provide similar or alternative personal satisfactions, are also involved. Pork or chicken may be a substitute for beef, or rice for wheat, etc. In the case of recreation, there are not only other areas at different locations but also, in some cases, literally intervening opportunities — parks driven or walked by in order to reach the destination. The alternative to outdoor recreation may be indoor activity of some kind.

4. Cost or price of the commodity or service demanded or consumed is another characteristic. For most commodities or services purchased, we consider only the money cost, although distance, time, and other factors in shopping may influence the amount, location, and/or price of the purchase. In the case of recreation, the price is the cost of bringing the user to the area — costs which may be, as we have noted, measured in dollars, time, travel time and distance, inconvenience, or other ways. In all cases, advertising may affect the knowledge of the consumer (user) and of his willingness to buy or to pay.

In each of these comprehensive characteristics, as well as in more detailed ones, the demand for outdoor recreation as an experience or activity closely parallels the demand for almost any other commodity or service. The particulars differ, and must be defined and measured for each.

The foregoing procedure provides an estimate of the demand for the whole recreation experience. The demand for the natural resources, including open space, used for this recreation experience can be derived from the demand for the whole experience. The process is illustrated in Table 2.

---

[10] An economic classification of outdoor recreation areas appears in Clawson *et al.*, *Land for the Future*, Chapter III.

Table 2.   *Estimated Number of Party Visits at Different Added Cost Levels, Lewis and Clark Lake, South Dakota, 1959*

Distance zone	Actual visits, 1959	Estimated party visits at added cost per party of:					
		$ 1	$ 3	$ 5	$10	$15	$20
		(. . . . .*thousands*. . . . .)					
Less than 50 miles	83	70	51	37	20	13	6
50–100 miles	91	85	69	58	28	12	12
100–150 miles	12	12	11	0	0	0	0
150–200 miles	40	30	5	0	0	0	0
Over 200 miles, in survey area	5	1	0	0	0	0	0
Total	231	198	136	95	48	25	18

A cost, which may be an entrance fee or other user charge, is added to the cost of visits from each zone of origin; it is assumed that users react to these added costs as they have reacted to other costs, and numbers of visits are reduced accordingly. In this example, an added cost of $1.00 per party cut the numbers of parties from 231,000 to 198,000; and an added cost of $3.00 per party cut the number of parties further, to 136,000; and so on, as shown in Figure 1. The whole area under the curve in this example is $1.4 million: this is the sum of the value of the recreation resource in this example to each individual user, or its total value to society. If a single entrance price had been charged, maximum revenues would have been received at an entrance price of somewhere between $5.00 and $8.00 per party; total numbers of parties visiting the area would have been between 60,000 and 100,000, and total revenues collected nearly $500,000. (In this example, and perhaps generally, the elasticity of demand for

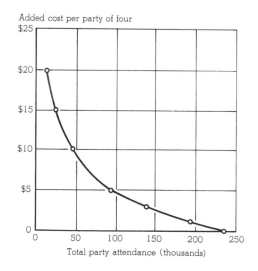

Figure 1.   *Estimated total party visits under varying added costs, Lewis and Clark Lake.*

the recreation resources is close to 1.0 for a considerable range near the maximum revenue point. Unless data are relatively detailed and accurate — more so than in this example — we cannot have much confidence in the determination of the exact point of maximum revenue.)

This is an extremely simple example. It is based on the assumption, among other things, that the methods of managing the recreation area are given. Modifying them might modify the attractiveness of the area, or the willingness of people to pay for its use. In particular, management methods might be modified if use were much smaller than that actually experienced, and in the process the recreation experience made more enjoyable. The whole recreation experience comes out of a mix of inputs, even at the site: additional management or labor input can substitute for natural resources, within some limits, and capital investment can make an area more attractive than it would otherwise be. Professional or technical skill, especially in design, can make a given area of land or body of water more attractive and hence enhance its value.

Under some circumstances, some of the benefits from an outdoor recreation area may not be measured by an analysis of data on visits to the area. If everyone who used the area was counted as a visitor, and if there were no service businesses in or around the area, then perhaps all the benefits would be included by an analysis of visitors. Sometimes, however, although their use of it is not likely to be counted in the visitor data, some people own vacation or other property in or around the recreation area, or their homes border on a park, or they otherwise obtain a benefit from the area. For instance, substantial increases in land value around some of the TVA reservoirs are attributable to recreation use of those reservoirs.[11] Likewise, there may be private business enterprises in a park, or near it, which do a considerable business with users of the area, and thus some property values arise which are attributable to the park. These values, which are wholly or largely additional to the values created directly by the users' visitation to or use of the area, can be estimated and added.

This methodology provides "shadow prices" for the outdoor recreation experience and for the space and other resources used for that experience. In the absence of market prices, these shadow prices may be reliable guides. The reliance that can be placed on them will be determined by the skill with which the necessary studies are made, but, if carefully estimated, such prices may serve as reliable guidelines for comparison with market prices of other commodities and services whose prices are determined in the market.

Before exploring the applicability of this methodology to uses of open space other than recreation, a few brief facts about recent trends in outdoor recreation may be useful.[12] The trend in attendance at all major types of public outdoor recreation

[11] Jack L. Knetsch, "The Influence of Reservoir Projects on Land Values," *Journal of Farm Economics* (February 1964).

[12] See Clawson and Knetsch, *Economics of Outdoor Recreation;* see also *Outdoor Recreation for America: The Report of the Outdoor Recreation Resources Review Commission* (U.S. Government Printing Office, 1962).

areas has been rather steeply and regularly upward since World War II; the annual increase has been in the general magnitude of 10 per cent for many types of areas. An upward trend of this magnitude must level off at some future date, otherwise it will lead to such absurdities as spending more days in outdoor recreation than there are days in the year; but no clear tendency to a flattening out in this growth rate is yet apparent. At the present time, the average American spends nearly two days annually at a national park, national forest, or federal wildlife area, more than three days at a State park or federal reservoir area, and visits a local park eight times or more during the year. A substantial proportion of all persons do not visit any of these areas, and very few visit all of them, so that numbers of visits by those actually going to such areas is much higher. There are no reliable statistics on recreational use of privately owned areas; it seems highly probable that their use is greater than that for all the public areas.

Participation in outdoor recreation at public areas declines with advancing age; persons over 65 years of age participate about half as much as those between 18 and 24.[13] Participation rises with increasing education, up to the level of high school graduation, and with increasing income, up to a point well above average income, but declines at the very highest income levels. Participation also rises with increasing amounts of paid vacation. Recreation, as an activity, is greatly influenced by the amounts and timing of leisure. Time budgets of the kind reported by Chapin and Logan in their chapter in this volume are very useful in this connection. The type of activity also shows some relation to these factors; in particular, participation in the more active sports declines with age while participation in the less strenuous types of activity may increase with age.

Although statistical data on the use of privately owned outdoor recreation areas are generally lacking — in particular, cross-classification data to show how much use of public areas is competitive with or complementary to use of private areas — it would appear that organized or consciously chosen outdoor recreation activity rises as availability of better homes and better private yards increases. Members of the upper middle class, socially and economically, both flock to public parks and buy single-family houses with yards in suburbs. For most of the population, more private closed space (in houses or apartments) is associated with more private open space, and more of each is associated with greater use of public open space for recreation. The situation may be different for the rich; they may substitute private open space for public open space.

In dealing with outdoor recreation a common misconception has been the confusion of attendance at public areas with demand for recreation, and especially the assumption that people demand most the activities they most often participate in. In fact, use depends upon supply as well as upon demand. If there are many attractive areas, then total usage is likely to be high; but demand, in the economists' sense of

---

[13] Data of this sort have come out of several studies; the source used here is Eva Mueller and Gerald Gurin, *Participation in Outdoor Recreation*, Outdoor Study Report 20 (Outdoor Recreation Resources Review Commission, 1962).

the word, may be no higher. Likewise, if swimming or some other sport is popular in one locality but not in another, the unwary may conclude that demand is much higher in the first than in the second; in fact, demand may be equal but supply much greater in one than in the other. People tend to want what they have known, not only in outdoor recreation but in many other aspects of consumption, and frequently the expressed demand for a good or service never known may seem slight or unimportant. These same relationships may well exist for forms of urban space other than for recreation; it should not be assumed that merely because people have not demanded some form of open space, there is no latent demand for it, but only that no one has had a chance to become familiar with it.

By application of the foregoing techniques, one could measure the monetary value of urban or other open space, or of natural resources generally, when used for outdoor recreation. Several such studies have been made or are in progress,[14] but they have applied generally to recreation areas outside cities and often to recreation associated with water development projects. However, it would be possible to make similar studies for recreation areas within cities. Costs would often have to be measured in travel time or in distance, including distances walked, and in many cases cash costs would be low or zero. Difficult problems would arise in reasonable conversion of the time and distance costs into monetary sums, but this is not insurmountable. Monetary values could be calculated for the whole area under the demand curve, as reflecting the total social value of a service or resource not sold in the market place. (This is the common practice with natural resource programs of many kinds, and the recreation values would generally be comparable with the irrigation, flood protection, electric power, or other values from such programs.) Or the monetary values could be calculated on the basis of the volume and price or value per unit which would yield the largest value sum, on the basis of a single price or charge — this would more nearly conform to the value of the land or site if used for private commercial use. In parts of cities where commercial, residential, and other land uses are highly intensive, recreational use of land would also have to be relatively intensive if the values of the site were to be equal to its cost or to its value in alternative uses.

This general approach to the value of open space might be applied to uses other than recreation, although there would be great difficulty in doing this and, as far as I know, no really serious attempt has been made to do so. Many, if not all, of the uses and forms of open space are in the nature of an amenity or amenity resource; the general problems and difficulties of dealing with such resources are explored by Atkisson and Robinson in Chapter 5. An attractive or a high amenity site may be compared to an unattractive or low amenity site in the same way that a top-quality beefsteak is compared to a low-quality one. If a significant segment of the total public is able to recognize differences, and to discriminate in some way in actions between one kind of open space situation and another, then values can be estimated, albeit

---

[14] See Clawson and Knetsch, *Economics of Outdoor Recreation*, especially footnote 2 on pages 48 and 49, where a number of such studies are listed.

with difficulty. In the case of many consumption goods, consumers register their preferences in terms of market prices paid. In the case of open space, they might indeed be willing to pay more for an office with a good view, in the same way that cottage owners around a lake pay more for this recreational location; or they might be willing to walk to the area, in order to enjoy it at the site; or, in a city district with good open space, the general character and values of the neighborhood might stay up, with less obsolescence than in one with poor open space.

Provision of light and air around buildings and provision of perspectives and vistas within a city have been listed as two uses of urban open space. In this regard, one might conceivably compare two cities, or groups of cities, with contrasting amounts of open space for these purposes, and study how far the difference in such open space affected any aspect of urban life in each city. It would be hard to isolate the effect of open space from the effect of many other factors which vary from one city to another. If in different parts of the same city, different but nearby streets or blocks varied in the amount of open space, perhaps one could identify some associated different patterns of activity and land use. The different effects of open space might not show up for some time; a new office building or group of buildings without space might seem as attractive as another group surrounded by more open space for a number of years, but might become obsolescent sooner.

Similar considerations would apply to the other uses of open space enumerated previously. Protection of ecological values, city-forming in the broadest sense, and other uses of urban open space may well have value, but it would be hard to set up tests, based upon public reactions, to measure these values. Instead, it may be necessary to resort to expert judgment — to get city planners, real estate appraisers, urban lending institutions, and others to express their judgment as to the effect upon value over the lifetime of a building or group of buildings, of different amounts and kinds of open space. A single office building built right to the outer inch of its property line, with no setback and no height limit, might produce one effect upon value, and a large group of office buildings so developed might have a very different effect.

Crowding and Space

Crowding is primarily a psychological phenomenon, only loosely related to the physical situation on the land or water. Daniel Boone is supposed to have felt crowded when he could see the smoke of a neighbor's cabin; the Forest Service has said that in a wilderness area one should not see more than two other parties daily; and I personally have canoed and hiked in areas where I felt gratified that no one else had been sighted that day. Although we customarily jam ourselves into buses and airplanes, literally touching our neighbors on either side, we often have a feeling of privacy if we can read without being interrupted by the telephone. In the modern apartment house, one is surrounded by strangers only a few feet away, yet — if the apartment is well constructed — without hearing or seeing them, and without conscious thought about their presence. Until the advent of mechanical transportation, people living in large cities inevitably had to be grouped in close proximity to others because distances were limited by walking times. Modern cities can be more spread out, and many are, yet modern technology also makes possible larger structures which, in turn, make higher population densities on the land possible — and found, in many large cities.

Hall has explored at length the effect on man, and other animals, of the space in which they find themselves, and their relationships with other individuals of their species when confined to some space.[15] He has classified space for human needs into four broad scales or categories: intimate, personal, social, and public, each of which has a close and not-close phase, and for each of which he has estimated distances measured in feet. He emphasizes that the individual's reaction to each of these scales of distance depends in large part upon his culture — upon what he has grown accustomed to throughout his life — as well as on his physical ability to see, smell, hear, or otherwise perceive another individual. Drawing on his own and other research, he shows how animals of different species react to crowding of various kinds; in many instances, their reactions are intense, including drastic declines in the birth rate in some cases, as well as increases in the death rate.

From these studies, Hall draws many conclusions for urban life in general, and particularly for the design of buildings and the spatial relationships between buildings. He places particular emphasis upon racial and ethnic cultures and the need to plan space in accordance with culturally determined demands. However, cultures change also, sometimes very slowly, but sometimes with much stress upon the culture and upon its members if the pace of change is too rapid. The modern city in the United States and elsewhere is almost certainly leading to the development of a wholly new way of life, and the culturally influenced or determined demands upon space may well be changing greatly also. The urban American of the next generation may have considerably different concepts of space, and considerably different demands for it, than either we or our ancestors have or have had.

Under what circumstances does one feel crowded by other human beings and by man-made structures? Perhaps no simple answer can be given, for surely there are numerous and highly personal situations, as well as generally determined cultural responses. One element common to most sensations of crowding, however, is the existence of a larger number and/or a wider range of sensations, primarily ocular, than the recipient is prepared to absorb. More people or more objects force themselves upon his attention — or at least are not rejected by him as irrelevant — than his perceptive ability is able to cope with. Thus the person who simply does not see other individuals, or accepts them as indistinct parts of the background, or the person whose perception of the physical world about him is limited to only that range of objects for which he has an interest, may not feel crowding under the identical physical circumstances which another person would find oppressive. Thus, one person may look into a single shop window on a busy street, enjoying what he sees there, oblivious to passersby, other shops, buildings along the street, traffic on the street, and other persons or objects well within his capabilities of vision. Or he may enjoy the sand of the

[15] Edward T. Hall, *The Hidden Dimension* (Doubleday & Co., 1966).

beach or the trees of the campground, shunting the horde of other visitors into a hazy distant background, while another may be so painfully aware of them that he can scarcely see the natural features of the landscape. The same relationships exist for sound, as anyone knows who has observed a teenager listening to blaring music while at the same time studying diligently.

Anyone who seeks to comprehend the whole or the major portion of many urban scenes, especially downtown areas, finds himself overwhelmed with ocular — and often auditory and perhaps olfactory — sensations.[16] In particular, he cannot perceive both that which is approximately on the eye level and that which is much higher, or that which is nearby and that which is distant, at a single steady look. Not only is the volume of ocular sensations far too great, but they spread over too wide a range, horizontally and vertically. It is here that open space may play such a decisive role; it enables the viewer to stand back, to get it all in. The problem is the same as trying to photograph a street scene with a normal camera — one simply cannot get all of it, or even a major portion, into one picture. The normal human eye has a limited range, vertically and horizontally: there is one range without movement of the eyes, another with movement of the eyes but not of the head, and still another with movement of the head. Distance from the object viewed reduces the amount of detail that can be perceived but greatly broadens the capacity to see the scene as a whole.

Faced with the enormous complexity of a normal street scene, the viewer either suffers feelings of crowding as he seeks to comprehend it all, or he retreats into a self-imposed selective perception of only a small part of it. Open space provides vistas and perspective; lack of open space produces sensations of crowding or a limitation in range of human interest. One might well imagine a rate of substitution curve, of crowding versus range of interest; or, rather, a family of such curves, each higher and to the right as the amount of open space increases. It is in considerations of this kind that the advocates of open space, who argue that it affects the quality of human life, have a real point.[17]

Closely related to this matter of too much to see, too close for it all to be seen, is a common absence of proper closings to the urban scene. We noted at the beginning of this chapter that open space implies a boundary, something to bring it to an end. The public square downtown is closed off by the buildings on the surrounding streets, but the downtown streets in the typical rectangular pattern stretch on and on. Such streets present no closing to the eye; what might be a meaningful open space is thus robbed of much of its potential value. The rectangular street pattern has many advantages for many purposes, but its streets do not serve well as open spaces to contrast with the built-up city. In newer residential areas, streets sometimes wind and curve, sometimes but not invariably producing pleasing effects to the walker or to the

[16] The implications for design in cities are discussed by Christopher Tunnard and Boris Pushkarev, *Man-Made America: Chaos or Control?* (Yale University Press, 1963); see also Christopher Tunnard and Henry H. Reed, *The American Skyline* (Houghton Mifflin, 1955).

[17] Garrett Eckbo, *Urban Landscape Design* (McGraw-Hill, 1964); Henry Fagin and Robert C. Weinberg (eds.), *Planning and Community Appearance* (Regional Plan Association, 1958).

motorist. As one walks along these streets, one may see ahead some shrubs, trees, and grass instead of endlessly stretching asphalt. But purposeful design of streets, making maximum use of them as open space, is still far from universal in residential areas, and rare indeed in commercial areas. The combination of straight streets which produce no attractive view at their end, and of tall buildings which cannot possibly be seen by someone on the street level, combine to force the person on the street to confine his attention to a few of the details at ground level.

Closely related to this inability to grasp the whole scene is a common lack in many cities of attractive eye-level views. The store front may display attractive goods, but the single-story store front may have as attractive goods as one located on the ground floor of a very tall building. The absence of attractive eye-level vistas is often marked for public buildings; seen in their entirety — if there is enough open space to provide such perspective — they may be attractive, but at the ground level they may be repelling. A great many of the larger structures in downtown business sections of major cities incorporate architectural design which would be impressive and might be attractive if only the average person on the street could see the building as a whole.

It is possible for greatly improved design to increase the feeling of spaciousness from the same area of land, not only in the downtown parts of cities but also in residential areas.[18] The single-family dwelling on a lot of standardized size is a voracious consumer of land, yet much of the land surface is divided into such small parcels or fragments that it has very limited usefulness, even to the owner of the lot and house. In general, extensive subdivisions of this type occupy large acreages of land yet there may be almost no open space; a flight over much of the Los Angeles basin is most instructive and depressing in this regard. By grouping houses somewhat closer, relatively little is lost in privacy and individual land usability, but a great deal can be gained in larger community open space. Fortunately, this idea has begun to attract the attention of house builders as well as of the buying public; and, in spite of many zoning and other obstacles, considerable experimentation with such subdivision ideas is under way.

Research into the problems of crowding might well be highly fruitful. If crowding is primarily a psychological phenomenon, as we have stated, then obviously the psychologists must be involved in such research; but, if design can affect the sensations of crowding, then equally clearly the architects, urban designers, and landscape architects must also be included; and since different designs will cost different amounts and produce different results, it would seem that the economist should be involved also.

One special aspect of this crowding problem, and of design as a means of relieving

---

[18] For an imaginative but very solidly based discussion of the possibilities of creating more open space in residential areas, by grouping of houses and leaving of open space between groups, see William H. Whyte, *Cluster Development* (American Conservation Association, 1964). For an important complementary or companion piece, see Carl Norcross, *Open Space Communities in the Market Place — A Survey of Public Acceptance*, Technical Bulletin 57 (Urban Land Institute, 1966). See also Urban Land Institute and National Association of Home Builders, *New Approaches to Residential Development: A Study of Concepts and Innovations* (Urban Land Institute, 1961).

it, is: Do people generally want what the experts want? Specialists in the various fields might — or might *not* — agree that certain designs were superior; but would people generally also accept them as superior? In thus raising this issue, we do not in the least mean to say that the raw untutored popular will should dominate, nor that popular taste is unchangeable. In appreciation for fine wine and good music, to take but two illustrations, we have long had expert taste which gradually filters down to popular taste; the whole advertising industry strives to modify popular taste, not always in directions that connoisseurs would approve. The whole public educational process affects public taste in innumerable and indirect ways. If the general public has had education on various forms of urban design, and has had opportunity to experience different forms or patterns of living, then perhaps the popular taste can be accepted to a greater degree.

Efficiency in Use of Open Space

The burden of our discussion thus far may be overly summarized by saying that open space, in its various forms, is both valuable and costly. Difficult problems are involved in measuring its value, and as a result there may be greatly differing estimates of the value of a particular open area within or adjacent to a city. But few social scientists would deny that open space in general, or a particular piece of open space, has some value — however much they might disagree as to the amount of that value. Open space, especially within the central built-up city, but also on its periphery, is also costly. The cost of the site reflects its alternative use values in some form of developed or built-up use. In this connection, it often makes a good deal of difference whether a unit of government or some other collective entity already owns the open space site or whether it proposes to acquire it, often by assembly of presently diversely owned sites. The alternative monetary value may be the same in either case, but the "turmoil costs" of land assembly can be very large, as anyone who has had experience with public land purchase knows. These costs are avoided when the open space site is already in government ownership but must be met when acquisition is necessary. The investment in improvements on urban open space sites is low compared to the investment on developed uses on similar sites — this is, after all, a basic characteristic of open spaces. But these investments may not be negligible, either, as any organization which has had experience in management of any kind of urban open space can testify.

From these simple facts seem to flow a few consequences connected with efficiency. First of all, some type of benefit/cost analysis should be applied to particular amounts and locations of open space for each of the open space functions. With urban open space, it is clearly not a case of "if some is good, then more is better"; on the contrary, the marginal value of additional open space declines at least beyond some range or point of open space availability. The whole city cannot be made up of parks or vista-producing open space. Most site area must be used for residential, commercial, or other urban purposes — otherwise there is no one to play in the parks and no object to see across the vista space. At the same time, the cost of additional open space is likely to rise, or at least to stay relatively constant, within the developed portions of cities. At some "volume" or area of open space, the declining marginal value curve must cross with the constant or rising cost curve. The practical problem is, where? This is essentially a problem of economic analysis, although the insights of other specialists may also be extremely useful. The specific answer will probably vary from one city to another, and surely by districts within a city.

For a city as a whole or for any major part thereof, the spatial arrangement of the open space and the developed areas is as important as the total area of open space. It is not only a matter of the number of acres of parks per thousand inhabitants, but the location of the parks with reference to where the people live; not only the area of vista-providing open space (whether streets or something else), but their location with respect to users of the urban area and with respect to the view which it is desirable to show; and so on.

In the second place, it would seem that for any of its functions, open space is or can be made subject to efficiency analysis, just as it can be made subject to demand analysis. Efficiency of use of urban open space, like efficiency in the production or use of any productive or consumption good or service, involves at least two aspects: organization and management. Organization of open space is more generally called design; the relation of one part to another, and of the open space to the surrounding area, whether it is park, vista-space, ecological area, or whatever. Within the open space, design is concerned with the structures (and there are almost certain to be some, even there); the lines of internal transportation (which may, in practice, mean the location of walkways); the kind and amount of vegetation; the location and form of rest areas (benches, etc.); the use of fountains; and many other features. Each of these features of internal design, and their combined effect, must be judged in relation to man and his capabilities for their enjoyment.

But open space must be managed also — there is no such thing as an unmanaged open space, any more than there is an unmanaged wilderness. The issues are the kind of management, the tools used, and the objectives; these can vary over a wide range, but some form of management is inescapable. Management of open spaces may be day-to-day (or even hour-to-hour), or seasonal, or on other schedules. How often, and at what cost, shall one pick up litter? How can the manager persuade users to place their litter in special containers, rather than scatter it about? How far shall he seek to maintain the vegetation of his park, by the use of "keep off the grass" signs as well as many other techniques, or how far shall he encourage the public to enjoy that grass by sitting on it or walking across it? Obviously, users cannot be encouraged to pick the flowers, but just how much shall our concern be for the vegetation and how much for the users' responses to that vegetation? Shall we encourage lively activity in our open spaces, or shall we regard this as undesirable commercialism? Shall we promote privacy, or may this merely encourage crime and antisocial actions in the more secluded parts of our open space? In a host of ways, the manager of the open space can affect its use; and almost anything that he may do has some effect upon how people use his area of open space.

The foregoing considerations are directly relevant to some of the analysis in the chapter by Perloff, including his Table 1 on the policy measures for various aspects of the urban environment. In that table he has five columns: indicators of the present condition; costs, both private and public, of environmental maintenance at present levels; costs or other adverse consequences, both private and public, of environmental abuses and shortfalls; costs, both private and public, of achieving standards at various levels; and benefits, both private and public, of achieving standards at various levels. In the vertical dimension, his table includes a consideration of the spatial environment, among others. Under this schema, open space (uncovered land) would be treated as part of this major category.

Three recent studies have come to my attention which, while not dealing precisely with the type of cost and benefit comparisons required for Perloff's Table 1, nevertheless have some calculations which border on it and which suggest methodologies for coping with the problems his table presents:

1. Lichfield estimates costs and benefits from different aspects of two alternative plans for redevelopment of the center of Cambridge, England, including estimates of the incidence of these costs and benefits upon various groups within the community.[19] He was fortunate in having a considerable body of data, as well as the benefit of extended public hearings with careful argument by the proponents of each alternative, which helped to evaluate the data on claimed costs and benefits. In spite of an impressive marshalling of theory, logic, and fact, at the end he still came out with some uncertainties and a large body of imponderability, particularly as to the effect of each plan upon preserving the unique cultural character of the city. While his analysis did not conclude with a neat simple unequivocal advantage of one plan over the other — indeed, it may be doubted if this outcome will ever result where the issues are complicated and highly debated — yet no decision maker could fail to gain from his analysis of the issues, costs, and values involved.

2. Levin has made a most interesting analysis of the factors affecting choices by local government, based on the amount of open space its citizens want and feel they can afford.[20] Starting from the heroic assumption that the acreage of municipally owned recreational lands accurately reflected the past judgments of citizens, expressed through the political process, he studied the relationship of various factors — such as per capita income, land prices, density of land use, and other factors — upon the per capita acreage in communities in New Jersey and in regions thereof, circa 1960. These variables "explained" most of the variation in acreage per capita for municipalities within Bergen County; somewhat less the variation between communities in a four-county area; and relatively little when all communities in the whole state were

[19] Nathaniel Lichfield, "Spatial Externalities in Urban Public Expenditures: A Case Study," in Julius Margolis (ed.), *The Public Economy of Urban Communities* (Resources for the Future, Inc., 1965).

[20] Henry M. Levin, *Estimating the Municipal Demand for Public Recreational Land* (unpublished manuscript, Economic Studies Division, The Brookings Institution, October 1966).

included in one analysis. Lack of data precluded estimation of costs and returns from various amounts of municipally owned recreation land, but the factors which presumably governed choices by citizens are revealed by this analysis. It should provide some helpful guides to planners and public officials in these communities in deciding how much recreational land to acquire.

3. The Howard County (Maryland) Planning Commission has prepared an extensive analysis of the public and private costs involved in suburban development of their county under three alternative design schemes.[21] One assumes that the whole expected development occurs in tightly organized new towns such as Columbia (which is located in the county); a second assumes that the same total development occurs in a highly dispersed fashion, similar to the present sprawling suburbs outside of Columbia; and a third assumes an intermediate pattern of development. The tightly organized new towns provide a saving of about $2,400 per dwelling unit, compared with the sprawled development, and at the same time provide more publicly owned recreation open space within the residential area. The open space associated with sprawl, in other words, is relatively costly. While no estimates are presented as to its value, it seems highly doubtful that it has significant, if any, values for the expected residents of the county.

While differing considerably in approach, these three studies do show that it is possible to make quantitative comparisons of open space, and suggest that this type of analysis might be pushed much further in the next few years.

It would be possible to treat each of the kinds or functions of open space, as described in this chapter, according to the kinds of information required by the five columns of Perloff's table, but this is not practically possible on a satisfactory scale of competence until a good deal more research has been done. One could show, for instance, the amount of area now available for recreation within specified distances from residences or, alternatively, what proportion of the population lives within specified distances of units of various kinds of recreation area, such as playgrounds. One could make some estimates of the costs involved in maintenance of the various kinds of open space areas now available; likewise, one could make some estimates of the costs of abuses and shortfalls, although this would be difficult. One could also make estimates of the costs of achieving standards, but the more rewarding estimates would be of the benefits from achieving either standards or some degree of movement toward them. The answers would probably differ for different cities, especially for cities of varying sizes; and they would almost certainly vary according to parts or districts of each large city. We lack specific data to fill in most or nearly all of Perloff's table, as far as open space is concerned; and, if we had the necessary data, their statement would probably involve more detail than would be appropriate for this chapter. But the task is one on which progress should be possible if research is aimed at this end over a period of years.

[21] *Howard County 1985*, a technical report prepared by the Comprehensive Planning Section of the Howard County Planning Commission (April 1967).

Landforms Best Suited for Open Space[22]

As already noted, one important purpose of open space may be to preserve important landforms from development. Some other uses of open space are largely indifferent to the landform. Some of the landforms where open space may be particularly important include:

1. River valleys, where floods are or may be a problem. Seriously damaging floods, by their very nature, occur at relatively infrequent and unpredictable intervals.[23] Occupancy of such areas may proceed in ignorance of the true hazard, especially during the relatively long intervals between serious floods. A number of studies have shown that all or many occupants of such areas seriously underrate the flood hazard to which they are exposed. Where the flood hazard is not great, the lands may be occupied if their values exceed the probable losses; but in many situations the flood hazard is so great that occupancy is highly uneconomic, is likely to lead to high public costs, and may result in unnecessary deaths. But such lands are often well-suited for use as recreation, city-forming, or perspective-providing open space.

2. Groundwater recharge areas, which are often but not always the same as the flood-hazard areas. In some urban areas, considerable reliance is placed upon groundwater for domestic, municipal, industrial, and other uses, and a major diminution in groundwater supply would have serious economic consequences. In some metropolitan areas, the groundwater recharge areas are rather limited in total extent, so that closing them to development would not severely restrict the area available for various intensive urban land uses. Development would generally seal off too much of the land surface from recharge, so that such areas should be kept wholly or largely open.

3. Marshes and swamps, which may provide either of the foregoing open space uses and/or may be important food producers for fisheries in fresh or salt water. They are also often expensive and difficult to build upon.

4. Excessive slopes (in excess of 15 per cent, perhaps — the exact slope depend-in part upon soil type), which would lead to severely accelerated soil erosion and

[22] Ian L. McHarg has studied several areas intensively and has written extensively on the relation of urban land use to landform. See "Ecological Determinism," in F. Fraser Darling and John P. Milton (eds.), *Future Environments of North America* (Natural History Press, 1966). For a major attempt to identify land and water forms worth preserving, and to show how their development and use could best be carried out, see F. Carlisle Towery, *The Lower Hudson* (Regional Plan Association, 1966); Walter Firey, "Ecological Considerations in Planning for Urban Fringes," in Paul K. Hatt and Albert J. Reiss, Jr. (eds.), *Cities and Society, The Revised Reader in Urban Sociology* (Free Press of Glencoe, 1957); William A. Niering, *Nature in the Metropolis* (Regional Plan Association, 1960).

[23] There is an immense technical literature on floods. For a report which draws upon some of that literature, interprets flood hazards into economic and land management terms, and suggests some programs for management of flood plains, see *Insurance and Other Programs for Financial Assistance to Flood Victims*, A Report from the Secretary of the Department of Housing and Urban Development to the President, as Required by the Southeast Hurricane Disaster Relief Act of 1965 (Public Law 89–339, 89th Congress, H.R. 11539, November 8, 1965), published as Committee Print, Committee on Banking and Currency, United States Senate, 89 Cong., 2 sess. (1966).

water runoff, if developed, and also often impose high costs for grading, road construction, water and sewer lines, and the like.

5. Other areas physically unsuitable for residential or other building, by reason of unsuitable soils, geologic faults, slide areas, and the like.[24] Not only are these likely to be costly, and the hazards to economic loss likely to be underestimated by builders and buyers alike, but hazard to safety and to life may exist also.

6. Unique ecological communities, which should often be preserved as open space for their own values.

While city planners are not ignorant of these values, there seems reason to suggest that such planners and various types of resource specialists might work together more closely.

Open Space as Part of Grand Urban Design[25]

Other chapters in this book deal more directly with matters of urban design than this one can, but one aspect of urban design in the large is the amount, location, and use of open space. On one hand, highways, residential areas, and other features of the urban complex materially affect the demand for open space; on the other hand, the location, form, and usability of open space affects the attractiveness of different areas of the whole urban region for different land uses, economic activities, and social values. We do not wish to pursue this matter further here, but only to remind the reader of the importance of these interactions.[26]

Parks, Playgrounds, and Similar Areas[27]

Within and near cities, parks, playgrounds, and similar areas are the kinds of open spaces used primarily for outdoor recreation, in the broadest sense of that term. Usually publicly owned, although sometimes privately owned, they are more or less

[24] Gerald W. Olson, *Application of Soil Survey to Problems of Health, Sanitation, and Engineering*, Memoir 387 (Agricultural Experiment Station, Cornell University, 1964).

[25] Arthur B. Gallion and Simon Eisner, *The Urban Pattern: City Planning and Design* (1963); Werner Z. Hirsch (ed.), *Urban Life and Form* (Holt, Rinehart and Winston, 1963); John A. Logan, Paul Opperman, and Norman E. Tucker (eds.), *Environmental Engineering and Metropolitan Planning* (Northwestern University Press, 1962); Regional Plan Association, *Race for Open Space* (New York, 1960); Stanley B. Tankel *et al.*, *The Region's Growth* (Regional Plan Association, 1967). Hans Blumenfeld, "Scale in Civic Design," *Town Planning Review*, Vol. XXIV (April 1953). For an example of one metropolitan area's effort to appraise its needs for open space, the relation of open space to the whole regional design, and the means for obtaining open space, see Baltimore Regional Planning Council, *Open Spaces*, Technical Report No. 5, 1960.

[26] For a semi-popular but extremely lucid and well-organized statement on the problems of urban expansion, see Mason M. Gaffney, "Urban Expansion — Will It Ever Stop?" in *Land, The Yearbook of Agriculture* (U.S. Department of Agriculture, 1958). For an attempt by political and intellectual leaders of a city to face the difficult problems of their city's design, see Mayor's Task Force, William S. Paley (chairman), *The Threatened City* (New York, 1967).

[27] The literature on outdoor recreation is voluminous, and only a few references can be cited here. The report of the Outdoor Recreation Resources Review Commission, *Outdoor Recreation for America*, and the 27 study reports which accompanied it (U.S. Government Printing Office, 1962)

permanently dedicated to this primary use, although intrusions for nonconforming uses are not unknown. A truly well-designed outdoor recreation system for a city or urban grouping consists of many parts, which are used for a relatively large number of specific activities, suitably located throughout the urban complex, and each of which are of a size and physical character suitable for its intended use.[28] At the most local level, there may be small parks, intended for quiet relaxation, often for the elderly or for the young matron and her children. Also at a very local level are playgrounds for children. Still more local are the sandboxes for the very small child; but these are usually in the individual backyard of single-family dwellings. Playgrounds are almost indispensable for schools, and the school playground can well serve at times other than when school is in session. High schools and junior high schools require larger playfields than do grade schools, since their range of sports is wider. Somewhat more widely spaced, yet still rather local in a truly well-planned outdoor recreation system, are the specialized sports areas — tennis and squash courts, golf courses, swimming pools, and the like.

Persons concerned with parks argue that *within* the city, and within each major part of it if its population exceeds a given figure (say, 50,000), there should be some rather large parks, with picnic areas, foot trails, bridle paths, and a generally more nearly "natural" environment. At the edge of the city or nearby, possibly a few miles away, there should be still larger parks for still more extensive activities, including a range of water sports if possible, and camping, as well as those activities of the closer-in parks. Urbanites also have a concern for the availability of state parks and other areas which are still farther away and require a major trip to reach — suitable for all-day outings or possibly short vacations. And at the farthest reach there is interest in the vacation areas — in the mountains, at the lakes, or at the seashore.

The capacity of each kind of unit in such an outdoor recreation system should be sufficient to meet the demand of people in the tributary area. The procedure for measuring demand was discussed earlier; causal factors include such things as per capita incomes, travel facilities, climate, and public tastes. The latter in turn depend to a major degree upon what people have known in the past.

If the capacity of each kind of area is not sufficient to meet the desires of local people — especially when they have had the opportunity to take part in a wide variety of outdoor recreation activities — then potential demand for one kind of area gets diverted to some other kind of area, or to activities other than outdoor recreation.

---

stand as a landmark in the field. Marion Clawson and Jack L. Knetsch, *Economics of Outdoor Recreation*, summarizes research and writings of these authors, as well as providing references to other works. Numerous state, regional, and city planning groups have prepared reports on outdoor recreation needs and opportunities in their respective areas.

[28] The system concept of park and recreation areas has been better developed on a national than on an urban scale. See William J. Hart, *A Systems Approach to Park Planning*, New Series, Supplementary Paper No. 4 (Morges, Switzerland: International Union for the Conservation of Nature and Natural Resources, 1966). But the same concept is applicable within the city, as within the nation.

Instances have been recorded when people flocked to scientific gardens or herbariums for such ordinary activities as picnicking, simply because adequate picnic facilities were not available elsewhere.

The capacity of various kinds of outdoor recreation areas cannot be judged on an annual basis, but rather must be looked at in terms of peak demand. Utilization of outdoor recreation areas is notoriously "peaked"— 90 per cent or more of the annual visits may come during the summer for some kinds of areas in some regions or, in some other kinds of areas, the Sunday demand may be more than half of the weekly demand, or the midafternoon attendance at the swimming pool may be several times the morning attendance on the same day. If every peak demand, no matter how extreme, is to be met by provision of adequate facilities, then the cost of the last units, divided by the small difference in use between the absolute peak and lesser peaks, may be large indeed. A simpler rule may be to provide capacity for all but the absolute peak, and at that time to permit some crowding or use beyond capacity or to turn some prospective users away. A campground may have capacity for a normal summer weekend, be half empty during most weekdays, and crowded beyond capacity at the Labor Day weekend, for instance.

All the parks, playgrounds, and similar areas within the city, and most of them nearby, are "user-oriented," in our terminology. That is, their location is determined primarily, and sometimes within very narrow tolerances, by where people live and work. Such areas are designed to be used daily, during clement weather, although they may get a heavier use on weekends than on other days. The physical characteristics of the site are nearly always secondary to locational factors. Time and cost of travel to such areas should be minimized as far as possible. Unless a playground is within half a mile, children of grade school ages will not use it; the rest park for the elderly must be at least as close, and preferably closer, if it is to serve its purpose. Safe transportation routes from home to recreation area are equally important, especially for young children, mothers with infants, and the elderly. Once the use of an area requires travel by car, much wider horizons open up — an extra mile is now less important. But even the day-outing area must ordinarily lie within two hours travel time of the homes of its users, and the after-school or after-work specialized sports area must lie much closer, in travel time, than that.

Outdoor recreation areas within cities must be used much more intensively than outdoor recreation areas lying in open country. The very same factors that force other kinds of land use within the city to be relatively intensive also force outdoor recreation to be intensive. This precludes altogether those outdoor recreation activities which require large areas of land — not only is the wilderness incompatible with the city, but camping and other relatively large uses of land are excluded from the city although they may be found around its edges. For any activity in the city, more people must ordinarily be crowded into a given area of land than would be necessary in a park in a rural setting.

If use of outdoor recreation areas situated within the city or close upon its borders is to be relatively intensive, this will require substantial investments of various forms and relatively large annual inputs of labor, cash, and management talent. If only a city block is available for a park that is to serve several hundred persons each day, then the use of each square foot must be planned carefully. Distance can no longer be relied upon to provide privacy, for instance; some privacy of users will have to be sacrificed but some can be retained by careful landscaping. If lawns, shrubs, and trees are to withstand heavy use, then unusual care in their maintenance is necessary. The ultimate in intensive use of small areas is perhaps to be found in the Japanese home garden where, on a plot about as big as an average Western dining table, the careful gardener produces much beauty and satisfaction for himself and his friends.

The whole field of outdoor recreation, and the provision of open space within the city to meet these needs, cries for hard-headed objective research. For a long time, political and other efforts in this direction were dominated by emotional and ideological appeals — there was no sound, objective basis for decisions on the amount of open space, its location, and at what cost it was economically rational, in comparison with other uses of the land and water and in the light of alternative wishes and desires of the public. Fortunately, some good research has been undertaken in recent years, although its volume is still much too small and its influence in decision making still too weak. A great deal of what is called "research" is either data-collecting or verbalizing.

Man-Made Water Bodies as Open Space

Man has created artificial water bodies for his use and enjoyment from earliest historical times, but modern technology of earth moving and construction equipment has greatly widened his opportunities and lowered the real costs of the necessary construction. In the past generation, more than 2 million farm ponds have been constructed, providing small water bodies where previously there had been none; while these are not urban in location, they do illustrate how common construction of artificial water bodies has become. During the New Deal public works days, a considerable number of artificial lakes were constructed as the centerpiece for state parks or other recreation areas; these, too, were not urban in location but they have provided a stimulus for more recent efforts in the same direction, and the areas so created have been used primarily by urban people.

Since World War II, artificial bodies of water have been created in growing numbers in strictly urban locations, often by private developers. The possibilities of creating such water bodies, and their cost, depend in considerable part upon the topography and the nature of the soil. In a rolling area of modest slopes, it is much easier and cheaper to construct an artificial water body than it is in nearly flat or in steeply sloping areas. Where soil types lend themselves to earth dams, construction is usually cheaper than where concrete dams are necessary. A dam must be located where it will intercept enough water to offset evaporation from the water surface and also provide some flow through the artificial lake, but where the volume of flow will not exceed the capacity of the dam and its spillway to cope with peak flows. These conditions can be met in many locations in the upland parts of the humid eastern half of the United States, but often cannot be met in the flatter areas or in the more arid western half of the country. Sometimes a marshy area or swamp can be converted to an artificial lake by means of a comparatively modest dam. Conservationists often deplore the destruction of swamps and marshes, but the general public almost surely values the lake more than it does the swamp or marsh. In some locations, as at Palm Springs, California, water bodies are so highly prized as part of a luxury housing and recreation development that they are created out of relatively unfavorable terrain and the reservoir area is lined with plastic sheets or with asphalt and subsequently covered again with earth, to reduce seepage loss to a minimum; and such artificial lakes are filled with relatively expensive water imported from the Colorado River or elsewhere.

It is likely to be considerably simpler to create an artificial water body than to maintain it in usable condition. Deposition of sediments from eroding land surfaces — which occurs, especially during the construction period of residential and other structures in growing suburban areas, from the accelerated runoff which results from the construction of impervious roofs, sidewalks, and streets — may reduce the capacity of the reservoir or water body or may create unattractive turbidity in the water, or both. If the watershed includes agricultural areas where artificial fertilizers are used in heavy volume, or if drainage includes urban wastes which have had secondary treatment (so that they present no serious health hazard but still contain a high volume of plant nutrients), then the water may gradually develop algae and other plant growths which may be most unattractive. In any case, what started out as a highly attractive new water body in a new urban area may, in a relatively few years, turn into something much less attractive — at the extreme, into a real nuisance. Sedimentation may, in some cases, be removed by dredging; Lake Barcroft, in the Virginia suburbs of Washington, has been dredged and will almost certainly have to be dredged at intervals in order to remove unwanted sediments. But the fertilizer problem cannot be dealt with so simply; the situation differs considerably from lake to lake.

The maintenance of water bodies, whether natural or artificial, in attractive condition, especially for recreation, presents many difficult technical and management problems.[29] Although hydrologists, biologists, ecologists, and others can point to the adverse influence of fertilizers and other chemicals upon water quality, the means for correcting these influences are by no means so clear. There is need for a greatly accelerated research program on this problem.

Even more difficult than the technical aspects of managing artificial water bodies may be the institutional and political aspects of their management. Burby found that

[29] For a comprehensive review of the pollution problem in small lakes, including the citation of relevant literature, see *To Save America's Small Lakes* (*Water Pollution Control and Abatement*), Third Report by the Committee on Government Operations, Union Calendar No. 226, House Report No. 594, 90 Cong. 1 sess. (1967). Another source of information about the problems of small water bodies is *Influence of Impoundments on Water Quality — A Review of Literature and Statement of Research Needs* (U.S. Department of Health, Education, and Welfare, Public Health Service, October 1964).

in North Carolina no agency of government exercised effective control over the building or the subsequent management of artificial lakes.[30] The builder of a residential subdivision typically constructs an artificial water impoundment, builds houses on the surrounding lots, sells them, and moves on to another subdivision elsewhere. In some instances, ownership of the artificial lake is left unclear or uncertain; in other cases, it is given to an association of property holders within the subdivision. But such associations frequently lack a clear purpose, able leadership, and any real intent or capacity to deal with problems as they may arise. An artificial lake might become a serious management problem in any one of several ways: its waters might contain so much plant nutrients that undesirable, perhaps foul smelling, build-ups of algae might occur; its water might get polluted, in the sense of containing harmful pathogens in critical numbers, inimical to human health; its shoreline might get littered with waste; its dam or retaining structures might need maintenance or repair; or other difficulties might arise. Any of these would require competent management and some funds, each of which might be lacking from the association of neighboring land-owners. There might be threats to invade the artificial lake or its shore with uses not compatible with the neighborhood; or, at the other extreme, it might be desirable to drain the lake and use the land for other purposes. Uncertainty about ownership of the lake, or lack of vigorous exercise of ownership responsibility, might lead to a misuse of the lake.

The economics of building artificial water bodies — especially for the private profit-seeking developer, but also for the public agency if it seeks an economically sound development — depend not only upon the cost of the dam and the attractiveness of the water body on a continuing basis, but also on the values created thereby. There has not, as far as we can learn, been any attempt to measure the influence of a body of water upon land values within a strictly urban setting. Knetsch found that TVA reservoirs created substantial values to lands bordering on them, but these lands are more rural than urban.[31] In addition to the matter of the total amount of values created by construction of an artificial water body, there is the matter of who gets these benefits. If the area of surrounding land benefited by the water body is in the control of the private group making the water development, then this group can gain these benefits. The private builder of a dam is gambling that the water body will make the surrounding land he owns so much more valuable than the whole area would have been in the absence of the reservoir that the additional costs of the dam and any

[30] Raymond J. Burby, III, *Lake-Oriented Subdivisions in North Carolina: Decision Factors and Policy Implications for Urban Growth Patterns — Part I — Developer Decisions*, Report No. 9, Center for Urban and Regional Studies, Institute for Research in Social Science (University of North Carolina at Chapel Hill, November 1967). See also Shirley F. Weiss, Raymond J. Burby, and Newton W. Andrus, *Lake-Oriented Residential Subdivisions in North Carolina: Decision Factors and Policy Implications for Urban Growth Patterns*, reprint from Research Previews, Volume 14, Number 2 (Institute for Research in Social Science, University of North Carolina at Chapel Hill, November 1967).

[31] Jack L. Knetsch, "The Influence of Reservoir Projects on Land Values," *Journal of Farm Economics* (February 1964).

other necessary works will be covered. Apparently a favorable relationship exists in many situations, or is thought by the developer to exist, since artificial water bodies are constructed by private land developers. But this obviously would not be true if someone else owned a considerable part of the benefited land — hence construction of artificial water bodies must be limited to rather large developers. Neither is it likely to be true for relatively modest residential or commercial development — the cost of developed land around the water body will be relatively high and hence only rather expensive housing will be built there.

Artificial water bodies in an urban setting may provide one or more of several open space values. They certainly provide vistas across the water and perspective to what lies on the other side, although this may not be the cheapest or best way of providing such vistas and perspective. Much depends on what is on the other side of the water, from the viewer's location. At the "new town" of Reston, near Washington, D.C., the initial lake is partly surrounded by relatively high buildings and the lake surely provides a better view of them than would have existed had the water area itself been built upon. If the artificial lake or reservoir is surrounded by residences, then their landscaping may greatly affect the view. Water bodies, even artificial ones if the shore line has reasonable pretensions to naturalness and if the water is not too offensively polluted, have their own charm and attractiveness, at least to many persons. The water surface itself, with its emphasis upon horizontal lines, appeals to many persons, quite irrespective of what lies on the other side. The water surface may provide recreation of various kinds; boating is usually possible, perhaps water skiing if the area is large enough, possible fishing under favorable circumstances, and more rarely swimming. Lastly, these artificial water bodies are uniquely effective as city-forming devices; building could hardly take place upon them, transportation across them is so much slower than transportation on land around them that they are most unlikely to become transportation arteries, and they effectively separate one part of the urban area from another. Their functioning in this latter regard depends primarily upon their size. Large water bodies would serve most effectively as city-forming devices, but would be least likely to be built by private land developers; a small lake in a new city center might actually serve as a focus of city activity, and hence serve to unite a city rather than to separate it, and thus might be built by a private developer.

An artificial water body has one pronounced characteristic as compared with an equal area of land: under pressure for other use, it is most unlikely to be invaded by nonconforming uses. One problem in establishing parks or other open spaces upon land is likely to be that they must continually be defended against invasion or conversion to other uses. For instance, superhighways can be built over parks with less displacement of low-income families and perhaps at less cost for the right of way. Various efforts have been made, and resisted, to permit the invasion of Central Park in New York with buildings of various kinds; and numerous other efforts, some successful and others not, have taken place elsewhere. But a water body is likely to be free of such attempts; its drainage would create serious problems and construction over the water is often costly or impractical. The city planner who wants to create a permanent open space would, therefore, be well-advised to advocate the building of an artificial water body if this is physically practical.

Research on management of natural and artificial water bodies is urgently needed. The chemical and physical problems of maintaining the water in a desired condition are difficult, but we surmise that the institutional and management problems of applying such knowledge are vastly greater. One complicating factor is that the bad results of various land and water management practices usually do not show up for some years; the fertilizer applied to the cropland slowly washes into the reservoir and stimulates algae and other undesired growths over a period of several years, for instance. In this illustration, as in others, externalities are present; one person commits the act, another bears the consequences. If natural and artificial water bodies are to achieve their potential as urban open space, then difficult management problems must be solved somehow.

Urban Open Space as an Externality Situation

The provision of open space within and near cities, like so many other natural resource management programs, involves externalities. The open space, once provided, is often available to others, without cost to them and without opportunity for the provider to capture all of the benefits flowing therefrom. This is especially true of open space designed primarily to provide perspective and vistas; if it exists at all, its benefits are available to everyone in the area. The same is true of open space that may be described as "general scenery"; each attractive yard in a residential area adds to the value of every other yard and of every home. Open areas interspersed in a residential area may add to the value of every property.[32] But their costs are shared most unequally among beneficiaries. A peculiar form of spreading costs over the whole public arises from the provisions of the federal income tax; the value of property donated to non-profit conservation organizations can be deducted from taxable income, thereby often making the real cost of the gift relatively small.[33]

Because the externality situation is so common in natural resource literature, and has been so widely discussed, we shall not pursue it further here.

Open Space on the City Margin[34]

Provision of open space within the city, especially near its heart, is unavoidably expensive and sometimes encounters other difficulties. While such space has great value if skilfully designed and managed, some kinds of activities are virtually precluded

[32] For a most imaginative effort by a local group to plan the development of their area to take full advantage of its natural features, and to develop a program to carry out their plans, see Green Spring and Worthington Valley Planning Council, Incorporated, *Plan for the Valleys* (Towson, Maryland, 1964).

[33] For an effort by a private group to stimulate private individuals to donate land for open space uses, and thereby to take advantage of certain provisions in federal income tax laws so that the net cost to the donor is low, see Open Space Action Committee, *Stewardship* (New York, 1965).

[34] See bibliography in appendix on the problems of the growing suburbs and adjacent open country.

because they require such large areas of land. In this age, when a major portion of the urban population is highly mobile through its individual ownership of automobiles, some of the desired open space may lie outside the city, but preferably rather close to it.

Many kinds of recreation areas can be located outside the built-up city and still be highly usable by city residents. Golf courses, which take relatively large areas of land, are a good example of a sport area which can be located near cities. Parks, for activities of many kinds, can be available for weekend use if located some miles outside the closely built-up urban areas. Such parks can permit activities which would be impossible or unduly costly in a park located within the city itself. The vital role that these parks can play in the total system of outdoor recreation areas has been discussed above.

A small proportion of the total population of an urban complex may live in the truly open country or in surrounding small villages, and can have open space more lavishly than is possible within a city. The number of people who can "solve" their open space problem in this way must be relatively small. In fact, a great deal of the post-war movement toward the suburbs and the open country has been self-defeating; the first ones who moved into the open country may have gained something, but later arrivals in large numbers have destroyed what each sought. Moreover, this solution to open space is not without its costs, private and public. The individual who chooses this route commits himself to time-consuming commuting and sometimes restricts his job opportunities as well, the cost of a dwelling and all necessary services may not be as low as he had hoped, and his family may find their social activities more circumscribed than they had expected. The public costs may include lengthy extensions of water and sewer lines, much greater traffic on roads and hence the need for roads of greater capacity, and generally higher costs of all public services because of the dispersed pattern of settlement. Nevertheless, with all of these limitations, true open country or small village living has its charms for many people who are prepared to bear the inevitable costs.

Some people have urged the retention of some farming near cities, out of nostalgia for their own past or out of a belief that somehow the future urban dweller would be a more nearly full man if he understood something of the natural, economic, and social aspects of farming. In fact, farming has tended to disappear near cities, even before the land was actually converted to urban use. Many erstwhile farms have become idle land, and have lain idle for some years before actual conversion to urban uses.

There are many difficulties to continued farming in an urbanizing area: gradual disappearance of supply houses for needed agricultural inputs, gradual weakening of agricultural marketing mechanisms, opposition of urban people to the smells and disturbances of farm operations, shortage and cost of agriculturally competent labor supply, and other difficulties. Increased taxes on land are often cited as a reason for discontinuance of farm operations, but this does not seem to be a valid argument. If continued farming were practical and profitable aside from taxes, it would provide some income — more than if the land were allowed to lie idle — and one would expect the land to continue to be farmed even if its income would not completely meet the real estate tax bill. The farmer is under pressure to sell; not only is continued farming difficult, but the price he can get for his land enables him to buy a much better farm elsewhere. Indeed, not a little part of the upward pressure on prices of farmland has come from erstwhile suburban farmers who now have more capital to invest in a farm more distant from the city.[35]

The farmer who gets a good offer for his suburban farm is not sure that he may get an equally good or better offer later if he chooses not to sell now. The virtual certainty that he will sell out at some relatively near future date makes the planning of his farming operations difficult — this is particularly true for the dairy farms, the most common type of farm near large cities. But the speculative purchaser of the suburban farm is under some pressure not to rent it back to the farmer, and he usually cannot operate it successfully himself. He wants to be free to take advantage of a good offer from an actual developer whenever this occurs, and not to be burdened with a farmer or farming operations.

If there is some social value to farm operations relatively near to cities — and the case is not fully proven — then some positive means should be taken to retain such farming.[36] Tax relief, especially without any reciprocal obligation on the part of the farmer, is likely to be ineffective, as well as a windfall for the owner of the land. Agricultural land would have to be zoned for continued agricultural use, and quite probably some compensation would have to be paid to the landowner for loss of development rights. Some measures might have to be taken to insure that farming remained profitable. But all of this would probably be inadequate from the social viewpoint; unless the remaining farming served as something more than vaguely distant scenery, its utility to the urban population would be very low. It would be possible to tie operating farms to schools for valuable instructional purposes, or to various social groups for real recreational and educational values. Unless some such linkage can be established between some major segments of the urban population and the retained farms, the latter serve little purpose that much more distant and more economic farms could not serve.

Any use of rural open space, relatively close to the city, as a substitute for or a supplement to open space within the city, has unfortunate effects in terms of income class participation. Truly poor people have no chance to live in the country and commute to work, nor to play golf in the country. These uses of rural open space are limited to middle and upper income levels. Moreover, if the more articulate and politically more active parts of the total population see such use of rural open space as one major solution to the open space problem, they may neglect or oppose costly programs which would provide at least some open space in the city centers where it is most lacking and most urgently needed.

[35] This subject is considered in some detail in Marion Clawson, *Policy Directions for U.S. Agriculture — Long-Range Choices in Farming and Rural Living* (The Johns Hopkins Press for Resources for the Future, Inc., 1968).

[36] Marion Clawson, "A Positive Approach to Open Space Preservation."

Public Control over Urban Open Space[37]

Urban open space involves groups of people, as contrasted with individuals, to an unusual degree. Urban open space is frequently publicly owned, or, if privately owned, it is nearly always under some form of public control or incentive which greatly influences private actions. If individually owned, urban open space is always "used" by more individuals or groups than its owners, and publicly owned urban space is typically widely used. The vista-forming or perspective aspect of urban open space is in the nature of a free economic good, open to all, incapable of being denied to anyone — once the space has been established, and as long as it continues. The recreational aspect of urban open space is generally open to everyone, although racial discrimination in use of city parks certainly existed until recent times and may still be known. With such heavy emphasis upon group action on both the supply and demand sides of the urban open space matter, the way in which such actions are taken has great importance.

The establishment and subsequent management of parks and other forms of open space has, in the past, been primarily a political issue with strong emotional or ideological overtones and with very little or no economic analysis. Parks and other open space have been advocated by those who believe such things are "good"; there has been no analysis to indicate whether the natural resources or the public revenues, if so used, would contribute more to the general welfare in this way than in any other. Indeed, until a decade or so ago, economists were virtually unanimous in saying that the values of urban open space, such as outdoor recreation, were unmeasurable in economic terms.[38] Although great advances in dealing with this problem have been made in economic analysis, the presently available technology is not completely understood and accepted, much less universally applied. Parks and other open space within cities are still advocated and supported on primarily emotional grounds.

Because it is not highly "improved" by structures or in other ways, urban open space has often appeared to have little economic value. Thus, it has been repeatedly open to attack by proposals for other use of the land. It is not enough to establish publicly owned urban open space, or privately owned space under public control or inducement; it must be continually defended. Here again, the lack of adequate economic analysis handicaps wise decisions on public action. In a great many cases, existing open space should be maintained because its value in this use, including its effects on the values of surrounding lands in other uses, is greater than its value in any alternative use; but sometimes it may well be sound public policy to change the use of open space — this use, as well as any other land use, can get out of date as time

[37] See references to the literature on this subject in the appendix to this chapter.

[38] In 1949, Roy A. Prewitt, in the employ of the National Park Service, circularized a considerable number of the leading economists of the United States, asking them how he could measure the value of outdoor recreation. With one exception (Harold Hotelling), they told him the problem was too difficult of solution or that it was impossible to place values on outdoor recreation. Roy A. Prewitt, *The Economics of Public Recreation — An Economic Survey of the Monetary Evaluation of Recreation in the National Parks* (National Park Service, Washington, 1949; mimeographed).

and circumstances change. Decisions on this point have rarely been guided by any careful economic analysis, weighing the costs and the gains from each alternative use of the area.

Aside from the deficiencies of public process in establishing and defending urban open space, the typical fragmentation of urban government makes the planning and establishment of a well-designed system of open spaces — such as we discussed previously for outdoor recreation — exceedingly difficult if not impossible. Downtown parks and other open spaces are used by residents of outlying suburbs as well as by residents of the city center; and the latter may well get a significant part of their outdoor recreation in outlying park areas as well as in downtown parks. If one unit of urban government establishes particularly good parks and other open spaces, it may be serving citizens and taxpayers of other jurisdictions to a major extent. The best park and open space plan for a whole metropolitan area might well include establishment and operation of parks in the outlying areas to meet the needs of people from the central city, yet it would scarcely be in the interest of the suburb or of the suburban county to establish such parks. Indeed, many suburban counties — Westchester County, New York, for example — have restricted the use of their parks, especially on Sundays, to residents of their county. In the San Francisco Bay area, the outdoor recreation demand primarily originates to the south of the city, down the peninsula, while some of the best areas of supply are north of the city, in other counties.[39] In regard to open space, as with so many other aspects of modern urban living, the inherited fragmented urban government is a major obstacle to wise social action.

The difficulties of co-ordinated and socially wise action for the whole of an urban complex are not limited to the establishment and management of parks and open space; this is the positive side of the problem, but there is also a negative side to it. Existing open space, especially in the suburbs and in the adjacent open country, can readily be despoiled and wasted without producing much offsetting value. A relatively few widely scattered and poorly planned small subdivisions, a few scattered hot dog stands and other roadside businesses, and a proliferation of blatant advertising signs can largely if not completely destroy whatever amenity values an open countryside possessed. The amazing thing is how little such "development" it takes to affect a relatively large area. As W. H. Whyte has said, "It takes remarkably little blight to color a whole area.... Five acres are being made to do the work of one, and do it very poorly."[40] The values added by such land uses are often small, in total. Relatively small additions to income for a small fraction of the area may greatly reduce the value of the whole land resource; this is the externality problem in a rather extreme form.

Despoliation of open countryside may take place in a physical sense also. Typical residential development procedures involve bulldozing existing tree stands, extensively reworking the land surface in many cases, and the resultant severely increased soil erosion and stream siltation. Land conversion almost unavoidably involves some dis-

[39] Frances W. Herring (ed.), *Regional Parks and Open Space: Selected Conference Papers* (University of California, Bureau of Public Administration, Berkeley, 1961).

[40] William H. Whyte, Jr., "Urban Sprawl," *Fortune* (January 1958).

turbances to the existing ecological and natural equilibrium, but these disturbances frequently need not be as severe as they are. Different methods of site conversion and preparation for residential construction are available at costs not much greater than those for the most indiscriminate reworking of the site. But suburban city and county governments have been loath to impose controls, partly for fear of diverting development to other areas and partly because of reluctance to impose any costs upon influential businessmen in their area.

As far as the development and management of a program for provision of urban open spaces is concerned, the fragmentation of urban government is serious in all parts of the urban area; but it is especially serious in the suburbs and in the suburban fringe, where the physical opportunities for open space are usually the best. The small and rapidly changing suburban cities often have too many other immediately pressing problems to be able to devote much thought and capital to establishment of open spaces. The suburban counties have nearly always lacked vision and frequently their governments have been in the hands of the very groups that would have to be controlled — landowners and builders, particularly. The voice of the future resident is not heard — indeed, it would be very hard to take his views into account, because he is not present and not identified, even to himself, in most cases. State governments have generally ignored most city problems, and those of the suburbs perhaps most of all. All in all, the situation has not been conducive to co-ordinated public action, with a careful weighing of costs and values of all alternatives, and a conscious choice for an alternative that seems to be in the best long-run interest of the total population. In the matter of open space, as in so many other aspects of modern urban living, a reform of government and of institutions seems essential.

Appendix: References to the Literature

I. There has been an immense volume of writing on the problems of the modern city, dealing explicitly or implicitly with open space, of a popular, semi-popular, and scholarly character. A catalogue of the chief items would be a major article in itself. At least five bibliographies, dealing more or less directly with the issue, have been published: Barbara J. Hudson, *The Urban Fringe Problem: A Bibliography* (Bureau of Public Administration, University of California, 1952); *Urbanization and Changing Land Uses — A Bibliography of Selected References 1950–58* (United States Department of Agriculture, Misc. Publication No. 825, 1960); Washington Center for Metropolitan Studies, *Open Spaces in Metropolitan Areas: Selected References* (1961); Urban Land Institute for the Urban Renewal Administration, *Open Space Land, Planning and Taxation: A Selected Bibliography* (1965); Michael A. Carroll, *Open Space Planning: A Selected Bibliography* (Bureau of Community Planning and Department of Urban Planning, University of Illinois, 1965; processed).

Several well-known writers have written books dealing with urban problems, including open space, of which the following are perhaps a fair sample: Peter Blake, *God's Own Junkyard* (Holt, Rinehart and Winston, 1964); Kevin Lynch, *The Image of the City* (M.I.T. Press, 1960); and Lewis Mumford, *The City in History — Its Origins,*

Its Transformations, and Its Prospects (Harcourt, Brace, and World, Inc., 1961). Urban America, Inc., has held two national conferences; the record of the first has been published by the organization as *The Troubled Environment: Business Examines Social and Economic Barriers to Improving Our Cities* (1965); and background papers to the second were made available by the organization in processed form under the title, *Our People and Their Cities* (1966). For a short but thoughtful article on open spaces in one metropolis, see Frederick Gutheim, "Open Spaces for the Washington Region," *Landscape Architecture* (January 1962). For a dramatic appeal for action, see Samuel E. Wood and Alfred E. Heller, *California Going, Going...*, published by *California Tomorrow* (Sacramento, 1962).

II. For some representative views about open space in general or for specific metropolitan areas, see John J. B. Miller, *Open Land in Metropolitan Chicago* (Midwest Open Land Association, 1962); Donald A. Cotton, "Land Use: Open Space: Its Values and Conservation in the Urban Environment," *Southern California Law Review*, Vol. 37, No. 2 (1964); National Capital Regional Planning Council, *Recreational Open Space Priorities* (Washington, 1966); Washington Center for Metropolitan Studies, *Open Spaces and Our Cities* (Washington, 1961).

III. There is a vast amount of literature on the characteristics and the problems of the growing suburbs and the adjacent open country; much of it is more oratorical than analytical; there is a notable deficiency of sharp economic analysis, which some of the current RFF projects seek to remedy. Some of the materials of interest in the present connection are: S. D. Clark, *The Suburban Society* (University of Toronto Press, 1966); Phillip H. Cornick, *Premature Subdivision and Its Consequences* (Institute of Public Administration, Columbia University, 1938); William M. Crosswhite and Gerald F. Vaughn, *Land Use in the Rural-Urban Fringe — A Case Study of New Castle County, Delaware*, Bulletin 340 (Agricultural Experiment Station and Division of Urban Affairs, University of Delaware, 1962); William M. Crosswhite, *Part-Time Farming and the Preservation of Open Space in the Penjerdel Region* [Penjerdel, Philadelphia, undated (after 1961)]; William G. Dobriner (ed.), *The Suburban Community* (G. P. Putnam's Sons, 1958); W. H. Geyer and P. Hanauer, *Preserving Agricultural Land in Areas of Urban Growth: A Look at the Record* (Interim Committee on Agriculture, California Legislature, Sacramento, California, 1964); Howard F. Gregory, "Urban Pressures on California Land," *Land Economics*, Volume XXXIII, Number 4 (November 1957); Robert R. Stansberry, *The Rural Fringe and Urban Expansion*, AER–43 (United States Department of Agriculture, 1963); Gerald F. Vaughn and Edward C. Moore, *Idle Land in an Urbanizing Area: The Delaware Experience*, Bulletin 349 (Division of Urban Affairs and Agricultural Experiment Station, University of Delaware, 1963); and Arley D. Waldo, "Farming on the Urban Fringe," *A Place to Live: The Yearbook of Agriculture* (U.S. Department of Agriculture, 1963).

IV. There is also a great deal of written material concerned with the problems of intergovernmental relations in the suburban fringe with zoning and other land use controls and with the means and the politics of group action; most of this, whatever its other characteristics, is not closely related to the problems discussed in this paper.

Some of the materials of perhaps greatest applicability include: Richard F. Babcock, *The Zoning Game — Municipal Practices and Policies* (University of Wisconsin Press, 1966); Advisory Commission on Intergovernmental Relations, *Alternative Approaches to Governmental Reorganization in Metropolitan Areas* (Washington, 1962); Advisory Commission on Intergovernmental Relations, *Governmental Structure, Organization, and Planning in Metropolitan Areas — Suggested Action by Local, State, and National Governments* (published as Committee Print, Committee on Government Operations, House of Representatives, 87 Cong. 1 sess., 1961); John Delafons, *Land-Use Controls in the United States* (Harvard University Press, 1962); for a rather comprehensive plan to deal with open space at the county level, see Fairfax County, Virginia, *The Vanishing Land — Proposals for Open Space Preservation* (1962); William I. Goodman, *The Implementation of Public Programs of Open Space* (Bureau of Community Planning and Department of Urban Planning, University of Illinois, 1965); Scott Greer, *Governing the Metropolis* (John Wiley and Sons, 1962); Charles M. Haar, *Land-Use Planning: A Casebook on the Use, Misuse, and Re-Use of Urban Land* (Little, Brown & Co., 1959); "Techniques for Preserving Open Space," *Harvard Law Review*, Vol. LXXV, No. 8 (June 1962); Peter House, *State Action Relating to Taxation of Farmland on the Rural-Urban Fringe*, ERS 13 (U.S. Department of Agriculture, 1961); Peter House, *Preferential Assessment of Farmland in the Rural-Urban Fringe of Maryland*, ERS 8 (U.S. Department of Agriculture, 1961); Morris Janowitz (ed.), *Community Political Systems* (Free Press of Glencoe, 1961); Jan Z. Krasnowiecki and James C. N. Paul, "The Preservation of Open Space in Metropolitan Areas," *University of Pennsylvania Law Review*, Vol. CX (December 1961); Jan Z. Krasnowiecki and Ann Louise Strong, "Compensable Regulations for Open Space — A Means of Controlling Urban Growth," *Journal of the American Institute of Planners*, Vol. XXIX (May 1963); Stanislaw J. Makielski, Jr., *The Politics of Zoning: The New York Experience* (Columbia University Press, 1966); National Capital Regional Planning Council, *The Law of Open Space in the National Capital Region* (Washington, 1965); John E. Rickert, *The Present and Potential Role of State and Local Taxation in the Preservation or Development of Open Space Land in Urban Fringe Areas* (Urban Land Institute, 1965); Shirley Siegel, *The Law of Open Space: Legal Aspects of Acquiring or Otherwise Preserving Open Space in the Tri-State New York Metropolitan Region* (Regional Plan Association, 1960); Ann Louise Strong, *Preserving Urban Open Space* (Urban Renewal Administration, 1963); William H. Whyte, *Open-Space Action*, Study Report 15 (Outdoor Recreation Resources Review Committee, 1962); William H. Whyte, *Securing Open Space for Urban America: Conservation Easements*, Technical Bulletin 36 (Urban Land Institute, 1959); Robert C. Wood, *Suburbia: Its People and Their Politics* (Houghton Mifflin, 1959); Robert C. Wood and Vladimir V. Almendinger, *1400 Governments* (Harvard University Press, 1961); and Roscoe C. Martin, *Metropolis in Transition: Local Government Adaptation to Changing Urban Needs* (Housing and Home Finance Agency, 1963).

5

Amenity resources for urban living

Arthur A. Atkisson and Ira M. Robinson

Arthur A. Atkisson is Executive Director of the Institute of Urban Ecology
and a Lecturer in Public Administration and Urban Planning,
University of Southern California.
Ira M. Robinson is Professor of City and Regional Planning and
Chairman of the Graduate Department of Urban and Regional Planning,
University of Southern California.

Amenity resources for urban living

Arthur A. Atkisson and Ira M. Robinson

As more and more people cluster into urban regions, what happens to the natural environment increasingly becomes a matter for public policy interest. Much of this interest is centered on the idea of "amenity resources"; although the concept of these highly valued resources remains vague. With growth in population, income, and leisure, pressures on such amenity resources can increase precipitously. Under such circumstances, the "management" of amenities becomes quite complex and can be extremely costly. Clarification of the concept of amenities and a better understanding of what might be called the amenity management process can contribute to public policy in this area. This is what we hope to do in this chapter.

It is helpful in this respect to conceive of the urban environment as a system with certain inputs and outputs and a set of conversion processes. Thus, if the outputs somehow fall short of our expectations, it becomes evident that we must look both at the quantity and quality of the inputs and at the processes by which they are being transformed, utilized, and related to the end states desired of the system. It also becomes clear that we must define the outputs we desire and the functions they are to perform.

It has been argued that such a coldly calculating approach to the design of systems which so deeply touch the quality of man's life does violence to man's very spirit and to the values of human freedom which underpin our society. To this, former Secretary of Defense McNamara has replied: "To undermanage reality is not to keep it free. It is simply to let some force other than reason shape reality. That force may be unbridled emotion, it may be greed, it may be aggressiveness, it may be hatred, it may be ignorance; it may be inertia; it may be anything other than reason."[1]

In this paper we suggest that responses to amenities make up one of the outputs derived from man's environmental system; that these outputs can be "managed"; and that decisional criteria and management systems can be developed to accomplish this task in a rational and socially responsible manner.

The Objects of Amenities Planning and Management

Although many distinguished writers on urban matters have discussed amenities, few have attempted to specify the boundaries of the subject, define the terms they use, or develop a conceptual framework appropriate for consideration of the topic. The different approaches to the subject are, however, suggestive.

We are indebted to our colleagues, Alan Kreditor and G. Thomas Kingsley, to Lowdon Wingo, Jr. and Blair Bower of RFF, and to other participants at the conference on the urban environment for their comments on the draft.— AUTHORS' NOTE

[1] Quoted in "A Changing City: Government," *Progressive Architecture* (August 1967), p. 123.

In a paper prepared for the President's Commission on National Goals, Catherine Bauer Wurster referred to amenities as including "the New England village," "the Gold Rush town," and "other pleasant communities with historic or merely rustic flavor," as well as natural amenities, such as open space for recreational use, clean air, and water.[2]

More recently, Jean Gottmann has argued that urban amenities include "physical and cultural" components related to the "good life" and has called for "a rapidly changing urban morphology, bringing more amenities, and an actually good life, into the cities." He refers to "physical amenities," as including attractive, climatologically pleasant surroundings and links the term with Riviera-type environments, good landscaping, and urban beauty.[3]

John Burchard has also linked urban beauty with amenities, and has described twelve amenity or urban beauty elements, including the weather and sky, lakes, river banks, parks, and squares.[4] He has also ranked various cities of the world in terms of an "urban amenity score sheet," based on twenty-four qualitative characteristics, among which are: fine rivers, lakes, great parks, trees and shrubbery, good air, generally pleasant climate, distinguished buildings, distinguished museums, fine libraries, diverse neighborhoods, visible past, and art in the streets.[5]

In discussing "the administration of the amenities," Jon Alexander has suggested that "those things beyond life's necessities which make human life meaningful, we call amenities. Their function is the development of that in us which is uniquely human.... Amenities programs may be distinguished by whether they primarily involve management of the environment, or primarily involve organization of activities of people."[6]

Linking the notion of amenities with economic development and population growth, Perloff and Wingo[7] have suggested that certain features of the natural environment affect the pattern of economic activity and distribution of population of a region. They suggest that amenity resources include that special juxtaposition of climate,

[2] Catherine Bauer Wurster, "Framework for an Urban Society," in *Goals for Americans*, The Report of the President's Commission on National Goals (Prentice-Hall, Inc., 1960), pp. 225–47.

[3] Jean Gottmann, "The Rising Demand for Urban Amenities," in Sam Bass Warner, Jr. (ed.), *Planning for a Nation of Cities* (M.I.T. Press, 1966), pp. 163–78.

[4] John Burchard, "Some Antidotes for Ugliness," *A.I.A. Journal* (April 1965).

[5] John Burchard, "The Culture of Urban America" (Paper given at 50th Anniversary Meeting of American Institute of Planners, February 1–6, 1968).

[6] Jon Alexander, "The Administration of the Amenities," *Public Administration Review*, Vol. 28 (January/February 1968), p. 55.

[7] Harvey S. Perloff and Lowdon Wingo, Jr., "National Resource Endowment and Regional Economic Growth," in John Friedmann and William Alonso (eds.), *Regional Development and Planning, A Reader* (M.I.T. Press, 1964); Harvey S. Perloff and Lowdon Wingo, Jr., "Planning and Development in Metropolitan Affairs," *Journal of the American Institute of Planners*, Vol. 28, No. 2 (May 1962); Harvey S. Perloff, " 'New' Resources in an Urban Age," in Harold F. Wise (ed.), *America's Private Construction Industry and the Future American City* (Proceedings of a Symposium sponsored by American Cement Corporation and Urban America, Inc., January 1966); and Chapter I of the present volume.

land, coastline, and water offering conditions of living which exert a strong pull on migrants from less happily situated parts of the nation. They view the concept in terms of a special constellation of environmental conditions that "affords conditions of life highly sought after in an affluent and mobile society."

In Great Britain the term amenity has been in common use among planners for a great many years. A standard British textbook on urban planning lists one of the objectives of planners as the "preservation, protection, and evolution of amenity," and defines this function to include "preservation of buildings of special architectural and historical interest; control of advertisements; concern with architectural appearance; preservation of trees and woodlands; protection of living or working conditions."[8] Sir William Holford, a highly respected British architect-planner, has stated that "amenity is not a single quality, it is a whole catalogue of values. It includes the beauty that an artist sees and an architect designs for; it is the pleasant and familiar scene that history has evolved; in certain circumstances it is even utility — the right thing in the right place — shelter, warmth, light, clean air, domestic service... and comfort stations."[9]

Reflecting agreement with this broad definition of the term, Gunnar Myrdal has called for "uniform standards in regard to all community amenities" which he then defines as including everything from "the provision of streets, parks, and playgrounds and their upkeep to the building of schools and the improvement of the level of teaching."[10]

Thus, an amenity can be defined in many ways. Some have linked it with qualities of desirability which lead to enhanced economic value of properties or which exert a lure to potential immigrants; some define it as any phenomenon which results in a pleasurable experience to those who are exposed to it; while others suggest that it is any comfort or convenience beyond the level of life's necessity. Some include man-made facilities in their definition while others confine the use of the term to certain natural features of the environment.

The definitional breadth which surrounds the use of the term is also revealed by Webster, where the range of definitions includes: "...the quality of being pleasant or agreeable...the attractiveness and aesthetic or non-monetary value of real estate... something that conduces to physical or material comfort or convenience or to a pleasant or agreeable life...an area or location that provides comforts, conveniences, or attractive surroundings to residents or visitors."

It therefore seems clear that any useful discussion of urban amenity resources must focus initially on the relevant meaning of the term and the phenomena which one wants to include. In this chapter, we have adopted a functionalist or behaviorist

[8] Nathaniel Lichfield, *Economics of Planned Development* (London: The Estates Gazette, Ltd., 1956), p. 32.

[9] Cited in Daniel R. Mandelker, *Green Belts and Urban Growth* (University of Wisconsin Press, 1962), p. 32.

[10] Gunnar Myrdal, "National Planning for Healthy Cities: Two Challenges to Affluence," in Warner (ed.), *Planning for a Nation of Cities*, pp. 3–22.

position and have sought to define amenities in terms of the attitudes and behavior evoked from human beings as a consequence of their interactions with their environment.

AMENITY RESPONSE SYSTEM

Some basic concepts from psychology are useful here. We are told that all that man learns throughout his lifetime is dependent on the effective operation of his five senses. As he moves from situation to situation he carries with him the cumulative experience derived from the operation of his five senses in other and earlier situations. Influenced by that experience, he reacts to the environmental stimuli which occur in each situation to which he is exposed. The perceived reaction of an adult to the environmental stimuli occurring at any point in time and space can therefore be viewed as a result of the operation of his senses in that circumstance as modified by his cumulative lifetime experience.

In a typical stimulus-response model, the five senses are shown as providing for human reception of environmental stimuli and as being responsible for the consequent experience of human sensations. Based on the sensitivity of the individual to the quality, intensity, extensity, and duration of the sensations evoked by the stimulus, the human organism experiences certain feelings which lead to the establishment of an *affective value* for the experience. Feelings involve such states as unpleasantness, pleasantness, tension, relaxation, excitement, or quiet. Of these, the feelings of unpleasantness and pleasantness characterize the "hedonic tone," or degree of satisfaction obtained from the subjective experience, and are the basis for establishment of affective value.

The affective value of sensations derived from a variety of stimuli have been measured through a number of techniques, including: (1) the scaler method, in which the observer judges the affective value of a stimulus on a subjective scale, extending from very unpleasant through indifferent to very pleasant, and usually involving five or more steps; (2) the serial method, in which the observer establishes the rank order to a set of stimuli with respect to affective value; (3) the paired comparison method, in which the observer judges the relative pleasantness of all possible paired combinations of a set of stimuli. The frequency with which a stimulus is preferred when paired successively with all others is considered a measure of its affective value.

Over time, the individual's feelings about particular sensations lead to the formation of *attitudes, motives,* and *habits.* Every attitude has an object as its focus and involves a feeling about that object. An attitude may therefore be defined as "a readiness to become motivated with respect to an object."[11]

Motives, drives, and attitudes involve some human valuing process by which appreciation or interest is expressed toward the quality of an object or phenomenon within the individual's sensory field, or which can somehow be related to that field. Value theorists suggest that *value* and the *feeling of value* are the same thing. Whether

[11] Aaron Quinn Sartain *et al., Understanding Human Behavior* (McGraw-Hill, 1958), p. 81.

expressed in the economic marketplace or in some other way, they have their roots in the feelings people express toward particular sensations. Because of this, feelings are studied experimentally as determinants of preference among various objects or events in the environment of human beings. Since the satisfaction of drives (motives) is usually pleasant, while frustration of them is unpleasant, feelings thus are related to motivation and to the whole field of economic behavior. Thus, the value a human being places on an experience, an object, or a phenomenon is based on: the attitudes he holds toward the commodity; the objects or goals which are motivating him; his preferential ordering of these goals in terms of past feelings about different sensations; and the other learning situations through which he has been processed.

A. H. Maslow has suggested that man's motives fall into an ascending hierarchy beginning with those oriented around his needs for survival, safety, and security and ending with those related to self-actualization which involve the maximum use of all his resources. The satisfaction of lower-level needs leads to a loss or reduction in their motivational power and to a reorientation of motives around the achievement of higher-level satisfactions. Thus, as the simple requirements for survival, safety, and security are satisfied, higher-level satisfactions are increasingly valued and become the basis of an individual's value and behavioral orientation.[12]

Drawing on these basic concepts, it can be said that *those stimuli which lead to feelings of comfort, pleasure, or joy may be referred to as amenities.* Since these feelings may be manifest in situations in which more basic, lower-order human needs are also being satisfied, a system or scale for classifying responses is needed. Because of this, it seems useful to conceive of a scale of human responses which are ordered around man's discernible hierarchy of motives and values, extending from survival at one end to self-actualization, comfort, and joy at the other. Since such a response scale has relevance to stimuli generated by environmental circumstances, it may also be appropriate for the measurement of environmental quality.

In similar terms, Frank Stead has suggested a scale involving four criteria by which environmental quality can be judged:[13] First, does it insure survival? Second, does it prevent disease and accidents? Third, does it help promote efficient or unusual human performance? Fourth, does it promote comfort, pleasure, or joy? In this chapter we will view Stead's fourth criterion in terms of an "amenity scale" along which might be ordered the several types of responses man makes to those circumstances in his environment which generate feelings of comfort, pleasure, or joy. Some of these responses may lead to heightened productivity or to such a relaxation of pressure, tension, and stress that they may be found to increase man's longevity or health. Other responses may be said to have economic value since they motivate the human being to purchase private amenity goods or to support community investments in public amenity goods. Still other higher-order responses may be psychologically

---

[12] A. H. Maslow, *Motivation and Personality* (Harper, 1964).

[13] Frank Stead, "Levels of Environmental Health," *American Journal of Public Health*, Vol. 50, No. 3 (1960).

valued by the individual but result in no clearly discernible behavioral manifestation, either economic or political.

An example of a simple amenity response system follows:

Amenity stimulus generator (or precipitant)	Hilltop bordering on an urban park
Respondent	Family in hilltop residence
Amenity	View of park View of hill contours Sound of breezes in hilltop trees and shrubs Smell of vegetation Quiet Privacy
Amenity response	Purchase of hilltop home Frequent walks on hilltop Potential support for zoning in surrounding area
Potential disamenities	Visually insulting introduction of highway through park Visibility-obscuring smog Noise-generating traffic routes Privacy-destroying developments on hilltop

The example makes clear the several components that are involved in any amenity-response system. The stimulus generator, which we shall call the precipitant (the park), generates a stimulus (a view of the park) which in turn provokes a sensation having affective value (pleasure, joy) to a respondent receiving the stimulus. For the sensation to occur, a respondent having sensitivity to and value for the stimulus must be brought into effective proximity (the hilltop) to the precipitant. In the model, it seems clear that the *view*, not the park or the hilltop, is the amenity. Factors, such as smog, which can interfere with the reception of the amenity (or stimulus) or which affect the capability of the precipitant to give rise to the amenity are here called *disamenities*.

In the model, the willingness of the hilltop resident to pay a higher price for his home there than for one in alternate locations can be viewed in three ways: as a measure of the intensity of his response to the amenities converging on that site; as an expression of his preference for that particular package of amenities versus others purchasable through a comparable investment; and as an indication of his ability to pay for amenity values in his environment. However, these expressions are simply indicators of his favorable response to this set of amenity stimuli, and are not to be confused with the amenity response itself; viz., the feeling of pleasure evoked by the view.

Since a variety of circumstances can lead to amenity responses, or can interfere with the generation and reception of amenity stimuli, an amenity-precipitant typology must include not only disamenities as well as amenities but should also cover several types of precipitants in each case. Thus:

	Amenities	*Disamenities*
Sociocultural precipitant:	Interactive (e.g., group activities)	Interactive ("not our kind of people")
	Artistic	Aesthetic "insults"
	Community services	Lack of community services
Physical precipitant:	Man-made (e.g., architectural artifacts)	Man-made (e.g., junkyards)
	Natural: basic environmental variables amenity resources areas (ARA's)	Natural (e.g., smog, noise, dust)

In this paper, the principal focus is on natural amenities and the disamenities which threaten enjoyment of them, although from time to time other types of amenities will be brought in for illustrative purposes.

In our view, then, the amenity value of any environmental configuration is determined by the human responses which it engenders. Thus, the concept of amenities relates to an entire system of stimulus-response variables; to the conditions which influence the occurrence of the stimuli — their intensity, extensity, and duration; and to the significance of these stimuli to human beings exposed to them.

In these terms, it becomes necessary to conceptualize the existence of both an "amenity response system" and a "disamenity response system." In one case, the stimulus is an amenity while in the other it is a disamenity. Each has a systemic reference and cannot be defined outside the context of a system consisting of a precipitant, a stimulus, and a respondent.

AMENITY RESPONSES AND RESPONDENTS

Within the context of the concept of the human stimulus-response system presented above, it is important to recognize that any measurable response attribute may have a wide range of variations. People differ in their response to music and drama, just as they differ widely in their response to the eye-irritating properties of photochemical smog. Where mixed cultural and biological factors are at play, as in the case of human responses to noise, similar wide variations in response patterns are observed. The threshold of amenity or disamenity experience may therefore be hypothesized to vary widely throughout a population, as may the intensity or significance of the experience. The process of socialization to which an individual has been exposed and the values of his family, his region, and his country can be viewed as factors important to the pattern of response he exhibits toward any environmental stimuli. Consequently, an understanding of these variations in human response patterns is a key aspect of urban amenity planning and management.

Since an amenity is measured by the response it evokes from human beings, the values, standards, and tastes of a population must necessarily influence the characterization, as amenities, of those environmental variables which impinge on the life space of that population. Since human perceptions are critical to the root concept, the amenity characteristics of an environmental variable, singly or in combination, may therefore vary from population group to population group, from place to place, and from time to time.

Response curves indicating the distribution of reaction of various population groups to amenity and disamenity precipitants would be helpful for environmental planning and management. However, we have found little hard data which could be used to construct such curves at this time. The task of developing scales of human response to environmental stimuli seems to us to be a most important and challenging one.

The factor of differences in response to amenity stimuli of individuals, groups, and communities might conceivably be measured by:

1. The proportion of exposed population experiencing a response;
2. The distribution of response intensity within the respondent group;
3. The willingness and capability of the respondent group to pay for any given level of the amenity value as a private good.

ECONOMIC AND POLITICAL RESPONSES TO AMENITIES

In a broader context, it is well to note that the amenity properties of an area or a specific natural environmental variable have value as private goods and are economically measurable through such indices as rates of inmigration, comparative property value, user charges, and consumer demand.

Edward L. Ullman has suggested that the "lure of amenities" is a key factor in human migrations.[14] He cites the massive population migration to southern California as substantiation of this premise. Referring approvingly to Ullman, Jean Gottmann examined migration patterns within the United States and concluded:

With the exception of Ohio, the net migration obviously flows toward areas at the periphery of the national territory that are richly endowed with either cultural or physical amenities, or both, as is now the case of California, which has received the most massive inflow for the last thirty years. That the "geography of amenities" plays an important part in the selection of location for people and a number of industries is increasingly recognized by students of statistics and by business managers. The lure of climate and landscape used to attract the wealthy,

[14] Edward L. Ullman, "Amenities as a Factor in Regional Growth," *The Geographical Review*, Vol. XLIV (January 1954).

the people of leisure, the aged who could afford it. Thus the fortune began of the "Rivieras" in France and Italy, of the Californian and Floridan coasts in America. Now these areas are bustling with young, busy people, and with a variety of economic activities.[15]

Gottmann points out that similar migration trends are at work throughout the world and suggests that the most rapid urban population growth is occurring in two classes of urban settlements: those which fall into the "megalopolitan" category and those which can be characterized as the "Riviera category." He argues that in the "Rivieras," growth has been stimulated principally by the amenity values inherent in the areas rather than by the lure of the agglomeration of commercial and industrial functions which have triggered the growth of megalopolitan centers.

Industries facing a highly competitive market for skilled labor and professional specialists have made plant location decisions to take advantage of the "lure" of amenity-loaded areas. The "think-tank" developments at Santa Monica, the IBM facility near Nice, the proliferation of electronic plants near Orange County's beaches are all suggestive of this trend. As Gottmann argues,

There is little doubt that as the new generation enters the labor force in the coming years, better educated, aiming at employment in the growing and more fashionable sectors of the economy, there will be an increasing concentration around the urban regions that will develop the most pleasant mode of life, offer a wide and attractive gamut of amenities. Such local conditions are largely man-made; they require a great deal of enthusiastic planning, investment, and care.[16]

Similarly, residential site preferences have been shown by Herbert and Stevens, and by others[17] to be influenced by the amenity values of alternative sites. These researchers have measured residential amenities in terms of such factors as the general appearance of the neighborhood, open spaces, views, greenery, the condition of yards, and the appearance of housing. They have found these factors to be important variables in residential site decisions.

In addition to those human amenity responses which may be characterized as falling directly within the economic market-place, there are also those which are manifest by overt political behavior (where economic factors come into play indirectly if at all). The formation of citizen groups to protect the "blueness" of Lake Tahoe, to

[15] Jean Gottmann, "The Rising Demand for Urban Amenities," in Warner, *Planning for a Nation of Cities*, p. 168.

[16] *Ibid.*, pp. 175–76.

[17] John D. Herbert and Benjamin H. Stevens, *Model for the Distribution of Residential Activity in Urban Areas* (PJ Paper No. 2, Penn-Jersey Transportation Study); an abridged version of which was published in *Journal of Regional Science*, Vol. 2, No. 2 (1960). See also F. Stuart Chapin, Jr. and Shirley F. Weiss, *Factors Influencing Land Development* (Chapel Hill: Institute for Research and Social Science, University of North Carolina, in co-operation with the Bureau of Public Roads, U.S. Department of Commerce, August 1962), and Arthur D. Little, Inc., "Amenity Attributes of Residential Locations," Technical Paper No. 3 of the San Francisco Community Renewal Program (Arthur D. Little, Inc., 1965).

Table 1. Amenity Response Patterns within an Amenity Resource Area

Precipitant(s)	Supporting precipitants	Function/uses	Amenity	Respondent(s)	Potential disamenities	Amenity infrastructure required, if any
Hilltop bordering on a large park	Congenial climate and weather	Site for residential, or commercial and/or industrial development	Views, vistas, panoramas, perspectives of park	Residents of and visitors to hilltop and park	Fumes, odors, smog	Clear trees
	"Pure" air		View of hill contours		Excessive wind	Build roads/tramway
	Vegetation, soils, wild life (e.g., trees, wild flowers, birds)	Viewpoint and natural landmark for residents and visitors to the park	The delight of natural sights, sounds, and smells; breezes through trees and song of birds	Bird-watchers, viewers, walkers, hikers, nature lovers, tourists	Foreground interference from roofs, walls, overhead wires, cars, backyards, trees, structures, signs, poles obstructing or distorting view of park	Install sewers and drainage systems
	Unique geological formations (e.g., cliffs, promontories, natural bridge)	Open area; limited development and use		Campers		Eliminate disamenities where possible
			Natural quiet		Visibility-obscuring smog	Minor roads to hilltop
			Privacy and repose			
		Camping and active recreation	Natural landmark		Noise-generating traffic	Hiking, riding, bicycling trails
			Communion with nature			Viewpoints
			Educational values		Privacy-destroying developments elsewhere on hilltop	Campsites
			Flora, fauna, wildlife, etc.		Levelling and denuding of hilltop	Stores, car parks, picnic areas
			Being able to get away from it all		Any development as required for residential, commercial, or industrial use	
			Active recreation			

preserve the primitive character of Mt. San Gorgonio, or to halt the intrusion of out-door advertising and other aesthetic "insults" within the urban community are examples of this type of amenity response. Within any community such behavior signals the existence of a reservoir of public opinion concerned with amenity protection and/or development.

AMENITIES, DISAMENITIES, AND THEIR PRECIPITANTS

As noted earlier (and as detailed in Table 1 opposite), it is necessary to distinguish between precipitants (which extend over very many natural and man-made features) and amenities (or stimuli).

Amenity planning and management should be concerned both with the amenity values of the basic natural resources (air, water, etc.) and with those *areas* in which a special juxtaposition of resource endowments and environmental quality characteristics converge at some point in time and space to result in the quality of "being pleasant and agreeable."

The qualitative properties of any basic natural resource, such as water, may be judged, at least conceptually, by an amenity scale. Similarly, some of the public concern over air pollution is directed at the visibility-reducing characteristics of a polluted air mass, characteristics which are aesthetically offensive to a substantial fraction of the population.

In contrast, the concept of an amenity resource *area* (ARA) is intended to refer to some point in time and space at which a special juxtaposition of environmental amenity precipitants occurs and which exhibits a complex pattern of amenity stimuli and response. Such a complex system is presented in Table 1, which deals with a hypothesized area consisting of a major precipitant, a hilltop bordered by a park. Within the area, a variety of supporting amenity precipitants are also discernible, each influencing detectable respondent groups. The population exposed to these precipitants responds to both single amenity variables and to combinations of those variables. The boundaries of any amenity resource area may be difficult to draw, but nevertheless seem to be prescribed by the pattern of stimuli and human reactions to them exhibited within the system.

Referring back to the question of measurement, these concepts suggest that for any amenity resource area, and for any level of amenity quality, there is:

1. a discoverable exposure group;
2. a discoverable respondent group;
3. a discoverable distribution of response intensity within that group;
4. a discoverable economic demand (value) for the amenity;
5. a discoverable cost for protecting and/or developing the amenity;
6. a discoverable economic gain or loss for protecting and/or developing the amenity.

Demand for Amenities*

Demand for amenities is related to both sociocultural and economic factors. The amenity demands of an individual at any income level are a function of his cultural experience, his social conditioning to environmental quality variables, and the attitudes and habits of other individuals within his life space.

An individual's life style and his concern with and demand for natural amenities within the urban community is influenced by the life style of his parents and family. Beyond these response-influencing processes, however, yet another force influences the level of demand for natural amenities within urban communities. We have called this influence the "acculturation factor," by which we mean to suggest that a growing fraction of our population is learning to appreciate particular amenities as a consequence of being exposed to them, perhaps for the first time. The rash of campers on our highways, the growing fleet of pleasure boats on our waterways, and the substantial sale of camping and hiking equipment is confirmation that this process is widely operative within our urban communities.

The environmental expectations of individuals at comparable income levels rise as a function of increases in these income levels. Galbraith has suggested that it makes no sense whatsoever to buy a Cadillac and then be forced to drive it over a rutty country road. Rising personal levels of economic affluence are matched by purchase of some private goods whose possession demands an escalating quality of the public environment.

We suggest, therefore, that a "ratchet-effect" is operative within our society in terms of our environmental quality aspirations. As income levels and economic affluence rise, we are motivated to satisfy new needs, quite unlike those which have traditionally motivated us. In short, Maslow's hypothesis concerning a hierarchy of human needs and motivations[18] seems to be operative within our economic marketplace.

Even if the present proportion of amenity seekers within our population remains constant, population growth alone will escalate amenity demands within our growing centers. Compound this escalation with certain inevitable losses in the absolute quantity of amenity resource areas within, and within reach of, our metropolitan centers, and the enlarged public amenity demand seems formidable indeed. Splice this with an enlarging proportion of amenity seekers whose levels of economic affluence have risen and who have been acculturated to value an amenity experience, and one begins to perceive the nature of future amenity demands.

Discussing the principle of "option demand" as a useful tool for economists and planners, Weisbrod hypothesized the existence of a privately owned park operated out of admission fees collected from its users. Unfortunately, the total costs of operating that park cannot be covered by such fees and the owner therefore faces the demands

---

Editor's note: For further elaboration of this point, with an emphasis on recreation, see Chapter 4, particularly pp. 143–52.

[18] Maslow, *Motivation and Personality.*

of allocative-efficiency which dictate that the park be closed. Given such a situation, Weisbrod suggests,

. . . a profit-maximizing entrepreneur would cease operating if all costs could not be covered— that is, if the present value of future costs exceeded the present value of future revenue. But it may be socially unsound for him to do so. To see why, the reader need recognize the existence of people who anticipate purchasing the commodity (visiting the park) at some time in the future. This "option value" should influence the decision of whether or not to close the park and turn it to an alternative use. . . . The potential consumer may have an option demand throughout his lifetime, and yet he may die without ever having purchased the commodity.[19]

Concluding with the view that public subsidies or investments may be necessary to meet the "option demand," Weisbrod states that:

The fact that the revenue of a private operator is limited, as a practical matter, to user charges, prevents his capturing the option demand of non-users. It follows that the inability of the operator to make a profit does not necessarily imply the economic inefficiency of the firm. If he had the power to tax he could supplement user charges with charges for the option services being generated. . . . Although it is only at the margin of closing down, or, in general, of curtailing supply, that the option demand is relevant, these are precisely the points at which the question is likely to arise; should the private firm be subsidized or possibly operated publicly rather than permitting services to be cut? The argument presented above does not imply an affirmative answer in all cases. It does imply that a negative answer is not necessarily justified, even on the grounds of allocative efficiency.

Can man-made features in large measure substitute for natural phenomena? Probably not. Technology will probably not advance to a point at which unique physical phenomena could be replicated or extinct species resurrected. Krutilla[20] has pointed out that while the landscape can be manufactured in a pleasing way under certain conditions — with artistry and the use of the large earth-moving equipment possible under today's construction technology (e.g., open-pit mines may be refilled and the surroundings rehabilitated in a way to approximate the original conditions) — these possibilities are limited, and in any case would still require "the co-operation of nature." He notes that although the supply of fabricated goods and commercial services is capable of continuous expansion from a given resource base as a result of scientific discoveries and mastery of techniques, the supply of natural phenomena is virtually inelastic. Moreover, even if it were possible to replicate unique physical phenomena or resurrect extinct species, it is not clear that fabricated replicas would have a value equivalent to that of the originals. Therefore, he argues, natural environments will represent irreplaceable assets of appreciating value with the passage of time.

[19] Burton A. Weisbrod, "Collective Consumption Services of Individual Consumption Goods," *Quarterly Journal of Economics*, Vol. LXXVII, No. 3 (August 1964), pp. 472–73.
[20] John V. Krutilla, "Conservation Reconsidered," *American Economic Review*, Vol. 57, No. 4 (1967).

There is a growing viewpoint that with the new technologies now on the horizon, the future should see much greater environmental control, and therefore should open up much greater opportunity with respect to the choice of living and working areas. For example, the Meyersons point to the possibility of an airconditioning shed being erected over an entire community, of irrigation tempering the landscape, and of bulldozers making hills or even mountains on a former flat plain.[21] They ask whether these developments will stop the migration of people to the areas of natural amenity and of pleasantest climate (in short, to Gottmann's Riviera-type urban amenity areas) and help to equalize population distribution throughout a region, state, country, or the world.

With these new technologies, it has been argued, man's environment can now be designed down to "a gnat's eyelash." In Dubos' words: "Modern man can almost orchestrate at will the nature and intensity of the stimulus he receives from the external world, and he can exercise some measure of control over his responses to them.... He can even live underground if necessary."[22]

Most persons would accept the argument, however, that the man-made environment cannot be a total substitute for the natural environment, and that, indeed, man requires daily links with the natural environment. For example, the lawyer-planner, Anne Louise Strong, has stated, "A need for amenity is not likely to be satisfied by a series of macadam-covered vacant lots equipped with basketball hoops."[23] Moreover, she suggests that while further research on the subject is needed, it probably can be assumed that "regular immersion of man in the natural environment, as differentiated from a passing-through encased in a climate-controlled car, train, or bus, is salubrious."

Furthermore, new technological developments should make possible a much greater concentration of population in our urban areas, which, in turn, should create a greater demand for urban natural amenities. New technological applications are likely to speed up the tendency, already in evidence, for families to "travel light."[24] These developments will make possible a style of living in which household appurtenances of all kinds are superfluous. Taking into account the space requirements entailed by storage of household equipment and of appliances today, it is clear — so goes the argument — that we can get by with considerably less space in the dwelling units of the future. Thus, these technologies will reinforce a trend already noted by many observers toward building patterns which are more dense, more nucleated, and more clustered.

Accompanying the tighter, denser development with stronger centers, there will be less private open space (that is, a much smaller fraction of the population will live

[21] Martin and Margy Meyerson, "Multiple Choices," in Nigel Calder (ed.), *The World in 1984* (Penguin Books, 1965), Vol. 2.

[22] René Dubos, *Man Adapting* (Yale University Press, 1965), pp. 270 and 279.

[23] F. Fraser Darling and John P. Milton (eds.), *Future Environments of North America, Transformation of a Continent* (The Natural History Press, 1966), p. 695.

[24] John Dyckman, "The Impact of Technological Change," *Forum on Neighborhoods: Today and Tomorrow* (Phila. Housing Association, No. 1, February 1958).

in single-family homes and thus there will be fewer small lots), and at every geographical scale of development there will probably be substantial open space, commonly enjoyed and publicly or commonly owned.

In light of these probable developments, Dyckman sees that we may, if we so
choose, have a reasonable degree of amenity at considerably greater densities than
exists in our cities today. He sees this prospect because of the possible great expansion
of the present trend toward two-house living:

It is economically possible and based on present cultural tendencies, socially not improbable,
that a pattern of living may evolve which entails living part-time in dense center cities, and
part-time in country semi-wilds or even perhaps in houseboats on lakes or rivers.[25]

The Amenity Decision System

Clearly, any environmental policy strategy for urban communities must be based
on the fact of continued urbanization and urban growth and not simply on current
situations. The massive city-building effort that yet lies ahead provides us with
numerous opportunities to readjust our traditional decisional practices and undeniably
would be enhanced by new sets of criteria concerned with the range of consequences
to environmental quality and life styles — optional patterns of land use, urban design,
population distribution, and other factors. One of the primary virtues of the systems
approach is the new visibility it may give to these consequences.

If the approach is to be made operational, however, attention must be given to
correction of the most grievous deficiencies of the present decisional system. If the
information fed back into the system is confined only to economic criteria, rather than
being concerned with the full range of human responses to environmental quality
conditions, then it seems likely that the system will behave in the future much as it
has behaved in the past, at least in respect to the protection and/or development of
natural amenities within our cities. The "social accounting" movement seeks to correct
this deficiency.

Also exerting pressure on the existing system is an increasing volume of citizen
protestation about the current quality of the urban environment and the lack of public
policy concern for our natural amenities. Throughout the country citizen groups have
risen in recent years to promote changes in traditional business and public policy
practices. Attacks on service station architecture, billboard jungles, aesthetically
offensive commercial strips, junkyards, the bulldozer rape of the cityscape, overhead
utility lines, and unlandscaped freeways have been mounted by citizen groups throughout the United States and are generating new demands for the public policy system
to concern itself with the amenity values of urban natural resources.

Each of these several forces is a part of the "decisional reality" within which the
amenity planners will function in the future.

[25] *Ibid.*, p. 3.

THE PHYSICAL CONTEXT OF AMENITY DECISIONS

It is our view that urban amenity planning and management must focus on the environmental subsystems, or "cells," which comprise the urban or metropolitan community. This follows Perloff[26] and others who argue that the urban community may be viewed as a set of interacting subsystems. We see man as an environmentally mobile creature who moves from sub-environment to sub-environment (from cell to cell) throughout the course of the day, the week, the year, and his lifetime within the metropolitan community. We have identified the *following* sub-environments which interface within a metropolitan community: (1) the *residential* environment, including the dwelling unit, its surrounding space, and the agglomeration of other dwelling places comprising any particular cell; (2) the *occupational* environment, including the work place and its surrounding service facilities, both interior and exterior to the structure or site within which the work is performed; (3) the *service* environment, including the institutions, organizations, commercial establishments, and other facilities which dispense commodities to urban man as he performs one or another of the functions associated with the other environmental cells; (4) the *leisure* or *recreational* environment, including all the places, facilities, and areas to which urban man transports himself for pleasure-seeking, rest, and respite — both within the urban environment and outside the urban complex itself, the latter comprising part of what Perloff refers to as "the environment of the urbanite"; (5) the *commuter* environment, including all the pathways followed by the urbanite in transporting himself from his residential environment to other environments within the metropolitan complex and to places such as leisure or recreational areas outside the metropolitan complex itself; and (6) the *background* environment. Each sub-environment is a "setting" for people's lives. The objective of environmental planning and management must be to enhance each of these settings, to bring out and heighten — not to submerge — the character of each sub-environment. The challenge is to produce delight in the whole fabric of the entire metropolitan landscape, not merely to pick out the highlights in the fabric.

The available literature suggests that the intensity and extensity of amenity responses within an urban population varies as a function of the sub-environment in which the response is measured. Thus, Robert L. Wilson suggests that people place more value on the environmental quality of their immediate neighborhood than on environmental quality variables which occur at the scale of the entire community.[27] Since his study focused on two comparatively small communities, these findings may be inapplicable to the giant metropolis; they nevertheless suggest the relevance of examining the significance of amenities as a function of the sub-environment in which they occur and the functions which that sub-environment is to serve, and of manipulating environmental variables on the scale of the sub-environment rather than of the whole city in any effort to increase its livability for most people.

[26] Harvey S. Perloff, Chapter 1 of this volume.
[27] Robert L. Wilson, "Livability of the City: Attitudes and Urban Development," in F. Stuart Chapin, Jr., and Shirley F. Weiss (eds.), *Urban Growth Dynamics* (John Wiley and Sons, 1962).

A MANAGEMENT SYSTEM FOR URBAN NATURAL AMENITIES

As suggested above, the amenity planner/manager must concern himself with certain key factors: the amenity precipitants, the pattern of amenity responses, the sub-environments in which they occur, and the decisional system within which amenity decisions are made.

The information collected and processed by the planner must meet more than some abstract standard of need; it must conform to the requirements of the decisional system in which the planner resides and the appetite of that system for various kinds and quantities of information.

We are currently engaged in a study of decision chains which impinge on environmental quality in several major sections of Southern California. One aspect of that study has been the decision chain through which proposals are processed for the subdivision of raw land, the subsequent development of physical facilities, and other improvements on the land. Results to date suggest that the people within the system have failed to perceive the "systemic" nature of their actions and the broad spectrum of environmental goals to which they might address themselves. Individually, they judge the quality of their decisions in terms of a very limited set of criteria — such as structural safety — and do not customarily concern themselves with other qualitative considerations, which they see as the function of "other professionals" or "other departments."

In view of the low amenity value of residential developments within Los Angeles County, the study suggests that something more is necessary than the insertion of new criteria into the system. If natural amenities are to receive attention, and if the competitive processes of our present decisional system are to act rationally with respect to urban amenities, then it may be necessary to build professional "amenity advocates" into the system. For example, Great Britain utilizes amenity planners whose professional task is to protect and/or develop amenities within the geographic zone of their concern. A similar step may be necessary in the United States if amenities are to receive the attention they deserve.

Operationally, it may be useful to adopt such practices as the conduct of amenity precipitant inventories, amenity demand surveys, attitudinal and opinion surveys of selected groups within the urban population, and research pointed at the development of predictive criteria appropriate for use by amenity planners and decision makers.

INVENTORY OF NATURAL AMENITY PRECIPITANTS

Before beginning any management system for urban natural amenities it is necessary to obtain information on the features that now exist in the urban or metropolitan community that may be considered potential amenities — in short, the nature, characteristics, and location of the amenity precipitants.

Because natural amenity precipitants are place-bound (since they are a function of the natural environment) and are not ubiquitous throughout the metropolitan community, and because they perform different functions and evoke different human responses depending on their location within the urban community, it would be helpful to inventory them for various subunits of the whole. Two localized differentiations should be considered: (1) within each of the sub-environments noted on p. 194; (2) within different geographic settings or scales; e.g., at the scale of the home, neighborhood, community, county, and metropolitan region.

That the function of natural amenity precipitants varies at different geographic scales is most clearly seen in the case of open space. Table 2 illustrates various types of open space amenity precipitants typically found at various geographical scales within a metropolitan region.

The open spaces under (1) are intensively used man-made spaces; e.g., yards, gardens, piazzas, plazas, etc.; those under (2a) and (2b) and some of those under (3) are semideveloped areas; e.g., parks, playgrounds, etc.; and part of those under (3) and practically all of those listed under (4) are basically natural areas and features; e.g., natural preserves, beaches, rivers, undeveloped mountain areas, private farms, ranches, or large grazing areas.

In short, while open space at the street scale is uniquely man-made, regional open space is the opposite, you can only take it the way it comes and that is the chief justification for its preservation. Therefore, it is not possible to specify standards for open space at the regional level. Some regions — e.g., New York, San Francisco, and Los Angeles — have a great variety of natural open spaces at the regional level; in Washington and Philadelphia, nature was somewhat less generous; Indianapolis and the Dallas–Fort Worth area, to cite but two examples, will have to be more inventive.

The open space immediately associated with homes and work places — i.e., at the street scale — is experienced more than all other open space. This is open space in microcosm. It is with us day in and day out. This dominance suggests that it has an impact on the role of other levels of open space. Open space at the street scale is also unique because it is the most man-made, both in its quantity and design. Nature can be of some help here — for instance, a few trees in a subdivision may save it from barrenness, or a location on a hillside certainly has many benefits — but for the most part street-scale urban open space is a creation of man. In particular, it is the creation of our architects, urban designers, and city planners, working within the framework and limitations of municipal zoning and subdivision regulations, and thus poses a challenge to these specialists.

AMENITY DEMAND CURVES

As Parr and others[28] have suggested, we need to plot the "behavioral topographies" associated with environmental quality variables, both singly and in the aggregate. More objective information is needed on how people actually respond to amenity and disamenity precipitants within the urban community. Can research instruments be developed and utilized by planners to detect changing response patterns? Can predictive criteria be developed by which planners may more precisely

[28] H. E. Parr, "Mind and Milieu," *Sociological Inquiry*, Vol. XXXIII (Winter, 1963); Raymond C. Studer and David Stea, "Architectural Programming, Environmental Design, and Human Behavior," *Journal of Social Issues*, Vol. XXII, No. 4 (1966).

Table 2.   Classification of Urban Open Space Amenity Resources by Geographic Scale[a]

Scale or level	Examples of open space amenity resources Land	Water
1. Street scale		
a) Building site	Yards; courts; gardens (i.e., sites less buildings)	
b) Group of buildings	Rights-of-way, streets, pedestrian ways, piazzas, plazas, residential commons, tot lots.	
2. Community		
a) Neighborhood	School grounds; playgrounds; small parks (up to 10 acres); hillsides; shopping center; squares.	Small lakes (natural or man-made), ponds, streams, lagoons.
b) Municipality	Parks up to 100 acres, play fields; civic center and other public squares; recreation roads and bicycling, riding, and hiking trails.	
3. County	Mountain and valley floor parks — 100–1,000 acres; shoreline parks; streamside preserves; golf courses; minor conservation areas (flood plains, watersheds, wildflower / bird /game preserves); scenic roads (driving, hiking, etc.); reservoir parks.	Large lakes, rivers, bays, inlets, water conservation reservoirs, islands.
4. Metropolitan region	Mountain and valley floor parks over 1,000 acres; wilderness areas; large conservation areas; private farms, greenbelts, woodland and other land on the urban fringe; coastlines and seacoasts; mountain ranges; milksheds; large institutional open spaces (e.g., university, college, hospital, sports arena, music center); scenic highways; historic natural landmarks.	Major water bodies; e.g., oceans, great rivers, major lakes; marine parks; harbors; islands; tidelands; marshland.

[a] Adapted from: Stanley B. Tankel, "The Importance of Open Space in the Urban Pattern," in Lowdon Wingo, Jr. (ed.), *Cities and Space: The Future Use of Urban Land* (The Johns Hopkins Press for Resources for the Future, 1963), Table 1, p. 61.

determine amenity demand levels, perhaps through inspection of such readily obtainable information as discretionary income levels?

We believe that it is possible to accomplish all this, although a good deal of hard work will have to be done before these planning tools will become available. Several specific targets seem appropriate for such an effort:

1. *Human Response Curves.* These may be thought of as human value or response scales. They should reveal the fraction of the population which responds to any environmental quality variable, or aggregation of such variables (i.e., amenity resources area); the social, economic, and other characteristics of that population fraction; and the distribution of response type and intensity within the respondent group. For example, a *disamenity-amenity* response scale might be constructed for a single environmental quality variable, such as the loading of suspended particulate matter in a cubic

meter of air. At the disamenity end of the scale, human respiratory discomfort and ill health would be measured by a particular range of particulate loadings for a specified respondent group. By relating such loadings to ambient visibility conditions, still further responses could be measured, in terms of human values toward optional conditions of visibility (10 miles, 5 miles, 3 miles, etc.). Through application of paired-comparison methods and other techniques, the utility function of responses to optional visibility conditions might be predicted for specific respondent groups. The intensity of public support for such specific environmental improvement measures as billboard removal, freeway landscaping, protection of primitive areas, etc., might be measured by these techniques and fitted into the response scales.

2. *Economic Demand Criteria.* As a special aspect of human responses to amenities, the economic behavior of urban populations in respect to amenity values deserves much more study. It seems clear that a substantial fraction of the public is willing to pay for amenity values as private goods and that substantial citizen support exists for public programs of investment in protecting amenity values and amenity resource areas. Nevertheless, at present it is difficult to compose precise statements that have predictive value to planners and managers in the public and private sector. For example, how much are people willing to pay to protect views now marred by outdoor advertising and overhead utility lines? Of what value to the purchasers in a subdivision is the protection of an adjacent open area, a hiking and riding trail, or a landscaped traffic collector route? Without new or unusual systems of public inter-vention into the private economic marketplace, the development of answers to these and similar questions would contribute much toward a more rational and socially responsible system of urban amenity management. Frederick Gutheim has pointed out:

In housing economics we have been able to attribute specific values to apartments with balconies, houses with fireplaces, and other design features having little to do with the raw facts of space and structure but much to do with amenity. We know that certain tenants will pay more for these features, and we know how much more they will pay. We also know that location has a specific value, one not always attributable to economic factors, but frequently linked to design. Here we tread more uncertainly; but it should be possible, for example, to compare a house in Georgetown with an identical house in the adjoining community of Foggy Bottom, and to disentangle what parts of the extra value of the Georgetown house are due to its location in a community with definite boundaries, quiet streets, shade trees, ample gardens, historical associations and architectural homogeneity, and what parts are due to its location in a community of high-income families, high property values and accessibility. We can also determine just which families will pay these premiums. Studies of aesthetic value can be usefully pursued at the point of decision when families move in or out, when they buy or sell. They should have a priority second only to experiments and demonstrations in the design of the urban environment itself.[29]

[29] Frederick Gutheim, "Urban Space and Urban Design," in Lowdon Wingo, Jr. (ed.), *Cities and Space: The Future Use of Urban Land* (The Johns Hopkins Press for Resources for the Future, 1963) p. 130.

RESEARCH INTO DECISION-MAKING CRITERIA

Of course, the development of amenity-precipitant inventories, measurement scales, response curves, and predictive economic criteria will not alone provide an improvement in amenity abundance and distribution which many now demand. For such an improvement we must look also at our traditional approach to the "unit" amenity decision. How have we traditionally decided on the allocation of land among competing user groups? How valid are these criteria in the modern urban community?

It is probable that much of the erosion in the amenity value of our urban communities has been produced by our orientation to goals related to short-term economic gains and losses. Given a tidal flat having potential for development either as a small-boat marina and waterfront residential development or as a petro-chemical complex, we often retreat into a "parochial" cost-benefit analysis. If the greatest economic gain accrues to the petro-chemical development, we argue with scientific pride that this is the "preferred" pattern of development. But is this really so?

In John Steinbeck's famous and still unspoiled Monterey–Salinas Valley in California, a recent public conflict focused on this very question. The Humboldt Oil Company desired to locate a major petroleum refinery at Moss Landing, which is located on a small bay at the upper northwestern end of the valley. Construction of the refinery would have resulted in a large economic gain to a limited group of landowners and might have presaged the migration of heavy industry into the valley. In terms of the typical complex of petro-chemical establishments which frequently surrounds refineries, one can predict that construction of the refinery might well have resulted in an enlarged pattern of industrial development throughout the area. Escalating land values, an expanded tax base, enlarged employment opportunities, and a higher level of income for the valley would have been the inevitable result. However, this pattern of development would have destroyed one of the last remaining unpolluted air sheds in California, and one of the most scenically rich resources of the entire state. The valley, and the Monterey Peninsula to which it is linked, are scenic favorites of many Californians residing hundreds of miles from the site. The area has value to these casual users, yet the dollars they leave behind after their infrequent visits probably amount to a much smaller sum than the possible economic gains from industrial, commercial, and intensive residential development of the area. If this area is finally developed, Californians, as well as tourists from the rest of the United States, will have lost a precious resource whose social value simply cannot be measured on an economic scale.

This case suggests that a community of interest may be identified and measurable in respect to any given amenity resource area and that the discoverable community may include nonresidents as well as residents, and casual visitors as well as habitual and frequent nonresident visitors; that, in some cases, the community may even include persons whose life-space is touched by the amenity even though they remain physically remote from it and who would bemoan their loss although they never have, and never will, personally and directly experience it (in short, they represent an "option demand").

In the Moss Landing case, there was a clear need for examination of the broad

Table 3. Information for Decision-Making in Amenity Resource Area (ARA) Planning and Management[a]

Public investment decisions	Allocative and regulatory decisions

1. Cost of acquiring, developing, and/or protecting the ARA in question;
   a. Present (T^1)
   b. Future (T^n).
	1. Reproducibility of ARA;
	   a. Cost of ARA
	   b. Cost of reproducing ARA at another location (ARA^1).

2. Cost of operating the ARA, T^1 to T^n.	2. Non-amenity use demands for ARA.

3. Size of potential respondent group;
   a. Present (T^1)
   b Future (T^n).
	3. Availability of alternative sites for non-amenity uses;
	   a. Cost of ARA site
	   b. Cost of alternative sites.

4. Expected exposure duration frequency distribution of potential respondent group.	4. Size of ARA potential respondent group;
	   a. Present (T^1)
	   b. Future (T^n).

5. Capital costs per respondent and per respondent exposure (T^1 to T^n).	5. Several of the items under "Public investment decisions" also relevant here.
6. Operating costs per respondent and per respondent exposure (T^1 to T^n).	
7. Comparative value of ARA to respondent group.	
8. Distribution of economic valuation of ARA, per unit of exposure, within respondent group.	
9. Distribution of ability to pay within respondent group.	
10. Absolute cost of developing and operating ARA.	

[a] A partial list.

range of potential costs, benefits, and optional solutions for a variety of groups. Excluding the consideration that this location had an undisputed amenity value for a large group of Californians, how many other sites within the state were appropriate for a refinery complex, and at what incremental costs or benefits? Given the loss of this amenity area, what could be done to replace it? What impact would the loss have on the "quality of lives" of the respondent groups?

These considerations suggest to us that the following dictum might be useful to environmental planners and managers: *Given equivalence in the economic potential of resource areas competing for development, such development should occur last in that area which exhibits the greatest amenity potential and in which the projected pattern of development would most adversely affect the area's amenity potential.*

Assuming that adequate inventories of potential amenity resource areas exist, the adoption of such a precept might permit incremental decision making without a gross dysfunction to amenity values.

Similarly, we suggest that a range of information is available to amenity planners, managers, and decision makers that can help with respect to the two broad clusters of decisional problems they face: (1) those dealing with public investments, and (2) those concerned with the public regulation of environmental quality and/or the allocation of amenity resources among competing users. Although it does not lead to any mathematical model appropriate for judging the final end-state decision, such information would expand our understanding of some of the consequences of our decisions. (See Table 3 for a preliminary classification.)

A more rational and socially rewarding system for the planning and management of urban amenities is sorely needed. The main intention of this paper is to emphasize that the development of such a system may be promoted through increased attention to the nature, functions, and systemic qualities of amenities.

6

Transport: key to the future of cities

Wilfred Owen

Senior Fellow, The Brookings Institution

Transport: key to the future of cities

Wilfred Owen

The greater mobility afforded by improved transport is highly valued by today's urban resident. Transport has made city dwellers the beneficiaries of more time, more space, and more opportunity for a fuller life. It may be called a resource-enriching (as well as a resource-using) element in urban life.

The radius of the city has now been extended to embrace new suburban development where the choice of a different kind of urbanism is offered to those who seek more room for living or for the location of industries. New circumferential expressways speed the motor vehicle from one side of the city to the other without passing through the center, and an entirely new urban geography has been introduced by the closer association of outlying communities.

Urban dwellers have greatly enlarged their job opportunities and social contacts as a result of the shorter travel times now possible, and the shopping center has introduced new methods of retail business and of housekeeping. Mobility for the city dweller has also meant more variety of recreation, more vacations, and more weekends away; and for many it has made possible both a house in the city and one in the country or at the beach.

The air age has introduced still further opportunities for those who live in cities, for the airplane has made it possible for businessmen to maintain contact with customers and associates throughout the country, and for professionals of all kinds to co-operate with one another to a degree that was impossible when intercity travel was confined to surface methods. Equally important, for millions of urbanites the airplane has opened the doors to the rest of the world, with resulting international exchanges on a scale hardly conceived of a few years ago.

These are some of the "new resources" and opportunities that transport technology has made available to an urban society. But there are obstacles to realizing their full advantage. The lowest income groups have not been able to afford automobiles or airline tickets, so that for them no new doors have been opened. For millions too poor to own a car or otherwise barred from driving, the trends have actually meant greater limitations on the degree to which urban life can be fully enjoyed. For these people the new patterns of urban development are not well served by public transport or by travel on foot, so that jobs, schools, entertainment, and recreation may all be inaccessible. Even those with the money to pay for mobility often find that the conflict between the space requirements of motorization and the constraints of urbanization result in congestion, loss of time and temper, and new kinds of transport problems. In addition, the provision of transport facilities has often been accomplished without regard for community values, resulting in a progressive deterioration of the urban environment for all residents of the city, rich and poor alike.

The changes brought about by the combination of increased motorization and urbanization have had other unfortunate effects. Those who own automobiles have used them to flee from the problems of the city, leaving the poor and the disadvantaged behind in the slums. Their flight has not only destroyed the true function of the city center but has led to an exploitation of suburban land that produces monotony and conformity in housing and in some cases a new kind of low-density slum. Travel routes from city to suburb have at the same time created roadsides that have polluted the land, in much the same way that urban traffic and industry have polluted the air. Thus a combination of affluence and poverty, of mobility and immobility, and of urban investments without comprehensive development planning has resulted in a strange mixture of run-down cities, disorderly suburbs, blighted landscapes, and in many cases, a poor quality of urban living.

The question, then, is how to reap the advantages of modern transport in order to enhance urban life and at the same time to minimize the deleterious side effects. To achieve these objectives will involve new designs for urban settlement, the appropriate selection of transport technologies, a desirable balance between public and private transport, and the use of transport facilities as a means of building better communities. What can be done will depend partly on the basic economic and social conditions governing urban living in future years, including the success of measures to eradicate poverty and to cope with racial injustice. But the future course of urbanization will also depend on how well we grasp the opportunities for innovations in urban living that modern technology makes possible, and especially the opportunities afforded by the technological revolution in transport.

Underlying Causes of Congestion

History tells us that transport problems have been a major part of the problems of cities for many years, regardless of the kind of transport technology. American cities undertook to relieve traffic congestion by constructing elevated railways and subway facilities before the motor vehicle appeared on the scene. Surface transit vehicles were usurping so much street space in Boston sixty years ago that a subway was constructed to clear the way for the horses and electric cars using the streets.[1] Traffic at rush hours was described back in 1905 as the number one problem of large cities in the United States, and pictures of urban traffic jams in the days of the horse and carriage testify that congestion was bad long before the motor vehicle made it worse. As early as 1902 it was suggested that solutions could best be found "by starting on a bold plan on comparatively virgin soil" rather than attempting "to adapt our old cities to our newer and higher needs."[2]

Contemporary geography provides us with additional evidence that transport problems cannot stem entirely from transport methods, and that they obviously have more deep-seated cause. Traffic congestion in cities has become acute all over the world. Tokyo, with its extensive commuter railways and rapid transit, is as overwhelmed by traffic as Los Angeles, with its automobiles and freeways. Delhi, with its

[1] Edward Dana, "Reflections on Urban Transit" (an address before the Canadian Club, Montreal, April 21, 1947).

[2] Ebenezer Howard, *Garden Cities of Tomorrow* (1902), p. 134.

bullock carts and teeming masses of people, is no less inundated by rush hour traffic than Bangkok, with its buses and bicycles. Istanbul is by no means a motorized city, but its traffic jams are no less exasperating than the more spectacular ones of Rome or Paris.

History and geography both tell us, then, that no matter how people move in big cities, there is almost always an uncomfortable degree of congestion and frustration. Often it seems that the more affluent a nation becomes, and the more advanced its technology, the less successful it is in coping with its traffic problems.

Why have cities allowed themselves to be the victims rather than the beneficiaries of the new mobility? Part of the answer lies in the failure to recognize that there are two aspects to the transport problem: the supply of transport capacity, and the demand created by the various activities taking place in the city. The only times we take both sides of the problem clearly into account is when a pipeline is laid or an elevator installed in a building. In both these cases the capacity of the transport facility is specifically related to the traffic that is to be generated, either by an oil refinery or by the predetermined use of a building.

Designing transport for a whole city is a much more complex task, of course, but the same conditions and solutions obtain. The basic cause of congestion lies in the failure to strike a balance between transport demand and supply. Failure to take the demand aspects into account will continue to make chronic congestion in big cities inevitable. "The time has already come when we are wasting our substance by attempting to squeeze more cars, goods, and people into smaller and smaller areas. The simple geometry of the plan will surely defeat us no matter how long we postpone the day by ingenious engineering."[3]

In the central areas of large cities today, restoration and rebuilding is taking place on a scale that has not been equaled for many years. But the efficiency of this new urban investment will be seriously impaired if the resulting densities and arrangements of urban structures are not accommodated by appropriate measures to facilitate the movement of people and goods. Either transport plans will have to be designed to cope with the congestion being created by urban building programs or the rebuilding itself will have to be tailored to what the transport system can accommodate. Tackling half the problem leads to no solution.

The key question is: What density of development and what systems of activity and land use are to be sought for urban areas under various circumstances in order to assure a satisfying urban environment in which people can move around? There are many reasons favoring a reduction of the congested living typical of most close-in areas of large cities, but it is also questionable whether today's typical suburb and disorderly sprawl are acceptable alternatives. Should urban size and density be reduced, as is often argued, in the interests of physical and mental health, civic order, recreation, scenic beauty, and convenience? Proposals have been made to restrict the size of

[3] G. Holmes Perkins, "The Regional City," in Coleman Woodbury (ed.), *The Future of Cities and Urban Redevelopment* (University of Chicago Press, 1953), p. 39.

cities on the grounds that "effective planning of a metropolis is impossible unless a limit is placed on its maximum size and population."[4] But too low a density denies the purposes of the city and has serious economic disadvantages as well. What size and shape and design of cities will be most satisfactory under various circumstances? Is not the answer to be sought first in asking what cities are for, how they came to develop as they did, why they have continued to grow, and what technological and economic factors appear to be altering some of the age-old concepts of what the city of the future should be like?

Originally men came together in cities because by closer association they were able to accomplish far more than would have been possible had the co-operation and interaction permitted by close urban living been denied. Every kind of goal — from walled protection to industrial production and the pursuit of science and the arts — has been achieved through the interaction of human beings in a community.

This community development in older times was possible only where nature provided the transport capabilities necessary to enable cities to feed themselves. The great cities of the world were originally dependent on water transport. Later, with the development of steam power, they also flourished at the junction of rail lines. Today, in an age of road and air transport — and telecommunications — it is possible for cities to grow at locations where neither water nor rail facilities are uniquely inviting. Yet the older cities continue to grow in total population and in geographic area, as if no basic changes in technology had taken place.

Large cities continue to expand both because of natural growth and because they are able to accept more and more people from the outside without noticeable strain. Growth by accretion has occurred because of individual decisions to take advantage of the urban infrastructure, its markets, and all of the external economies available in a settled community. But these decisions are made without appropriate actions to compensate for the resulting social costs. For instance, a new plant coming to New York benefits from existing markets and infrastructure, and from the great variety of service industries already there to meet its requirements and reduce its risks. The fact that this newly arrived enterprise may increase the congestion and costs of urban living for everyone does not influence the location decision. The city continues to grow because newcomers can still benefit, even if their arrival is detrimental to those already there. The transport situation deteriorates, like everything else, and extensive new public investments can often do no more than maintain standards of service at levels that are barely tolerable.

New technology now makes it likely, however, that some other pattern of urban settlement would make more economic and social sense. For if the original purpose of cities was to enable men to be in closer proximity, and thus communication, with one another, have we not reached the point where the very size of urban agglomerations makes human interaction increasingly difficult and costly? And does not tech-

[4] William A. Robson (ed.), *Great Cities of the World: Their Government, Politics, and Planning* (Macmillan, 1954), p. 103.

nology make it possible to achieve these interactions through more extensive transport and communications rather than simply through togetherness and more intensive crowding? The time has arrived for a new kind of urbanization that avoids the dense-packed continuous buildup, yet gives more freedom of communications than ever before.

Urban Development and Transport Technology

We are now on the threshold of very great advances in the art of transport and communications, and in the capacity of man to enjoy this new order of mobility. Looking first at intercity transport, we see that very soon the airplane will evolve into a vehicle of giant dimensions capable of carrying many hundreds of people at low cost, and many tons of freight at rates competitive with surface transport. These developments could have enormous influence on the spatial distribution of industry.

Two opposite trends in the speed of transport will also influence the design and location of cities. One is the acceleration of aircraft movement to supersonic speeds, which will bring people all over the world within very short travel time of each other. The other is deceleration of aircraft movement to zero miles an hour by new techniques of hovering. The latter will bring air travel to large numbers of cities that previously were too small to support scheduled service.

Along with these potentials are the possibilities of high-speed intercity ground transport. One is the air cushion vehicle, which may attain speeds of up to 250 miles per hour. Another is the automated highway to permit high-speed motor traffic through electric propulsion and electronic guidance. These methods of movement, combined with low-cost transmission of voice and picture by satellite communication systems, could make possible geographically extensive regional cities and close association among widely dispersed centers of population. It may prove easier to maintain contacts through high-speed transport serving large numbers of moderate-sized communities than to journey through the continuous built-up areas of a small number of super-cities. High-speed intercity transport may offer an antidote to low-speed city transport.

This, in fact, is what has been happening to date in the air age. People complain about how much time it takes to get to and from the airport, and that more time is spent going short distances on the ground than long distances in the air. They conclude from this that speeding up the airplane is not going to be much help; that what we need to do is to speed up ground transport.

From another viewpoint, however, speeding up the airplane can help to compensate for the fact that transport on the ground is so bad. And it is far easier and cheaper to improve performance in the air. For improving conditions on the ground involves not simply improving transport but rebuilding the whole urban community. The point here is not that ground transport improvements should be neglected, but that high-speed intercity travel can be and often is a desirable economic trade-off. The trip to the airport in many cities is annoying, but the fact that jet-propulsion has cut flying time in half often makes it seem worthwhile.

But new transport technology also offers the possibility of improving local circulation, either on the ground or in the air, and this could help to make high densities more feasible. Automated highways, for example, will permit many times the number of vehicles presently accommodated by a lane of ordinary highway. Parking may also be automated in great storage areas. Electric vehicles can overcome the problems of noise and fumes, and new techniques of tunnel construction, such as the laser beam, may help to develop lower-cost underground transport systems. Urban transit will also be able to take advantage of the air cushion principle to provide quiet and vibrationless movement without wheels, and computer control of bus routing may permit surface pickup and delivery of passengers at costs as low as one-fourth to one-tenth of taxi costs. Local air bus service with vertical take-off and landing capabilities also offers hope for metropolitan area transport.

In the movement of freight, equally promising methods may ease the burden on city streets. One is the substitution of non-transport solutions for what once were transport problems. Already the use of gas and electricity has appreciably reduced urban traffic in fuel. Now solid wastes are being either incinerated or ground and moved by pipe. Other transport-saving devices may be developed through food processing, nuclear power, and the shift from petroleum to electricity for automobile propulsion. Freight movement may also be facilitated by underground belt conveyors, the movement of solids by pipeline, and the extension of container transport systems. Higher buildings and the use of high-speed elevators introduce further possibilities of making supercities manageable.

Vertical development has become increasingly attractive as the cost of building high structures has declined. Tall buildings offer the advantage of conserving ground space and making it economically feasible to maintain large surrounding areas of open land. The skyscraper can also be used for a variety of purposes, including work places as well as living space, schools, recreation, and services. Transportation among these activities by elevator provides low-cost automatic service that is designed from the start to meet the demand. This vertical system of urban-living-with-a-view accomplishes many of the goals of urban design that have been frustratingly difficult to achieve on a horizontal plane.

It seems fair to say, therefore, that the new transport techniques and other technical innovations at our disposal offer a wide set of options, from greater dispersal to still greater concentration. But other factors need to be taken into account, and in particular the anticipated changes in population and in economic and social conditions.

The Implications of Economic Growth

Economic trends will combine with technology to change the character of urban settlement. First of all, we confront a very sizable expansion of the urban economy. Between 1966 and 1985 the population of the United States is expected to increase by 50 million. Gross national product in two decades may be double what it is today, so that within less than a decade, the average family income in the United States may rise to $10,000 per year. Together these two factors mean that a great deal of new urban development will be taking place which potentially can be of much higher quality than the cities of the past. In about a decade and a half we will be building the equivalent of 1,000 new cities, each with a population of 50,000.[5]

What is in question is the extent to which we will in fact be building new communities to meet the new demand, focusing growth in existing large metropolitan areas, or expanding exurbia beyond the limits of today's urban boundaries.

One of the most significant influences will be the effect of affluence on the expansion of private transport. Automobile ownership will continue to increase more rapidly than population in the next two decades as a general increase in economic activity is accompanied by a more equitable distribution of income. As families move up the income ladder, increased expenditure for transportation always follows. For example, in 1966 only 28 per cent of families with annual incomes of between $1,000 and $2,000 owned an automobile, but 93 per cent of families with incomes of $7,500 to $10,000 were car owners, and 30 per cent of them owned two cars or more.[6] In the low income brackets, less than 6 per cent of consumer expenditure went for transport; in the highest brackets, expenditure was between 12 and 15 per cent.[7]

How much of an increase in automobile registrations is likely can be judged to some extent by past relations between car ownership and population. There was one car for every 2.4 persons in the United States in 1965, compared to 4.8 persons per car in 1948. Over the next two decades better cars and better roads, along with economic growth, may be expected to produce a still greater density of automobile ownership. The upward trend in motoring has been closely comparable to trends in gross national product, which, together with the further growth of the suburbs, will mean an increasing number of multiple-car families. The possibility of one car for every two people appears to be a conservative expectation and would mean a total of some 130 million cars by 1985. The probable addition of 20 million trucks would raise total 1985 registrations to the 150 million mark.

The outlook for more motorization makes the prospects for high-density living less inviting, for, granted the other factors that might make good circulation more feasible in large urban agglomerations, the presence of great numbers of additional private vehicles will certainly favor a more open type of urban design. Other forces may be expected to press in the same direction. They include the demand for more urban space per person, both at home and at work, as well as additional space requirements for the new machines and processes of automated offices and industries. Space requirements per person may also be expected to increase with the decline in working hours, for leisure time will expand the requirements for recreation.

Along with the deconcentration that will be encouraged by these trends, indus-

---

[5] Robert C. Weaver, "The Significance of Public Service in American Society" (Address to the 50th Anniversary Celebration, Institute of Public Administration, University of Michigan, May 25, 1964), p. 5.

[6] Automobile Manufacturers Association, *Automobile Facts and Figures* (Detroit: AMA, 1967), p. 39.

[7] *Household Income and Expenditure Statistics No. 1, 1950–1964* (Geneva: International Labour Office, 1967), p. 247.

trial location decisions will be made with less concern for transport and more concern for climate and recreational opportunities. This will mean a continuing decentralization of activities throughout the country. For good transport and communications are making it possible for economic activities to be situated over wide areas of the country recently considered inaccessible.

Within this general framework of deconcentration and decentralization, we can expect to find that very different kinds of urban patterns will emerge. The giant city will be encouraged to grow still bigger by the increasing ability of transport to feed and supply large urban populations, by the growth of vertical structures and vertical transport by elevator, and by the low-cost exploitation of underground space. At the same time, there will be the opportunity to accommodate new urban growth in more moderate-sized cities, which either are entirely new or have been created through the expansion of existing towns. These settlements might offer most of the advantages of the larger cities, and some additional advantages as well. They would introduce an urban pattern that might be called the new regional city — a whole region of urban development that includes countryside as well as more densely built-up urban areas. As Lewis Mumford has envisioned, the farmer and the city man, separated through all history, could be brought together in the regional city, where rural residents could enjoy the same benefits of education, medicine, and cultural activities as the urban dweller, and where the apartment dweller could enjoy the advantages of the open country.

Such new towns could be designed and built from the start to incorporate a balance between transport supply and the traffic-generating activities of the community. The new towns could also serve as a necessary supplement to renewal of the old; for the satisfactory deconcentration of existing cities will require alternative sites for industry and housing outside the old built-up areas.

Still another direction for the coming urbanization will be much wider extensions of exurbia, so that people can live in the country yet lead a life that is essentially urban and urban-related. Transport and communications, together with innovations in power, will permit dispersal of urban living over the entire countryside.

All of the alternatives for the urban future appear to meet a need, and to reflect what, in fact, is already taking place. Yet each of these solutions, if it was the only one offered, might be quite unsatisfactory. The supercity, for example, may reach a practical limit at which increasing marginal social costs cannot be sustained. The opposite course of unrestrained dispersal may also prove too costly — especially in the sense of restricting human interaction, and of devouring open space. The concept of the regional city, on the other hand, may make allowance for both concentration and dispersal, and for the old cities as well as the new towns associated with them.

What seems to be called for is both many kinds of urban settlements and further experimentation with new forms, in order to offer a variety of options that will suit a variety of tastes. And the selection of how and where one lives will necessarily dictate the choices of transport that can be made available. Cities need to be very different places for different kinds of people who are doing different kinds of things.

Transport needs will vary accordingly. Maximum fulfillment for an individual may mean different things. For instance, for a painter, it may mean living in the largest city and communicating with other painters locally but also on a world-wide basis through works displayed in museums. For another individual engaged in scientific research, and participating perhaps with people similarly engaged in other countries, the concept of city is global, and his work calls for intercity and intercontinental mobility. Urban location and transport needs also vary with different age groups, different family sizes, and different levels of income. Some have reasons to be close to the city center, and others to stay farther out. The degree of dependence on one form of transport or another will be contingent on these conditions, and on a large number of other variables that will make the choice different for different occasions.

What we are concerned with is accommodating variety and making options available for those who live in cities, whether the setting is supercity, small city, suburbia, or exurbia. To meet these requirements we will need to develop a strategy for urban settlement that encompasses the whole nation. We need a national policy for urbanization that permits us to have supercities that can be lived in and moved in; dispersal that does not preempt the growing requirements for open space and recreation; suburbs that provide a more open type of development, yet avoid isolation; new towns that profit from the lessons of old towns; and groups of urban places in regional associations linked together by modern transport and communications. But if one option is not to interfere with the realization of another, there must be broad standards and policies for the whole.

National Policy and Urban Planning

The role of transport in a nation's total economy is better understood than its role in the city. At the national level there is more awareness that transport is an essential ingredient of almost everything to be accomplished. It opens up the land for cultivation and enables the expanding population to be fed. It makes accessible natural resources and helps to make their exploitation economically feasible. In rural areas, mobility enables the doctor to visit and the children to get to school; and it helps to overcome the isolation of the village. Transport is also an important adjunct to industry, for it supplies the raw material inputs for the factory and enables the products of industry to be made available to consumers.

Thus when we view the intricate systems of economic and social activity that operate on a national scale, we see quite readily how important is man's ability to move himself and his goods with relative economy and ease. But what is so obvious for an entire nation is less so for cities, even though the situation is comparable. The city is such a complex economic organism that even its inhabitants seem unable to grasp the many things that are going on all at once. Very few people in a big city know or care where their food comes from, how it gets there, and by what local distribution network the community is assured of eating. More is known about passenger transport because we all experience it directly, but again we have only a limited understanding of the complicated patterns of travel required by different categories of urban residents and the underlying economic and social conditions and spatial arrangements of cities that create travel demands.

In national development plans it is necessary to articulate the broad goals and specific targets that a society is striving to achieve, and then, in the transport sector, to translate these goals into what will have to be moved. Perhaps the goals will need to be modified when transport requirements are taken into account.

In some cases the need for transport may be better satisfied by non-transport solutions. For example, it may be that the peak transport problem during the harvest can be handled more economically by adding to storage capacity and processing facilities. Or the burden of transporting fuel may suggest locating power plants close to the sources of energy and transmitting power by wire. Changes in the location of proposed industrial developments may also help to resolve transport problems.

These approaches and conditions have their counterparts in urban areas. Cities, as well as countries, need to articulate their goals. The task is to build the kinds of communities that will provide maximum opportunities for human development through economic, social, and cultural enhancement. To this end cities will need housing, schools, libraries, hospitals, parks, recreation facilities, and a host of services that help make employment productive and leisure time an asset. And they need to be pleasant places in which to work and play. This means that they should be desirably situated, they should have ready access to the country and to other cities, and they should provide a sound basis for supporting themselves, including transport and other infrastructure.

In a world in which space is being rapidly compressed by high-speed transport and instantaneous communications, one approach to a national policy for cities should be to focus on the land and how it is used. There should be general agreement on the tentative boundaries of lands to be left in forests, farms, recreation areas, and useful open space. This in turn may influence policies as to how the expansion of urban areas might best be directed, how cities could be kept from running into each other, which cities should be encouraged to expand, and what sites should have priority for the building of new towns.

Once the general contours of a total urban system are envisioned for the nation, the next step is to lay out the kinds of transport facilities needed to tie the urban system together and to make the metropolitan regions and individual cities themselves mobile. This obviously requires different approaches for cities of different size and character, so that a high degree of diversity would be achieved within the broad outlines of national urbanization policy. But some broad guidelines can be enumerated:

1. Transportation is so shrinking the dimensions of the nation that in terms of elapsed time we are rapidly becoming a nationwide metropolitan area. Thus national transport policies and the provision of intercity transport services will have a significant influence on the nature of urban problems and their solution.

2. Within urban areas, the scarcity of available land suggests that transport facilities be carefully designed to conserve and protect land or to make it serve multiple purposes.

3. Large amounts of land will be used for transport in any event, and this land and adjacent properties comprise the parts of the city seen most often by the largest number of people. For this reason, land devoted to transport should be made to enhance the city and the lives of its inhabitants.

4. Transport facilities are a means of attaining urban goals, and should be built to promote specific objectives. This means making transport programs an integral part of programs for housing, education, health, industrial development, commercial operations, and recreation.

5. Since transport is not an end in itself, the arrangements and interrelations among land uses should be designed to reduce unnecessary transport. Cities should maximize the opportunities to move but minimize the necessity for movement.

6. People spend a considerable amount of time in transport vehicles and in terminals. These are accordingly an important part of the urban environment. Vehicles should be made cheerful and comfortable, and responsive to the requirements of human dignity. Terminals should be attractive, instructive, and inspirational both to travelers and to the neighborhood.

7. Many of the uses of the transport system are in conflict. These conflicts should be avoided by separation of uses where this will help to achieve more effective transport operations.

8. Since transport systems comprise a variety of methods, these should be so interrelated that they provide complete and physically integrated services.

9. Variety in transport facilities and services needs to be maintained to provide options that will meet the different types of transport demand created by different ages, incomes, occupations, weather conditions, times of the day, and other circumstances.

The question that has to be answered in every city, then, is how can improvements in transport help to achieve the goals of better urban living. And conversely, how can the city avoid the creation of unnecessary transport demands? Since resources are limited and goals virtually unlimited, there is obvious need to strike an appropriate balance among the many different programs of capital improvement in order to assure that the improvement of transport does not conflict with the attainment of basic goals.

To illustrate, an elevated highway to speed commuter traffic may destroy the goal of developing an attractive downtown and persuading people to live closer in to avoid commuting. A poorly located highway can make an urban renewal project impossible, and the noise, fumes, and unsightliness of some traffic solutions can defeat the goal of attracting new industries. Cities, like countries, have to seek internal consistency in the measures they adopt, and transport provides more than its share of opportunities to produce inconsistent results.

Traffic Patterns and Their Meaning

If the transport program is to be oriented to urban goals, and if the goals themselves are to reflect what is needed and wanted, we need to learn more about how people use the city. The elaborate studies made in recent years of why people travel can help us to understand urban activity and to visualize the transport solutions they call for.

The greatest volume of movement on city streets is caused by people getting to work and back home again. In the Baltimore metropolitan area, this home-to-work travel accounts for 38 per cent of all trips by all transport methods, and the situation is roughly comparable in other big cities. Some people also travel while on the job, either in sales or services, or in freight delivery and passenger transport. Total work-oriented trips thus account for 47 per cent of urban travel. Another 16 per cent are shopping trips and family business, including trips to the doctor. An additional 16 per cent are for social and recreational purposes: visiting friends and relatives, going to the movies, a restaurant, concert, museum, or to church, or just going for a ride. School trips make up another 10 per cent of passenger trips on a typical day in Baltimore.[8]

How these trips are taken reveals the diverse requirements for transport under different conditions. Most trips in the metropolitan area are by automobile — 70 per cent in all — while 18 per cent are by public transit vehicles and 7 per cent on foot. These are overall figures that reflect the fact that by 1966 the number of people using mass transit facilities in the United States, including buses and rail facilities, had fallen to less than half the 1952 level of patronage. But for certain kinds of travel, and at close-in locations, mass transit continues to play a major role. This is especially true of home-to-work travel focusing on the center. In Manhattan, at the extreme among cities, 74 per cent of all persons entering the downtown area during a 24-hour period travel by mass transit. Mass transit patronage is even greater between 7 A.M. and 10 A.M., when 85 per cent travel by bus, subway, or train. In Philadelphia, mass transit accounts for 50 per cent of all trips made throughout the day, but in the evening rush hour the proportion of transit riding rises to 72 per cent.

Altogether, on an average weekday, transit facilities in the United States still provide some 25 million rides. These transit services are generally inadequate from the standpoint of comfort and convenience and, at the very least, steps need to be taken to provide more acceptable accommodations for those who use these facilities. In addition, transit ought to be made more attractive for those who would like to use it but who find it too costly, difficult, burdensome, confusing, or distasteful.

There is reason to believe that the decline in transit may be nearing an end. Thus far the downward trends have been the natural result of improved economic conditions, for every family able to do so has purchased an automobile as soon as income permitted. With many millions of families yet to move out of the poverty class, there is still further potential for a rise in car ownership relative to population. At the same time, however, an opposite trend toward more riders is being created by the growth of population and the growing importance of age groups dependent on transit.

In 1966 there were 55 million adults over 65 and children between the ages of

[8] Wilbur Smith and Associates, *Baltimore Metropolitan Area Transportation Study* (Wilbur Smith and Associates, 1964).

5 and 13. This was an increase of 26 million over 1940. By 1970 the number of these potential transit riders will increase to 70 million.[9] Thus, as new automobile registrations slow down relative to population growth, the effect of these rising numbers of young and old should begin to be felt. The resulting increase in transit patronage may be augmented by improvements in transit equipment, service standards, and operating techniques.

Changes in income distribution and efforts to assist the lowest income groups will also tend to increase transit riding. Among the poor, many more trips would be made today if people had the money to pay for them. We know there are jobs that are not taken because they are too far away or too costly to reach. We also know that both old people and young are prevented from enjoying many of the recreational and cultural possibilities offered by the city because the public transport services they depend on are not available. The goals of living in a community are often unattainable because people are unable to negotiate the distances that separate their living quarters from other parts of the city.

Traffic studies fail to reflect these unmet demands, and they also neglect to tell us how many trips might have been avoided if destinations had been more convenient. For example, more shopping for everyday needs might be performed on foot if convenient neighborhood shopping areas were provided, and car trips to recreation areas might be less frequent if there were parks and play space close at hand. And since peak traffic volumes reflect in part the city worker's efforts to flee the downtown area at night, those too could be reduced substantially by a combination of better housing, better schools, more job opportunities, and a more satisfactory environment close in.

Thus, the study of traffic data and of traffic potentials points to important approaches to meeting urban needs and to overcoming the conditions that underlie transport problems. They indicate that the goals of the community need to be furthered by improving both automobile and public transport capabilities, and that despite the predominance of the automobile in the total picture, public carriers will continue to be essential for specific groups, times, and places.

Horizontal, Vertical, and Time Separation

As soon as we view all the transport problems together, as an integrated system, it is clear that on many routes there needs to be a separation of conflicting operations to achieve reasonable standards of efficiency. On many streets, for example, the attempt to use a limited width of traveled way for both parked and moving vehicles cuts down effective traffic capacity by one-third to one-half. Additional conflicts result from mixing local traffic with through traffic. In many cities, vehicles not destined for the center are forced to pass through the city to get from one side to the other, causing unnecessary congestion where roads have the least capacity. The mixing of pedestrians and motor vehicles is another conflict of street uses that has had unfortunate results. A

[9] *Economic Report of the President* (U.S. Government Printing Office, 1967), p. 235. For the year 1985, an average was computed for series A and D population projections.

quarter of a million walkers, the majority of them in cities, have been killed in the United States during the past 25 years. Much of the inefficiency of transit, too, is the result of buses being forced to share the streets with large numbers of automobiles that slow down service and increase operating losses.

Innovations in the design and financing of off-street parking facilities are needed to provide a satisfactory low-cost solution to this aspect of traffic congestion. Removal of parked cars will be feasible only when garages are built at frequent intervals to provide an alternative to leaving cars at the curb. This should be done wherever the social cost of parking on the street exceeds the cost of furnishing space off the street. In addition to parking charges, other sources of revenue for off-street facilities could include vehicle fuel and servicing outlets included within the buildings, and the use of rooftops or top floors for neighborhood recreation and community activities.

In downtown areas, a network of existing streets designated for bus use only might alleviate public carrier problems during peak hours of the day. Commercial truck traffic could be excluded during morning and evening rush hours, or deliveries confined to rear entrances. Private cars passing through the area might be excluded entirely. Or bus traffic could be separated from other traffic by providing reservations on the side or in the middle of main boulevards, as was once done for the streetcar, and in Europe still is.

These types of solutions require better measurement of their cost and effectiveness for the system as a whole. They also introduce the need for new technology. Satisfactory operation in congested areas suggests a quiet electric-powered motor vehicle, and improved bus operations for downtown circulation suggest the use of smaller buses on more frequent schedules. The large, awkward, noisy bus that appears at infrequent intervals is not designed to furnish good urban service.

What is needed in total is a system of streets, garages, sheltered bus stops, and buses designed to accommodate short-haul passengers with frequent service. There should also be appropriate communications to monitor bus operations, to keep riders informed, and to speed up car storage and delivery.

Horizontal separation to improve traffic efficiency should include the isolation of pedestrians from motorized transport. Excellent examples are found in downtown shopping centers and pedestrian malls in Boston, Philadelphia, Hartford, Rotterdam, Milan, The Hague, Berne, and other cities, as well as in the new towns of Britain. In Venice, pedestrians have exclusive use of a land network of walkways, plazas, bridges, and stairways covering the entire city. Automobiles owned by Venetians and visitors are left in a multi-storied garage and parking area next to the railway station, at the entrance to the city.

Renewal areas and new suburbs can be designed with separate transport systems for pedestrians and motorized traffic. By so doing it is possible to overcome the slowdown and inefficiency of mixing motor traffic with people, and suffering the consequences in congestion and accidents.

Vertical separation through the use of tunnels and elevated structures can also segregate vehicles and pedestrians. Where transport facilities are depressed, the use of air rights over them may make it possible to design platforms for pedestrians, for local traffic, and for parks. This approach has been successful in many instances through the use of space above railway tracks and rail yards, as well as express highways. Vertical separation is also being accomplished effectively by underground rapid transit systems. The cleanliness, quiet, and attractiveness of the new subways in Paris, Milan, Montreal, and other cities have demonstrated how subway transport can be combined with underground shopping facilities and pedestrian walkways for improved circulation in major cities.

An additional type of traffic separation is time separation, which can be accomplished in two ways. One is the pricing of transport services to encourage off-peak use and to discourage peak-hour traffic. The other is the staggering of work hours to achieve the same effect. While much has been said about the impracticability of these approaches, they have had considerable success in the limited degree to which they have been tried. This is especially true of staggered work hours. The need for simultaneous arrivals and departures has not been convincingly demonstrated, and shorter hours of work may provide added opportunity for experimentation.

Non-Transport Functions of Transport Facilities

While movement is the primary purpose of the transport system, transport facilities have another important function. Transport is a major user of space, and therefore the properties devoted to movement need to be designed to enhance the environment, and to avoid types of adjacent development that reduce community values. Along many highways, for example, the uncontrolled encroachment of commercial activities not only reduces the safety and efficiency of transport but undermines the quality of the environment.

Space devoted to transport includes roads, parking areas, motor vehicle sales and service facilities, repair shops, rail yards, airports, and other terminals. At least 25 per cent, and in some communities 30 per cent, of all urban land is used to keep the metropolis moving. If anything is to be done to improve the aesthetics of the city, the task begins with transport. For this network is constantly seen and used by the people who live in urban areas. Transport also influences a wide band of additional land adjacent to transport routes, where transport-created land pollution is despoiling large areas that are the most visible part of the city.

Urban roads are the main corridors and front parlors of the city. They should be built to please the eye of both those who travel and those who live in the environs, and they should reduce to a minimum the discomfort caused for those who live close to the traveled way. In addition, wherever possible, transport facilities should be combined with other land uses to become an integral part of the functioning of the area. The space and investments used for transport facilities can be an important contribution to the desirability of the city as well as to the mobility of its people and goods.

The European city offers many examples of how the street performs these extra-transport functions. Along the waterfronts in Geneva, Lausanne, Hamburg, and

Stockholm, the highway might have been designed as an ordinary waterfront artery for the movement of traffic, without concern for the needs of the non-motoring public and the functioning of the neighborhood. From a strictly transport point of view, such a facility would have met the criterion of a least-cost solution. But waterfront highways can be designed to fulfill a very different function. Their broad tree-lined sidewalks, adjacent lawns and flower gardens, sidewalk kiosks and eating places, all combine to make the right of way serve not only the movement of vehicles but also the social and recreational needs of the people and the aesthetic enhancement of the downtown area. These boulevards are not conceived simply as highway projects, but as combined highway, recreation, park, and pedestrian mall.

This use of waterfront space is in sharp contrast to the use of space along the Potomac in the Georgetown area of Washington, D.C. There, the least-cost solution to moving traffic was an elevated highway designed only to move traffic. This solution made no attempt to enhance the neighborhood, but instead added to its aesthetic inadequacies. It took no advantage of the possibilities of using the waterfront for recreation and relaxation, or of making use of the area for shops and restaurants. New institutional arrangements will be needed to permit transport investments to become part of a total scheme for the joint use of urban space.

There are less spectacular ways to improve the many miles of streets that are not susceptible to heroic treatment. Shade trees are the most important embellishment. Well-designed commercial architecture and good taste in the use of signs are also necessary. Inconspicuous curbside fuel tanks attractively landscaped can make a difference when substituted for the offensive retail outlets now used by the major oil companies.[10] Where service stations must be larger, one solution is to make them integral parts of an office building or other structure, as is frequently done, with good results, in Europe.

There are other variations in the development of streetsides. Along a city block it is possible to remove the fronts of buildings or to set back new construction to provide an indented area for a park and shopping center, relieving the monotony of the block and providing a sitting and walking place for pedestrians. The redevelopment of the blighted close-in areas of American cities could readily incorporate such islands of green along streets that have become drab and colorless.

To improve the appearance of the roadside will require extending the area of public interest beyond the street itself to the zone on both sides influenced by the traveled way. Just as the approaches to airports are protected by public authority, control should be exerted over land uses adjacent to major streets. Where controlled access is not possible or desirable, controlled roadsides are. There is need to assure that the public investment in streets is not lost through undiscriminating land uses that reduce the safety of transport and destroy the appearance of the city.

An illustration of the aesthetic role of transport facilities is provided by transport

---

[10] The notable exceptions are on toll roads, where higher standards have been part of the contract. The practice should be universal.

terminals. They can and should furnish a monumental entrance to the city for the traveler. Their structures and surroundings should be assets to all who frequent the area. The railway station once performed this historic function, and now the airport does. The Union Station in Washington, for example — overlooking its current state of maintenance — is an aesthetic asset. So are the railway stations in Milan, Rome, Venice, and Copenhagen, and many other rail and airport buildings around the world.

But there are all too numerous examples of how the terminal is a source of blight to the neighborhood and of depression to those who travel: Midway Airport in Chicago, Boston's North and South railway stations, London's Euston Station, the bus terminals in Washington, and in fact nearly every bus depot in the United States. The American bus terminal is perhaps the dingiest part of the twentieth century transport system, and the worst offender from the standpoint of the traveling public and the community both. Greyhound and Trailways provide wretched facilities where the low-income traveler, in contrast to those who travel by air, is denied minimal facilities for human decency. Public provision of long-distance bus depots, such as the Port of New York Authority bus terminal, appears to be the appropriate recourse.

Perhaps the greatest opportunity to provide better terminal space is in the parking of private automobiles. Europe has not achieved notable success in providing adequate off-street parking capacity, but where parking facilities are provided they are often tree-shaded and landscaped and supply welcome green space for the neighborhood. The effect is relatively pleasing compared to large expanses of paved surface on makeshift temporary lots.

Transport Solutions through Urban Design

Just as transport programs can make a major contribution to better cities, urban design can go a long way toward alleviating transport problems. Whether the accommodation of future urban growth is predominantly through the renewal of old cities or the extension of the suburbs, or through the development of essentially new towns, these new investments can be designed with built-in solutions to the transport problem, much in the same way that tall buildings under the guidance of the architect are equipped with an elevator system that generally performs as it was intended to.

Designing a city that solves rather than creates transport problems must be the basic approach for the future. The approach is to design for people's wants and to estimate in advance the extent to which these wants are to be satisfied. This can be accomplished by spatial arrangements that bring desired functions within reach of those who seek them, or by transport arrangements that move people to where the functions are. There are many examples of urban redevelopment projects in the United States that approach the transport problem in this way. But the best examples can be found in new town development.

Britain's twenty-two new towns in various stages of development furnish significant lessons of what should and should not be done to take advantage of transport and space in order to create better conditions of living. These new settlements have their shortcomings, but each has gone a long way toward achieving an attractive and cheerful urbanization with open space, recreation facilities, access to employment, and convenient shopping and service areas.

Within these new towns, transportation plays a major role in urban design. Internal circulation systems emphasize the preservation of quiet neighborhoods with pedestrian walkways between residential areas and commercial centers. The latter are in varying degrees reserved for shoppers on foot, with adjacent parking areas attractively landscaped.

The transport system is not simply a means of vehicular and pedestrian movement, but functions as part of the framework of the town, delineating housing space, and providing trees and landscaping along the streets and in the parking areas. Under these conditions the transport network becomes an asset in itself, in addition to facilitating movement.

The journey to work is reduced by shortening the distance between home and job. Recreation areas of major size are close by, and neighborhood play space is immediately adjacent to housing. Daily shopping needs are readily met at village centers within easy walking distance, and it is generally but a short ride by bus or car to the major shopping center. Schools for the lower grades are located within the immediate neighborhood, and can be reached without crossing the street.

The possibilities of minimizing travel are illustrated by methods of moving in Stevenage, England, fifteen years after its construction. This town of 60,000 persons (the next set of new towns will be larger) has one car for every two families. About 87 per cent of employed Stevenage residents now find work within the town. Of all trips made within the town limits, 43 per cent are made on foot, while 12 per cent are by bus and 24 per cent by automobile. Bicycles and other two-wheeled vehicles account for about 20 per cent of all trips.

Note that individual transport by all methods, walking included, make up 87 per cent of the journeys, and that public transport is the least important method of travel. Where distances are short, both old and young can make their own way on foot. On a typical Saturday, nearly half of all shopping trips are made to neighborhood shopping centers, while somewhat over half of shopping trips have destinations in the larger town center pedestrian plaza. Of the total number of Saturday shoppers, 59 per cent arrive on foot. Three-quarters of all schoolchildren walk to school and one-eighth go by bicycle. Of trips in the social and recreational category, 42 per cent are by foot.

The principal explanation for so high a degree of dependence on foot travel is that 75 per cent of all trips are less than 2 miles in length. By contrast, in other large cities in England only about 25 per cent of daily trips are so short. In these latter cities, one-third of all trips extend more than five miles one way, while little more than a tenth of trips by Stevenage residents are that far. Perhaps the main success of the Stevenage plan is that three-quarters of its workers live less than two miles from their jobs.[11]

[11] Raymond C. Bunker, "Travel and Land Use in Stevenage" (University of Birmingham, Department of Transportation and Environmental Planning, 1966).

In all of these new towns, the streets form the framework of the community, and the commercial areas and living areas are given their unique character by the separation of motorized traffic and pedestrians. The roominess thus created would undoubtedly result in a jungle in the same amount of space in unplanned areas of the same size. The new towns have made transport facilities play the dual role of moving traffic (with due regard to volume) and at the same time of forming an integral part of the commercial and residential neighborhood plan.

In the United States, the new town movement will need to be aided by a national policy on the use of land, by financial assistance and power of eminent domain to permit the acquisition of new town sites, and by good intercity land and air transport to assure the necessary ease of interurban communications. In addition, government investments in schools, industrial sites, and community facilities of all kinds will have to finance the basic infrastructure necessary to stimulate growth patterns considered desirable.

There is also a case in most instances for preventing existing urban settlements from coalescing with each other and with new towns. It is in the interest of city dwellers to have ready access to the country, which may mean preserving open spaces in present uses, in order to maintain the rural character of the land. It may well prove less costly and more efficient to provide intercity connections through areas kept rural than to permit these areas to become urbanized and to require high-cost arteries that are essentially urban streets.

Needed Institutional Changes

There are no easy solutions, few clear prescriptions, and substantial opportunity for divergence and experimentation. One area in which there is particular need for improvisation and for a fresh approach is the field of public administration and public-private co-operation. For transport is being administered in most cases by government institutions that were made obsolete by the very technologies they are trying to cope with. And because obsolete institutions seldom cover either the total system or the geographic area involved, the solutions being offered are necessarily partial and unsatisfactory.

The present compartmentalized approach to transport planning, administration, operation, and financing is especially irrelevant to the tasks that urban areas now confront. The isolation of transport responsibilities from the urban development planning of which they are a part creates additional obstacles. At the local level the transit company operates mostly over public thoroughfares which were not designed and are not now operated with their needs in mind. State highway departments concerned for the most part with the engineering aspects of getting from one city to another are left to reconcile their objectives with the very different goals of urban communities. A mixture of private and public interests keep the parking problem from any serious chance of acceptable solution. The relation of all these transport efforts to urban housing, health, industrial development, recreation, and other community goals is often minimal.

How do we begin to reorient our thinking, and to devise the institutional innovations that must replace the old ways of doing things? We need to start at the federal level, where the new Department of Transportation (DOT) and Department of Housing and Urban Development (HUD) offer hope that a simultaneous attack on problems of urban transport and urban living can be successfully mounted.

If the United States is to embark on a program to rescue the cities, the compelling need is for national urban policies that can establish the broad goals to guide DOT, HUD, and all of the other agencies that have a vital role in the future of urban development, including the Department of Health, Education, and Welfare (HEW), the Department of the Interior, and, as it becomes increasingly apparent, the Department of Agriculture. In an increasingly urban society, the economic and social development of the nation is the concern of everyone.

We need to begin, then, in the Executive Office of the President, with a National Development Council. One of its priority tasks should be to establish the broad outlines of the future of urban America, in co-operation with state and local officials and civic, business, and educational leaders. Initially the attempt must be made to decide where urban trends are leading, whether this is where we want to be going, and what we need to do to assure, twenty-five years from now, that we are closer to the goal.

We will have to overhaul present federal aid programs for transportation. What is needed is aid for urban transport to help realize the stated national urban goals and the patterns of urban settlement that these goals imply. Federal aid for transport would be only one of many federal efforts, including programs for open space, recreation, housing, renewal, industrial development, and all the rest.

We have now arrived at a point in history where conventional federal aid for highways has come to the end of its useful life. For nearly half a century it has made good sense, but now good sense suggests that we move on to the new transport tasks confronting us. In the urban areas themselves, these tasks are essentially to make transport facilities of all kinds an integral part of urban rebuilding.

The anomaly of a Department of Transportation with responsibility for urban highways but not for urban transit has now been resolved. As new systems of combining individual and mass transport develop, the separation of the two was destined to be impractical. A systems approach to total passenger movement makes it logical that all aspects of urban transport technology should be combined in the Department of Transportation. But it could also have been argued the other way — that urban transport is such an integral part of urban structure that transit should have stayed in HUD. But if this argument made sense, then urban highways, too, should have been under HUD's jurisdiction.

The latter solution was not appealing, however, any more than the argument that urban health or welfare activities should be transferred from HEW to HUD. And making HUD a transportation agency had a more basic defect. It is confronting the most massive task in the history of the United States: the task of providing the intellectual leadership by which combined government and private efforts are to rebuild America's cities. The transportation agency makes it possible to avoid a preoccupation in HUD with technical transport problems that would divert it from doing what no one else is going to be doing: deciding how transport can be used to achieve urban goals, and how urban design can help achieve transport solutions. It is already possible for HUD to influence transport policies more effectively through its comprehensive planning responsibilities, and the establishment of a National Development Council would reinforce this primary policy role of HUD in the urban area.

For the investment funds needed to modernize urban transport, innovations in finance will have to accompany changes in federal aid. Urban residents are concerned with the total system of transport available to them and with the options at their disposal. They are continually affected, as motorists, by the efficiency or inefficiency of transit and, as transit riders, by the degree of automotive congestion. Just as public transit and private automobiles cannot be viewed as physically separate problems, it follows that financial separation is equally unsatisfactory. The effective provision of one service will mean more effective operation of the other. The use of motor vehicle tax revenues for transit has already been approved in several states, and the time has come for pooling revenues and integrating price policies for all transport and parking in urban areas.

A Program of Research

The first objective of urban transport research should be to identify trends and assess their meaning. Is transport in cities getting better or worse? How does the situation differ from city to city, and what do these comparisons reveal about the success and failure of alternative public policies?

For those who travel by automobile, there are indications of improvement. The car itself is more comfortable. The heater, the air conditioner, and the radio, together with the quality of the ride and the ease of operation, all help to make the trip more pleasant and the traffic more tolerable. And although traffic has increased enormously, its impact has been dissipated by the expansion of the urban area, by the construction of limited access highways, and by the extension of off-street parking.

People who live along busy thoroughfares, and travelers who have to look at what borders them, must find the index of satisfaction on the way down. The frequency of attractive architecture and pleasing commercial developments is declining, and from nearly every angle there is less beauty per block. There are more signs, more fumes, and fewer trees. But on many miles of controlled access roads, driving can be a satisfying experience.

For transit riders the trends appear to be mixed. There is no striking evidence of reduction in running time or in waiting time, or of less crowding in buses and on rapid transit. Buses, however, are generally of more recent vintage than was the case some years ago, and air conditioning has eased the ride substantially. More attention is also being paid to station aesthetics and to providing information to guide the passenger. But there is no evidence that transit riding has undergone the substantial upgrading that has affected automobile riding.

The situation is obviously different in different cities, and one cannot be sure of what the trends have been. This suggests that specific indices should be established for measuring the pleasures and pains of moving. These should be used to compare cities and to indicate those that are above average or below, and which are gaining or falling behind. For this purpose, specific routes might be selected in various cities and periodic measurements made of the following considerations:

Volume of vehicles and people accommodated;
Elapsed travel time by automobile and transit;
Number of cross streets;
Number of fatalities and injuries per year along the route;
Number of protected pedestrian crossings;
Percentage of pedestrian traffic moving on exclusive rights of way;
Average age of transit equipment;
Percentage of travelers in air-conditioned transit;
Per cent change in transit fares;
Frequency of service, or average length of wait;
Noise and fume levels at the noisiest and most toxic locations;
Number of trees per mile along the right of way;
Linear feet of grass plots and gardens along the public right of way;
Number of poles, billboards, and free-standing commercial signs per mile;
Number of substandard buildings en route;
Number of cars parked on the traveled way.

Studies are also needed to project the transport situation, assuming continuation of present trends or the introduction of specific changes in social, technological, and economic conditions. Among the future possibilities to be tested are different population projections; shorter hours of work; acceleration of automated processes; higher real incomes; some type of minimum annual income; the elimination of racial discrimination in housing; a major reduction in defense expenditures; and new technology, such as the introduction of electric automobiles, low-cost air bus operations, and automated mass transport.

Studies of the impact of these and other assumptions about the future will help to indicate the sensitivity of the transport system to selected changes and therefore will show which potentials should be encouraged or avoided.

Another set of studies is needed concerning the relative costs and satisfactions of various sizes, densities, designs, and groupings of urban places. Are size and density significant factors in the extent to which cities are agreeable and efficient? Or are internal designs and arrangements of land use and urban activities more significant?

In addition to comparing cities of different sizes, comparative studies should be made of cities in the same size category throughout the world, to shed light on what factors are most conducive to satisfactory urban life, including housing, jobs, neighborhood design, cultural opportunities, schools, recreation and open space, aesthetics, mobility, and accessibility.

A third area for research concerns institutional innovations that can help cities cope with transportation problems. Innovations are required at all levels of government, including effective partnership of the public and private sectors, regional arrangements to keep pace with the new urban geography, innovations in transport financing, changes in federal-aid legislation, new machinery for federal-state-local co-operation, and new approaches to relating transport and other urban developments.

In Conclusion . . .

If the quality of America's cities is to be commensurate with the nation's wealth, construction will be required on an unprecedented scale to provide new neighborhoods, adequate housing, schools, commercial areas, health facilities, and recreation facilities. Transport arteries, terminals, and services will be necessary to provide access to these developments and to furnish urban residents with the mobility that makes it possible to take advantage of the city and what lies beyond it. This is the obvious function of the transport system: to provide the means of accomplishing the many goals of daily living through ease of moving.

Less obvious, but equally important to the urban future, is the use of transport investments to help design and redesign the city. The very large outlays to be made available for transport modernization can be an integral part of slum clearance, housing, recreation, and renewal programs. In addition, urban designs that are transport-minimizing can resolve many of the most vexatious transport problems through built-in transport solutions. Finally, since transport absorbs and affects such a large proportion of the land in urban use, any serious effort to improve the urban environment will depend to a major degree on a broad community approach to providing transport.

7

The value of urban land

Edwin S. Mills

Chairman of the Department of Political Economy,
The Johns Hopkins University

The value of urban land

Edwin S. Mills

Urban land is an important resource in modern production, transportation and transfer, and consumption activities. Therefore, the value of land is a matter of prime importance. In fact, land value has been of interest to economists over a long period of time.

Classical and Neoclassical Land Rent Doctrine

Ever since economics was an identifiable subject, land rent has provided major analytical difficulties. Early writers, who thought price to be mainly determined by cost of production, found it especially difficult to explain how a product — land — to the production of which no resources has been committed, could command a price. And how should the fact that some land commands a higher price than other land be explained? Do land values help determine commodity prices, or is causation in the opposite direction? What will be the effect of technical progress on the distribution of income between land rent and returns to other factors of production?

But closely related to these analytical problems were many social issues about which economists and others sometimes held very strong views indeed. What, if any, is the moral justification for the payment of a return to a non-produced factor? And how could society expropriate whatever part of the return to land lacked moral justification without impairing the efficiency of resource allocation?

It is not possible here to survey the interesting history of land rent doctrine — the job has been done by others.[1] Hence, I shall confine myself to a Cook's tour through the countryside, pointing out some of the more interesting landmarks to my fellow tourists.

Ricardo is correctly attributed with the most fundamental insight concerning land rents in the history of economic thought. Indeed, progress during the 150 years since the publication of his *Principles*[2] has consisted of a gradual sharpening and extension of analytical tools and a gradual separation of scientific analysis from the related social issues. To say that progress since Ricardo has been evolutionary and lineal rather than revolutionary is not to say that progress has been insubstantial. Indeed, to compare a careful modern statement of rent theory with Ricardo's is to affirm that economics is a cumulative science.

The research reported in this paper was supported by a grant from Resources for the Future. The author has benefited greatly from comments by Mason Gaffney and Irving Hoch on an earlier draft.— AUTHOR'S NOTE

[1] Joseph A. Keiper, Ernest Kurnow, Clifford D. Clark, and Harvey H. Segal, *Theory and Measurement of Rent* (Chilton Company, 1961).

[2] Piero Sraffa (ed.), *The Works and Correspondence of David Ricardo*, Vol. I (Cambridge: The University Press, 1951).

Ricardo is best known, of course, for the view that land rent arises from differential fertility, the least fertile land in use receiving zero rent. Ricardo thought entirely in terms of agricultural land, and that is understandable for one writing in 1817. The domination of agricultural land in the thought of much later writers is less easy to understand. Alfred Marshall was one of the first major writers to devote substantial attention to urban land values and rents. John Stuart Mill, for example, mainly followed Ricardian doctrine regarding agricultural land rents, but apparently believed that urban land rents were entirely the result of monopolization. Whatever it is that makes central business district (CBD) land in a metropolitan area worth one hundred times as much as suburban land twenty miles away, it is clearly not differential fertility. What is really important is differential marginal revenue productivity (MRP), and differential fertility is no more than an example of a circumstance that will account for differential MRP. Differential transportation cost to the market is a second example. Ricardo realized this, even if his literal-minded successors did not. In fact, it is not even necessary that fertility be different on different plots of land to account for rent. All that is necessary is that demand outstrip the available supply at zero rent. Suppose, for example, that all the land available for agriculture in England was of uniform fertility and that distance from the market was unimportant. Then all this land would be used and would command a rent.

The above bare-bones statement of Ricardo's basic idea does not make a distinction that came to dominate the best writings on land rent for nearly a century. By my reading, there are really two views of rent in Ricardo. One is that rent is a residual which just absorbs the excess of revenue over returns to other factors priced on, say, competitive markets, The other view is that land rents, like other factor prices, are determined by factor supply and productivity conditions. Careful readers of Ricardo may dispute my opinion that both views are to be found in the *Principles*. But it is clear that subsequent writers tended to take one view or the other. And there was a tendency during the latter half of the nineteenth century to shift to the productivity view as marginal productivity theory became better understood, and as the symmetry between land and other inputs was recognized. But it was Wicksteed[3] who, in 1894, argued that under competition and constant returns to scale, the two views amount to the same thing. In other words, if all input and output markets are competitive and if the production function has constant returns to scale, then a payment to each input equal to the value of its marginal product will just exhaust the firm's total revenue. Wicksteed cleared the air of half a century of confused controversy. The issue of whether factor payments exhaust revenue from sales has come to be known as the "adding up" problem, and Wicksteed's result is an easy consequence of Euler's theorem.

Although Wicksteed had the fundamental insight, his demonstration was inadequate. It was Wicksell[4] who shortly provided a careful demonstration of the product

[3] Philip H. Wicksteed, *An Essay on the Co-ordination of the Laws of Distribution* [1894] (Reprinted, London School of Economics and Political Science, 1932).

[4] Knut Wicksell, *Lectures on Political Economy*, Vol. I (London: Routledge, 1935).

exhaustion theorem. He also showed that as long as perfect competition forces firms to produce at the minimum point on their long-run average cost functions, competitive factor pricing will exhaust revenues regardless of the presence of constant returns (provided only that the production function is such that a minimum point exists at a positive output).

The work of Wicksteed and Wicksell provided the tools to solve the mysteries concerning land rents that troubled nineteenth-century thinkers. Take just one example. Henry George's concern that land rents would swallow up the fruits of technological progress is now seen to be basically a conjecture that technological progress is non-neutral in a peculiar way such that it raises the marginal product only of land. Nobody now believes that to be the case.

Wicksteed and Wicksell also provided the tools for a unified treatment of agricultural and urban land rents. The key to land rents is the value of land's marginal product (assuming a competitive product market). In agriculture, the most important influences on land's productivity are presumably fertility and distance from the market. Farms more distant from the market cannot charge a higher delivered price than farms producing the same product closer to the market. Since transportation is not free, the f.o.b. price must be lower for farms further from the market. If other inputs are no cheaper for more distant farms, land rents must be lower in order to make it possible for distant farmers to break even.

The same principles apply to urban land rents. Urban land rents are determined by the value of the land's marginal productivity. And, as in agriculture, the land's productivity is determined by the characteristics of the land itself and by transportation costs to relevant markets. Of course, the characteristic of urban land that is relevant to productivity is not fertility. Usually it is topographical features. The view from the Santa Monica Mountains in Los Angeles or from a lake front property in Chicago may be important for residential land. Or grade and drainage may be important for industrial property. For urban land, the set of markets to which transportation costs are relevant is more numerous and complex than for agricultural land. But the principle is the same. Goods and services produced on a given plot of land must compete with similar products produced on other land, and a piece of land will be able to claim less rent if it is more distant from markets than competing land.

These basic ideas are now well understood by economists. And the process of sorting them out has been a notable accomplishment in the development of economic doctrine. By themselves, they do not, of course, provide us with a model of urban land values. For that purpose it is necessary to incorporate land rents into a model that describes the demand and supply of urban land for all uses. The crucial characteristic of urban land is the great complexity resulting from the fact that supply and demand for different parcels of land are related in significant and poorly understood ways. In other words, an urban economy is a complicated general equilibrium system. Understanding the relationships among the various sectors of the urban economy is the key to better understanding and better public decision making in urban areas. For example, an increase in property taxes in the central city relative to those in the suburbs will affect the locational advantages and presumably the land rents in the two sectors. As a second example, improved radial transportation will alter the relative advantages of locations at different distances from the city and will presumably affect land values. In both examples, major public policy issues depend on the effect of public actions on land uses and land values. Such effects can only be evaluated within a general equilibrium model. The models discussed in the remainder of this paper constitute a beginning at thinking about urban problems in a general equilibrium context. Although none of the models is sufficiently detailed to evaluate the kinds of policies that are discussed in other papers in this volume, they indicate a promising direction for future research.

Land Rents in Recent Models of the Urban Economy

We saw above that two basic ideas have dominated the historical development of land rent doctrine. First, the equilibrium rent of a piece of land should just absorb whatever revenues are left over after other inputs have been paid at whatever prices the market dictates. Second, land rents should guide the allocation of land: in competitive markets, the value of the marginal product of any use of land should just equal the land's rent. We also saw that the culmination of the long period of development of production theory was the demonstration that these two basic ideas are consistent if all input and output markets are competitive and if production functions display constant returns to scale (or, to use Wicksell's generalization, if markets are competitive and the production function yields a well-defined minimum to the average total cost curve). Although these conditions are important both theoretically and empirically, they are clearly not the only conditions in which economists should be interested. Whether any other set of conditions exists in which land rents can play both roles is an open question.

Within the last decade, several attempts have been made to incorporate these basic ideas in explicit mathematical models of land values and land uses in urban areas.[5] Although these models differ in important ways, they share some basic ideas.

In all these models, the crucial assumption concerns the reason for variation in the value of the marginal product of land from place to place within an urban area. As was reported above, physical differences among different pieces of land can cause differences in productivity. Although it has been introduced in some empirical studies to be discussed below; as far as I know no one has introduced this factor into a mathematical model.

Instead, most writers assume that distance from the city center incurs a "penalty" in the form of transportation or communication costs. The penalty may take the form of an assumption that everyone works in the CBD and those who commute from

[5] William Alonso, *Location and Land Use* (Harvard University Press, 1965); Edwin S. Mills, "An Aggregative Model of Resource Allocation in a Metropolitan Area," *American Economic Review*, Vol. 57, No. 2 (1967); Richard Muth, "Economic Change and Rural-Urban Land Conversions," *Econometrica*, Vol. 29, No. 1 (1961), pp. 1–23; Lowdon Wingo, Jr., *Transportation and Urban Land* (Resources for the Future, 1961). Many other publications have, of course, dealt with the theory of urban land values. Those referred to here are among the most recent and explicit.

farther away must incur greater transportation costs. Or it may take the form of an assumption that goods produced anywhere in the urban area must be shipped to the city center for distribution either within or outside the urban area.

Now these are extremely simple and useful assumptions. In conjunction with additional assumptions concerning technology, costs, demand, and land availability, they make possible the deduction of testable conclusions about the rent distance function and about land uses in various parts of the urban area. Any alternatives to them that I have seen or attempted appear to result in models that are so complicated as to be of questionable value. And I believe in "sticking to one's last" with simple models if they are useful. Thus, a major question is how much of the variability of land values and land uses can be explained by models whose crucial assumptions relate to penalties incurred because of distance to the city center. I will return to this question in the next section.

Here, I want to ask to what extent we should expect centrality to be a useful assumption. I believe that there are two quite different sets of assumptions that will produce centrality.

First, assume that the world is a homogeneous plain, but that at least some industries have increasing returns to scale at sufficiently small levels of output.[6] Such an industry will produce a substantial output at a single location, and may "export" some of its output to other areas. Then industries vertically related to such an industry will have an incentive to locate near it. ("Vertically related" includes selling to the firm or its employees, and buying from the firm.) Then the firm with scale economies will form the focus of an agglomeration of production and population. I believe this is an important set of conditions, and the model is based on them. As a technical matter, the presence of increasing returns deprives one of the Wicksteed-Wicksell theorem, and special devices must be used to produce a consistent theory of rent at the focus, or CBD, of the urban area. More important, modern urban areas do not seem to be focused on industries with major internal scale economies, as the model assumes. At least, large manufacturing plants, where scale economies are presumably of greatest importance, are increasingly located in the suburbs, and sometimes outside the metropolitan area altogether.

Second, assume that the heterogeneity of land provides advantages to particular locations. Here there are two sub-cases. In sub-case A, production functions for goods differ from place to place. The production function for coal mining differs from place to place depending on whether coal is below the earth's surface, and similar factors. And more inputs, such as fuel, are required to produce given levels of some goods in cold climates than in warm climates. Clearly, firms have an incentive to locate where production functions for goods they produce are especially favorable. And vertically related firms will have an incentive to locate nearby. In sub-case B, the land heterogeneity is the presence of rivers, harbors, or other topographical features that make transportation to other areas especially cheap. Clearly, a firm that wants to ship part

---

[6] For a fuller discussion, see Mills, "An Aggregative Model...."

of its output away from its immediate surroundings has an incentive to locate where transportation is cheap. To account for agglomeration, sub-case B must include assumptions that make intercity transportation desirable. But, provided some such assumption is made, the firm in question and others vertically related to it have incentives to agglomerate in a particular locality.[7] The difficulty with the second set of assumptions is that much of what is now exported from urban areas is not transported via railroad or harbor. Rather, it leaves the area by road without going into the city center.

The analysis in the last two paragraphs suggests that simple models of centrality are inadequate. And their inadequacy becomes greater as urban areas become more decentralized. Some writers have even suggested that postwar developments in road transportation between cities and elsewhere have completely destroyed the basis for agglomeration of economic activity. But this is going too far. Powerful forces are pulling an increasing fraction of population and economic activity into urban areas.[8] What is really needed are models that explain the attraction of population and economic activity to urban areas, but are not dependent for the explanation on complete centrality. We still await the first model with both characteristics.

The preceding comments apply to all the mathematical models referred to above. All of them assume or imply an urban area with a single focus of all economic activity. Nevertheless, these models differ in many important respects. I conclude this section with a number of comments about specific models.

Muth's model[9] has the great advantage that it starts from explicit (Cobb-Douglas) production functions for the goods produced in the urban area. Its disadvantage is that it assumes f.o.b. price to fall off exponentially with distance from the city center. It would be preferable to introduce intracity transportation explicitly, with appropriate production and demand equations. Then one could examine the circumstances in which f.o.b. prices of goods would behave in the way assumed.

Wingo[10] introduces explicitly the assumption that land rents must just offset differences between transportation costs to the city center from one part of the urban area or another. Also, he makes the demand per family for residential land a function of land rent. These assumptions plus the assumption that the urban area is just large enough to contain its exogenously given population are sufficient to derive the rent distance and population density functions. A good deal is said about the nature of intracity transportation costs, but the effect of different kinds of transportation cost functions on rent distance and density distance functions is not investigated. Nor are

----

[7] If there are scale economies in the production of, for instance, rail transportation, then proximity to a railroad may play the same role as proximity to a natural transportation mode in sub-case B.

[8] Forces are also pushing population and other resources off the farms. But we still require an explanation of the fact that such resources are moving to large urban areas rather than to small towns or to rural nonfarm employment.

[9] Muth, "Economic Change...."

[10] Wingo, *Transportation and Urban Land.*

transportation, housing, and other economic activities viewed as competing for a limited amount of land around the city center. A final comment is that, although Wingo considers the effect of land rent on the demand for residential land, he does not introduce the important possibility of substituting capital (in the form of structures) for land in the production of housing.

Alonso[11] considers not only the possibility of substitution between land and commuting, but also the possibility of substituting between either of these and "other goods." It is, of course, desirable to start from fundamental conditions of utility maximization, but economists' unwillingness to commit themselves to specific functional forms prevents them from deducing many testable implications about rent distance and density distance functions. Most writers are therefore inclined to work directly with demand functions. Furthermore, my view of the facts is that substitution between structures and land in producing housing is more important than substitution between land and "other goods." In other words, I believe that the elasticity of substitution between land and structures is much larger than that between land and any other set of commodities. Alonso focuses carefully on the competition of producers for rings of land at various distances from the city center, and makes good use of rent offer functions in so doing. Although Alonso starts with utility functions in analyzing consumers' behavior, in analyzing producers' behavior he starts with cost rather than production functions. This precludes consideration of substitution between land and other inputs in the productive process. Alonso does not complete the model with equations that could determine overall city size.

Writing after the other researchers referred to above, I was able to build on their work. "An Aggregative Model of Resource Allocation in a Metropolitan Area"[12] starts with explicit production functions for three industries: CBD goods, housing, and intraurban transportation. Substitution between land, labor, and capital is considered, as is the competition of all three industries for the limited supply of urban land. The demand side is treated less fully than by Alonso, only the substitution between capital and land in housing being introduced explicitly. Explicit forms of the rent distance and density distance functions are deduced.

Empirical Studies of Urban Land Values

In this section I return to the question posed above: How much of the variation of land rents and values from one part of an urban area to another can be explained

---

[11] Alonso, *Location and Land Use.*

[12] Two technical deficiencies of this model are as follows. First, although the model implies that CBD land rents (and other factor payments) just exhaust the revenue of the industry located there, the model does not preclude the possibility that a CBD worker might be able to bid away from the CBD industry a piece of land in the interior of the CBD for residential use. I am indebted to W. M. Gorman for this point. Second, all workers are assumed to receive the same gross wage. CBD workers are nevertheless in equilibrium wherever they live in the suburbs because land rents just offset transportation costs. But some workers are employed in the suburbs and they are obviously better off than CBD workers living in the same neighborhood. I am indebted to Ann H. Coffey for this point.

by simple models emphasizing centrality? And what other factors can be introduced to improve the explanatory power of the model? There are, of course, dozens of empirical studies of urban land values. I make no attempt to survey the field. Rather, I restrict my comments to a small number of recent studies that shed light on the centrality issue.

1. E. F. Brigham studied a sample of land values in the Los Angeles metropolitan area.[13] Three rays were drawn emanating from the Los Angeles CBD. Each block through which a ray passed was treated as a sample point. Land values were taken from assessments for tax purposes. Three accessibility variables are used to explain land values: air line distance to CBD, roadway distance to nearest freeway exit, and a weighted average of employment levels in various employment centers within the urban area (weights are inversely related to distance to the employment center, and involve parameters that are estimated from the sample data). Other independent variables are "amenities" (income levels, per cent non-white population, crowding, and average building values), topography (a one-zero dummy variable to differentiate between mountainous and other sites), and one-zero dummies to differentiate the three rays. Only linear regressions are reported.

It is interesting to note that the smallest correlation coefficient between any pair of the three accessibility variables was 0.89, and that air line distance to CBD was the most useful of the three in explaining land values. This strongly suggests that more complex accessibility variables are not worth the cost of computing. Furthermore, distance to CBD proved to be a consistently important variable in explaining land values. The partial correlation coefficient between land value and distance to CBD varies from -0.49 to -0.89 in Brigham's major regressions. The squared multiple correlation coefficients vary from 0.59 to 0.89. The fact that centrality is so important in Los Angeles, which is presumed to be the most decentralized of large U.S. cities, suggests that this variable should not be excluded from any model.

Most of Brigham's other variables appear to be plausible contenders for the role of explaining land values. But with at least some, there is a serious question of whether they should be included. For example, it is hardly surprising that building value and land value should be highly correlated. But high building values are at least partly a consequence rather than a cause of high land values. Where land values are high, land is expensive relative to capital (structures) and users economize on land by employing a high capital-land ratio. High-value buildings cannot be used as an independent explanation of high land values. In more technical language, land values and the capital-land ratio are both endogenous variables, and each should be explained by regression on the predetermined variables in the system.

The same criticism can be levied against the inclusion of some other variables in Brigham's regressions. But for some — e.g., the percentage non-white population — it may be difficult to decide whether they are appropriately treated as endogenous

[13] E. F. Brigham, *A Model of Residential Land Values*, Memorandum RM–4043–RC (The RAND Corporation, August 1964). The same study is more accessible in his "The Determinants of Residential Land Value," *Land Economics*, Vol. XLI, No. 4 (November 1965), pp. 325–34.

or predetermined. This criticism applies equally to the other studies discussed below and can be met only by explicit consideration of simultaneous equation models.

2. Rickert sampled land values from one-mile segments of twenty radial lines emanating from Washington, D.C.[14] Adjusted tax assessments were used for land values. Unfortunately, the study is limited to sample observations outside the District of Columbia.

Three distance variables were tried as independent variables: air line distance to the CBD, shortest road distance to the CBD, and shortest road distance to the nearest highway intersection. The preferred regressions are linear in logarithms. Air line distance is the preferred distance variable and its logarithm explains 57 per cent of the variance of the logarithm of land values. In the preferred regression its partial correlation with land value is -0.41.

Other variables included in the regression analysis were measures of physical amenities (presence of utility services), social amenities (nearness to shopping, etc.), parcel size, and dummy variables to represent the county in which the parcel is located. Multiple R^2 in the preferred logarithmic regression was 0.84.

Two final points are worth noting. First, Rickert's study includes taxable property, regardless of whether its use is residential or other, whereas Brigham's sample was restricted to land in residential use. Rickert's regressions include dummy variables for the type of land use. Second, the size of simple, multiple, and partial correlation coefficients can be greatly affected by averaging of the dependent variable. Values of individual parcels show the most erratic variation, and these are used by Rickert. Brigham used averages for the block in which the sample point lay, and this procedure should be expected to average out a good deal of erratic movement. Averaging over larger areas would probably eliminate even more of the erratic nature of the data.

3. Alonso includes in his *Location and Land Use* a regression analysis of a small sample of land values in Philadelphia. Rejecting assessments as measures of land values, he uses parcels for which transactions prices are available during a short period of time. (Transactions prices are not necessarily good estimates of "true" land values. Price may be overstated as reported for conveyance taxes, and there are "straw" sales for a variety of purposes.) He also restricts his sample to transactions in areas in which the market has been active, and apparently selects his sample partly on the basis of the sign of the correlation coefficient between land values and income. Since income is an independent variable in his regression, this is clearly not a legitimate procedure.

The dependent variable is average price paid for all sales in the sample, within a particular census tract. Independent variables are median family income in the tract and air line distance to the CBD. Only transactions in predominantly residential areas are included. Only a linear regression is reported. Income has a positive coefficient and distance a negative coefficient. R^2 is 0.48.

[14] John E. Rickert, *The Present and Potential Role of State and Local Taxation in the Preservation or Development of Open Space in Urban Fringe Areas* (Urban Land Institute, December 1965).

It is unclear why Alonso used total expenditure as dependent variable rather than quantity of land purchased or price per unit of land. (The latter is clearly relevant for a regression intended to explain land value, but it is surprising that few writers distinguish carefully between price and total expenditure in empirical studies of land values.) His remarks make it clear that the regression is viewed as a demand relation, but a properly formulated demand equation would contain quantity as dependent variable and price, income, and distance as independent variables.

4. Wendt and Goldner studied a sample of land value estimates in Santa Clara County at the southern tip of San Francisco Bay.[15] Of the four investigations surveyed in this section, only this one starts with a presumption that centrality is unimportant in explaining land values.

The dependent variable is price per square foot of land as estimated from FHA appraisals. Three distance variables are employed: air line distance to the CBD, "constructive mileage" to the CBD, and an index of job accessibility. The last of these is a weighted average of employment at different centers in which weights are distances from the land parcel to the employment center. It should be noted that the first two distance variables are from the San Jose CBD rather than from the San Francisco CBD. Other independent variables are size of lot, value of improvements, an FHA-estimated site desirability index, and median family income in the census tract. The preferred regression includes the job accessibility index and all the other independent variables except those related to distance. Its R^2 is 0.737. Only linear regressions are reported.

Wendt and Goldner apparently believe that only the job accessibility index among their three distance variables is useful in explaining land values. I find this conclusion implausible for the following reasons. First, distance is measured only from San Jose, and no estimates are reported of the influence of distance from San Francisco. Second, they dismiss air line distance and constructive mileage on the basis of low simple correlation coefficients with land values. More relevant would be the sizes of partial correlation coefficients in preferred regression equations. Third, the job accessibility index is hard to defend theoretically. Whereas Brigham weighted employment levels inversely to distance, Wendt and Goldner weight them directly proportional to distance. Their index implies that a given employment center has more effect on land values the farther away it is. Surely, distance to an employment center and the level of employment there should affect land values in opposite directions.

The criticism made above of Brigham's inclusion of the value of improvements as an independent variable applies equally here. Further, I find it hard to understand how lot size could have the inverse effect on price per square foot that Wendt and Goldner claim to have found. An owner of a large lot always has the option of making it into small lots and presumably would do so if he could get a better price by so doing.

[15] Paul F. Wendt and William Goldner, "Land Values and the Dynamics of Residential Location," in *Essays in Urban Land Economics* (University of California, 1966).

There is, of course, some saving in transaction costs in large sales, but it is hard to believe that this is a major factor. Zoning may prevent division into small lots, but if that is the explanation, then zoning variables would be more informative than a lot size variable in the regression. My guess is that lot size serves as a proxy for some other disadvantage in these regressions. Finally, one can hardly be surprised that FHA appraisals of land values are correlated with an FHA-estimated site desirability index.

A Model of Urban Land Values

In this section I present a mathematical model of urban land values whose assumptions are motivated by the analysis and comments in previous sections. This is followed by an attempt to estimate and test some implications of the model. The model that follows, although similar to the one in my earlier paper,[16] is simpler and differs in significant respects. The city described by this model is focused on a single center, but — unlike some of the models discussed above — it is not assumed that all workers are employed in the CBD or that all output is produced there.

The basic motivation for the model is the idea that many urban areas owe their prominence to a point or small area which forms their focus and from which intercity (possibly international) transportation is especially cheap. Intercity trade is justified from this point either because production costs for some products are lower here than elsewhere (perhaps owing to proximity to some natural resources) or because enough can be sold from this point to exhaust scale economies. If the latter is the case, it is assumed that the city expands by adding new productive facilities of optimum size so that the city's total productive activity behaves as if it were subject to constant returns to scale. (See the discussion of Wicksell's theorem above.)

It is assumed that homogeneous land stretches out from the city center in all directions except for a pie slice of $2\pi - \theta$ radians ($0 \leq \theta \leq 2\pi$). This at least approximates most major U.S. cities. Land is available for urban uses as far away from the city center as urban users are able to outbid agricultural (or other non-urban) users for it.

For simplicity, it is assumed that only one product, called output, is produced in the urban area. Although it makes the analysis highly aggregative, this assumption is extremely useful for many purposes. Actually, if one retains the basic assumption of centrality, it is not difficult to introduce an arbitrarily large number of products into the model. But the implication is that each product will have exclusive use of one of a series of concentric rings around the city center. This leaves unaltered the basic conclusions about the nature of the rent distance function, and is extremely artificial in the context of a modern urban area, so the multiproduct generalization has not been used.

The production function for output will be written

$$X_1(u) = \bar{A}_1 L_1(u)^{\alpha_1}\, N_1(u)^{\beta_1}\, K_1(u)^{\gamma_1} \quad \alpha_1 + \beta_1 + \gamma_1 = 1 \tag{1}$$

[16] Mills, "An Aggregative Model...."

where X_1 = output, and L_1, N_1, and K_1 are inputs of land, labor, and capital respectively. The u following a variable indicates the value of the variable at a distance of u miles from the city center. $X_1(u)$, for example, means the output produced u miles from the city center. Equation (1) is well known as the Cobb-Douglas production function. Its properties are constant returns to scale, unit elasticity of substitution between any pair of inputs, and an elasticity of output with respect to each input equal to the exponent of that input. With the assumption of competitive markets, the exponents also equal the shares of factor remuneration in total revenue.

The other competing urban land use is for intracity transportation. It is assumed that its production function has the form, but not necessarily the parameter values, of (1).

$$X_2(u) = \bar{A}_2 L_2(u)^{\alpha_2} N_2(u)^{\beta_2} K_2(u)^{\gamma_2} \quad \alpha_2 + \beta_2 + \gamma_2 = 1 \qquad (2)$$

$X_2(u)$ means the number of passenger miles (or ton miles) of intracity transportation produced u miles from the city center. (2) requires a few words of justification. There is, of course, a considerable possibility of factor substitution in transportation through choice of alternative modes. Most forms of mass transit economize on land and (to a lesser extent) labor inputs, but use a great deal of capital. Private automobiles economize on capital, but are land — and labor — intensive. And in most large cities, mass transit is used most heavily in downtown areas where land is expensive, and automobiles are heavily used in the suburbs where land is relatively cheap. It is less widely recognized that the same kind of factor substitution occurs within a particular mode, such as automobiles, and for the same reason. Downtown, where land is expensive, congestion has the effect of economizing on land relative to labor (in the form of travel time). In the suburbs, land is much less expensive relative to labor, and land is substituted for labor by reducing the intensity of road use and thus speeding up traffic. The foregoing does not prove that (2) is the correct form of the transportation production function, but it makes the assumption plausible.

It will also be assumed that transportation inputs and outputs are bought and sold on competitive markets. (It is equivalent to assume that a transportation "authority" pays competitive prices for inputs, and charges full cost for transportation services.) The assumption implies that the value of the marginal product of each factor is equal to its price:

$$\text{(a) } \alpha_2 p_2(u) \frac{X_2(u)}{L_2(u)} = R(u) \qquad \text{(b) } \beta_2 p_2(u) \frac{X_2(u)}{N_2(u)} = w \qquad \text{(c) } \gamma_2 p_2(u) \frac{X_2(u)}{K_2(u)} = r. \qquad (3)$$

Here $p_2(u)$ is the price per unit distance of transportation u miles from the center; $R(u)$ is the rental rate on land u miles from the center, to be determined by the model; w and r are the wage rate of labor and the rental rate of capital, assumed to be determined outside the model and to be the same at all points in the urban area. [From (3) it is easy to deduce Wicksteed's theorem that factor payments exhaust revenues, and to show that factor shares are α_2, β_2, and γ_2.] From (2) and (3) it is also easy to show that

$$p_2(u) = A_2 R(u)^{\alpha_2} \qquad A_2 = [\bar{A}_2 \alpha_2{}^{\alpha_2} \beta_2{}^{\beta_2} \gamma_2{}^{\gamma_2}]^{-1} w^{\beta_2} r^{\gamma_2}. \qquad (4)$$

That transportation price per unit distance should vary directly with land rents is not implausible, although it may appear so at first sight. Where land rents are high, congestion makes travel slow, increasing the time costs of travel.

The foregoing has dealt with the supply side of the transportation system. The demand side will be based on the assumption that each unit of output generates a certain demand for transportation to the city center. This can be expressed as

$$X_2(u) = \rho \int_u^k X_1(u')du' \tag{5}$$

where k is the distance from city center to edge of suburban fringe (to be determined by the model) and ρ is the transportation to city center demanded per unit of output. (5) says that the total demand for transportation at u is proportional to the output produced beyond u. When output is goods, the assumption can be interpreted to mean that a certain fraction of goods is transported to the city center. When output is housing services, the assumption can be interpreted to mean that a certain amount of commuter traffic is generated per household. Whatever output is not shipped to the city center is either consumed locally or exported from the urban area directly from its point of production.

Firms producing output and shipping it to the city center sell it there at a competitive price of p_1. The price received at the factory door is then $p_1 - T(u)$, where

$$T(u) = \int_o^u p_2(u')du'. \tag{6}$$

$T(u)$ is the cost of shipping a unit of output a distance u to the city center. Adding the assumption that the output industry buys factors of production on the same competitive markets as does the local transportation industry, we have the following marginal productivity conditions:

$$\text{(a) } \alpha_1[p_1 - T(u)] \frac{X_1(u)}{L_1(u)} = R(u) \qquad \text{(b) } \beta_1[p_1 - T(u)] \frac{X_1(u)}{N_1(u)} = w \tag{7}$$

$$\text{(c) } \gamma_1[p_1 - T(u)] \frac{X_1(u)}{K_1(u)} = r.$$

These are analogous to (3). Analogously to (4), we get the following relationship between p_1, $T(u)$ and $R(u)$:

$$p_1 - T(u) = A_1 R(u)^{\alpha_1} \qquad A_1 = [\bar{A}_1 \alpha_1^{\alpha_1} \beta_1^{\beta_1} \gamma_1^{\gamma_1}]^{-1} w^{\beta_1} r^{\gamma_1}. \tag{8}$$

Although the output industry is competitive, its total sales are a decreasing function of p_1:

$$p_1 = a_1 X_1^{-\lambda_1} \tag{9}$$

where

$$X_1 = \int_o^k X_1(u)du. \tag{10}$$

(10) defines X_1 as the urban area's total output, and (9) asserts that the demand for total output has a constant price elasticity equal to λ_1. The assumption that the price

of the urban area's output is a decreasing function of its volume is reasonable because, among other reasons, the more output the city sells the further it must go for customers, thus increasing transportation costs and reducing f.o.b. price at the city center.

Two more equations complete the model.

$$L_1(u) + L_2(u) = \theta u \qquad\qquad 0 \le u \le k \tag{11}$$

Equation (11) says that production and transportation must exhaust available land at every distance u within the urban area's boundaries.

$$R(k) = R_a \tag{12}$$

(12) says that the urban area's boundary, k miles from the center, occurs where urban users can just bid the agricultural rental value of land, R_a.

The model is now complete. Despite its drastic simplifications, it is a model of some complexity. Its exogenous parameters are R_a, θ, ρ, the four parameters in each production function, the two parameters of the output demand equation, and the rental rates for capital and labor. From it can be deduced the rent distance function, the prices of output and transportation, land use and density-distance functions, and k or any related measure of the size of the urban area.

The major advantage of this model over the one I presented in "An Aggregative Model of Resource Allocation in a Metropolitan Area" is the greater simplicity of the present model. This one has only two sectors instead of three, and avoids the artificial distinction between CBD and suburb. In fact, output (including, but not restricted to, housing) is produced throughout urban areas and there is no distinct CBD boundary in most large cities. In addition, input substitution in intracity transportation is handled more satisfactorily and more symmetrically with the output industry than in my earlier paper.

For purposes of the empirical study in the next section, primary interest focuses on the rent distance and related land use functions that are implied by the model. The rent distance function is the key to solution of the entire model.

If we substitute the right hand side of (6) for $T(u)$ in (8), we get

$$p_1 - A_2 \int_0^u R(u')^{\alpha_2} du' = A_1 R(u)^{\alpha_1}$$

Differentiating once, we get a different equation in $R(u)$:

$$AR(u)^{\alpha} + R'(u) = 0 \tag{13}$$

where $A = \dfrac{A_2}{\alpha_1 A_1}$, $\qquad \alpha = 1 + \alpha_2 - \alpha_1$

For $\alpha \ne 1$, this equation has the solution

$$R(u) = [C - A(1 - \alpha)u]^{\frac{1}{1-\alpha}} \tag{14}$$

where C is a constant of integration. Now $1 - \alpha = \alpha_1 - \alpha_2$, so $1 - \alpha$ will be positive or negative depending on whether α_1 is greater than or less than α_2. In either case, rent is a decreasing function of u, falling off rapidly near the city center and less rapidly as one moves away from the city center.

α_1 and α_2 are the shares of land in output and transportation. Little is known about their relative magnitudes, but it is probably a good guess that they are not very different. To the extent that they are similar, the solution of (13) when $\alpha = 1$ is a good approximation. In this case the solution is of the simple negative exponential form:

$$R(u) = R_o e^{-Au} \tag{15}$$

where the constant of integration R_o now has the interpretation of land rent at the city center. Although the negative exponential function has been used in many studies of urban rents and densities, to the best of my knowledge this is the first time it has been deduced from a general equilibrium model.

From (3) and (7), it is easy to see that all land use densities are proportional to land rent. We have, for example,

$$\frac{K_1(u)}{L_1(u)} = \frac{\gamma_1}{\alpha_1} \frac{R(u)}{r}. \tag{16}$$

This says that capital per acre of land devoted to output production is proportional to land rent. Analogous results hold for other inputs and for land used for transportation. Hence, if the negative exponential function is a good approximation for the rent distance function, it is an equally good approximation for land use density functions.

The final result to be established in this section is that output per acre of land is also related to land rent in a simple fashion. From (7a) and (8), we get

$$\frac{X_1(u)}{L_1(u)} = (\alpha_1 A_1)^{-1} R(u)^{1-\alpha_1}. \tag{17}$$

Again, a similar result holds for transportation. Equation (17) says that production per acre of land devoted to output is an increasing function of land rent. If $R(u)$ is negative exponential, $X_1(u)/L_1(u)$ will be as well.

Empirical Estimates and Tests[17]

In this section I report on some extensive regression analysis I have undertaken with data on land values[18] and uses in the Chicago metropolitan area. Chicago was chosen mainly because of the ready availability of excellent data. However, an additional advantage of Chicago is that it satisfies the assumptions of the model in the following ways: The reason for its location is clearly the availability of cheap inter-

---

[17] Mrs. Ann Coffey supervised the calculations reported in this section.

[18] Nothing has been said in this paper about the relationship between land values and land rents. The latter are relevant in theoretical models, but data are usually estimates of the former. At any given time, it is reasonable to assume that the capitalization rate differs little from one place in an urban area to another. Thus values and rents will be in a constant ratio. But through time or across great distances, capitalization rates may vary substantially. In such cases the ratio between values and rents will also differ.

city transportation; land of highly uniform topography extends for long distances from its center; and its only obstruction, Lake Michigan, forms an almost perfect pie slice (of about 180°). A possible disadvantage is the recent encroachment on each other of the Chicago and Gary metropolitan areas.

Three distinct sets of regressions are presented: first, a set of regressions involving virtually the only comprehensive historical data on land values available for any U.S. city; second, a set of regressions involving contemporary land values; and third, a set of regressions involving contemporary land uses.

1. Homer Hoyt published comprehensive estimates of land values in Chicago for five years: 1836, 1857, 1873, 1910, and 1928.[19] The urban area was divided into square mile grids and an average land value was estimated for each grid. Data came from a variety of sources and are undoubtedly of uneven quality. Nevertheless, no comparable historical series has come to my attention for any urban area, and the importance of comparing land value patterns over long periods of time justifies the analysis.

Three regressions were estimated for each year. First, land value was regressed on distance from city center. Second, log of land value was regressed on distance. Third, log of land value was regressed on log of distance. Values are in dollars per acre, and distance is air line miles from the intersection of State and Madison Streets.

The first regression involves no transformation of the variables. The second is the logarithmic version of the exponential function deduced in the preceding section. The third is the logarithmic version of the equation

$$X_2 = aX_1^b$$

and provides a natural comparison with the exponential form.

Results are in Table 1 (*t*-values are shown in parentheses beneath the coefficients of the distance variables). R^2 is the square of the multiple correlation coefficient and, in this table, is of course the same as the square of the simple correlation coefficient.

In all cases, the linear regression provides a poor fit. Cursory inspection of the data, and of land value theory, strongly suggest a nonlinear equation. The two nonlinear equations provide much better fits.[20] The distance variable coefficient has the correct sign and is highly significant in each regression. There is little to choose between the two nonlinear equations. R^2's are of similar magnitude, though that for the log version is larger for three of the five years. In the log equation, the constant term is the log of estimated land value at the city center, and its steady increase through time is as expected.

[19] Homer Hoyt, *One Hundred Years of Land Values in Chicago* (University of Chicago Press, 1933).

[20] R^2 is not comparable for the linear and nonlinear equations. For the former, R^2 measures the percentage of value explained, whereas for the latter it measures the percentage of log of value explained. Since the two nonlinear equations have the same dependent variable, their R^2's are directly comparable.

Table 1.   Chicago Historical Data

Year	Regression	Constant	Distance	R^2
1836	linear	1016	−101.6 (−3.2782)	.0503
	log	5.799	−0.3986 (−27.1104)	.7836
	log–log	6.272	−1.936 (−31.3073)	.8284
1857	linear	6011	−575.1 (−6.9412)	.1911
	log	8.792	−.4874 (−35.3627)	.8597
	log–log	10.40	−2.873 (−34.1262)	.8509
1873	linear	24920	−2333 (−7.2494)	.2009
	log	10.05	−.3300 (−22.4327)	.7066
	log–log	10.34	−1.543 (−20.3243)	.6640
1910	linear	139800	−19220 (−4.4658)	.1386
	log	10.84	−.3275 (−13.2685)	.5867
	log–log	10.70	−1.300 (−16.3365)	.6828
1928	linear	182400	−15590 (−4.2650)	.1150
	log	11.05	−.2184 (−11.7969)	.4985
	log–log	11.96	−.9886 (−10.8135)	.4551

Many writers believe that land rent gradients should become flatter through time as transportation improves.[21] This is borne out in Table 1 in both the nonlinear equations. In the log version, for example, the absolute value of the slope falls from 0.3986 to 0.2184 during the 92-year period. In both equations, 1857 is an exception to the rule. In both nonlinear equations, there is a gradual decrease in R^2 through time. In the log version, 1857 again forms the only exception. In the log-log version, the pattern is less regular, but the trend seems clear. I conjecture that this results from the process of decentralization discussed at length in previous sections. As time passes, the urban area grows, and centers of economic activity other than the city center

[21] This is not, however, a consequence of the model in the preceding section. In (15), faster technological progress in transportation than in output production implies an increase in the ratio of A_2 to A_1 and a steeper gradient.

Table 2. Chicago Data, 1966: Lots on Major Streets

Regression	Constant	Distance	Zoned commercial	Zoned business	Zoned services	Zoned manufacturing	Zoned residential	R^2
linear	3228	−217.8 (−3.4726)	−1531 (−1.6557)	1997 (1.8720)	−1262 (−1.2443)	−1335 (−1.2194)	−732.8 (−0.6904)	.2924
log	6.505	−.1147 (−4.8754)	−.3016 (−.8693)	.8990 (2.2465)	−.04778 (−.1256)	−.2422 (−.5899)	.2588 (.6800)	.3196
log-log	6.692	−.6071 (−9.4496)	−.2217 (−.7729)	.2707 (.7878)	.0365 (.1153)	−.3060 (−.9040)	.3316 (.9993)	.5276

Table 3. Chicago Data, 1966: Residential Lots on Rays from City Center

Regression	Constant	Distance	Per cent not dilapidated	Ray I dummy	Ray II dummy	Ray III dummy	Single or multiple zoning	Predominant zoning	R^2
log	4.294	−.0184 (−.8759)	.0094 (2.1258)	−.1778 (1.3745)	−.2627 (−2.2627)	.0960 (.7449)	.0381 (.2913)	.0772 (.7815)	.3022
log-log	4.299	−.0304 (−.2007)	.0080 (1.4582)	−.1650 (−1.2733)	−.2706 (−2.3172)	.1108 (.8489)	.0921 (.7504)	.0694 (.6977)	.2904

become more important, with the result that distance from the city center explains less of the variability in land values.

2. The second set of regressions is based on data sampled from *Olcott's Land Values*[22] for 1966. Olcott is one of the most authoritative sources of land values in the United States. It is published annually and covers the entire Chicago metropolitan area.

The first sample was chosen by identifying eight major streets that pass through or near the center of the CBD. Each of these streets was marked off in one-mile segments. At each mark, an observation was chosen by taking Olcott's estimate of land value for the parcel in the middle of the block in which the mark fell. This procedure was followed as far out from the center as Olcott's tabulations go, and yielded 132 observations. The dependent variable was dollar value per front foot of a lot of standard depth. Independent variables were road distances from the center of the CBD measured in miles, and five zero-one dummy variables to indicate the zoning classification of the lot in question.[23]

The results are shown in Table 2. The regressions are the same as those estimated for Hoyt's data, except that the log-log regression includes the log only of distance among the independent variables; the zoning dummies are the same zero-one values used in the other regressions. The distance variable coefficient has the right sign and is significant in all three regressions. It is difficult to know what signs should be expected for the coefficients of the zoning dummies a priori. In the two nonlinear regressions, only one of their t-values exceeds one. The most surprising result in Table 2 is the relatively low R^2 for the log regression compared with the log-log regression.

A second sample was drawn by drawing four rays in different directions from the center of the CBD. One-mile segments were marked off on each ray. The dependent variable consisted of Olcott's estimate of the land value per front foot of the nearest residential lot to each mark. Again, the lines were extended as far from the city center as Olcott's data went. The sample size was fifty-one. The major purpose in analyzing these data was to obtain results that would be comparable with other studies of residential land values referred to above.

Other studies of residential land values suggest a large number of variables that might be included in these regressions. My preferred regressions are in Table 3. Results were extremely poor for the linear regressions and they are not presented. The log-log regression includes the log only of distance among the independent variables. The distance variable is again air line miles to the city center. "Per cent not dilapidated" is the percentage of residences in the census tract in which the sample observation lies which the 1960 Census reported as not dilapidated. Each of the three ray dummies assumes a value of one when the observation is on that ray and zero otherwise. Single or multiple zoning is zero if the property is zoned for a single-family

---

[22] *Olcott's Land Values Blue Book of Chicago 1966* (Chicago: G. C. Olcott & Co., 1966).
[23] A few lots were zoned for two categories.

residence and one if it is zoned for a multiple-family residence. Predominant zoning takes the value zero if nonresidential zoning predominates in the block, and one if residential zoning predominates. Its compilation involves an element of judgment.

All coefficients have the expected signs, though few are highly significant. (Degrees of freedom are scarce in this sample.) There is little to choose between the two regressions shown. The low R^2's led to the search for variables that would improve the fit. An access variable was constructed which measured the distance to the nearest highway interchange or commuter railway stop. It was highly correlated with the distance variable and had the wrong (positive) sign in all regressions. Per cent of white residents in the census tract was correlated with per cent not dilapidated, and was of little significance. A zero-one dummy to indicate whether the lot was in or out of the city of Chicago had the wrong sign and was not significant. More complex dummies to indicate the kind of nonresidential zoning that predominated in the block were of little help.

It is important to try to determine why the results in Table 2 are more satisfactory than those in Table 3. One reason undoubtedly is that restricting oneself to residential lots arbitrarily throws out a great deal of the variance in land values that is explicable in terms of distance and other available data. A second reason may be that some erratic behavior is eliminated by restricting observations to main streets, as was done in Table 2. A third factor is that a lot fairly near the center of a large city may be used for residential purposes because it has a defect which makes it worth little for any purpose. For example, suppose a lot in a commercial area is too small for profitable commercial use. Then it may remain in residential use even though its location makes it undesirable for that purpose. These considerations lead me to the conclusion that it is undesirable to restrict oneself arbitrarily to residential land in investigating urban land values.

3. It was shown in the previous section that the intensity of land use is closely related to land rent in the model considered there. Equation (16) shows that the capital-land ratio is proportionate to land rent. Therefore, the former should follow the same pattern within an urban area as the latter.

The market value of structures has been used as a variable in several regression studies of land and building values. But estimates of market values — tax assessments, transaction prices, and appraisals — all suffer widely recognized defects. It is therefore desirable to compare results using value measures with those employing physical measures of capital. Among various physical indexes, floor space is probably the most desirable on theoretical grounds.

Fortunately, floor space measures are available from the Chicago transportation study.[24] The transportation study divided the metropolitan area into half-mile grids. These in turn were aggregated into districts whose area varied from 1 square mile in the CBD to almost 150 square miles at the edges of the metropolitan area. For these districts, land in use and floor space were published for several major uses: manufac-

---

[24] Chicago Area Transportation Study, *Final Report*, Vol. I, *Study Findings* (Chicago, 1959).

turing, commercial, residential, and public buildings. After eliminating districts for which floor area data were incomplete, twenty districts remained, ranging in size from 1 square mile to 16.5 square miles. The data are in Tables 20 and 21 of the study. From the published data it was possible to compute floor area per acre of land used for each of the above categories. Air line mileage was measured from the CBD to the center of each district.

Table 4 shows the results of regressing floor space per acre of land used for each of the above four categories on distance from the CBD. Also shown are regressions of total floor space per developed acre on distance. The linear regressions are again the least satisfactory. The nonlinear regressions have high R^2's on the whole, for cross-sectional data. Interestingly, the log-log regressions have uniformly larger R^2's than the log regressions.

Table 4. Chicago Land Use Data, 1959

Regression	Constant	Distance	R^2
Manufacturing			
linear	191.2	−22.63	.3599
		(−3.1811)	
log	5.084	−.2210	.6920
		(−6.3586)	
log–log	5.181	−.8541	.8776
		(−11.3626)	
Public			
linear	139.5	−15.40	.3402
		(−3.0463)	
log	4.654	.1639	.5110
		(−4.3371)	
log log	4.848	−.7134	.8228
		(−9.1407)	
Commercial			
linear	172.2	−21.35	.3141
		(−2.8711)	
log	4.702	−.2075	.5159
		(−4.3798)	
log–log	4.933	−.8935	.8126
		(−8.8352)	
Residential			
linear	211.0	−26.68	.2932
		(−2.7325)	
log	4.931	−.2290	.5790
		(−4.9752)	
log–log	5.116	−.9403	.8292
		(−9.3473)	
Developed			
linear	124.6	−14.42	.3530
		(−3.0458)	
log	4.665	−.2043	.6265
		(−5.3395)	
log–log	4.748	−.7809	.8086
		(−8.4751)	

The regressions for different uses are remarkably similar. For example, the slopes for the five log regressions vary only between $-.1639$ and $-.2290$. The constant terms in the log regressions, which are logarithms of estimated densities at the city center, vary only between 4.654 and 5.084. The log-log regressions have a similar uniformity. Two conclusions are suggested by this similarity. First, all users appear to be responding to much the same set of incentives to high- and low-density use. Second, it does not appear that a great deal is lost by a highly aggregative model, as was employed in the previous section.

Concluding Comments

There seems to be little doubt that rather simple general equilibrium models can be used to explain the general pattern of variation in land values and land uses from one part of an urban area to another, from one urban area to another, and from one time to another. In this study, simple regression equations have been deduced from a general equilibrium model and used to explain Chicago land value and land use data. Considering the cross-sectional nature of the data, the results are reasonably satisfactory.

The only exceptions to this conclusion are the regressions involving residential land values along rays from the city center. Although these results are certainly disappointing, it seems likely that they are mainly caused by the arbitrary restriction to residential properties. If, as seems likely, lots tend to be zoned for the uses to which the market would allocate them, then restriction of a sample to residentially-zoned lots arbitrarily excludes the most valuable parcels of land. This is equivalent to throwing out most extreme observations in a sample and casts grave doubt on the results obtained in many studies of residential land values. It may be somewhat less serious in a study restricted to parts of an urban area where zoning is predominantly residential, but that procedure still excludes some of the most important variability to be explained.

Concerning the particular form of the regression equations, the only simple conclusion is that the linear form is uniformly unsatisfactory. As between the two nonlinear forms, no simple pattern emerges. With some data, the negative exponential form is better, whereas with other data the log-log form is better. Certainly, there is no persuasive evidence in the data studied here for the superiority of the negative exponential form, even though it follows from an important special case of the theoretical model. What model would lead to the log-log form of the rent distance function is an open question.

It is easy to see why the linear form is unsatisfactory. If production functions were of the fixed input-output coefficient type, then the rent distance function would be linear. But that production function ignores the enormous amount of substitution between capital and land that takes place within a metropolitan area. I do not believe that any model whose production functions have non-zero elasticities of substitution between capital and land will yield a linear rent distance function.

DATA AVAILABILITY

I will conclude this paper with a few remarks about data pertaining to urban areas. No economist can work long on urban matters without acquiring a strong sense of the inadequacy of available data. Unlike some subjects, the problem is not simply the paucity of data. In fact, large amounts of data are available for many metropolitan areas in the United States. The problem is that much of the data is collected by local governments for specific purposes, such as transportation studies, and data are not comparable between metropolitan areas. Land use data, which are of top-priority importance in urban studies, are available for many metropolitan areas. But the data differ from one metropolitan area to another as to coverage (e.g., whether unimproved land is included and whether the data pertain to the entire metropolitan area or just the central city); methods of classification (e.g., whether single- and multiple-family residences are distinguished); degrees of aggregation (e.g., whether the data are presented for the area as a whole or for sections of the area); nature of the data collected (e.g., whether measures of intensity of land use are included); and the timing of surveys. Value data (pertaining to unimproved and improved values of land, and to inputs and outputs in productive processes that take place on the land) are much worse, as they generally lack adequate measures of *intensity* of land use.

Much better data on all these items are needed not only for research, but also for policy making. The fundamental need is for comparability, and this can only be achieved if the major responsibility is assumed at the federal level. It is now common for local agencies to redo land use surveys almost every time a major issue of public policy (such as slum clearance or mass transit) comes up. Successive surveys lack comparability, and it is not uncommon for two or more agencies of the same local government to undertake noncomparable surveys at almost the same time. The contrast with population data is striking. The decennial U.S. Census provides a large volume of useful and comparable population data for all major metropolitan areas. Local governments find these data adequate for many purposes, and when additional data are needed the attempt is usually made to design surveys so that census data can be used either for comparison or as benchmarks.

Comprehensive *value added* data for metropolitan areas are also urgently needed. At present we have metropolitan area value added data only for manufacturing, and broken down only by central city and suburban fringe. We should have data on value added by industrial origin by census tract.

Only with data of this type — and comparability — can we hope to develop a comprehensive picture of the reasons behind land-value variation, certainly a key question both for research and for the making of urban policy.

8

Location, size, and shape of cities as influenced by environmental factors: the urban environment writ large

Brian J. L. Berry and Elaine Neils

Brian J. L. Berry is Professor of Geography and Director of the
training programs of the Center for Urban Studies at The University of Chicago.
Elaine Neils is a graduate student in geography at The University of Chicago.

Location, size, and shape of cities as influenced by environmental factors: the urban environment writ large

Brian J. L. Berry and Elaine Neils

"...the race is not yet fully aware of what its resources are."
— Robert Murray Haig, "Toward an Understanding of the Metropolis,"
Quarterly Journal of Economics, No. XL (1926), 199.

This is a paper about the interrelations of location, size, and shape of cities and environmental factors — about the national urban system, its development, and about the characteristics of the urban environment. The purpose is to provide a general vantage point from which to understand the nature of the new resources that are of increasing significance in an urbanized age.

The topic has been addressed many times. It was of particular significance during the formative years of urban studies in the late nineteenth and early twentieth centuries. A fresh look is warranted today on several grounds, however. Broader geographic and historical frameworks provide much higher ground from which to view the issues involved. In the earlier studies — inevitably myopic — a Newtonian stance was typical. Explanation proceeded from simple monolithic causes. It now becomes clearer that a systems framework which incorporates a wide range of variables and deals with both persistence and change is essential for such studies. In this kind of framework, the system becomes part of the predictions, causes merge into consequences, and these consequences in turn become causes.

The complexity is awesome, yet there is need to contend with it, to introduce order to gain insight. One route is that of the last two decades of location theory, which, following disapproval of early environmental orientations, took refuge in the world of ceteris paribus. The result has been that many of today's urban location theorists find solace in models of urban systems and city structure constructed on unbounded uniform plains, and delight in the beautiful tessellations of the central-place hierarchy and graceful negative exponential distance-decay patterns. For them, environmental issues are conveniently sidestepped.

Yet no amount of assumption can avoid the fact that there is an environmental context within which behavior occurs.[1] As Perloff notes on p. 4, one view of the urban environment is "as a contained (but not closed), highly interrelated system (or subsystem) of natural and man-made elements in various mixes." At the interface of the natural and man-made elements one finds the urban resource endowment.

What constitutes this resource endowment is rooted in the determinants of final demand — in consumer preferences and income distribution, and in the current

---

[1] To quote Norbert Wiener, the environment might best be conceived as a myriad of "To whom it may concern" messages, putting emphasis on the necessity for selection. *The Human Use of Human Beings* (Houghton Mifflin Co., 1964). See also Emrys Jones, "Cause and Effect in Human Geography," *Annals of the Association of American Geographers*, Vol. 46 (1956).

organization and technology of production. As they change, so does the resource endowment. Several stages of "natural resources that count" can be cited in the history of the American economy.[2] In the agricultural period, the most valued natural endowment was arable land with environmental components of climate and water. During industrialization, a new set of mineral resources became important. In the twentieth century, service activities and amenity resources have exerted an increasingly strong pull on industry and on people.

If natural resources, in a socioeconomic sense, are those elements of the natural environment that have use to man but whose supply falls short of demand, in the contemporary urbanized age these "new resources" include pure air and water, three-dimensional breathing space, adequate open space, and other amenity features. These are the resources that count in crowded urban areas. Since the last third of the twentieth century seems destined to become a period of conscious urban development, it seems appropriate that we should begin to understand the nature of the system in which these new resources have been defined, their interrelationships within that system, and the extent to which they are direct products of system growth and change.

Is there a way to introduce order without retreat to the uniform plain? One can order a complex universe in several ways, for example:

1. by creating typologies, classifying and arranging examples;
2. by tracing common developmental processes, despite many differences between types.

In this paper we do both, but the typologies are shown to be logical outcomes of the growth processes. The thrust is thus toward a general field theory, getting away from symptoms and syndromes of symptoms and focusing on processes that deal with interactions of elements, including how the system became what it is, how it works, persists, and changes.

We focus first on the evolution of the American urban system and the relations of its regional growth patterns to changing definitions of natural resources. Certain system characteristics are then outlined and a general theory of polarized development for system maintenance and change is discussed. Finally, the main categories of city-environment relations in the present urban system are discussed. Such understandings are a necessary ingredient of experiments with institutional arrangements designed to achieve agreed-upon social goals for our cities.

Evolution of the American Urban System

MERCANTILE BEGINNINGS

America's oldest cities were mercantile outposts of a resource area which was exploited by the developing metropolitan system of Western Europe. The initial impulses for independent urban growth came at the end of the eighteenth century,

---

[2] This framework is Perloff's. See Harvey S. Perloff, "Modernizing Urban Development," *Daedalus,* Vol. 96, No. 3 (1967), pp. 789–800; see also his introductory statement in this volume.

when towns were becoming both the outlets for capital accumulated in commercial agriculture and the centers of colonial development of the continental interior. Arable land was the resource that counted in regional growth. Regional economies developed a certain archetype: a good deepwater port as the nucleus of an agricultural hinterland well-adapted for the production of a staple commodity in demand on the world market.[3] Growth potentials of regions depended on the extent and richness of the hinterlands accessible to the ports (Figure 1), and the distribution of economic activity before 1840 was a function of the expansion of nucleated agricultural regions into the vacuum of the unsettled continent (Figures 2–4).

It was during this expansion phase that New York established itself as the national metropolis (Figures 3–4), a position it was never to lose, by setting the terms under which exportable surpluses were marketed and imports obtained, and by which interior industries could secure credit. New York was the only colonial center which had the advantages of good interior connections for both exports and imports. Boston and Charleston were prevented from exploiting the interior by physical barriers. Baltimore and Philadelphia were able to import with ease, but trans-Appalachian movement of exports to them was too costly. New Orleans was well suited to control the riverine internal trade, but was far distant from the growing supply areas of domestic manufactures and the heart of the domestic consumer market.[4] The prototypic American metropolis thus was a port at a strategic location on long-distance oceanic or riverine trade routes, providing a range of mercantile services, and determining the terms of trade. Much of the early theory of urban location was written about exactly such cities.

This agricultural resource-dominated (but city-centered) expansion of the economy set the stage for subsequent developments by establishing a geography of markets, transport routes, and labor force that conditioned the nature of succeeding growth. The system that developed persisted as a leading part of the environmental context of changes that followed.[5] The process of population increase and spread continued, and with rapid construction of the railroads and expansion of processing industries, new rail transportation-manufacturing centers such as Cincinnati, Chicago, and St. Louis grew up at "gateways" from which the agricultural regions of the Midwest could be organized. As in the East, shipments of goods demanded by the agri-

[3] Harvey S. Perloff and Lowdon Wingo, Jr., "Natural Resource Endowment and Regional Economic Growth," in Joseph J. Spengler (ed.), *Natural Resources and Economic Growth* — papers presented at a conference sponsored jointly by Resources for the Future and the Committee on Economic Growth of the Social Science Research Council (jointly published by RFF and the Committee, 1961), pp. 191–212.

[4] Beverly Duncan and Stanley Lieberson, *Metropolis and Region in Transition* (unpublished manuscript). John R. Borchert, "American Metropolitan Evolution," *The Geographical Review*, Vol. LVII, No. 3 (July 1967), pp. 301–32.

[5] William Warntz, *Macrogeography and Income Fronts* (Regional Science Research Institute, 1965); also "Macroscopic Analysis and Some Patterns of the Geographical Distribution of Population in the United States, 1790–1950," in *Quantitative Geography* (Northwestern Studies in Geography, 1967).

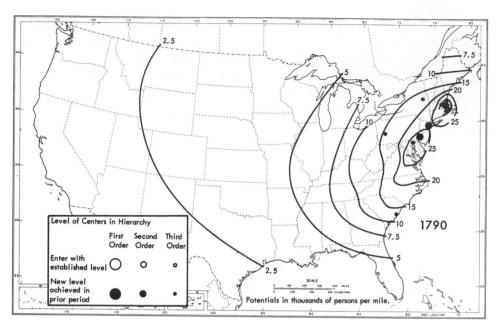

Figure 1. Status of urban centers in 1790 related to population potentials in that year. Potentials at any point i were calculated by William Warntz in thousands of persons per mile as $p_i = \sum_j (p_j/d_{ij})$. Level of centers in the urban hierarchy estimated by John R. Borchert. See references in footnotes 4 and 5.

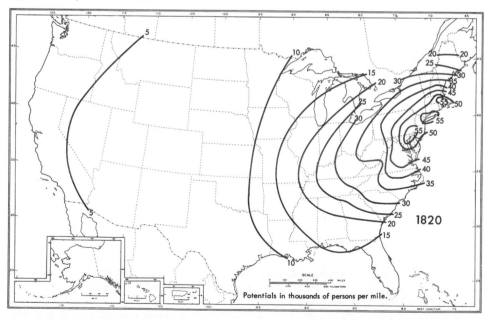

Figure 2. Population potentials, 1820. Note the increasing densities along the East Coast and the westward spread. Whereas Boston had the peak potentials in 1790, three East Coast metropolises now share that role.

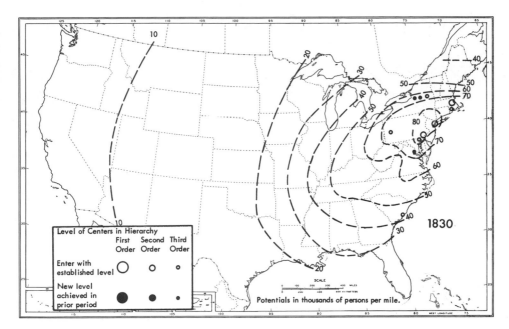

Figure 3.   Status of centers in the hierarchy, 1830, related to population potentials of 1840. Open circles indicate centers whose level in the hierarchy remained unchanged between 1790 and 1830. Black circles show centers rising to new status (along the Hudson-Mohawk route).

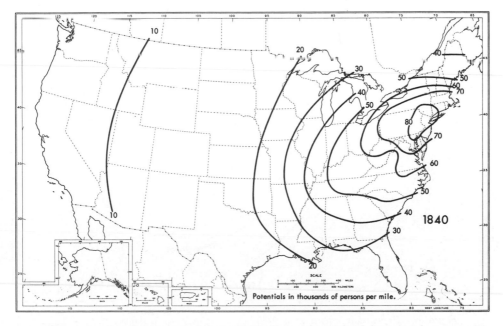

Figure 4.   Population potentials in 1840. The peak potential has already centered in New York, and the trans-Appalachian spread of population continues.

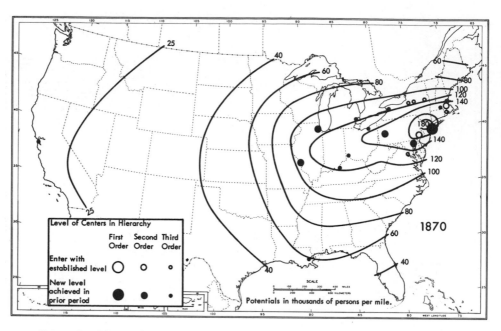

Figure 5. Many urban centers achieved new status in the 1830–1870 period. The manufacturing belt and agricultural Midwest stand out clearly in this growth. New York has moved ahead to first order status, and population potentials outline the northeastern heartland.

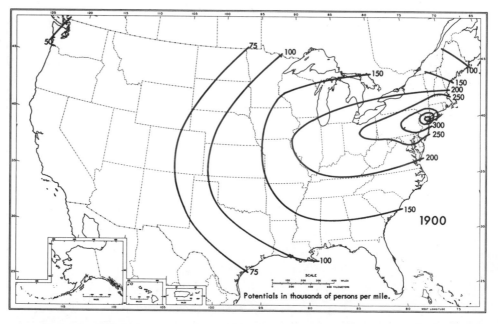

Figure 6. Population potentials in 1900. The northeastern heartland and the New York peak are again emphasized.

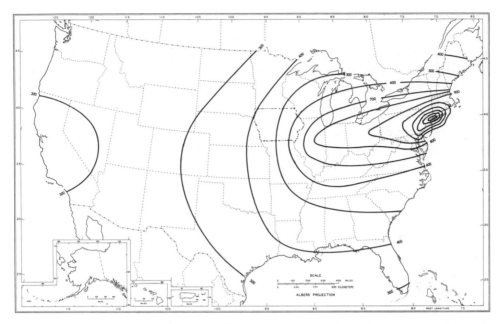

Figure 7.   U.S. income potentials, 1956. Note that this measure of access to the national market is patterned in the same way as population potentials.

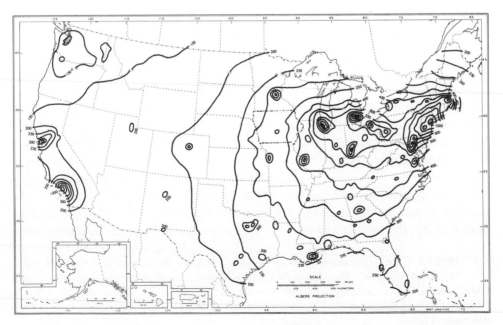

Figure 8.   Details of U.S. population potentials, 1960. County data were used by William Warntz to generate this surface, to show local metropolitan peaks on the overall configuration. See reference in footnotes.

culturalists and the assembly of agricultural products for regional, national, and international markets took place to and from the national and regional metropolises through the organizational medium of a central-place hierarchy comprising regional capitals, smaller cities, towns, villages, and hamlets.[6]

INDUSTRIAL TRANSFORMATION

New resources became important from 1840–50 onwards, and new locational forces came into play. Foremost was a growing demand for iron, and later steel, and along with it rapid elaboration of productive technologies. Juxtaposition of coal, iron ore, and markets afforded the impetus for manufacturing growth in the northeastern United States localized by both factors in the physical environment (minerals) and system-related environmental components (linkages to succeeding stages of production). Manufacturing cities such as Buffalo, Cleveland, Detroit, and Pittsburgh grew on bases that were spatially distinct from the earlier centers that dominated long-distance trade, although some of the commercial metropolises were able to capture a share of the new manufacturing base. The "heartland" of the American manufacturing belt developed westwards from New York in the area bounded by the Lake Superior iron ores; the Pennsylvania coalfields; and the capital, entrepreneurial experience, and engineering trades of the Northeast; while at the same time New York cemented its dominance by accentuation of its financial, entrepreneurial, and specialized manufacturing roles. This heartland became not only the heavy industrial center of the country, but has since remained the center of national demand, determining patterns of market accessibility (Figures 5–6).[7]

CUMULATIVE HEARTLAND-HINTERLAND RELATIONSHIPS

This heartland had advantages of both excellent agricultural resources and a key location in the minerals economy. With development, it grew into the urbanized center of the national market (Figures 7 and 8). Subsequent metropolitan growth has been in a pattern organized around this national core region. Since 1869 there has been a stable pattern of growth in manufacturing employment among the states.[8] Continued spread of population and agriculture over the continent pulled processing and servicing activities and new urban growth with them (Figure 9). However, the developmentally-dominant effects still came from growth of the minerals economy until well into the twentieth century, so that a process of "circular and cumulative

---

[6] Brian J. L. Berry, *Geography of Market Centers and Retail Distribution* (Prentice-Hall, 1967).

[7] Chauncy D. Harris, "The Market As a Factor in the Localization of Industry in the United States," *Annals of the Association of American Geographers*, Vol. 44 (1954). Edward L. Ullman, "Regional Development and the Geography of Concentration," *Papers of the Regional Science Association* (1959).

[8] George H. Borts, *Patterns of Regional Economic Development in the United States, and their Relation to Rural Poverty* (Report to the National Advisory Commission on Rural Poverty, U.S. Department of Agriculture, 1967).

causation"[9] strengthened and maintained the relations of the national heartland and hinterlands — of core and periphery — and the new metropolitan centers that did emerge did so in sequence with the overall growth of the economy.

Before 1900, New Orleans, San Francisco, and Minneapolis grew as commercial "gateways" for the Gulf and the Mississippi basin, the central valley of California, and the mid-continent plains, respectively. Between 1900 and 1940, Los Angeles grew as the trade and service center for southern California, and Kansas City emerged in the Central Plains. Since 1940, Seattle has grown in the Pacific Northwest and Dallas, Houston, and Phoenix in Texas and the Southwest. These represent elaboration and deepening of subnational economies, building upon the geographic pattern of activity brought about by interregional resource shifts after 1850, although also reflecting the relative decline of mineral resource activities in the national economy and the increasing significance of the service sector (Figures 9–10).

In each case, the basic conditions of regional growth were set by the heartland. It acted as the lever for successive development of newer peripheral regions by reaching out to them as its input requirements expanded, and thereby fostered specialization of regional roles in the national economy. The heartland experienced cumulative urban-industrial specialization, while each of the hinterlands found its comparative advantage based on narrow and intensive specialization in a few resource subsectors, only diversifying if the extent of specialization permitted achievement of some threshold scale. Flows of raw materials inward and finished products outward articulated the whole.[10]

The spatial dimensions of the national economy have thus become a

...great heartland nucleation of industry and the national market, the focus of large-scale nation-serving industry, the seedbed of new industries responding to the dynamic structure of national final demand, and the center of high levels of per capita income. Radiating out across the national landscape are the resource-dominant, regional hinterlands specializing in the production of resource and intermediate inputs for which the heartland reaches out to satisfy the input requirements of its great manufacturing plant. Here in the hinterlands, resource endowment is a critical determinant of the particular cumulative advantage of the region, and hence its growth potential.[11]

AMENITY RESOURCES AND THE SERVICE SECTOR

The post-1950 growth of the various regions has been associated with the growth of the service sector; the increase in the number of footloose industries, such as the

[9] Allan Pred, *The Spatial Dynamics of U.S. Urban Industrial Growth, 1800–1914* (The M.I.T. Press, 1966).

[10] Edward Ullman, *American Commodity Flows* (University of Washington Press, 1957).

[11] Perloff and Wingo, "Natural Resource Endowment and Regional Economic Growth," pp. 211–12.

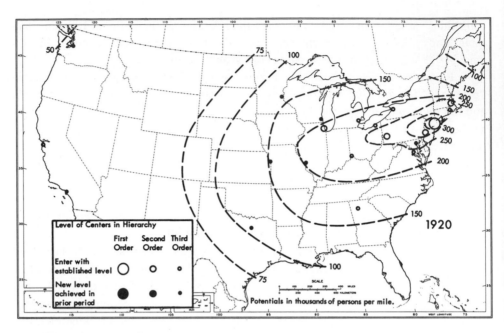

Figure 9. New urban growth in the 1870–1920 period. Note emergence of the commercial metropolises of the Plains and the West Coast.

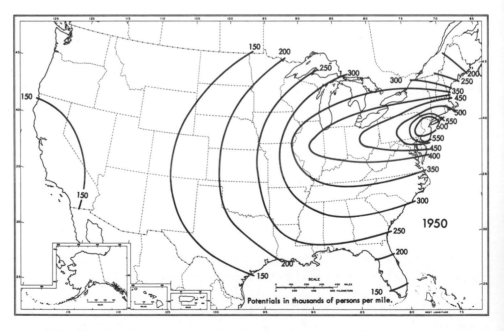

Figure 10. Population potentials in 1950. Emergence of a Californian "rise" is a new feature of the pattern.

aircraft, aerospace, and defense industries, and research and development; the expansion and interregional migration of the non-job-oriented population; and overall rising real incomes. As a result of these developments, new amenity resources have moved to the forefront of the national economy. New advantages for economic growth have been found around the "outer rim" of the country, in regions and places relatively well-endowed with such amenities.[12] The advantages have been cumulative, for regional growth within the context of the national pattern of heartland and hinterland had brought these regions to threshold sizes for internal production of a wide variety of goods and services at the very time that changes in the definition of urban resources made rapid advance possible. Hence the explosive metropolitan growth of the South, Southwest, and West (Figure 11).

Studies of employment shifts in the national economy in the 1950–60 decade provide graphic evidence of the bases of this growth, within the context of continuing heartland dominance, but with the added dimension of relative center-to-periphery shifts *within* the largest metropolitan areas. Factor analysis is an appropriate exploratory method of data analysis in this context because we are interested in "factors... the elements that co-operate to make a given situation."[13]

The analyses employed here are based upon industry-mix and competitive-shift coefficients for thirty-two two-digit industries. One analyzed changes over the more than three thousand counties of the country; the second dealt simply with the SMSA's, as defined in 1960.[14]

[12] Edward L. Ullman, "Amenities as a Factor in Regional Growth," *The Geographical Review*, Vol. 44 (1954), pp. 119–32.

[13] Factor analysis is a multivariate procedure in which a data matrix consisting of *n* observations, for each of which measurements on *m* variables have been made, is analyzed to determine (a) groups of highly correlated variables displaying essentially the same patterns of variation over the observations, and (b) factor scores for the observations, indexing the common behavior of the variables in each group. Output from the analysis includes a statement that there are *r* groups of variables, where $r \leq m$, that each group may be represented by a single common pattern of variation (the factor related to the group), an $m \times r$ table of factor loadings showing which variables fall in each group, and an $n \times r$ table of factor scores providing indexes for each observation on each factor.

The quotation is from Robert E. Park *et al.*, *The City* (University of Chicago Press, 1925).

[14] The coefficients were produced by a shift analysis — a simple analytical approach based on study of the three main components of regional growth: that part attributable to national growth, that part attributable to the rate of growth of the mix of industries in the region, and that part due to differences between rates of growth of industries within a single region and rates of growth of the same industries in other regions. Symbolically, this may be expressed as:

$$d_{ij} = g_{ij} + k_{ij} + c_{ij} \qquad (1)$$

where: g_{ij} = the national growth element for industry i in region j;

   k_{ij} = the industry-mix effect for industry i in region j;

   c_{ij} = the regional competitive effect for industry i in region j;

   d_{ij} = the absolute change in employment between two points in time for industry i in region j (that is, $E_{1960} - E_{1950}$).

Both analyses produced the same eight-factor structure (in the county analysis, a ninth factor characterized agricultural change), with the first two components of greatest interest, and six industry-specific effects. The first factor in both cases recorded *relative change due to industry mix* in a wide variety of sectors covering market-oriented manufacturing, wholesaling, retailing, and services — from 1950 to 1960, the dominant element in the changing employment patterns of the United States was clearly whether or not an area had been fortunate enough in 1950 to possess 1950–60 growth sectors.[15] This change has resulted in continuing *centralization* of growth in the larger urban centers of the manufacturing belt; however, the southern and western rims of the country have also developed because of their specialization in newer growth industries (compare Figure 12 with Figure 11), so that, based on industry mix alone,

For example, considering industry *i* in region *j* between 1950 and 1960, the following might apply:

Year	April 1 employment (*thousands*)
1950....................	42.8
1960....................	59.0
Absolute change.........	16.2

Now, the national overall rate of growth between 1950 and 1960 was 0.1548. For industry *i* it was 0.3112. And for industry *i* in region *j* it was 0.3787.

Letting: r = the national overall rate of growth (0.1548)
  r_i = the national rate of growth in industry *i* (0.3112)
  r_{ij} = the rate of growth of industry *i* in region *j* (0.3787)

with: E_{1950} being employment in 1950
  E_{1960} being employment in 1960.

Then:

$$g_{ij} = E_{1950} \times r$$
$$= 42.8 \times 0.1548 = 6.6 \text{ thousand}$$
$$k_{ij} = E_{1950} \times (r_i - r)$$
$$= 42.8 \times (0.3112 - 0.1548) = 6.7 \text{ thousand}$$
$$c_{ij} = E_{1950} \times (r_{ij} - r_i)$$
$$= 42.8 \times (0.3787 - 0.3112) = 2.9 \text{ thousand}$$
$$d_{ij} = E_{1960} - E_{1950}$$
$$= 59.0 - 42.8 = 16.2 \text{ thousand.}$$

Finally, we have: $d_{ij} = g_{ij} + k_{ij} + c_{ij}$
$$16.2 = 6.6 + 6.7 + 2.9.$$

I performed the factor analysis of the shift-share data for Edgar S. Dunn, Jr. As yet, his complete study is not available, and I am grateful to him for letting me make use of them. A preliminary report on the county analysis is in Brian J. L. Berry, *Strategies, Models and Economic Theories of Development in Rural Regions* (U.S. Department of Agriculture, 1967).

[15] It is thus no accident that Wilbur R. Thompson gets excellent results using industry mix as his principal independent variable in predicting income levels, distribution and stability, and city growth behavior. See "Internal and External Factors in the Development of Urban Economies," in Harvey S. Perloff and Lowdon Wingo, Jr. (eds.), *Issues in Urban Economics* (The Johns Hopkins Press for Resources for the Future, 1968).

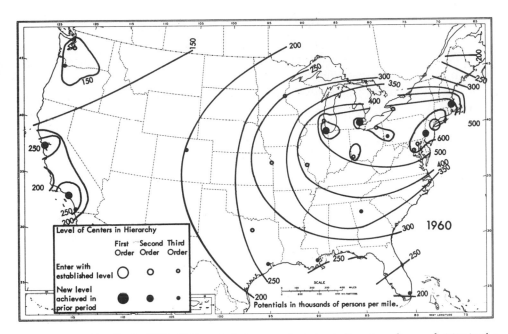

Figure 11. In the 1920–1960 period, the manufacturing belt metropolises and cities in the Far West, Gulf Coast, and Florida rose to new status. Population potentials reveal several western peaks and greater local differentiation within the northeastern manufacturing belt heartland.

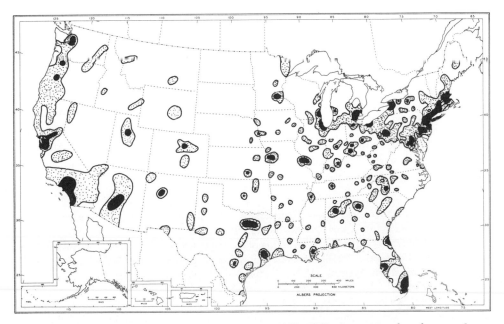

Figure 12. Growth due to industry mix, 1950–1960. Intensities based upon factor analysis of shift-share data.

continued centralization has been accompanied by deconcentration of activity from the national heartland to the outer rim of the continent.

The second factor isolated complementary *competitive shifts in the light manufacturing and service sectors.*[16] What is most important about this factor is that the county-level analysis revealed competitive shifts in favor of the outer rim of Florida, the Southwest, and West, as did the metro-level study, but it also showed the same shifts in favor of the suburbs of the older metropolitan areas of the Northeast. Relative losses were registered by the largest older central cities (Figure 13). Thus, additional *deconcentration* on the national scale and *decentralization* on the urban scale have the same competitive bases.

By far the majority of U.S. cities changed in much the same way that the nation changed in the 1950–60 decade — simply on the basis of the relative growth of the industries already there.[17] However, there were a few groups of SMSA's which showed substantially different trends. The largest group was of cities in Florida, Arizona, Texas, and California, plus Denver, Las Vegas, and Reno. These have been the main beneficiaries of the competitive shifts. Most of the other changes are industry-specific (for example, in the textile towns of Fall River-New Bedford, Paterson-Clifton-Passaic, Pawtucket-Providence, and in the mining towns of Wilkes-Barre, Johnstown, and Scranton) or spectacular military-related shifts (in San Diego, Seattle, Norfolk, and Washington, D.C.). Finally, the nation's principal metropolises — New York, Chicago, Los Angeles, Detroit, Philadelphia, Boston, San Francisco — experienced continued growth due to industry mix, but were characterized by competitive declines at the center and growth at the periphery.

Patterns of Urbanization and Urban Influence in 1960

Although by the 1960's only a relatively limited part of the nation's area was characterized as metropolitan by the Bureau of the Budget (Figure 15), in fact the residents of most of the populated parts of the country journeyed to metropolitan employment opportunities on a daily basis (Figure 16). Many segments of the country lay simultaneously within more than one of these commuting areas (Figure 17), although of course the degree of local labor market participation dropped off in each case with distance (Figure 18).[18]

[16] That is, growth in these sectors in particular regions at rates more rapid than expected on the base of national and industry growth trends alone.

[17] This is consistent with the systems notion of growth based on a "law of proportionate effect," as inferred from existence of parallel rank-size regularities in 1950 and 1960. See Brian J. L. Berry, "Cities as Systems within Systems of Cities," *Papers of the Regional Science Association*, Vol. 13 (1964), pp. 147–63.

[18] Figure 16 is a generalization of Figure 17, which in turn is derived from Figure 18. The latter map was produced from a detailed study of the commuting behavior of the U.S. population in 1960, on a consistent national base. See Brian J. L. Berry, *Metropolitan Area Definition: A Re-evaluation of Concept and Statistical Practice* (U.S. Bureau of the Census Working Paper, 1968).

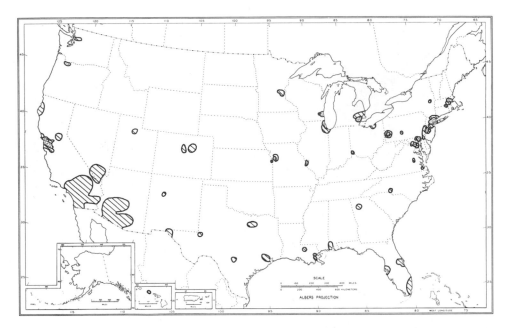

Figure 13. Change due to competitive shifts, 1950–1960. Dotted areas experienced relative losses; cross-hatched areas in metropolitan suburbs, the Southwest, and South gained.

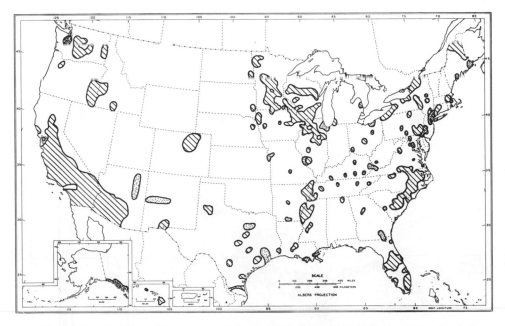

Figure 14. Relative change in agriculture, 1950–1960. Lines indicate areas of relative competitive gain; the dotted areas were those of competitive losses (both within the framework of overall decreased dependence on agriculture as a source of employment).

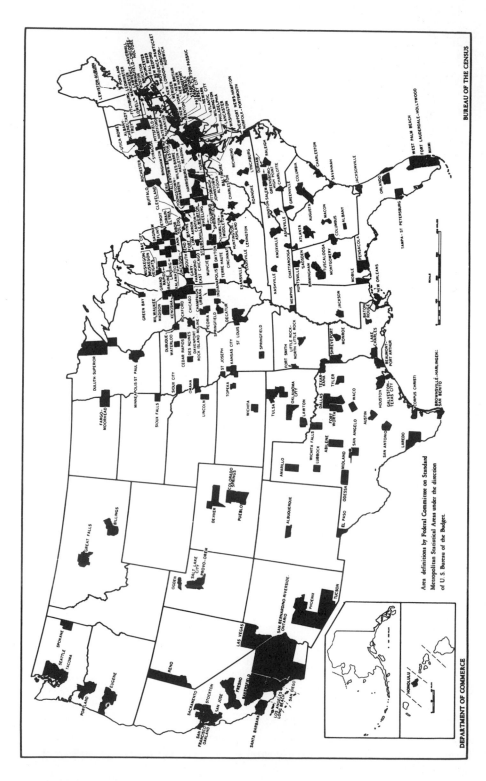

Figure 15. Standard metropolitan statistical areas, 1960. The zones shaded black covered the counties designated as "metropolitan" in 1960 by the U.S. Bureau of the Budget.

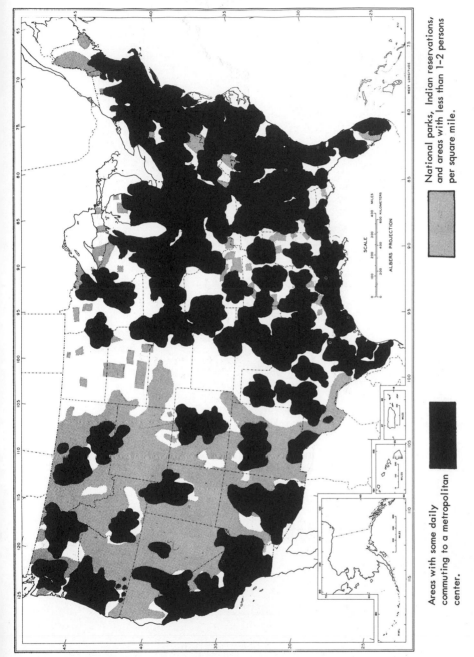

Areas with some daily
commuting to a metropolitan
center.

National parks, Indian reservations,
and areas with less than 1–2 persons
per square mile.

Figure 16. Areas with daily commuting to a metropolitan center in 1960. Studies at the University of Chicago indicate that most of the populated parts of the country lay within metropolitan fields of daily contact in that year.

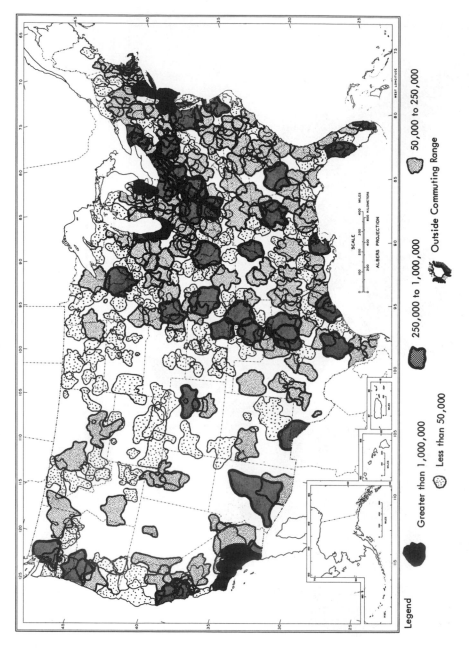

Figure 17. Extent of individual commuting fields in 1960. Areas in daily contact with metropolitan and smaller urban centers are indicated, by size of center. Note the extensive areas with commuting to more than one metropolis, revealing the complexity of urbanization.

Varying rhythmically with degree of participation in metropolitan labor markets were a variety of other variables: population densities, value of farm land and buildings, income and educational levels, migration rates, patterns of population change, and degree of unemployment (Figures 19 and 20 provide examples). Clearly, metropolitan influences mold social life throughout the nation, in well-marked gradients of urban orientation. Urban centers with a population of less than 25,000 generally have no local impact on the gradients. The patterns are involuted within the inner-city ghettos of the nation's largest cities, dropping inward from the inner suburban ring.[19]

On the other hand, the economic base of urbanization varies in the heartland-hinterland manner. A factor analysis of county employment structure in 1960 produced relevant maps.[20] The industrial heartland stands out (Figure 21). A dominant orientation to agriculture remains only in the Plains and the western basin (compare Figures 14 and 22 with the unshaded areas in Figure 16). Urban areas in the Plains, West, and South show the highest degree of dependence on the tertiary sector (i.e., the wholesale, retail, and service industries) (Figure 23) and the Appalachian, southern, and western interurban peripheries have the lowest degrees of such dependence (compare Figure 24 with Figure 26). Similar relations are seen in the familiar functional classification of cities (Figure 25). The manufacturing heartland is surrounded by mixed retail-industrial metropolises, whereas urban centers whose economic base is in the retail and service sector occupy the southwestern and southern rims. Each group reflects a phase of growth and the particular pattern of resource orientation during that phase. Because manufacturing agglomerations led to regional clusters of cities, the heartland evidences the greatest complexity of commuting patterns (Figures 17–18), whereas the hinterlands, with the widest spacing of metropolises and the greatest interurban peripheries, have the greatest concentration of counties in economic distress (Figure 26).

The heartland-hinterland patterns are perhaps best indexed by the population or income potentials measures, which show accessibility to national markets. Tideman has shown that potential maximization, under certain elasticity conditions, produces profit maximization (generally, where marginal production cost is insignificant compared to unit transport cost)[21] which is reason enough for maintenance of the manufacturing belt.[22]

[19] Brian J. L. Berry, *Degree of Metropolitan Labor Market Participation as a Variable in Economic Development* (Economic Development Administration, 1968). The gradients in Figures 19 and 20 were produced by plotting the changes in census characteristics of counties along principal transportation routes joining the urban centers indicated. Approximate centers of counties were used as plotting points.

[20] Analysis again completed for Edgar Dunn. See Berry, *Strategies, Models and Economic Theories....*

[21] Nicholaus Tideman, "Transport Cost Versus Market Potential" (unpublished paper, Center for Urban Studies, University of Chicago, 1967).

[22] Chauncy D. Harris, "The Market as a Factor...."

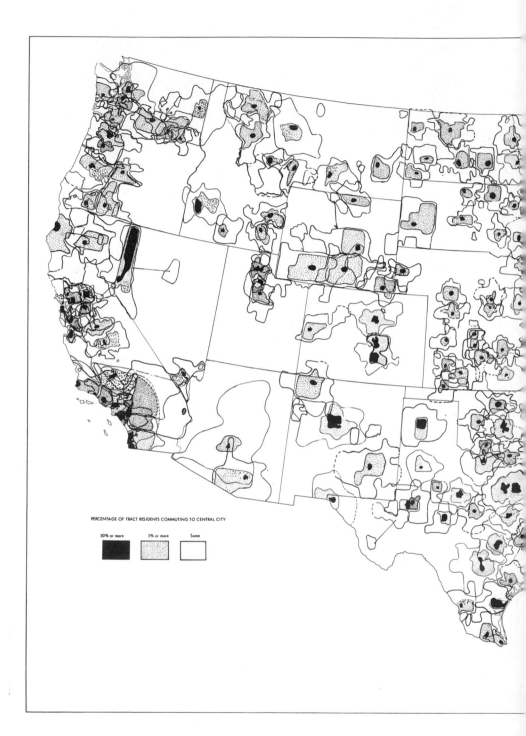

Figure 18. Intensity of individual commuting fields in 1960. Variations in the propor-

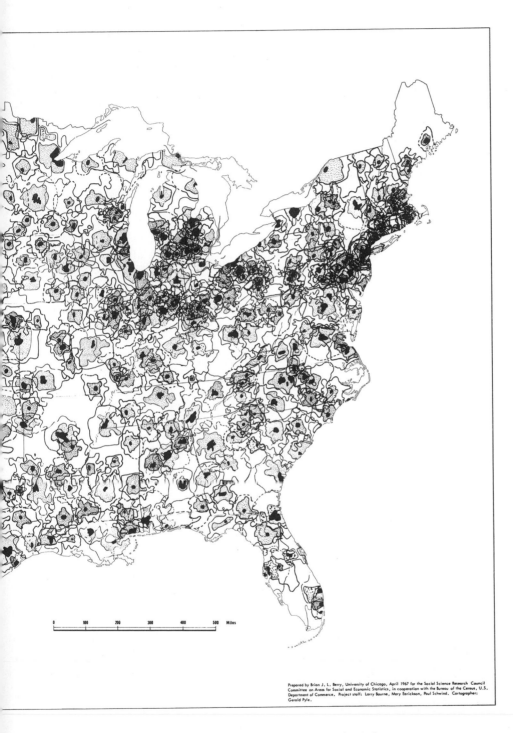

Prepared by Brian J. L. Berry, University of Chicago, April 1967 for the Social Science Research Council
Committee on Areas for Social and Economic Statistics, in cooperation with the Bureau of the Census, U.S.
Department of Commerce. Project staff: Larry Bourne, Mary Earickson, Paul Schwind. Cartographer:
Gerald Pyle.

n of tract or minor civil division commuting to urban centers are indicated.

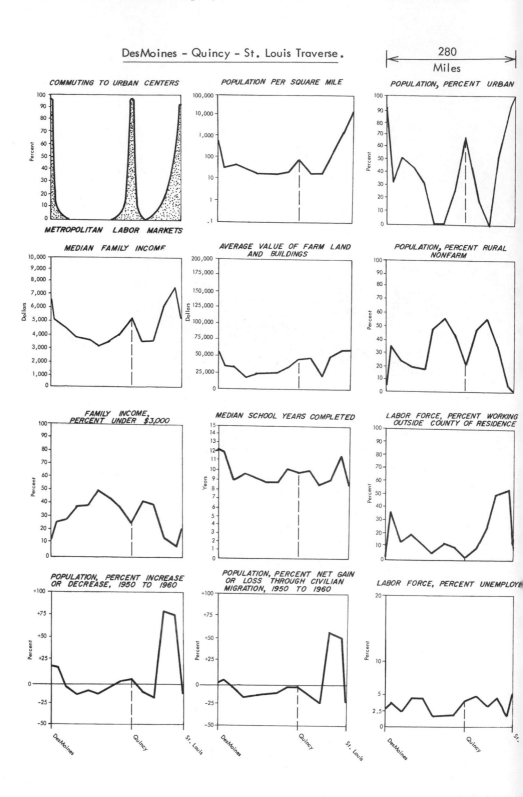

Figure 19.   *Gradients of urban influence on a traverse from Des Moines to St. Louis.*

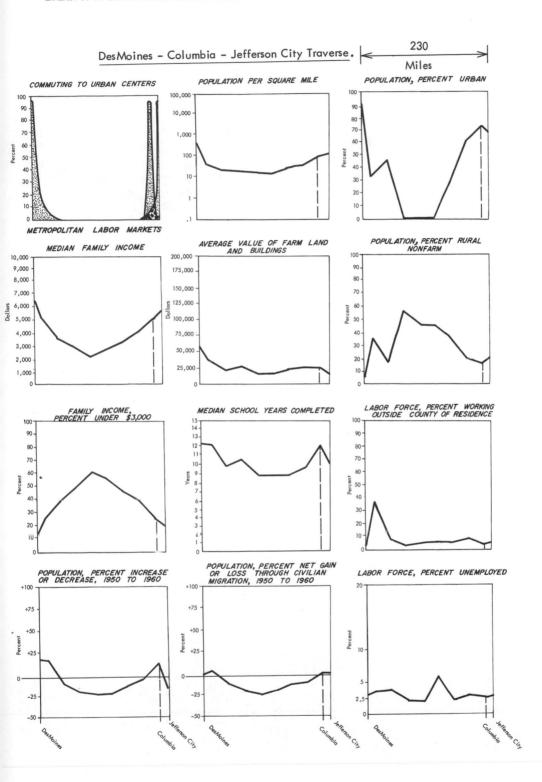

Figure 20.   Gradients of urban influence between Des Moines and Jefferson City.

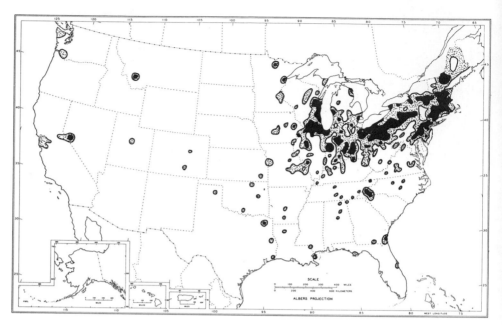

Figure 21. Areas with least dependence on agriculture, 1960. The intensities are based upon factor scores created in a principal axis factor analysis of county employment data, 1960.

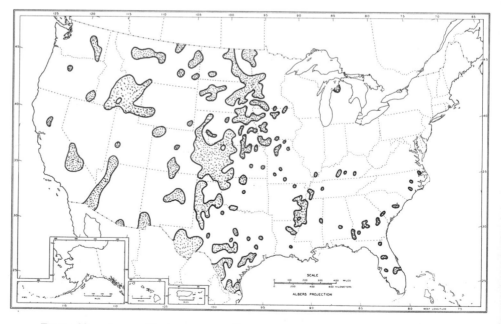

Figure 22. Areas with the greatest reliance upon agricultural employment, 1960.

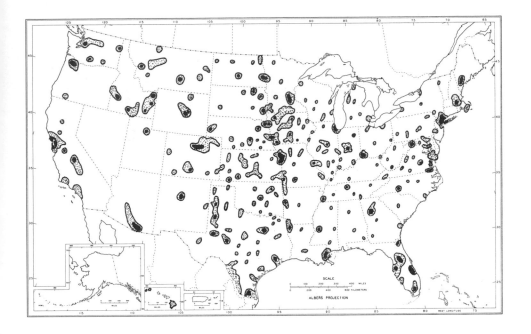

Figure 23.   Areas with the greatest reliance upon employment in the tertiary sector, 1960.

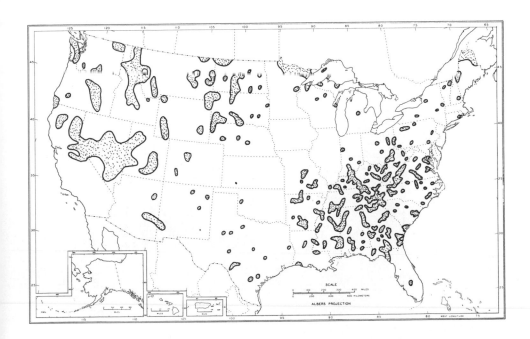

Figure 24.   Areas with the least reliance upon tertiary employment, 1960.

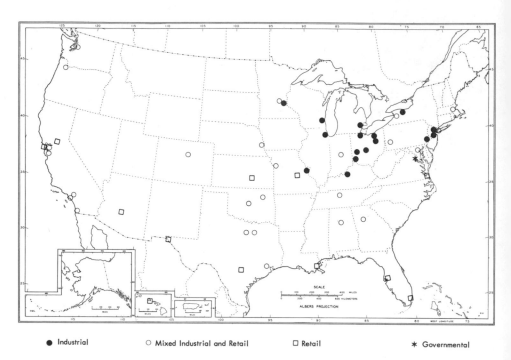

● Industrial   ○ Mixed Industrial and Retail   □ Retail   ✳ Governmental

Figure 25. Principal functional classification of cities over 250,000 in population, 1960. The source is the International City Managers' Association, Municipal Yearbook *for 1967.*

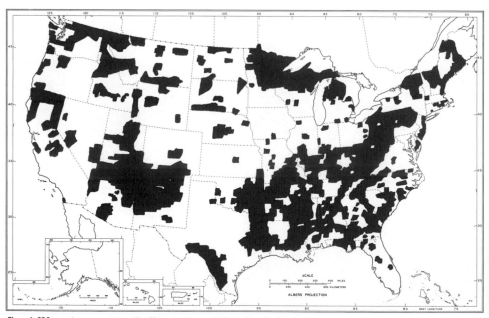

These 1,225 counties -- containing 49 million people -- qualify for federal public works grants and regional development aid, by reason of high unemployment and low average income.

Figure 26. Counties in economic distress in 1964. Note the inverse relationship in low income and high degrees of participation in metropolitan labor markets.

The Duncans and their colleagues go further.[23] They show the proportion of land in farms, the proportion of farmland in crops, and density of farm population to be functions of accessibility to the national system as indexed by potentials, and a measure of land quality. On the other hand, per acre value of crops and farmland values (indicating intensity of production) vary with proximity to a metropolitan center. Yet the correlation of densities and land quality is negative: farm densities are higher in the Northeast, where general access is higher, than in the naturally better-endowed Midwest and South, so that lower natural endowments are offset by opportunities for off-farm work.

Similarly, nonmetropolitan manufacturing drops off with general accessibility: this relationship is stronger for fabricating than for processing industries. The association between level of activity and general accessibility to an urban center is weaker but significant for other resource-extracting activities — such as coal mining — although location of the activity is obviously tied to availability of the resource.

There is yet another type of patterning to be noted at the regional level. On a uniform plain the hierarchy of market towns shows a regular tessellation of sizes and locations, with the town-ratio varying by organizational principle (supply, transportation, administration) and by layout of the transport network (linear alignment, triangular-hexagonal, rectangular-rhomboidal).[24] Traditionally, this norm was affected environmentally in two ways:

1. Many "centers" were not geometrically central to their tributary areas, because of break-of-bulk functions — as in the case of a port or metropolis which grew up at a river crossing.

2. As population densities dropped in a progression toward agricultural areas of increasing aridity and decreasing productivity, the tessellations of the central-place hierarchy were "stretched," although not at the rate needed to maintain a constant size of market, so that activities performed by smaller centers in more densely-populated areas centralized to higher-order centers where densities were less. Centers of comparable rank in the hierarchy were smaller in population and weaker in functions than those in more densely populated areas.

Both cases have received extensive documentation. The second, of course, shows the "stretching" of the urban hierarchy that occurs systematically outwards from the nation's core to its periphery. In the nation today, however, a transformation of settlement is taking place as part of a general urbanization process in which people are shifting from farm to nonfarm occupations, centralizing from farms and small trade centers to large urban areas in selective, age-specific migration, and dispersing from built-up city areas into neighboring suburbs and the countryside beyond. Where inward migration to the city dominates, population densities are falling and the urban hierarchy is centralizing; where outward flow of commuters dominates, new centers

---

[23] O. D. Duncan *et al.*, *Metropolis and Region* (The Johns Hopkins Press, 1960).
[24] See Berry, *Geography of Market Centers and Retail Distribution*.

are being established. These changes are occurring regardles of locations within the country, in a pattern that transcends environmental differences and is molding central-place hierarchies more closely to the shape of the commuting fields of the country's metropolitan centers (Figure 18). Only at a much grosser level do the traditional environmental differences appear. The essentially unpopulated parts of the country lying outside the metropolitan fields are mountains, forests, or deserts — national parks, Indian reservations, and areas with population densities of less than two persons per square mile. On the other hand, the heartland has the greatest overlap of commuting fields. The growth directions within these urban fields apparently are toward zones of superior amenities, including recreational zones within a one-day travel radius of the central city (and where such zones are scarce, they are being created around artificial lakes and open space reservations.[25]

The System of Cities and the Characteristics of Different Categories

The cities form a national system. Above a population of approximately 250,000, the size-distribution of the labor markets approximates a steady state (shown by the rank-size distribution, Figure 27).[26] A city's area varies directly with its population S_c and inversely with system location (population potentials, P).

$$\log A = 0.78 + 0.82 \log S_c - 0.396 \log P$$
$$r^2 = 0.80$$
$$S_e = 0.196$$

Further, the population of the city's labor market S_M varies directly with size of the legal central city S_c and potentials P. (See Figures 28 and 29.)

$$\log S_M = -0.2 + 0.71 \log S_c + 0.53 \log P$$
$$r^2 = 0.81$$
$$S_e = 0.21$$

Internally, population densities drop off with distance from the city center, providing one element to the gradient of the urban field:[27]

$$d_x = d_o e^{-bx}$$

where d_x is density at distance x

d_o is central density, as extrapolated, and

b is the density gradient

---

[25] Raymond J. Burby, III, *Lake Oriented Subdivisions in North Carolina: Decision Factors and Policy Implications for Urban Growth Patterns* (University of North Carolina, Institute for Research in Social Science, 1967).

[26] Berry, "Cities as Systems within Systems of Cities." Also Wilbur R. Thompson, *A Preface to Urban Economics* (The Johns Hopkins Press for Resources for the Future, Inc., 1965).

[27] Brian J. L. Berry *et al.*, "Urban Population Densities: Structure and Change," *Geographical Review*, Vol. 53 (1963), pp. 389–405.

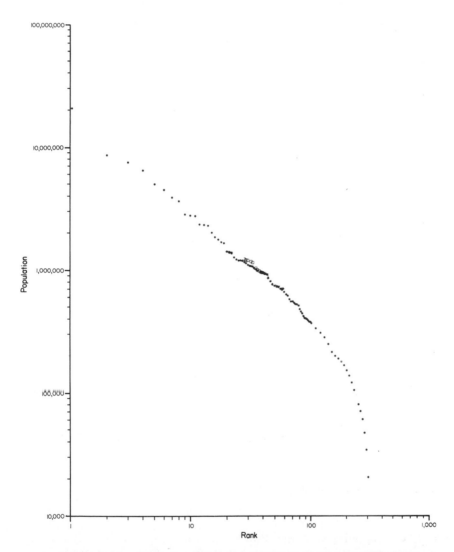

Figure 27.   Rank-size distribution of labor markets in 1960. Labor markets defined by relative closure as either consolidated urban regions or functional economic areas. See Brian J. L. Berry, Metropolitan Area Definition. A Re-evaluation of Concept and Statistical Practice (*U.S. Bureau of the Census, 1968*).

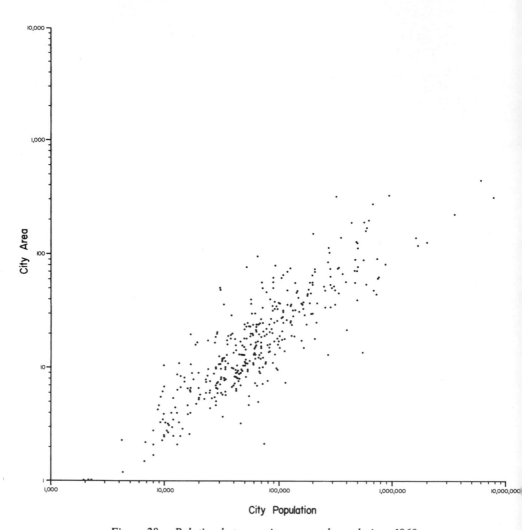

Figure 28. Relation between city area and population, 1960.

But the density gradient also varies inversely with size of city:

$$S_M = 10^5 \, b^{-3}$$

where S_M is population of the SMSA. Also, if the density gradient is integrated to yield total population, one obtains:

$$2d_o\pi b^{-2} = S$$

so that central density is derivable as a product of the density gradient and city size.[28]

If the density gradient varies with size of city, however, the degree of participation of workers within the labor market in the central city's employment opportunities

[28] Herbert K. Weiss, "The Distribution of Urban Population and an Application to a Servicing Problem," *Operations Research*, Vol. 9 (1961), pp. 860–74.

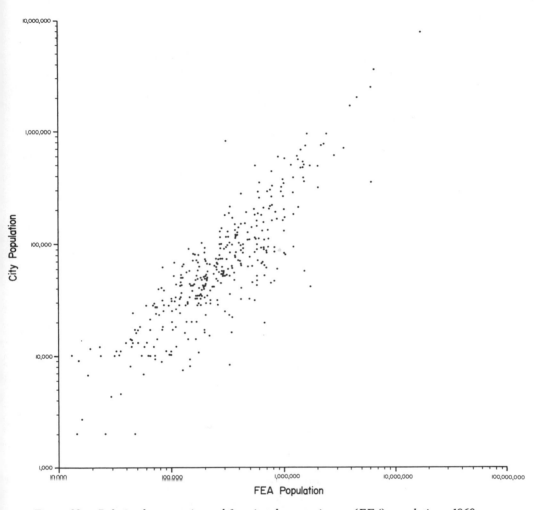

Figure 29.   Relation between city and functional economic area (FEA) populations, 1960.

does not, outside an inner zone roughly coterminous with the radius of the central
city. Analysis of the complete set of commuting fields plotted in Figure 18 showed the
gradient *c* in the model

$$W = k(D - R)^{-c}$$

(where *W* is the percentage of resident workers commuting to the central city,
       D is the distance from the CBD,
and   *R* is radius of the county containing the central city)

to have a mean of *c* = 2.0. This distance exponent varied systematically over the
country's cities neither with size of city nor location within conurbations nor where
obvious physical features such as lakes, mountains, rivers and sea cut off part of the
available area, nor by sector radiating from the CBD. Degree of participation in the

central city labor market evidently obeys a universal inverse distance-squared rule. The expected value of c is 2.0, with a standard deviation of 0.6 and an observed range of 1.1 to 4.8. Variations in numbers of commuters from various distances into central cities of different sizes are thus a function of the density gradient and not of the central labor-market participation rate.

There are other regularities to the internal patterning of cities within the system. The classical concentricity of the Burgess ideal-type and the axial arrangements of Hoyt's model of urban ecology, together with the segregation and concentration studies of the "Chicago School" are known well enough not to need elaboration. Likewise, the family structure, socioeconomic status, and segregation dimensions revealed by social area analysts have been replicated in enough studies to be recognized as general properties of urban ecology. The synthesis of the two is the essence of the "new ecology."[29]

Briefly, the ecology of the city appears to represent the summation of three principal elements:

1. Stage of families in the life cycle, which determines family size, type of housing and location of residence selected, attitudes to density, open space, use of the personal automobile, etc. It is this syndrome that leads to concentric patterns of land use, and declines of densities with change of housing type at increased distances from the city center.

2. Socioeconomic status of individuals, involving educational background, type of employment, level of income, quality of residence, etc. This factor varies (in Hoyt fashion) by sectors, with lower status sectors following job axis and higher-status sectors seeking out superior residential amenities.

3. Segregation — the restriction of certain groups to particular communities within the city, where communities can be defined by the intersection of concentric patterns (a), and axial patterns (b), as relatively homogeneous social groups.

TYPOLOGY OF CITIES, 1960

These system regularities characterize all American cities. But because the nation's development process led to regional growth patterns based upon particular resource endowments and industry mixes, because each urban area consists of a series of "layers" reflecting initial epoch of growth and subsequent competitive position, and because differing industry mixes support different social mixes through the medium of the income level and distribution, there are also distinctive types of cities in different

[29] Brian J. L. Berry, "Internal Structure of the City," *Law and Contemporary Problems* (Winter, 1965). Janet Abu-Lughod, "The City is Dead — Long Live the City: Some Thoughts on Urbanity," (resource paper for the 1966 AIP meetings). Robert A. Murdie, *The Changing Social Geography of Metropolitan Toronto* (forthcoming in 1969 in the Research Series, Department of Geography, University of Chicago). John W. Dyckman, "City Planning and the Treasury of Science," *Environment for Man* (Indiana University Press, 1967), pp. 46–47.

regions, with varying growth histories, and substantially different resource-orienta-
tions both historically and contemporaneously.[30]

This internal differentiation is of major importance for our evaluation of "new
resources in an urban age," because of the substantial regional differences in valued
resources that are implied. Thus, it is appropriate to explore a recent typology of
standard metropolitan statistical areas which has been developed using 1960 census
data and related series.[31]

Mayer used some sixty-six variables to capture the main elements of differentiation of the SMSA's. These included characteristics of the urban economy; the social,
economic, and demographic characteristics of the population; certain indices of recent
change; measures of relative location; some simple characteristics of the physical
environment; and the like. Twelve components, which were identified by a principal
axis factor analysis of these data (the variables required logarithmic transformation;
simple structure was approximated by normal varimax rotation), capture the principal types of differentiation of the metropolitan areas.

Earlier factors in this type of analysis span more of the variance than later ones,
and each factor represents a complete *scale*. Table 1 summarizes the factor structure
and provides the factor loadings (correlations of original variables and the factors).
Thus, on factor 1 — socioeconomic status (SES) — centers can be arrayed from those
with the lowest (low incomes, housing values, educational levels, housing qualities) to
those with the highest. Factor 2 scales cities by age, size, and their correlates. Factor 3
picks out differentiation according to population composition; factor 4 according to
recent service-oriented growth, etc.

In a related study exploring urban pathologies, Maloney[32] has identified similar
components, and related specific urban problems to them. For example, unemployment rises as the SES of a city drops (factor 1); governmental fragmentation, and
per capita city service costs rise with size and age of city (factor 2); the crime rate
is greatest in the largest and the most rapidly growing cities (factors 2 and 4); riot-
prone cities are, on the other hand, the largest and oldest (factor 2) with the greatest
Negro concentrations (inverse factor 7). There is much that is socially meaningful,
therefore, in the typology.

Taken together, the twelve factors provide a "space" within which the similarities
and differences of the metropolitan areas can be studied simultaneously, on the basis
of the "distances" between centers located as points in this space. Use of numerical
taxonomy then enables a meaningful typology of the metropolitan areas to be derived.
(See Table 2.)

Apparently, within the twelve patterns of differentiation of the SMSA's, there
are clear regional clusters arranged from the manufacturing belt heartland outwards

[30] Richard E. Engler, Jr., *The Challenge of Diversity* (Harper and Row, 1964).

[31] This study was undertaken by Harold M. Mayer, and is as yet unpublished. I am indebted
to Professor Mayer for permitting me to draw on his results.

[32] John C. Maloney, "Metropolitan Area Characteristics and Problems" (Working materials,
Medill School of Journalism, Northwestern University, 1967).

Table 1. Factor Structure: Mayer Study of U.S. Metropolitan Areas, 1960

Factor	Variables represented by factor	Factor loading
Socioeconomic status	Median rent	0.869
	Value of homes	0.784
	Median family income	0.907
	Per cent white-collar workers	0.567
	Median school years	0.754
	Per cent with high school education	0.720
	Per cent families < $3,000 income	−0.821
	Per cent families > $10,000 income	0.881
	Per cent homes with plumbing	0.758
Age and size	Population	0.974
	Age	0.648
	Per cent using public transportation	0.643
	Per cent population Jewish	0.626
	Proportion SMSA urbanized	0.911
	No. of railroad connections	0.571
	No. of airline passengers	0.888
	Tons waterborne commerce	0.722
	No. of vacant units	0.911
	Production workers in manufacturing	0.954
	Value added in manufacturing	0.957
Population composition and demography	Fertility rate	0.627
	Death rate	−0.644
	Family size	0.712
	Median age	−0.857
	Per cent population under 5 years	0.891
	Per cent population working age (21–64 years)	−0.602
	Per cent population old (over 65 years)	−0.755
	Population per housing unit	0.852
	Labor participation rate	−0.560
Growth 1950–1960	Per cent homes built since 1950	0.867
	Per cent homes with two cars	0.538
	Per cent population change 1950–60	0.837
	Per cent population moved 1950–60	0.767
	Per cent population migrated 1955–60	0.788
	Distance to state capital	0.591
	Temperature range	−0.686
	Mean annual temperature	0.677
	Per cent payroll from manufacturing	−0.550
	Per cent labor force in manufacturing	−0.523
Commercial vs. manufacturing orientation	Per cent workers white collar	0.609
	Manufacturing payroll, per cent	−0.550
	Retail payroll, per cent	0.659
	Manufacturing labor force, per cent	−0.667
	Trade labor force, per cent	0.784
	Transport (etc.) labor force	0.666
	Finance (etc.) labor force	0.641

Table 1 (Continued)

Foreign-born population	Per cent foreign born	0.867
	Per cent of foreign parentage	0.845
	Per cent homes single family	−0.635
	Per cent vote for Kennedy	0.584
Relative upland interior location	Per cent population non-white	−0.508
	Average annual rainfall	−0.679
	Elevation above sea level	0.798
Institutional or military population	Per cent population living in group quarters	−0.853
Location relative to SMSA	Distance to nearest SMSA	0.893
	Distance to nearest SMSA with 1 million population	0.774
Use of public transport	Per cent employees using public transport	0.502
	Per cent employees residing in another county	0.597
Low density	Per cent urban area in central county	0.611
	Average density of urbanized area	−0.527

Table 2. Typology of SMSA's, 1960

A. *New England, eastern New York, and New Jersey cities*

Intermediate to higher SES, older and/or larger, slow growth 1950–60, substantial commercial orientation, foreign-born population, substantial use of public transport and cross-commuting.

Aa. *New England subgroups* (e.g., Fall River, New Bedford)
Low status, older residual populations, crowding, etc.

Ab. *New York* (special case — modest status, old, large, commercial orientation, foreign born, public transport, etc.)

B. *Manufacturing belt cities*

Older and/or larger, industrial, slow growth 1950–60, high density, substantial foreign-born, use of public transport.

C. *Mining towns* (Pennsylvania, West Virginia, Duluth).

Low SES, older populations, substantial use of group quarters, public transportation.

D. *Cities of agricultural Midwest and Plains*

Younger populations, slow growth 1950–60, commercial orientation, relative isolation, little use made of public transport.

Da. *Chicago* (special case — older, larger, manufacturing)

E. *Smaller towns of Pennsylvania, Ohio, Southern Indiana and Border South*

Average or modest on all factors, few foreign-born, somewhat older population, weaker commercial bases.

F. *Larger Mason-Dixon line cities, plus Atlanta, Richmond, Roanoke*

Some manufacturing, younger populations, slower growth, fewer foreign born.

G. *Southern cities*

   Low SES, young populations, growing, weak commerce, few foreign born, substantial Negro population.

H. *Florida*

   Older populations, rapid growth, commercial, many foreign born, relatively isolated, low density.

I. *Texas and Arizona*
   Ia. *Texas Gulf coast*
      Low density, substantial Negro populations and institutional or military base. Populations youngish, few foreign born.
   Ib. *Mexican border towns*
      Very low SES, very young populations, commercial, many foreign-born, many institutional, military.
   Ic. *West Texas and Arizona*
      Higher SES, younger populations, very rapid growth, automobile-oriented, low density.

J. *Mountain States cities*
   Young cities, young populations, commercial, few Negroes, relatively distant.
   Ja. *Denver and Colorado Springs*
      Same, except larger, growing more rapidly, more use of public transport.

K. *West Coast cities*
   Higher SES, commercial, substantial military involvement.
   Ka. *Los Angeles* (special case — older, larger, more rapid growth, less commerce, absence of public transport).

L. *Other groups*
   La. Principal "institutional" metropolitan areas — Ann Arbor, Champaign-Urbana, Lawton.
   Lb. Las Vegas
   Lc. Midland-Odessa
   Ld. Honolulu

to the periphery. Major contrasts are drawn between manufacturing and commercial cities. Rapid growth in the 1950–60 decade is largely at the periphery — in Florida, Texas and Arizona, and on the West Coast. (See Figures 30 and 31.)

System Generating and Maintaining Mechanisms

Thus, we note that the relevant definitional planes are of the national, regional, and local scales: (1) growth of the nation at large, leading to polarized development, a heartland and hinterlands, and a national system of metropolitan centers; (2) an urban hierarchy within each metropolitan region; and (3) urban "fields" or gradients of influence of each urban center on its surrounding hinterland. The different regional types of cities arise from age and stage of development within this matrix — from the manner in which innovation and diffusion processes have operated in this systems framework.

One can view development as a series of elementary innovations which merge into innovative clusters and finally into linked systems of evolutionary innovations

Figure 30. Regional patterns, SMSA typology of 1960.

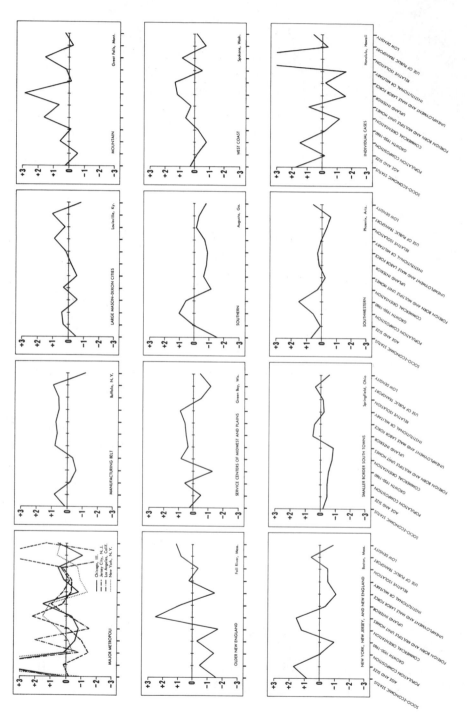

Figure 31.   Factor profiles of sample cities, SMSA typology of 1960.

that replace one sociocultural paradigm by another as they cumulate to an "epochal innovation" that produces "revolutionary" change in paradigms.[33]

The frequency of innovation is a function of the probability of interaction or information exchange in open systems — particularly large cities or urbanized regions — so that what develops in one phase of growth becomes the environment of subsequent phases, and powerful pressures for system-maintenance are generated. The development process therefore has its origin in a relatively small number of poles of change, or core regions, and spreads outwards from these to peripheral areas. Core region or heartland development is, as a result, self-reinforcing in a pattern of circular and cumulative causation,[34] due to such feedback elements in the development process as net flow of natural, human, and capital resources from hinterlands to heartland; information flows due to size and change at the core; linkages involving innovations that breed others by creating new demands; creation of necessary conditions for innovation; transformation of values into those accepting greater change through innovation; scale, urbanization, and localization economies.

Viewed spatially, then, polarized development can be seen to have taken place in the United States in a system with New York at its apex, with a core industrial region in the northeastern manufacturing belt, spanning a variety of urban places supported mainly by their manufacturing function. Connections between this heartland and the specialized hinterlands surrounding it have been maintained by a network of commercial metropolises that have articulated commodity flows between core and periphery and have set the terms of trade. Beneath them, successively lower orders of central places have organized the supply and assembly functions for surrounding peripheral areas.

The rate of innovation is greatest in the heartland, and is systematically transmitted outwards from it into the hinterlands. Thus, in the United States, one should expect change to take place (1) nationally, outwards from the manufacturing belt, (2) down the urban hierarchy; and (3) outwards from any urban center into its surrounding urban field. However, it should be recognized that newer centers have the propensity to adopt innovations and assume new forms more rapidly than older centers of comparable size located in regions which grew at an earlier time, for, following the analysis of Perloff and his colleagues:[35]

1. Relative change in the urban system at any time-period is based upon activities and resources new in the national economy, rather than upon redistribution of existing activities—this is the basis of the emergence of new centers and regions and the shift in relative size of the old.

---

[33] John R. P. Friedmann, *Regional Development Policy* (The M.I.T. Press, 1966), and "A General Theory of Polarized Development" (draft manuscript, Santiago: Ford Foundation Urban and Regional Development Advisory Program in Chile, June, 1967).

[34] Allan Pred, *The Spatial Dynamics....*

[35] Harvey S. Perloff *et al.*, *Regions, Resources, and Economic Growth* (The Johns Hopkins Press for Resources for the Future, 1960).

2. New centers, growing rapidly in a particular phase of urban growth, always have a concentration in the newer lines of economic activity—the "growth sectors" of the current phase of technology—and are found in regions well-endowed with resources valued by those growth sectors.

3. City character and structure are a record of (a) the epoch of initial growth and (b) subsequent success in capturing lines of activity new upon the national scene.

4. Since the phase of growth associated with iron and steel, the dominant national pattern in the American urban system has been that of a manufacturing belt heartland and surrounding resource-oriented hinterlands, complemented at the regional level, for each metropolitan center, by an analogous center-periphery (or distance-decay) phenomenon, which is then repeated at the successively more local scales of each level of the urban hierarchy downward from the metropolis.[36]

An example of the processes operating can be seen in the sequences and transitions of technology used to move people and goods within cities, and the way they relate to (1) the national growth process, and (2) diffusion mechanisms, with net results in the typology of cities to be seen today.

Borchert identifies four principal epochs in American metropolitan growth, separated by changes in technology crucial in the location of urban development and the internal features of urban morphology: (1) "sailwagon," 1790–1830; (2) "steamboat and iron horse," 1830–1870; (3) "steel rails and electric power," 1870–1920; (4) "auto-air-amenity," 1920–present (internal combustion engine and shift to services).[37] Much of the earlier discussion has been devoted to the growth and change of the national urban system as the country developed through these phases. However, paralleling the system transformation, there was also a series of shifts in internal structure — from the pre-industrial walking-and-wagon form, to the industrial city in which jobs remained centralized but residential areas had spread and differentiated, to the post-industrial forms of decentralized residences and workplaces.

In the pre-industrial phase there had been water-related expansion of the national urban system along the Mississippi-Ohio system and the Great Lakes and the beginnings of the blanketing of the country by a network of railroads and rail-related commercial centers. But in both of these, internal growth of cities was constrained by internal means of transportation — essentially walking or horse and wagon. Urban activities were, despite good reasons for decentralization in prices of land, labor, and capital, forced by primitive means of moving goods short distances overland to remain as close as possible to port facilities and, later, to railroad terminals.[38] Workers of all grades were forced to live close to work in crowded, mixed, residential-commercial-industrial areas.[39]

---

[36] Berry, *Geography of Market Centers and Retail Distribution*, and Peter Haggett, *Locational Analysis in Human Geography* (London: Edward Arnold, Ltd., 1965).

[37] Borchert, "American Metropolitan Evolution."

[38] Leon Moses and Harold F. Williamson, "The Location of Economic Activity in Cities," *American Economic Review*, Vol. LVII (May 1967), pp. 211–22.

[39] Gideon Sjoberg, *The Preindustrial City* (The Free Press, 1960).

But at the same time that the economy was being transformed industrially and the dynamics of industrial growth were being added to commercial-related expansion of the urban system, the first street railway was installed in New York in 1851. Although workplaces were still confined by use of horses and wagons to port- and railroad-related locations at and radiating from the city center, this revolutionary innovation permitted residences to decentralize.[40] The industrial city came into being not simply because of the new economic base, but because the industrial transformation coincided with a new means of moving people, and this in turn led to separation of land use types and socioeconomic differentiation of residential areas according to principles of both centrality and axiality. According to Hurd, this meant cities in which:

The land which is most convenient is first utilized, and that which is less convenient is made of service in accordance with its diminishing facilities. Since convenience means economy in time and cost, the value in any piece of land will represent the cost saved and the pleasure obtained by its use, as compared with the use of land worth nothing multiplied by the number and economic quality of the people for whom the saving is made. Thus the value of all urban land ranges from that which least serves the smallest number of people of the lowest economic quality, up to the highest economic quality.

Since value depends on economic rent, and rent on location, and location on convenience, and convenience on nearness, we may eliminate the intermediate steps and say that value depends on nearness. The next question is, nearness to what?—which brings us to the land requirements of different utilities, their distribution over the city's area and the consequent creation and distribution of values.[41]

New York installed its street railway in 1851. By 1865, the largest of the older cities and the now industrial and commercial-manufacturing centers of the emergent heartland had also adopted it (Figure 32). By 1897, the pattern of adoptions had spread outward from the heartland to replicate that of the system of population potentials that was to characterize the United States until 1950. Early adopters used horses or mules as motive power. Later, steam was applied, but steam facilities were seldom constructed in small hinterland centers after the invention of electricity (Figure 33). Not only did diffusion take place from heartland to hinterland, however; it was also in evidence down the urban hierarchy (Figure 34). Additionally, two other elements affected the diffusion sequences: smaller hinterland centers that were growing rapidly were more likely to adopt street railways than heartland cities of comparable size; and the closer a small city was to a metropolis that had already adopted a street railway, the greater was the probability that it would adopt one at an earlier date than more distant places within the urban field.[42]

[40] Arthur J. Krim, *The Innovation and Diffusion of the Street Railway in North America* (M.A. Thesis, University of Chicago, 1967).

[41] Richard M. Hurd, *Principles of City Land Values* (New York: The Record and Guide, 1924).

[42] Krim, *The Innovation and Diffusion of the Street Railway* . . . .

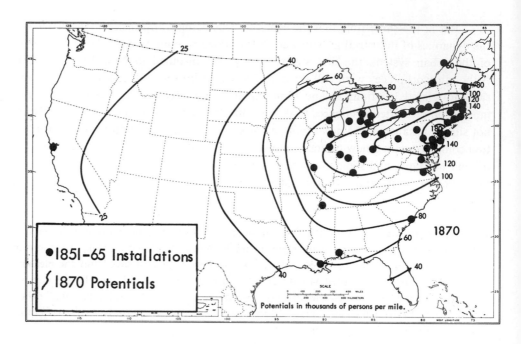

Figure 32.   Urban centers installing street railways, 1851–1865.

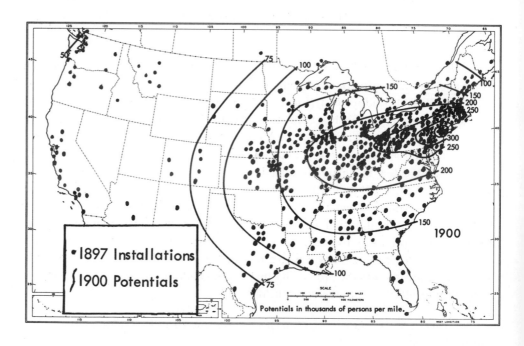

Figure 33.   Street railway installations in 1897.

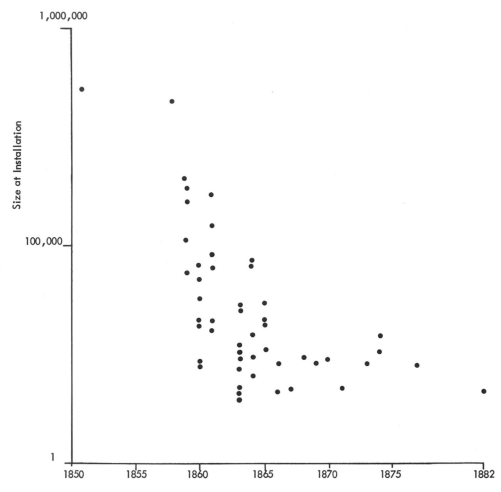

Figure 34. Diffusion of street railway adoptions down the urban hierarchy, 1851–1880.

A similar heartland–large city pattern characterized electric interurban railway installations. These permitted further residential decentralization until the 1930's, when their function, and that of the street railways, was gradually replaced by buses and the private automobile in the areas shown in Figure 35. For cities of more recent growth, the automobile dominated from the start.

Each of these subsequent developments in personal transportation took place within the context of the industrial city. They were *evolutionary* innovations permitting increased residential differentiation based on life cycle, social status, and ethnicity, and given the central-axial layout of places of employment and the concentration permitted by the inventions in building technology of the 1870's and 1880's (for example, steel-frame skyscraper, elevator), they supported the familiar ecology of the industrial city.

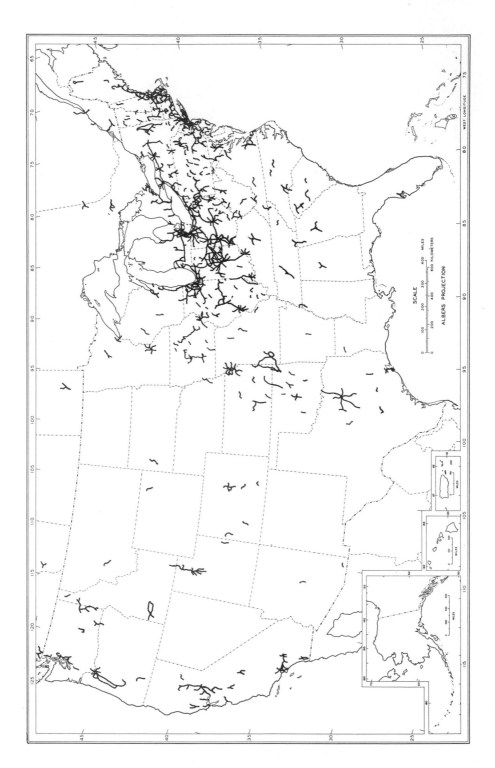

Figure 35. All known electric interurban railway routes.

It was not until the combination of truck transportation and new interstate high-ways was felt in the years after World War II, at a time when new economic growth was based on footloose industries in the final stages of processing and in the service sectors, that places of employment began to decentralize substantially. It was this combination of elements that led to the next urban *revolution:* growth of the post-industrial city in which industries, employees, and the non-job-oriented population have all been seeking out new amenity resources, and the overlapping commuting fields depicted in Figures 17 and 18 grew. The process involves both push and pull, for the essence of the large industrial city has been concentration and high densities —absence of open space, crowding, increasing problems of environmental pollu-tion, etc. Large industrial cities have also been the principal sources of blue-collar employment, with attendant accumulations of members on the lowest rungs in the status system in deteriorating crowded slums. New industries and the white-collar middle class characteristically avoid such areas, so that the revolutionary innovations of the post-1950 period imply substantial changes in system form, rather than the system-maintenance of evolutionary sequences. There is growth of certain parts at the expense of others. In either case, however, it is the system that provides the environmental context for the changes.[43] The challenges that result are substantial and many. For, at the very time that the pull of new urban resources is towards decentralization within urban regions and continued deconcentration by hinterland growth along the southern and western rims of the continent, Jean Gottmann con-cludes that for the nation's great urban concentrations "increased crowding has become the indispensible alternative to decay."[44]

City and Environment under Post-Industrial Conditions

We find in the end, then, that there are significant relationships that tie the smallest local developments to broad-scale national developments. Thus, the face of North America varies by broad physiographic and climatic province and by myriad differences of site and microclimate. Overlaid on the continent is a national urban system with a manufacturing heartland, integrated by a set of industrial and commer-cial metropolises, articulated intraregionally by central-place hierarchies, patterned by the regular rise and fall of gradients of urban influence, and structured by individual locational choices and their accumulation into the urban ecology. An outcome of the overlay is a set of locations, sizes, and shapes of cities.

The basic pattern has been laid down under multiple influences of environment, technology, and resource use. It is now so strong that it is generating its own change, under post-industrial conditions that call for growth of certain parts and decay of

[43] Borchert, in "American Metropolitan Evolution," notes the increasing problem of residual structures dating from earlier growth epochs. Ironically, Andrew Wilson notes that the immigration to Tucson in response to the climatic advantages has contributed to that city's high unemployment rates. See also W. R. D. Sewell, *Human Dimensions of Weather Modification* (University of Chicago, Department of Geography Research Paper No. 105, 1966).

[44] Jean Gottmann, *Megalopolis* (Twentieth Century Fund, 1961), p. 632.

others. Revolutionary innovations are now demanding that the system change form in certain key aspects. Under these conditions, questions emerge as to configurations of new urban resources that may have been defined by the innovations, their relationships to the urban system on the one hand, to the physical environment on the other, and to feedbacks between the emerging urban form and the new urban resources.

Concern in the post-industrial context is as much with negative impacts of the system on environment and with environmental factors related to decay and the possibilities for rejuvenation as it is with new resources promoting growth. The issues are as much qualitative as they are quantitative, and they must probably be addressed differently for each of the different types of cities that have emerged in the evolution of the urban system. For the different types have different economic bases that support different income levels and mixes and therefore markedly different populations in terms of social status. And since the perception of new resources is socially-relative, then relations of city and environment must be examined with reference to type of city.

Within the cities themselves, at the local scale, there are significant micro-environmental relations. For example, the density-gradient has been shown to be lower in higher-status residential sectors, and Hoyt has pointed out that these high status sectors have sought out zones of superior residential amenities — views, higher ground, slopes, trees — and away from industrial areas and railroad yards (which followed the valleys as they converged on CBS's). Low status groups, on the other hand, have been compelled to follow the industrial axes for dual reasons — they could not compete for superior residential amenities and, by virtue of their lower incomes, they were required to reside closer to their work in the heavy industries that provide most blue collar employment.

The role of amenities in locational choice is of increasing importance today because generally rising real incomes and improved transportation is breaking down the closeness of the ties to workplace in all but the lowest income groups. Advantages of site and microclimate (Hurd's "pleasurable" features of the use of land, in distinction to simple nearness) are hence of increasing significance. They are "new resources" in that with increasing demand they are more valued. On the other hand, the oldest and most crowded environments have, in effect, reduced the supply and therefore increased the value of other new resources — in particular, open space, fresh air, and pure water.

Growth and decline are both thus characteristics of system development and transformation. Increased awareness of and orientation to the new resources nationally, regionally, and locally has, in effect, led to greater public awareness of their absence in the great industrial cities that epitomized all that was desirable in the previous epoch of urban growth.

9

Patterns of time and space use

F. Stuart Chapin, Jr., and Thomas H. Logan

F. Stuart Chapin, Jr., is Research Director of the Center for Urban
and Regional Studies and Professor of Planning at the
University of North Carolina.
Thomas H. Logan is a graduate student in the Department of
City and Regional Planning at the University of North Carolina.

Patterns of time and space use

F. Stuart Chapin, Jr., and Thomas H. Logan

In order to develop an optimal scheme in the use of "new resources" in the urban environment, policy intervention must, to a significant extent, take into account the living patterns, thoughtways, and value systems of urban residents. What constitutes "quality" in this environment is a function of the human filtering process called "perception," and in turn perception is shaped by man's experience with a whole range of behavior systems interacting with the environment. Indeed, the problems of resources exist because of the interaction of an organized human productive machine with the resources the earth offers up to it. But the complex organization of the modern city gives the human organization side of the equation a heightened importance, a new urgency in the eyes of those who must deal with resource problems.

Perloff has emphasized that the city is the productive plant of our society. Berry points to the dynamic of the nation's system of cities in generating its own growth and shaping the physical environment. These views should remind us to look at the effects of this productive machine on human as well as physical resources; and to look at the effect of human as well as physical resources on the productive machine. For people are the crucial resource in the productive system, the important element in the city, and the beneficiaries or victims of progress. Meier made this eminently clear in his classic proposal for using time budgets as an accounting system in the study of urban growth.[1]

This paper suggests a way of analyzing the behavior systems of people in ways which can contribute to knowledge of how the productive machine and the urban environment interact. The unit of analysis is the "episode" in people's patterns of activity, and it is used to measure and analyze their reaction to their environments. The conceptual framework embodies a systemic view of people in routine interaction with the environment. At this stage in the work the research strategy has of necessity emphasized time patterns. But sufficient work has been done in relating spatial aspects of activities to time patterns to indicate how both facets of this way of conceptualizing a city offer a means of relating urban resource policy to the living patterns of people who are presumed to benefit from such policy. Some brief extensions of the time analysis to the spatial analysis will be brought into the discussion below.

The findings presented in this chapter were made possible by two research studies at the Center for Urban and Regional Studies, University of North Carolina at Chapel Hill. The data were obtained as part of Project 8-6, "Individual Preferences for Alternative Dwelling Types and Environments," National Co-operative Highway Research Program, and the analysis and computation runs were made possible by support from Project CH 00116, "Household Activity Patterns and Community Health," U.S. Public Health Service.— AUTHORS' NOTE

[1] Richard L. Meier, "Human Time Allocation: A Basis for Social Accounts," *Journal of the American Institute of Planners*, Vol. 15, No. 1 (February 1959), pp. 27–33.

This perspective for the study of new urban resources offers a number of avenues for exploration. This kind of research can help us to understand how people use the city-machine, how the complex human organization affects them, how they respond in their daily lives. Do they have increasing leisure? How do they use what they have? Do they pursue social activities over the entire extent of the city, or mainly near home? What kind of recreational facilities do they use, and what effect does their availability have on the total pattern of activities? How does the time spent driving to work affect other activities? Can we get an idea of the degree of segregation or integration of land use types which is most functional?

In brief, then, this chapter examines patterns in time and space use in the urban environment as key elements in evaluating how the resource aspects of the environment influence when and where human activity takes place, and how, in turn, experience in this respect feeds back and provides a basis for shaping and modifying policy to accomplish a new equilibrium. It views metropolitan areas in terms of behavioral systems in which processes surrounding the activities of such entities as firms, governments, households, voluntary organizations of various kinds, and other institutions clustering in the city and using the city as a base of operation are the focus of interest. These systems and subsystems are seen to consist of flows — flows of goods, services, information, and actions of various kinds, according to the nature of the system under consideration. In this discussion, one such behavioral system is singled out for attention — a system developed around human activity routines. As distinct, then, from activities of firms, governments, and other entities, this paper will give special attention to activities of the residents of metropolitan areas, particularly the decision-making members of households, typically heads and spouses. In brief, the approach taken here centers around the flow of events in the life of urban residents over some set span of time. In roughing out a model of such a behavioral system, particular attention is given to the interrelationship between human activity patterns and spatial structure of metropolitan areas. To explore even the most elemental implications of such a view of metropolitan areas is, of course, an enormously complicated task, and in a presentation of this kind, it is possible to treat the concepts involved only in a very summary and tentative form.

The chapter is organized in three parts. The first provides a conceptual view of this behavioral system, giving particular attention to the significance of household activity patterns for the study of urban spatial structure. In the second part, a summary view of the daily activity patterns of residents of metropolitan areas in urban America is presented; in the third, the implications of observations concerning these living patterns for policies and decisions in the use of urban resources are considered.

Household Activity Patterns as a Behavioral System

The notion of studying a metropolitan area in terms of the activity patterns of its residents and viewing these in the framework of a behavioral system overlaying other such systems — for example, economic activity systems — has some interesting potentialities. First of all, as an area of theoretical investigation it offers promise of supplying some conceptual guidelines for relating resident behavior patterns to the spatial organization of the city. Thus if, as seems to be the case, there is a source of order to activity routines — an evolutionary sequence to activity choices over some unit period of time — and if this order also extends to the way in which residents "use" their city, it is a matter of great interest to examine these activity patterns juxtaposed with respect to the physical structure of the environment and the spatial organization of land uses. Such a framework may provide the means of relating human behavior in the city to the urban environment which may then become an important means for defining planning criteria or standards which heretofore have existed largely as ad hoc rules of thumb.

A second and not entirely unrelated potential of this kind of approach is the possibility of linking up planning goal formulation, policy making, and political action concerning the urban environment to the value systems and preference patterns of urban residents. In the past few years a great deal of effort in city planning has been going into defining goals for growth and development. A variety of approaches for identifying goals has been experimented with, ranging from the establishment of public commissions where members' own wisdom, experience, and observation are used to define goals; to bringing in panels of experts; conducting attitude surveys; all the way to holding elaborate sequences of community forum discussions staged at different locations and given some central sense of continuity through a TV hook-up, with each forum session culminating in a questionnaire search for consensus in attitudes or preferences. One purpose of the latter approach is to make political action on public improvement programs more sensitive to the preference patterns of various segments of the population, although it must be added that perhaps these efforts have greater significance as techniques for broadening the base of citizen understanding about the problems of cities — making participation an educational experience. The point here is that these efforts constitute a search for a means of making environmental planning decisions more responsive to highly diffused and often ill-defined preferences of urban residents. In terms of the mission of this paper, it can be argued that there is still another approach to defining preference patterns — an approach based on the study of activity choices. It can be argued that when there is discretionary choice in what activity is to be engaged in and where it is to take place, the choice that is made constitutes a reflection of preference in some conscious or subconscious form. Indeed, as Godschalk and Mills have demonstrated, this kind of effort is adaptable to the public decision-making process through what they call a "collaborative approach" in which the household activity study is adapted from a primarily analytical tool to a two-way educational medium.[2]

Whatever emphases emerge in the applications of work centering on household activity routines, this kind of study offers in a very general sense a means for identifying resident demand for community facilities — what has come to be called "user-defined

[2] David R. Godschalk and William E. Mills, "A Collaborative Approach to Planning Through Urban Activities," *Journal of the American Institute of Planners*, Vol. XXXII, No. 2 (1966).

requirements" as opposed to those determined from the supplier point of view; for example, requirements prescribed by a recreation commission, a health planning council, or some other policy-making group which has responsibilities for estimating the demand for some form of community facility. If the survey of activity systems should become a focus of effort equal to that which city planning agencies now expend on land use inventories, there would then be an opportunity to organize analyses of community facilities around supply and demand relationships and to determine how an equilibrium can be achieved in the spatial distribution of these supply and demand relationships. It would then be feasible to think in terms of developing modeling systems in which both the demand and supply considerations in locating community facilities could be treated in a more systematic way and become the focus for testing out policy alternatives.

The notion of developing a behavioral system around the activities of metropolitan area residents can be made clearer by developing the rationale in further detail. This will be done first by sketching it out in a micro-level form, and then, in recognition of compromises that become necessary in making the rationale feasible to apply and economical to carry out, a macro-level approach will be blocked in. This will reflect data realities and resulting aggregation and simplification which must of necessity be introduced into the framework.

THE CONCEPTUAL FRAMEWORK AT THE MICRO LEVEL

The underlying organizing concept of this behavioral system is based on the notion that every urban resident's life consists of a flow or a series of more or less interconnected events which have an essential order and follow predictable sequences. The energizing phenomena for this flow is seen to be the individual's sense of destiny and his felt needs to fulfill this destiny as prompted by considerations of security, achievement, status, and other norms of the social system.[3] Drawing on choice theory, each single episode is seen to be the output of the choice process, where the input consists of some set of values the individual holds — a set of motivations relative to the norms of the social system. In this application of choice theory, then, the input set of values constitutes the person's objectives, whether or not these have ever been articulated as objectives per se. The output, the event that occurs following his choice among some set of alternatives, is loosely referred to here as an activity. Actually, an activity is a classificatory term for episodes of an essentially homogeneous character. Thus, for example, the term "socializing" might be used as an activity classification to include a whole range of visiting and related episodes such as dropping in on the neighbors, having dinner and spending an evening in a friend's home, going to the club, going to a cocktail party, going out with the boys to the poolroom, meeting

---

[3] This and the ensuing discussion are paraphrased from the framework as set forth in F. Stuart Chapin, Jr., "Activity Systems and Urban Structure: A Working Schema," *Journal of the American Institute of Planners,* Vol. XXXIV, No. 1 (1968).

the fellows at the corner, and so on. In the micro-level framework, discrete events are examined, and it is only when an aggregative adaptation to this framework is used that the term "activity" comes into usage.

Applying choice theory to the phenomena under discussion, it may be stated that an individual makes his choice on how he spends his time by consciously or unconsciously searching for an optimal combination of satisfactions based on the suboptimization of security, achievement, status, and other needs essential to his sense of well-being. His tradeoffs at a particular time in each suboptimal combination of choices are determined by the levels of satisfactions-dissatisfactions anticipated, within such constraints as income, stage in the life cycle, and knowledge of the options open to him. It may be stated further that a person's choices will be prompted by some set of values which have been shaped by norms of the social system but modified by his past experience and his response to the social system as he perceives it.

Now, using these episodes as building blocks, a dynamic representation of a person's life sequence theoretically can be constructed, with each successive episode conceived of as a link in this chain — what has been described above as a flow of events. Given a sufficient sweep of time, it is seen that this sequence tends to follow a certain order divisible into at least three time scales: the daily and weekly sequence, the seasonal sequence, and the life sequence.[4] In each of these sequences, time is measured by a somewhat different unit. For example, in the daily and weekly sequence, hours provide the most meaningful measure; in the seasonal sequence, days are more appropriate as a measure; and in the life cycle, years become the unit of measure.

If episodes are conceived of in terms of a flow, some interesting causal chains suggest themselves which, in fact, offer promising hypotheses in the study of urban spatial structure. For example, it may be hypothesized that moving behavior in the third time scale is in part generated by response patterns in the first time scale. Imagine going through a series of many episodes of going to work, going to the doctor's, going to the store, or visiting one's best friends. It is not difficult to see that some kind of response pattern will begin to develop, and intuitively we see that some notion of accessibility will emerge relative to the accumulated satisfactions-dissatisfactions experienced in pursuing these activities. Given a ripeness in certain other circumstances, for example, a change in family size, an increase in income, or a change in some other relevant factor, it may be hypothesized that the cumulative response patterns in the first time scale will prompt a person to begin house-hunting, an activity which we associate with the third time scale because it corresponds more with key changes in needs during the life of a family than with daily or seasonal pursuits. When response patterns of a felt need to move are hooked up with response patterns concerning wanted environmental qualities, it may be hypothesized that a house-hunting

---

[4] In previous references, four time scales have been cited, in which daily and weekly time are listed separately. Here we combine these two as one general time scale, thus yielding three well-differentiated time scales.

cycle in the choice mechanism will be activated which may then lead to a second cycle culminating in a decision to move or to stay put.

In the context of housing market analysis, the foregoing discussion is dealing with housing demand, and, in effect, it has traced out a sequence of events serving to generate demand. Indeed, if this framework were to be used in housing analyses, it is at this juncture that the supply and demand aspects of the housing market would be examined in determining what the outcome of the housing decision would be. Thus, subject to constraints of the pocketbook and the size of dwelling accommodation required, the housing choice can be expressed as a function of some "mix of accessibilities," some "mix of living qualities" sought by the household, and some residual representing other factors involved in the choice. The human activity routine under discussion in this paper is the key to determining how the accessibility component in housing demand comes to be defined.

A MACRO ADAPTATION OF THE SCHEMA

Very clearly some simplification is necessary in order to apply this behavioral system to aggregates of people of the order of magnitude involved in a metropolitan area. Simplification is achieved largely through aggregation — aggregation of episodes into activity classes, aggregation of persons into classes of population, and aggregation of time relative to a particular class of activity and a particular class of population. In making these aggregations apply to the rationale discussed above, it is necessary to shift one's thinking from conceiving of a *unique flow of episodes* tied to one person to looking at a *typical flow of activities* associated with a particular class of population.

The flow sequence of activities is called an activity routine, and when the activity makeup of a routine is found to be typical to a class of population, the choices reflected are said to consist of an activity pattern. Thus, a pattern to the activity routine of some class of population implies an aggregation of episodes into activity classes, a fitting together of activity categories into a sequence, and the identification of a characteristic composition of activity choices which goes with the life style of that class of population. As the term implies, activities included in a routine exhibit a tendency to recur over some selected unit of time under study. Thus, for a working person, a typical routine for the waking period of his day between the time he gets up and the time he goes to bed generally includes such general activity categories as meals, work, and leisure-time activities.[5] It will be noted that the routine includes what might be thought of as obligatory and discretionary activities — meals and work being obligatory and leisure-time being discretionary, in the sense that a person is free to engage in family-related, cultural, socializing, recreation and relaxation,

---

[5] Trip-making behavior can be treated as an instrumental form of activity for facilitating a person's ability to take part in a primary activity. Clearly there is a relationship between time-distance to and from an activity and the act of choosing to engage in an activity.

church, organizational, or other activity.[6] This distinction is important in exploring regularities in routines, for obligatory activities provide a kind of structure to a routine that assists the analyst in discovering an order to the discretionary areas of the routine. Thus, it can be hypothesized that, in establishing the nature of choices made in the leisure-time portion of an activity routine, it makes a difference if the work activity is sedentary or physically active.

In aggregating people into classes of population, it is useful to think in terms of sampling metropolitan area households. In any complete reporting system covering all household activity, the sampling would identify patterns of all members of the household — children, teenagers, parents, members of the extended family present, and even unrelated members of the household such as roomers. In the study summarized in this paper, persons interviewed were heads of households and spouses, chosen on an alternating basis. This was done in part as a cost restraint on this particular study, but it was also a purpose of the research design to narrow the focus to members of the household who make housing decisions. In any event, aggregating the respondents into population classes enables the analyst to pursue the hypothesis that members of these classes have different life styles which involve different activity patterns. This is a hypothesis of interest in the national study discussed below. It should be noted that the concept of life style extends to the *manner* of carrying on overt activities. In concentrating on the barest essentials of activities, the studies covered in this paper will only touch on the patterns of living known as life styles.

The mean time devoted to an activity has been introduced into household-activity analysis to permit the analyst to deal with aggregated episodic phenomena in finite time durations for particular activity classes. In the macro adaptation of the activity schema, we wish to be able to define activity routines for a range of types of urban resident identified according to life styles as noted above. Thus, instead of dealing with actual persons, the intent is to define activity systems that differentiate between archetypes in the population. The mean time concept is therefore introduced to attribute a duration to activities of these archetypes. It should be noted at this juncture that the significance attached to duration must be interpreted in terms of the activity classification system used. Thus, the higher the degree of aggregation in activity classification, the more variability is to be expected around the mean duration. To a lesser extent, another source of variation will be the amount of person-aggregation involved in identifying the archetype itself; i.e., whether a few or a large number of life-style or archetype classes of persons are identified in the metropolitan area population.

[6] This is a distinction that requires operational definitions, for upon reflection it is clear, for example, that meals, while obligatory for human survival, have discretionary aspects, such as the timing — when the meals will be eaten; the degree — how many will be eaten, whether there will be, let us say, two instead of three meals; and where the meal will be eaten — whether at home, in the lunchroom on the job, or in a restaurant. Similar observations can be made with respect to other obligatory activities.

Keeping these distinctions and limitations in mind, it is possible to think of a metropolitan area in terms of, say, half a dozen activity systems, each coalescing with or overlying the others, each with an evolutionary aspect (i.e., a flow of activities structured around the routine that goes with its particular life style), and each with a spatial locus defined with respect to the residential locations of persons falling in the sample for that particular life style. The definition of spatial loci of activities permits the analyst not only to identify broad service areas associated with particular community facilities, but also to determine to what extent different life styles support different "activity communities."

To give each such system the dynamic quality identified in the micro version of the conceptual framework, it is necessary to conceive of the routine of each system as evolving into subsequent routines, and in the process being successively modified by some measure of the satisfaction-dissatisfaction response that feeds back into the choice process through subsequent cycles of the activity routine. In a macro version, this would call for a continuous inventory approach to data collection. Using a subsample of each life style class of population as a respondent panel, subsample residents could be revisited on a longitudinal sampling basis and readings could be taken on changes in activity routines and satisfaction-dissatisfaction levels associated with changes in activity routines. If measurements were reasonably accurate, it might well be possible to design and calibrate a system of models for simulating these activity systems.

At this point, it may be of interest to refer to an experimental technique which has been used in some studies to get a more direct measure of preference than may be reflected in the choice of activity itself. It can be argued that, if they had the opportunity to engage in other activities, people would make different choices. In an attempt to give some recognition to this aspect of activity routines, in several activity surveys the interview has included a "game" in which respondents are asked to simulate their choices under certain hypothetical circumstances.[7] Game choices are then compared to actual choice patterns with the thought that differences in broad areas of choice may be useful in anticipating changes in activity patterns. In short, the game may be useful in exploring prospective choices, should restraints be modified; for example, should a shift in the stage of the life cycle occur, an increase in family income be achieved, or some other circumstances arise which would give the respondent a free choice of activities in the discretionary area of his routine.

It may seem that the possibility of developing a model system for simulating activity routines is still far in the future, and this may well prove to be the case. However, while many problems remain unresolved, a prototype system of simulation is being tested by Hemmens in a series of experiments which use a transitional probability approach in a semi-Markov type model.[8] To take account of the time element,

[7] A prototype version of this game can be seen in F. Stuart Chapin, Jr., *Urban Land Use Planning* (2nd ed.; University of Illinois Press, 1965), pp. 250–52.

[8] George C. Hemmens, *The Structure of Urban Activity Linkages* (University of North Carolina at Chapel Hill, Center for Urban and Regional Studies, September 1966).

Hemmens proposes to construct an activity sequence using two matrices. First, he would apply a matrix of transitional probabilities which show for each possible activity what the probability is that each of the other activities would be the next choice; he then would use a second matrix consisting of time-distribution functions for each activity transition to determine the elapsed time that activity would have before the next activity commences. By using matrices of these kinds for different classes of households and applying them over a particular cycle of time, it would thus be possible to simulate activity routines for a range of household classes in a metropolitan area.

To carry this analysis a step further and simulate the spatial pattern of distribution would involve still another operation. Where these activities take place in the metropolitan area is dependent on a given pattern of land uses and the locations of established community facilities within this pattern in relation to the locations of places of residence of households. Given the residential distribution of each class of household and given a set of community facilities within certain time-distance standards, it is not difficult to conceive of an extension of the foregoing approach, in which after the time matrices are applied, spatial distribution functions are applied. For example, for those activities that have a propensity to focus in distinct centers, it would seem reasonable to introduce an intervening opportunities model to establish what the probabilities are at each center for drawing users generated in different time spans from each class of household within each time-distance zone.[9] It is thus only a step further to make use of such a system of models to explore the implications of pursuing various public investment policies and facility location alternatives; for example, investment policies and locations for systems of multiple-purpose neighborhood centers or systems of public health clinics.

In bringing this part of this chapter to a conclusion, it may be observed that, while still in an early stage of conceptualization, household activity analysis has moved to a stage of development which offers promise not only for the study of urban spatial structure, but also as a behavioral system of some theoretical utility in the study of metropolitan areas in a larger social systems sense. Be that as it may, we turn now to an examination of data obtained from a national sample of SMSA households. Since this study represents only one cross-section in time, the emphasis will be more on the activity patterns in the data than on the dynamic aspects for identifying routines and following their cycles through time.

A Snapshot View of Household Activity Patterns in the United States

The sample used to obtain data for this analysis consisted of 1,467 households drawn to be representative of urban households in the standard metropolitan statistical areas (SMSA's) of the forty-eight states in 1960. It was drawn so that it would

---

[9] See Hightower's formulation in F. Stuart Chapin, Jr., and Henry C. Hightower, *Household Activity Systems — A Pilot Investigation* (Center for Urban and Regional Studies, University of North Carolina at Chapel Hill, May 1966), pp. 65–70.

be distributed proportionately to urban households in the four major census divisions in the forty-eight state area and, within each division, proportionately to the urban households resident in the central city and the rest of each SMSA. Respondents were chosen by alternating heads of households and spouses where spouses were present.

The data on daily activities were obtained by asking the respondent what activities he or she had engaged in the day before.[10] The interviews were evenly distributed over the seven days of the week. The time at which each activity was begun was entered with the activity mentioned. Travel time was included in out-of-home activities, rather than being entered separately. The activities were coded after the survey was completed according to a previously established system of activity classification. For purposes of analysis, these codes were collapsed into thirty categories in which the following distinctions were maintained to the greatest extent possible:

1. The location of an activity in or out of the home;
2. The degree of discretion possible in choosing it;
3. The extent to which an activity was "sociable"; and
4. The degree to which it was active or passive in nature. (See Table 1.)

Within these thirty categories, starting times of activities were subtracted from each other to obtain the durations of activities.[11]

THE ANALYSIS

The analysis of the national activity data obtained in this study is necessarily exploratory. The conceptual framework discussed above is intended to indicate directions of exploration but is not to be construed as limiting analysis to any one particular method of getting the information sought on activity patterns. The nature of the choice process in this kind of research is not yet well enough known for the researcher to chart a sure-footed way through a day's routine and emerge from the analysis with clear-cut conclusions on patterns. Moreover, the activities of urban residents are not yet well enough understood for the analyst to be able to recognize immediately what is important.

Thus, activity analysis seeks patterns characteristic of groups of people as an aid in making conditional predictions of what activities will be pursued under given

[10] Diaries are being used in some of the work at the Center for Urban and Regional Studies at Chapel Hill. For this study it was not feasible to use diaries as a basis for obtaining activity data.

[11] The durations thus obtained cannot be regarded as altogether accurate in all cases, for in order to retain all of the cases and therefore to maintain the representativeness of the sample, starting times of certain activities — especially rising, retiring, and in-home activities lumped together by the respondent — were estimated in the coding process. The choice between maintaining the representativeness of the sample and the purity of the data was made in favor of the sample. Inaccuracies introduced by coder estimation must be borne in mind as a qualification to conclusions drawn about these categories of activity. Fortunately, the activity choices of direct concern in this research were not those primarily subject to this source of inaccuracy.

Table 1.   Activity Classifications Used in Preliminary Analysis

---

Income related activities
1. Primary full-time job
2. Other income-earning and related activities

Family related activities
3. Child care and child-centered activities
4. Family activities (except visiting) and pet care
5. Family visiting

Recreation and relaxation activities
6. Resting, napping, and general relaxation
7. Reading the paper, a magazine, or a book
8. Television and radio
9. Individual creative activities
10. Casual diversions[a]
11. Sports
12. Education

Religious activities and organizational participation
13. Church services
14. Other church-related and organizational participation

Socializing activities
15. Visiting in the neighborhood
16. Visiting outside the neighborhood
17. Other socializing
18. Telephoning and writing letters

Subsistence activities
19. Meals and snacks at home
20. Meals and snacks out
21. Convenience goods shopping
22. Other shopping
23. Sick in bed
24. Medical services (for self, accompanying others, etc.)
25. Housework
26. Home, yard, and car maintenance (including moving)
27. "Taxi" service
28. Errands
29. Out-of-town activities
30. Rising, retiring, and personal care

---

[a] Includes going to movies, theater, concert, museum, or library; strolling, window-shopping, stopping at the bar or tavern, dropping in at the pool hall, meeting friends at the corner, driving around town, etc.

circumstances in the future. However, before this stage is achieved, it must be possible to describe activities in order to know better what characteristics of individuals are most relevant in grouping the population for analysis.

Using choice of activity as a dependent variable, the analysis summarized here explores respondent choices successively according to location and according to the discretionary, passive, or sociable character of the activities. Each of these groupings of the dependent variable is tabulated against various background characteristics of the population which, in this initial phase of the research, are considered as independent variables. The analysis seeks to see if respondents fall into distinct groups which show significant differences in the frequency or duration of activities. The independent variables consist of such standard categories as sex, race, stage in the life cycle, educational attainment, employment status, family income, size of city, and the Duncan scale of social status.[12]

The size of the sample limits the number of factors which can be held constant in such an analysis. The number of cases rapidly becomes insignificant as categories are nested. The suggestions made as to the characteristics which may be significant are therefore quite tentative. It has not been possible to apply the desirable range of controls in the analysis, although appropriate statistical tests have been used.

Where social characteristics appear to explain part of the variation in the activity data, an effort has been made to search for clusters of activities which show similar variations among the same population groups. It has not been possible to carry this kind of analysis as far as would be desirable. For example, no factor analysis has yet been made. What has been done, however, indicates the directions in which classification and grouping of activities can be pursued in the analysis of overall activity patterns in the next stages of the research.

FINDINGS — AN OVERVIEW

One of the most striking things about the data is the essential homogeneity of results across the categories analyzed. The social scientist is so attuned to searching for differences that he may tend to overlook similarities. The fact is that in their most overt form (at the levels of aggregation shown in Table 1), the daily activities of the various groups in the population as they are customarily divided are very much the same. A quick review of the frequencies shows that the most popular discretionary activities were television viewing and radio listening. Over two-thirds of the sample engaged in one or both of these activities. Runners-up are activities — or the lack of them — characterized as resting, napping, or taking it easy. About half of the respondents reported these. A little under a third did some sort of reading. Roughly 10 per cent of the respondents had engaged in family activities, family visiting, and visiting in and out of the neighborhood. A little over 5 per cent engaged in individual creative pursuits, casual diversions, church services, other church-related and organizational participation, various social activities not classified as "visiting," and in telephoning and correspondence. Education and sporting activities claimed the attention of about 2 and 3 per cent, respectively.

The split between the races, which is associated with so many differences in American society, reveals no huge differences here. Just about a quarter of each group shopped for convenience goods each day, for example, and each averaged about an

[12] Otis Dudley Duncan, "A Socio-Economic Index for All Occupations," Chapter 6; "Properties and Characteristics of the Socio-Economic Index," Chapter 7; and Appendix B; in Albert J. Reiss, *Occupations and Social Status* (The Free Press of Glencoe, 1961).

Table 2.   Percentages of Heads of Households and Spouses Engaging in Activities[a]

Activity	Percentage engaging in activity	
	Heads	Spouses
Child care and child-centered activities	8.5%	47.1%
Resting, napping, and general relaxation	55.0	42.6
Casual diversions	6.8	6.2
Reading the paper, a magazine, or a book	32.1	27.4
Watching television or listening to radio	68.0	67.3
Socializing		
Visiting in neighborhood	4.6	7.6
Visiting outside the neighborhood	7.0	8.8
Telephoning, writing letters	1.2	7.4
Shopping		
Convenience goods	17.9	29.4
All other shopping	13.1	17.3
Health-related activities		
Sick at home	2.6	1.4
Seeing, or accompanying others to, doctor	4.7	8.3
Housework	18.8	91.0
Home, yard, and car maintenance	22.2	9.2

[a] Survey instructions called for interviews with heads of households and spouses of heads on an alternating basis. If spouses were not present, the heads were designated to be respondents. The two classes of respondents split into 54 per cent heads and 46 per cent spouses.

hour and a half a day at this activity. About two-thirds of each group watched television for somewhat over three hours a day. One of the more perceptible differences — the fall in the proportion of those watching TV and listening to the radio with rising education — shows a range of from just over 70 per cent for the lowest level of educational attainment to just under 60 per cent for the highest level, with average time durations of those watching ranging from 2½ to 3¾ hours. Without a doubt these are significant differences, but they do not appear to indicate a deep split in the population according to their overt behavior. Perhaps the most noticeable differences are found between heads of households and spouses of heads — the basis on which subjects were drawn from sampled households (see Table 2). But even here there are strong similarities, especially in discretionary activities. It may be fruitful to examine these activities, searching for matters of style and other more subtle aspects in them in order to identify significant differences among social groups and classes. Or, as suggested earlier, notions about security, achievement, social status, and similar factors used in conjunction with conventional background variables may prove to be better predictors of activity choices. These tentative observations suggest that activities may need to be examined in relation to broader ranges of considerations that people take into account in "using" their environments. It has also become evident that, because the relationships found are not very strong, the analysis of differences in these overt aspects of behavior as related to the social characteristics of the population must be carefully controlled. A second point to be made is that while there may be considerable homogeneity in activities among classes of the population, there is also considerable variation within classes. It was not uncommon in the analyses of durations and of proportions of time spent in various types of activity to find standard deviations which were larger than the means.[13] Many activities were engaged in by only very small proportions of the members of any group. In each group there was clearly a large number of people who did not engage in a given activity, even though others in the group did. Both in terms of the dichotomy of engaging or not in given activities, and in terms of durations, there is considerable difference within categories. Each category of persons is heterogeneous within itself.

This indicates the need to look beyond social characteristics in order to explain more of the variation in activity patterns. In addition to looking at social and psychological variables, a promising factor for study is the physical environment, the facilities it offers and the costs it places on engaging in various activities. But that is for the future; the present task is to see what social characteristics may explain.

FINDINGS — CLUES TO DIFFERENTIAL ACTIVITY CHOICES

In the tabulation and testing of activity data, particular attention was given to activities which were considered to be discretionary. As shown in Table 1, these include the activity categories listed as recreation and relaxation, religious activities and organizational participation, socializing activities, and the family activities and family visiting categories listed under family-related activities (excluding child care). Child care, shopping, and medical care received some attention as activities conceivably subject to considerable variation and often important out of the home in their relation to community facilities. Housework was considered because of its importance in relation to other home-oriented activities. Because of the focus on discretionary activity choices, gainful employment and certain standard subsistence activities have been neglected for the present.

At this stage of the analysis, very simple statistical tests were used. Through use of a package computer program, chi-square tests were used for the analysis of differences in proportions, and the value of "F" was calculated to test differences in means.

GENERAL MEASURES

Discretionary Aspect of Activities.   One level of analysis of these activity choices dealt with such aspects as their location, the degree of discretion possible in choosing them, and the extent to which they are sociable and active or passive. A search for patterns in the distribution of these aspects was made among groups in the sample. One such measure was the difference in the proportion of the 24-hour day occupied by the discretionary activities defined above. Time spent on a primary job, employment status, stage in the life cycle, and income all are related to the proportion of the day spent in these discretionary activities.[14] All of the proportions vary around 20 per cent.

---

[13] Collapsing activity codes probably accounts for some of this intra-class variation.

[14] These differences are all significant at the .01 level.

With longer working hours came a smaller proportion of discretionary activity, varying from 11.4 per cent for those who spent over ten hours on the job to 27.6 per cent for those who worked for less than three hours. The data for employment status express the same basic facts. The unemployed spent a third of their time in discretionary activities; nonworking housewives, 27.9 per cent; part-time workers, 24.7 per cent; and full-time workers, 19.8 per cent. Of full-time workers, females had more discretionary time than males in this category, but the nonworking male had more than the nonworking female. When not controlled for employment status, sex had no significant effect.

The lower income group (under $5,250) had more discretionary time by about four percentage points than the upper group ($8,750 and over). Finally, the elderly, with 32.5 per cent, led both people under 35 years of age without children (24.8 per cent) and those over 35 without children or with grown children (24.2 per cent). Those raising children had about 20 per cent of their time free for discretionary activities.

Location Index. Because the sample was not distributed in a spatially random manner in each of the forty-two SMSA's falling in the sample, no attempt was made to pinpoint locations of activities in relation to the home. However, a simple index —the percentage of total discretionary time which was spent outside of the home —was used for a minimal location analysis. This location index was found to be related to time spent on gainful employment, the stage in the life cycle, income, and social status as measured by the Duncan scale.

The relationship between time spent on the job and discretionary time spent away from home is similar to the relationship between working hours and the total amount of time spent on discretionary activities. The proportion of time spent out of the home falls with rising hours of work. Those gainfully employed for less than three hours, however, spent a smaller proportion of time out of the home than did those working from three to six hours.[15] This may reflect a tendency for housewives to be tied to the home.

While the elderly had the most discretionary time available, they spent a smaller proportion of it out of the home (15 per cent). People under 35 years of age without children spent the most time away from home (36 per cent), followed by those over 35 without children under 22 at home (19 per cent), again followed by those raising children (around 18 per cent).[16] Except for the elderly, these proportions follow those for the amount of discretionary time available.

Income and social status factors are similar to each other in their effects. The middle income group ($5,250 to $8,750) and our next-to-highest group on Duncan's 100 point social status scale (30–49) spent the highest proportion of their discretionary time out of the home (about 22 per cent). The highest income and status groups were two or more percentage points below this.[17]

[15] These differences are significant at the .01 level.
[16] Significant at the .01 level.
[17] Significant at the .05 level.

Sociability Index. The sociability index expresses the proportion of discretionary time spent in socializing activities. These are defined as including the following activity codes: family visiting (activity group 5); visiting in the neighborhood (group 15); visiting outside the neighborhood (group 16); other socializing (group 17); and telephoning or writing letters (group 18). Factors associated with sociability were: sex, time spent at work, and stage in the life cycle.[18]

Time spent at work and sociability are related in the same direction as are time spent at work and time spent on out-of-home activities; those who worked from three to six hours engaged in such activities for the largest proportion of the time. Women spent more time than men in these activities. Also, stage in the life cycle had the same effect as it had on the location index, with young childless people highest, and the elderly lowest.

Active-Passive Index. This index expresses the proportion of discretionary time spent on the active pursuits — creative activities, sports, education, and organizational participation. It is not too clear conceptually, since the degree to which these or other pursuits are active or passive is debatable. Sports here includes spectator as well as participant activity, because of the aggregation of activity categories.

Perhaps a better definition would yield better explanations as well. Race is the only background variable significantly associated with variation in the index, with whites using an average of 8.4 per cent of their discretionary time on active pursuits and nonwhites using 4.5 per cent.[19]

MEASURES OF SPECIFIC ACTIVITY CATEGORIES

When the activities are taken one by one, sex, stage in the life cycle, income, and education prove to be the factors with significant power to explain variation in the data. In reference to the proportion of people in a given class who engage in an activity, employment status and the Duncan social status scale are not significantly related to the variation in any of the discretionary activities. City size has an effect only on the activity class called "casual diversions." A larger proportion of residents of cities with a population of over one million engaged in these activities than in smaller cities. Race had a significant effect only on reading: more whites than non-whites reported this activity.[20]

Only a little more explanation of differences can be found when the other dependent variable — the average duration of activities among those who engaged in each activity — is used. The unemployed seem to spend more time at resting and in neighborhood visiting than do those employed or doing housework.[21] Social status

[18] Significant at the .01 level.
[19] Significant at the .01 level.
[20] Significant at the .001 level.
[21] Due to an imbalance in the number of cases in each employment category, these tests may be suspect.

Table 3. *Percentages of Men and Women Engaging in Selected Activities*

Activity	Per cent engaging in activity[a]		Level of significance
	Men	Women	
Child care and child-centered activities	8.3%	39.8%	.001
Family-related activities (except visiting)	6.8	10.1	.05
Family visiting	9.6	17.0	.001
Resting, napping, and general relaxation	55.3	43.9	.001
Religious activities and organizational participation	3.3	8.2	.001
Neighborhood visiting	4.9	12.4	.001
Visiting outside the neighborhood (high income)	4.6	9.5	.05
Convenience goods shopping	17.8	28.9	.001
Non-convenience goods shopping (middle income)	12.9	22.4	.01
Medical services			
(middle income)	4.6	9.8	.05
(high income)	4.6	9.9	.05
Housework	19.0	87.5	.001

[a] Percentages for men and women shown here may differ from the percentages for head and spouse shown in Table 2 because some women respondents were heads of households rather than spouses.

appears to be related to the time consumed by television and radio.[22] Those lower on the scale spent longer periods on these activities. Nonwhites spent longer periods in visits outside the neighborhood than did whites.[23] There was a split on family visiting, in that among males, whites spent more time, whereas among females, nonwhites spent more time at this activity.[24]

Effects of Sex. On the other hand, sex is related to variations in a number of activities. Significantly higher proportions of women than of men engaged in child care, family activities, family visiting, organizational participation, neighborhood visiting, housework, and convenience-goods shopping. For visiting outside the neighborhood, shopping for goods other than the convenience type, and seeking medical services, only in the middle or high income groups (over $5,250) did the women exceed the proportion of men engaging in the activities. The men should be chastened to learn that only in the "resting" category did they outdo the ladies. Except in the penultimate three categories in Table 3, all of these differences were significant even when only those of each sex who worked full time were considered.

Among those who engaged in these activities, men spent more time on television and radio, casual diversions, and neighborhood visits (except for those with children aged 14–22, where the women spent longer periods). Women spent longer periods at the housework than did men, when stage in the life cycle was controlled.[25]

[22] Significant at the .01 level.
[23] Significant at the .05 level.
[24] Both when the effects of educational level were controlled and uncontrolled.
[25] Significant at the .01 level.

Table 4. *Percentages of Men and Women in Various Stages of the Life Cycle Engaging in Selected Activities*

Activity	Sex	Per cent participating by stage in life cycle[a]						Significance level
		1	2	3	4	5	6	
Child care	Males	0	21.8%	9.0%	3.8%	0.7%	0.8%	.001
	Females	0	80.2	50.3	17.8	5.0	1.3	.001
Reading	Males	22.9%	29.7	26.0	31.3	30.9	43.2	.05
	Females	15.6	22.9	26.6	37.6	28.1	35.0	.05
Television and radio	Males	45.8	64.9	70.0	66.3	69.8	80.3	.001
	Females	60.0	64.3	61.5	69.3	71.2	82.5	.05
Creative activities	Males	6.3	4.5	4.0	2.5	3.6	9.1	N.S.
	Females	2.2	7.4	6.3	9.9	9.4	21.3	.01
Casual diversions	Males	18.8	9.4	5.0	2.5	11.5	11.4	.05
	Females	17.8	3.1	6.3	8.9	6.5	1.3	.01
Sports	Males	12.5	3.5	1.0	1.3	1.4	0	.001
	Females	13.3	0.4	1.4	1.0	0.7	0	.001
"Other socializing"	Males	18.8	6.9	6.0	8.8	5.0	3.8	.05
	Females	11.1	5.4	6.3	8.9	7.9	2.5	N.S.

N.S. = Not significant.

[a] Column 1 — Respondent under 35 years old, no children;
Column 2 — Respondent has children under 6 years old;
Column 3 — Respondent has children aged 6–14 years;
Column 4 — Respondent has children aged 15–22 years;
Column 5 — Respondent 35–65 years old, no children under 22;
Column 6 — Respondent over 65 years old.

Effects of Stage in the Life Cycle. There are several activities which are affected by differences in life cycle stage. An obvious one is child care. Those with the youngest children engaged in child care in the largest proportions, and — among the men — for the longest average durations. It is notable, however, that among women, those with children aged 14 to 22 spent longest with their children. People over 35 with no children or with grown children spent very small proportions of their time on child care.[26]

Recreational and relaxation activities fall into two groups in the way they are affected by the life cycle. Reading, watching television or listening to the radio, and individual creative activities are engaged in least by young people without children and most by those over 65 years of age (except that among women, those over 35 with children between 15 and 22 years of age read more than those over 65; and differences for creative activities were significant only among women).[27] People over 35 years of age who rested, napped, or took things easy around home also spent more time at it than did the younger groups.[28] Casual diversions and sports (for both sexes), and other

[26] Figures for frequency of participation are significant at the .001 level.
[27] Significant at the .05 level or better.
[28] Significant at the .01 level.

Table 5.   *Percentage of Men and Women in Three Income Classes Engaging in Selected Activities*

Activity	Per cent participating by income			Level of significance
	Under $5,250	$5,250–$8,749	Over $8,750	
Women				
Child care, etc.	28.2%	53.3%	42.5%	.001
Family activities (except visiting)	6.4	10.3	14.3	.01
Family visiting	17.4	22.0	12.3	.05
Visiting outside the neighborhood	6.4	14.0	9.5	.05
Non-convenience goods shopping	12.4	22.4	16.7	.05
Men				
"Other socializing"	6.4	4.2	10.1	.05
Housework	23.5	19.2	14.2	.05

socializing and individual creative activities (among the men) show the young childless group with the highest participation rate and the elderly group with the lowest.[29] Those without minor children spent longer periods at shopping for convenience goods and shorter periods at housework than did those who were raising children.[30]

Effects of Income. Because sex was seen to have an effect on a number of the activities studied, this factor was controlled in the analysis of income. Child care, family activities, family visiting, visiting outside the neighborhood, and non-convenience goods shopping showed that differences were related to income only among women. More women in the high-income group (over $8,750) than in the middle-income group ($5,250–$8,749) participated in family activities. For other activities, the middle-income group had the highest participation rate, followed by the high-income group. Among men, the catch-all, "other socializing," showed increases with income, while housework was more common among the lower-income group.

Effects of Education. The explanatory power of the educational attainment factor is not very impressive. To approximate a balance in the number of cases, a simple dichotomy between those who had completed high school and those who had not was used for statistical tests.[31] There was a difference of about nine percentage points among women and about four among men in the proportion of those engaged in child care.[32] The higher proportion held among those who had at least completed high school. People with higher education were also more likely to engage in activities of

[29] Significant at the .05 level or better. The differences for men in individual creative activities were not statistically significant.

[30] Significant at the .05 level and .01 level, respectively.

[31] This may not have been adequate, although examination of a more detailed breakdown did not suggest any greater explanatory power.

[32] Significant at the .05 level.

the "other socializing" category. This follows the pattern for men of higher income. Among men there is a difference of some six percentage points,[33] among women, of about four.[34]

Among those who engaged in the activities, people with less education spent longer periods at rest, watching television or listening to the radio, and visiting in the neighborhood.[35] Perhaps surprisingly, men who had not graduated from high school engaged in individual creative activities in significantly higher proportion than did those with higher education.[36]

INTERPRETATIVE OBSERVATIONS

To what extent does any general picture emerge from the study? It must be admitted that it is too early to draw general, trustworthy conclusions about what characteristics of individuals and of the social group determine the activity pattern. Yet certain general observations can be made which may help to direct further work.

Passive Nature of Discretionary Activities. First, this analysis supports the observation that the bulk of most people's time is spent in obligatory activities and passive pursuits. As the Hungarian Central Statistical Office points out, "during the so-called leisure time people are not doing what they should prefer but they often follow the line of the 'least resistance,' i.e., they choose the type of diversion involving the least effort and preparation, the one which is just near at hand."[37]

Our analysis of "active" activities showed that only about 7 or 8 per cent of the time spent on discretionary activities was spent on active pursuits. When related to background variables, very little deviation from this proportion was found. The extremes were 11.2 per cent for people under 35 years without children and 4.4 per cent for nonwhites. This finding is consistent with those of other studies. A study of British housewives found the most popular leisure activities to be television viewing, reading, chatting with friends and family, and radio listening, in that order.[38] Reviewing results of multi-national comparative time-budget research, Szalai claims that "in most countries it is the use of mass media that occupies most of the working people's free time."[39] And the Hungarian analysis found participation and the desire to participate in sports and walks to be almost insignificant.[40]

---

[33] Significant at the .001 level.

[34] Significant at the .05 level.

[35] Significant at the .01 level.

[36] Significant at the .01 level.

[37] The Hungarian Central Statistical Office, *The Twenty-Four Hours of the Day: Analysis of 12,000 Time Budgets*, English version (Budapest, 1965), p. 52.

[38] "The Housewife's Day," in *Mass Observation Bulletin*, No. 54 (June 1957).

[39] Sándor (Alexander) Szalai *et al.*, "Multi-National Comparative Social Research," *American Behavioral Scientist*, Vol. 10, No. 4 (December 1966), p. 30.

[40] The Hungarian Central Statistical Office, *The Twenty-Four Hours...*, p. 56.

The Effect of Major Responsibilities. An intuitively obvious but interesting factor in the choice of activities is the nature and magnitude of one's major responsibilities. As studied here, these responsibilities were indicated by the number of hours spent in gainful employment, a respondent's employment status, and his stage in the life cycle (which indicates child-raising responsibilities).

The general measures in this study showed that the longer one spends at work, the smaller will be the proportion of the day that is spent in discretionary activities (which is to be expected) and the smaller will be the proportion of these activities devoted to out-of-home activities and socializing. Where employment status is significant on these measures, it follows the same pattern. Szalai also found that, in Hungary, longer working hours contracted recreation and study time more than sleep time.[41]

Consistent with the present analysis, Lundberg and his associates found that non-working "suburban housewives are conspicuously of the leisure class," although he suggests that there is something lacking in the quality of their leisure which causes them to deny it.[42]

Stage in the life cycle affects the pattern of activities as well. The general measures in this analysis show that those who do not carry the responsibility of raising children spend a larger proportion of the day on discretionary activities and — except for the elderly — more of that time out of the home and on sociable activities. Stoetzel, in a study of women in urban France, shows that the mean time spent daily on both in-home and out-of-home distractions goes down as the number of children goes up.[43] The Hungarian study found that out-of-home activities are more common among young people than among older age groups.[44] In a somewhat related finding, Szalai comments that "marriage reduces everywhere, in every country, participation in continuing education and in occupational training on the one hand, and participation in civic and collective activities on the other."[45] He goes on to say that the time spent in the home is generally increased with marriage.

The Traditional Role of the Woman. The present study appears to show the heavy hand of tradition pressing down upon the brow of the modern woman. To be more explicit, even when the factor of sex is controlled for employment status, women carry a much greater share of household and family-related tasks than do the men. The men, on the other hand, are found napping and "idling"— as some studies have put it — in larger proportions than is true of women. Evidence also points to a some-

[41] Sándor (Alexander) Szalai, "Differential Work and Leisure Time-Budgets as a Basis for Inter-Cultural Comparisons," *The New Hungarian Quarterly* (Budapest), Vol. 5, pp. 105–19 (Winter 1964).

[42] George A. Lundberg, Mirra Komarovsky, and Mary Alice McInerny, *Leisure: A Suburban Study* (Columbia University Press, 1934), p. 88.

[43] Jean Stoetzel, "Une Étude de Budget-temps de la Femme dans les Agglomérations Urbaines," *Population* (Paris), Vol. 3 (jan.–mars 1948), pp 47–62.

[44] The Hungarian Central Statistical Office, *The Twenty-Four Hours...*, p. 49.

[45] Szalai *et al.*, "Multi-National Comparative Social Research," p. 24.

what predominant role for women in social activities of various sorts. Perhaps women tend to act as the "social chairmen" of their families.

Measures of Status. The most notable thing about the measures of social position used here is how little they show. In summary, the only indications of significant differences in activity patterns based on social position are that higher-income groups may be more busy and more family centered while the lower-income group appears to have more uncommitted time; whites seem more "active" in their discretionary activities than nonwhites; and average time spent on mass media is greater in the lower levels of social status than among the higher.

Limits of the Factors Studied. It is clear from the foregoing discussion that the characteristics of individuals and social groups do not go far in explaining the variations in the data. They yield some insights and can give some direction to future work. However, other dimensions of activity systems could profitably be explored in continuing work. Some are suggested by other work which has been done on time-budgets. Szalai, Lundberg, Chombart de Lauwe,[46] and the Hungarian Central Statistical Office, for example, all did some beginning work on what may be called "elasticity analysis." Here the focus is on the question of which activities are most likely to expand or contract when the time taken by certain obligations is varied. Such analysis can add materially to a thorough knowledge of the nature of activities themselves. Closely related is what one might term "replaceability" analysis. The study of British housewives noted the activities which appeared to replace television viewing for those who did not own sets. Other possibilities might be the differences in the patterns of Sundays among those who did and did not attend church services, or the differences in activity systems between those who frequently engage in a sport and those who seldom do.

In pursuit of a more complete knowledge of the activities, Lundberg suggests that "the most meaningful difference lies in the qualitative variations between the activities which we have been compelled to classify under the same captions."[47] A more adequate inquiry into people's attitudes toward their activities might yield useful ideas about the factors that matter. Although their sample was inadequate to yield representative quantitative findings, Sorokin and Berger pursued the motivational aspects of activity choice intensively.[48]

Other work at the Center for Urban and Regional Studies in Chapel Hill is being concentrated on attitudes toward social contact, status transfer through residential location, and other aspects of the dynamics of residential space demand. Such work could be extended to study the interaction of activity desires, activity systems,

---

[46] Paul Henri Chombart de Lauwe, *La Vie Quotidienne des Familles Ouvrières* (Centre National de la Recherche Scientifique, 1956), p. 48.

[47] Lundberg *et al.*, *Leisure* . . . , p. 124.

[48] Pitirim A. Sorokin and Clarence Q. Berger, *Time-Budgets of Human Behavior*, Harvard Sociological Studies, Vol. 11 (Harvard University Press, 1939).

and the facilities available for various activities. This approach would lead to studies of the environments and facilities of particular cities.

The rhythm of activities through the day, the week, and the year may, as noted earlier, be substance for fruitful analysis. Chombart de Lauwe shows graphic displays of typical days, depicting both durations and placement during the day of various types of activities.[49] This or other graphic techniques could aid in conceptualization, and some might be devised which could show the cumulative effect of individuals' choices on available facilities. A number of previous studies have analyzed variations through the week. The Hungarian Central Statistical Office, for example, has devised a formula which yields an "index of structural difference" between two days of the week in activity patterns.[50] It does not seem presumptuous to say that many possibilities are open to the interested investigator.

Implications of Activity Patterns for Policy

The foregoing interpretations from this study of activity patterns in the metropolitan areas of the United States prompt some brief concluding observations on two subjects. First, it is appropriate to indicate the importance of taking both a time *and* a spatial view of human activity. So a brief note on the interrelatedness of time and spatial dimensions to activity patterns is introduced. Second, it is fitting to return to the central theme of this volume and relate what has been brought out about these behavioral systems in the resources frame of reference.

A NOTE ON SPATIAL PATTERNS OF ACTIVITY

In the discussion above of the rationale behind activity investigations, it was emphasized that the spatial aspect of activities is an integral part of activity analysis. While the study reported here has been concerned primarily with the range of variation in factors influencing temporal patterns which could only be provided by a national study of the kind discussed in this chapter, this glimpse of activities in a time context has served to point up the importance of viewing activities in both their time and spatial aspects.

Indeed, it is a fundamental premise of the activity system approach to the study of the spatial structure of metropolitan areas that to a significant extent the spatial loci of activities which people choose to pursue and which form the core routines of urban households serve to influence location decisions, even while the pattern of existing land use is also serving to influence the spatial pattern of activities. Clearly these behavioral systems are interacting with land use systems or, broadly, with the environment. It must therefore be evident that land use analysis is incomplete without a concurrent activity analysis, for to ignore the interplay between the two is to enter upon policy decisions based on supply considerations without relating them to demand aspects.

[49] Chombart de Lauwe, *La Vie Quotidienne...*, p. 53.
[50] The Hungarian Central Statistical Office, *The Twenty-Four Hours..*, Appendix IV, 3, pp. 95–97.

The out-of-home activity consists of several functional concerns in the day-to-day routine of members of the average household, according to the role each such member performs in the household and the life style in which the household falls. For the head of the household and increasingly for the spouse, at least in the later stages of the life cycle, the work activity dominates this routine. Also important and frequently shared with the spouse are out-of-home socializing, entertainment, and various recreation activities. Although the head may share in, and in some cases perform, some of the various activities commonly ascribed to the homemaking spouse, the non-working homemaker generally pursues a quite different out-of-home activity routine. Depending on the particular life style, this may consist of shopping, volunteering time for organizational or civic work, and pursuing activities which involve the utilization of various health- and education-related services — such as visits to the doctor's office, taking the children to school, the library, and other places. For the children, the out-of-home activities consist largely of school and play, with the latter activities changing to dating and entertainment as they reach adolescence and move into early adulthood.

At the macro level, the shared and the various independently pursued out-of-home activities fall into two groups: (1) activities which focus in particular nodes with clearly defined land use components — employment concentrations, retail centers, and such community facilities as schools, theaters, museums, and libraries; and (2) activities which are more diffused in their patterns of distribution — such as visiting and other forms of socializing — and various kinds of unorganized outdoor recreation and play. As indicated in the discussion of the simulation of activity patterns, experimental work is in progress to examine the facility-oriented activities in the framework of an intervening opportunities model. For activities with the more random patterns, some kind of diffusion model seems more appropriate.

But in addition to seeing the locus of human activity in macro forms, there are important micro-level spatial patterns which, when differentiated by household life style and family-member role functions, offer still other perspectives for analysis and policy consideration. Thus, if spatial patterns could have been documented as systematically as time patterns have been in the survey reported above, it is quite probable that the network of neighborhood patterns of the spouse in the homemaking role in the course of neighboring or convenience shopping, and the activities of children in going to school or out to play, would describe an overall living pattern that is highly home- and neighborhood-centered. Various studies indicate that these patterns vary according to suburban and central city locale and life style of households found in these areas. Thus, in the central city ghetto, doorstep neighboring, backlot play, and street corner society could be documented and differentiated from the activity patterns of the Beacon Hill, Gramercy Park, or Rittenhouse Square enclaves; and these patterns in turn could be differentiated from those found in localized activity communities of the great expanses of residential neighborhoods extending across the gray areas and into suburbia.

The neighborhood networks of activity differentiated by life style are by no means an unknown phenomenon. In the thirties, Lundberg used time budget techniques to describe distinctive suburban patterns,[51] in the fifties Whyte supplied some free-ranging impressionistic studies of kaffeeklatch patterns of interaction among suburban housewives,[52] and in the sixties Gans has provided participant observation perspectives of neighborhood life.[53] Nor are interaction patterns of central city residents overlooked, as evidenced by the free-wheeling commentary of Jane Jacobs about street life in Greenwich Village type neighborhoods on Manhattan,[54] or Horton's reports on street life in Watts (where clock time is shown to be wholly shorn of meaning),[55] or even the activity patterns of the hang-loose ethic of those found in the Haight-Ashbury district.[56] The perspectives growing out of these studies and commentaries clearly indicate that if there are indeed identifiable spatial communities of these kinds, it is important that policy aimed at modifying or shaping land use take into account the effect that regulatory, renewal, or other similar measures to change land use have on the mosaic of fine-grain patterns of activity in the urban scene. Just as the macro patterns of activity provide insight for decisions concerning transportation systems and the location and intensity of land use, the micro-level activity patterns provide a basis for decisions relating to public services and community facilities. Localized networks of activity bear a direct relation to the allocation of governmental resources to family services and to day-care centers, health clinics, recreation centers, and other neighborhood-serving facilities.

The results of the analysis reported above show that research into the patterns of space and time use will not be uncomplicated. The differences among individuals are extensive and are not easily explainable in terms of social groups and characteristics. And, as research moves from an emphasis on time use among broad classes of the population to one on time use in response to particular spatial arrangements, research strategies will be more complex.

Imagination will tell us that the possible cross-effects of time-use habits and spatial arrangements on each other are endless. What must be sought is a set of hypotheses tapping the effects which seem most important in formulating space and resource policies.

Some variation of *ex post facto* experimentation seems called for. Groups of people, who are similar in characteristics shown to be significant in this and other studies, but who are placed in different spatial arrangements or have access to different facilities, would be compared. If carefully handled, such a strategy could assess the effects of the different spatial arrangements on activity patterns. Alternatively, study of similar physical settings populated by different kinds of people could sharpen the kind of analysis of the effects of social characteristics presented here. Even an approxi-

---

[51] George A. Lundberg *et al.*, *Leisure....*

[52] William H. Whyte, Jr., *The Organization Man* (Simon and Schuster, 1956).

[53] Herbert J. Gans, *The Levittowners* (Pantheon Books, 1967).

[54] Jane Jacobs, *The Death and Life of Great American Cities* (Random House, 1961).

[55] John Horton, "Time and Cool People," *Trans-action*, Vol. 4, No. 5 (April 1967), pp. 5–12.

[56] J. L. Simmons and Barry Winograd, *It's Happening* (Marc-Laird Publications, 1966).

mate picture of the complex relationships between time habits and spatial arrangements will require carefully controlled research to spot the independent effects of social imperatives and of physical opportunities and constraints.

Thus, behavioral systems in both time and spatial perspectives, functioning within constraints of existing land use as laid down over time by the operations of the market system and the social system, have significance for the underlying concerns of this volume. They offer a means of evaluating how policy positions with respect to the new urban resources singled out in Perloff's chapter and discussed in subsequent chapters will affect living patterns of the city. To an important degree, the impact of new policies on residential living patterns may determine their acceptance, especially where radical changes are under consideration.

ACTIVITY SYSTEMS AND ENVIRONMENTAL RESOURCES POLICY

In balance, several observations can be made on the applications of this work to policy and decision making with respect to new urban resources. From the analyses above, in the broad aggregate picture, two rather fundamental behavioral patterns come through. One stems from the analyses of the time dimension and has to do with the dominance of home-centered activities among discretionary choices made by American households. The other has to do with the two quite different spatial patterns involved in out-of-home activities.

While not documented in data presented from the national study reported above, undoubtedly there are other activity dimensions in both time and space definable around role functions and life styles which would bear further investigation. These dimensions may include both the intensity of enjoyment of the activity and its function in relating the person to his community and to defining that community. For example, an out-of-the-neighborhood social event for one person may involve other neighborhood residents and be a fairly intense experience cementing the solidarity of the group. For another, leaving the neighborhood may involve a relatively cosmopolitan experience in a theater or night club.

With respect to the time dimension, from the data in hand one very clear message is the disinclination of American households to use their so-called "free time" for activities away from home. For the 1,405 respondents reporting time spent on discretionary activities, 77 per cent of the 5.7 mean hours available as discretionary time by the definition noted earlier in the chapter, was spent in the home. This allocation to the home varies with employment status, sex, and stage in the life cycle in so far as heads of households or their spouses are concerned, but the general pattern in the commitment of leisure hours of a person's "time budget" to the home is strong enough to carry overtones of significance for decision makers.

If the concept of "home" is extended to homemaking activities that go on in the immediate neighborhood environs, it may well be found that time-worn concepts used as the basis for resource allocation in the past are no longer entirely valid. While other factors — such as experience (in the sense of previous frequency and intensity of experience) and patterns of preference for these home-centered or localized patterns of activity choice — require careful investigation in order to establish how likely they are to continue into the future, the home-centered patterns are sufficiently pronounced in this one-time cross-sectional survey at least to raise the question of whether the community facility systems being built today actually fit activity patterns. It also raises, again, the question of the scale of area which is identified by the individual as constituting his "community." Further study might illuminate the question of the extent to which "merit goods" are ignored because they are offered in the wrong place, as opposed to simply not being desired.

Assuming that this home-centered pattern of the commitment of time persists — and there are no reasons to expect any major change in this allocation — a whole range of policy and public investment decisions concerning community facilities may need careful reappraisal in many metropolitan areas. Policy makers might well find that entire new approaches to the provision of public services and the development of community facilities are needed to conform more closely to home-centered and localized networks of activity. Perhaps the city-within-city concept embodied in Chicago's Marina City is more than a novel real estate venture. Indeed, if no overriding normative considerations are involved, as dictated by needs from a welfare, physical, or mental health viewpoint, policy makers might well wonder whether the future use of any community facilities can be justified without careful study of user demand as determined from activity analysis of the kind discussed in this chapter. Such an analysis not only describes how these facilities, as presently designed, are used but can also be applied to study how community facilities of varying designs and differing spatial distributions might be used.

With respect to the spatial dimension, and particularly the nodal and dispersed patterns mentioned above, one very obvious conclusion concerns the design of a transportation system which more nearly serves these polar forms of out-of-home leisure-time behavior. Assuming that public investment decisions are made after utilizing activity analysis to evaluate the relative emphasis to be given to leisure-time transportation needs as opposed to transportation to and from work, shopping, and various essential services, these decisions can also be made in the light of the cost-benefit aspects of providing the highway or public transportation system needed to optimize opportunities for pursuing both nodal and diffused leisure-time activities in space. There is already a developing scientific capability to estimate the spatial impacts of public investment decisions. If the calculus is to take into account the widely forecast reduced length of the work week for the period 1985 to 2000,[57] various conditional forecasts on the use of the presumed increase in leisure time might be cycled through

---

[57] It should be remembered that the activities which will replace time spent at work are not easy to predict. De Grazia points out that the time gained from the job in the last hundred years has not gone largely to leisure activities, but rather to moonlighting, transportation, household tasks, and so on. This finding emphasizes again the need for an "elasticity analysis" for the various activities of life. Sebastian de Grazia, *Of Time, Work, and Leisure* (Anchor Books, 1964), Chapter III.

the activity systems models discussed in this chapter,[58] and cost-benefit functions re-examined for various re-weighted leisure, work, shopping, and service facility activity demands on the transportation system.

If visiting and other forms of socialization are to achieve policy recognition as an essential part of social policy planning in preventing breakdowns in urban behavior of the kinds witnessed in the mid-sixties, it then becomes important to recognize in public investment decisions what has customarily been considered to be a concern of the private sector. The so-called "many-to-many" solution to public transportation (a system designed to deliver riders directly from scattered origins to scattered destinations) might well receive more public policy support than the "many-to-one" solution (a system for assembling riders at origin points on some mass transportation system and their subsequent distribution at selected destination points). The applications of activity analysis thus offer a variety of possibilities in developing the calculus needed in re-evaluating cost-benefit criteria for resource allocation to public services and facilities.

The specific way in which activity analysis is used in public investment decisions is not particularly important for the purposes of this discussion. The key element that this chapter has sought to introduce into the discussion of urban resources is the underlying importance of testing policy positions taken with respect to policy measures of the kind Perloff has suggested against the living patterns, thoughtways, and value systems of the people whose interests these measures are presumed to represent. In the search for more objective ways for evaluating policy proposals, an essential part of this search should be the development and use of evaluation techniques which can relate policy more directly to behavior systems of urban residents.

A final caution should be offered. It will be easy to acquire a little knowledge, but not enough, about the patterns of activities of large numbers of people. We must be wary of giving too much credence to what appears on the surface. At the turn of the century, because it had not yet probed below the surface, science gave support to racist theories; similarly, activity analysis could all too easily discredit poorly used facilities by attributing lack of interest to the populace, when some other reason was at the base of the lack of use. In any use of activity analysis for evaluating programs, alternative explanations for the findings of the analysis must be considered if irreparable damage is not to be done through the use of misleading partial knowledge.

---

[58] In passing, the observations noted earlier concerning the "elasticity of demand" for leisure time facilities would need to be considered. For example, Alexander Szalai discovered in European time-budget studies that time freed up from work does not get transferred to purposeful leisure-time pursuits on a one to one basis: at least some of the new free time is absorbed in taking more time in transportation. Also there is a tendency for small increments to be added to TV-watching and other present patterns in use of time.